SEÁN LEMASS
DEMOCRATIC DICTATOR

Dr Bryce Evans is a historian based at the Humanities Institute of Ireland, University College Dublin. A graduate of the University of Warwick and the NUI, he teaches modern Irish and European history in the School of History and Archives, UCD. A regular contributor to the *Sunday Independent*, his doctoral thesis appraised Lemass's Department of Supplies (1939–45) and has appeared in part across various media.

'Powerhouse' by Jon Everitt

SEÁN LEMASS
DEMOCRATIC DICTATOR

BRYCE EVANS

The Collins Press

First published in 2011 by
The Collins Press
West Link Park
Doughcloyne
Wilton
Cork

British Library Cataloguing in Publication Data

Evans, Bryce.
  Sean Lemass : democratic dictator.
  1. Lemass, Sean. 2. Statesmen--Ireland--Biography.
  3. Ireland--Politics and government--1922-
  I. Title
  941.5'082'092-dc22

ISBN-13: 9781848891227

Typeset in Bembo by Carrigboy Typesetting Services
Printed in Sweden by ScandBook AB

Cover photographs
Front: (main) a young Seán Lemass; (top) first Fianna Fáil cabinet, 1932; (bottom):
Gabriel Hayes' depiction of the Shannon Scheme (courtesy Fionnbharr Ó Riordán).
Back: (first and third from top) Gabriel Hayes' drawings of Irish aviation and of
the Shannon scheme; (second and fourth from top) panels depicting shipbuilding
and the Celtic god Lugh on the Department of Industry and Commerce building
(all courtesy Fionnbharr Ó Riordán).

Contents

To Marian, and my parents

Acknowledgements

I owe a particular debt of gratitude to my good friend, colleague and critic Stephen Kelly; to my father, Peter Evans; to the long-suffering Marian Carey; and to the extraordinary generosity of that fine historian, John Horgan.

My sincere thanks to the following people for their assistance in the course of my research: Lisa, Hugh and Victor at the Military Archives; Rosemary at the Allen Library; Paschal at the Arts Council Archive; Séamus, Orna, and all at UCD Archives; the staff of the National Archives of Ireland; of the National Archives of the United Kingdom; of the Ó Fiaich Memorial Library and Archive (in particular Séamus Savage); and those who work in the Dublin Diocesan Archive; Trinity College Manuscripts Collection and Early Printed Books Department; the National Library; Dublin City Libraries; the Public Record Office of Northern Ireland; the Irish Newspaper Archive; and the Irish Architectural Archive.

Special thanks to those who allowed me to interview them: Seán Haughey, Ulick O'Connor, Michael D. Higgins, Des O'Malley, Tony O'Reilly, and Harold Simms. For their support, encouragement and advice I wish to thank: the straight-talking Diarmaid Ferriter, my mentor Susannah Riordan, Clara Cullen, Mary Daly, Michael Laffan, Michael Kennedy, Lindsey Earner-Byrne, Liam Collins, Kieran Allen, all at The Collins Press, Aonghus Meaney, Eunan O'Halpin, Paula Murphy, Ivar McGrath, Bryan Fanning and Robin Okey; the talented Jon Everitt, Eileen Lemass, Liam Delahunt, Ann de Valera, Éamon de Valera, Maureen Haughey, Fionnbharr and Róisín Ó Riordán and Angela Rolfe; Úna MacNamara, Greta Evans, Ros Evans and all my family, especially my grandparents Nora MacNamara and John and Eileen Evans; Anne O'Grady, Dennis O'Grady, Ed Carey, Anthony Carey, Peter Tighe, John O'Connor, Frank Kelly, Doney Carey and Máire Nic an Bhaird, Liz Dawson, Adam Kelly, Sarah Campbell, Fintan Hoey, Aoifie Whelan, Ashling Smith and Paul Hand.

Lastly, thank you to my colleagues and friends in the Department of History and Archives, UCD, and the Humanities Institute of Ireland, particularly Marc Caball, Valerie Norton and my office-mates down the years.

Introduction

The Use and Abuse of the Lemass Legend

'Not another biography of Lemass!' Many of the people who have subsequently provided me with help in researching this book initially uttered these words. Their reaction is understandable. Seán Lemass (1899–1971) has been the subject of no fewer than five published full biographical studies.[1] The publication of this, the sixth, coincides with the fortieth anniversary of his death.

The very fact that this book has been commissioned illustrates the lasting allure of Lemass. Unlike the majority of his political predecessors, peers and successors, 'the architect of modern Ireland' enjoys an unsoiled status in the popular imagination. For a long time Irish historians were preoccupied with the debate on 'revisionism', a term describing the subjection of national myths to critical scrutiny. Lemass, though, has consistently escaped the revisionist's noose. How?

Firstly, Lemass is acknowledged as an extraordinary historical figure. He held key ministerial appointments in every one of Éamon de Valera's Fianna Fáil administrations from 1932 onwards, went on to become Tánaiste and, between 1959 and 1966, Taoiseach. He orchestrated two critical economic transitions in twentieth-century Irish history: the construction, and dismantling, of protectionism. A moderniser who, for his time, was exceptionally receptive to change, Lemass's workaholic commitment is striking. His achievements have been extolled in the ample literature that has grown up around him. This 'Lemassiography' is at times cloying, but his qualities shine through in any work dedicated to him, and this book is no exception.

It would be trite, however, to ignore a major factor in Lemass's enduring popularity: his place in the politics of memory or, to put it plainly, the use and abuse of Lemass's name by Ireland's elites. In recent history, successive taoisigh have realised the political capital that comes with paying Lemass lip service. Charles Haughey used to impress visitors to his lavish Kinsealy mansion with a prominently displayed oil painting of his father-in-law, which now hangs at the top of the stairs in Leinster House. The portrait of Lemass in the Taoiseach's office is said to survive all changes of government.[2] In his autobiography Albert Reynolds described Lemass as his 'hero';

his successor Bertie Ahern, who himself launched two of the canonical books in the Lemassiography, said of his fellow Dub: 'I never miss a chance to state my belief that Lemass was in the vanguard of almost every great event and decision that shapes the Ireland in which we live.'[3] Launching the latest biography of Lemass in 2009, Ahern's successor, Brian Cowen, used Lemass to urge support for the government's bailout of the banks and endorsement of the second referendum on the Lisbon Treaty.[4]

During the belle époque of the Celtic Tiger boom, a period overseen by Ahern and Cowen, Fianna Fáil, the political party Lemass helped to found, projected itself as the spearhead of national progress. This 'modern Ireland', much like a newly emergent state, needed a creation myth. Éamon de Valera, the post-independence colossus of party and nation, was increasingly seen as peculiar and twee, 'de Valera's Ireland' grim and anti-materialistic. At the same time revelations about the corruption of the modern 'Boss', Charlie Haughey, the bon viveur antithesis to the frugality preached by de Valera, were uncomfortably close to home. Lemass, however, fitted the bill. In the popular imagination he came to be contrasted with his close political ally, de Valera, and his son-in-law, Haughey. Lemass was invoked as the embodiment of the march of progress, a visionary free trader who kick-started progressive, cosmopolitan, secular, neoliberal Ireland.

When interviewed for this book Tony O'Reilly, Ireland's first billionaire and arguably the greatest success story of Ireland's 'economic miracle', said of Lemass, his personal hero: 'He had what every great politician needs – he was an extraordinarily good poker player!'[5] O'Reilly's reflection is an astute one. Like many political leaders of the twentieth century, most notably former US president Richard Nixon, Lemass was an avid poker player. The story of Lemass's life is enduringly compelling because it combined all the elements of the game he loved: intelligence, skill and courage on the one hand; cunning, ruthlessness, luck and deceit on the other. The former aspects of Lemass's game are familiar, but the latter much less so.

To the historian, the darker arts deployed in the game should naturally demand attention. But when it comes to Lemass an entire generation of Ireland's historians have neglected them in favour of a tasty dichotomy. De Valera, we are told, stood for an Ireland 'pious, disciplined and folksy', 'a real-life version of *The Quiet Man*'.[6] Dev's

Ireland was 'a few comely maidens and the occasional athletic youth', full of 'asexual mothers of ten nodding approvingly, not an impure thought or an orgasm in sight'.[7] Lemass's Ireland was, by contrast, radical and modernising and 'promised at long last to banish to the rubbish dump of history the wailing of Kathleen Ni Houlihan, the champion whiner of the western world, the princess of the begging bowl'.[8]

The construction of this gulf between two men who had worked alongside each other for the best part of forty years involved a considerable amount of airbrushing, particularly of Lemass's career before he became Taoiseach in 1959. Most historians now recognise that the 'Age of de Valera' interpretation inhibited a fuller under-standing of Ireland in the last century.[9] The same cannot be said for its corollary, the 'Age of Lemass', which is loosely applied to pre-Troubles, Swinging-Sixties Ireland and remains popular with Irish historians.

Recent works celebrating Lemass, most prominently Tom Garvin's 2009 biography, have clung dear to a 'Whig history' of the man, in which a narrative of progress and development obscures other considerations. Essentially, Garvin presents the reader with the same story as found in the biographies of Lemass by John Horgan (1997), Michael O'Sullivan (1994) and Brian Farrell (1983). The thrust of these books resembles all too closely and uncritically the upbeat tone of 'Lifting the Green Curtain', the famous 1963 *Time* magazine piece on Ireland:

> The nation is at last facing up to its future . . . signs are every-where: in the new factories and office buildings, in the Irish-assembled cars fighting for street space in Dublin, in the new TV antennas crowding the rooftops, in the waning of national self-pity . . . The nation's new mood is that of Sean Lemass, who four years ago succeeded Eamon de Valera as *Taoiseach* (Prime Minister). Though Lemass has been de Valera's protégé and heir apparent for three decades, the two men could not be more dissimilar. 'Dev', the aloof, magnetic revolutionary with a martyr's face and a mystic's mind, was the sort of leader whom the Irish have adored in every age. Sean Lemass, a reticent, pragmatic planner . . . is by temperament and ancestry more Gallic than Gaelic, and represents a wholly new species of leadership for Ireland. In de Valera's shadow, the new

Taoiseach (pronounced tea-shook) has labored single-mindedly
for decades to break the vicious circle of declining living
standards and dwindling population that threatened Ireland's
very survival as a nation.[10]

The celebration of Lemass as the father of boom Ireland started
around this time and is epitomised by Garvin's much later book
which, fittingly, was composed as the Celtic Tiger was starting to
limp. To a number of influential commentators in between, the
influx of foreign capital into Ireland was a sort of *deus ex machina*
which resolved all the country's problems. Lemass's role in this
process led to a tendency among historians to resort to ahistorical
post hoc, ergo propter hoc reasoning when looking at Lemass's life prior
to his reforms as Taoiseach. And this, in turn, begat the intellectual
laziness of hero worship.

It is significant that the first biography of Lemass (which all
his subsequent biographers have drawn on but which remains
unpublished) does not share the same philosophy as the later works.
Liam Skinner wrote the unpublished *Seán Lemass: Nation Builder*
before Lemass became Taoiseach in 1959. Skinner's book verges on
hagiography, but takes a dramatic and unexpected U-turn halfway
through when he launches an unbridled attack on the 'evil and
pernicious tendency' towards the welfare state and socialism. He lays
the blame for the 'octopus-like extent' of state control squarely at
Lemass's door, accusing him of paying lip service to private
enterprise while clamping down on it at every opportunity.[11]

How are we to view Lemass, then? Proto-neoliberal? Socialist? A
heady mixture of both, or neither? The recent abrupt demise of
Ireland's economic boom may have brought few welcome results,
but it has provided a fitting time to appraise Lemass fairly. The
material wealth and cultural confidence of the Celtic Tiger era has
dissipated and the Catholic Church is in a downward spiral. 'Where
did it all go right?' has become 'Where did it all go wrong?' And
the answers to both questions, not merely the former, involve Seán
Lemass.

This book is intended as a critical accompaniment to John
Horgan's seminal *Enigmatic Patriot*. Yet it also seeks to balance the
scales: to jettison the machismo mystique of Lemass, the 'man of
action'; to get beneath his personal ascent, consolidation and exercise
of political power; to shed light on under-researched episodes in his

life; and, most importantly, to explode Tom Garvin's contention that Lemass was a 'cultural revolutionary'.[12] It highlights the condescension inherent in the tendency to look nostalgically to the Fianna Fáil 'golden age'; while no 'hatchet job', neither does it paint Lemass as icon or iconoclast.

Tim Pat Coogan, author of biographies on both Éamon de Valera and Michael Collins, considered writing Lemass's biography, but confessed that his 'prosaic businessman persona' did not enthuse him. Coogan found his prospective subject neither colourful nor romantic enough.[13] This reflection only reinforces Lemass's success in concealing this side to his character because his story runs deeper than its sober, pragmatic facade. To borrow one of the many platitudes from an RTÉ documentary on him, 'The story of Seán Lemass is the story of modern Ireland.'[14] And it begins, overleaf, in the year 1899 . . .

1

The Shadow of a Gunman

Capel Street, the Christian Brothers and the Rising

In the summer of 1899 the heavily pregnant Frances Lemass travelled with her husband, John, and her midwife to Dun Laoghaire, south County Dublin. John and Frances were sufficiently well off to be able to regularly hire a large cottage belonging to a dairy farmer in nearby Ballybrack which they used as the family's summer house. It was here that Frances gave birth to Seán Lemass on 15 July 1899. After two months the baby was christened and John and Frances returned to their home on Capel Street, in the heart of middle-class commercial Dublin.

Twelve years later a census was conducted across Ireland. The return for number 2 Capel Street, the family business and home, provides a snapshot of Seán Lemass's early life. Seán had three sisters and four brothers in total; another sibling had been lost in infancy. John, a hatter by trade, was forty-three years old in 1911. Frances was thirty-nine. The oldest of the children was the sturdy Noel (thirteen). Next there was Seán, aged eleven and listed as 'John'. Then there was Alice (ten), Clare (seven), Patrick (four), and Mary (one).[1]

This early glimpse of Seán Lemass's life is indicative of his relatively comfortable upbringing. At the time Dublin contained some of the most unsanitary slum housing in Europe. By contrast Seán Lemass's background was affluent. His father, John, ran a gentleman's outfitters in a prosperous area of the city, and was listed in Thom's commercial directory.[2] When Frances gave birth it was in the country retreat and in the company of her own nurse.[3] The Lemasses were also wealthy enough to have a domestic servant, a young woman called Elizabeth Kelly, who was aged nineteen in 1911.[4]

The eleven-year-old Seán Lemass was a pupil at the nearby Christian Brothers school in North Richmond Street, Dublin. He had followed his older brother there from convent school; Seán and Noel had enrolled together two years previously.[5] Seán was a well-behaved, rather introverted and nervous child. Mathematics was his favourite subject. Outside of school he loved to play in the workshops in his father's business.[6] His older brother, Noel, by contrast, was taller and more outgoing.

A fellow student of the Lemass brothers in North Richmond Street was Ernie O'Malley. In later life he achieved fame as a republican militant and writer; he and Seán Lemass were to take up arms together in the Civil War a decade later. A slightly younger colleague was Brendan Bracken, later Viscount Bracken, and Minister for Information in the British cabinet during the Second World War.[7] As an adult Bracken discarded his Irish roots for the altogether more advantageous identity of an English public school boy and became a sycophantic favourite of Winston Churchill. In London in the 1920s Bracken was approached in the street by another former Christian Brothers pupil who claimed to remember him, recalling from his face an odd childhood memory – the smell of his corduroy trousers at school. Characteristically, Bracken feigned ignorance and walked away.[8] The man left standing in the street was Emmet Dalton. Dalton, a pupil in the same North Richmond Street school, played and studied alongside Seán and Noel.[9] As they sat at their school desks none of these boys could have foreseen the different directions their lives would take, nor that the name Emmet Dalton would become linked with the untimely death of Noel Lemass.

In the Dublin of these boys' youth, history and politics were fields of lively contention. In the year of Lemass's birth Britain went to war with the Transvaal and the Orange Free State. The Boer War, as it became known, elicited much anti-imperial feeling in Ireland. The concentration camps Britain erected for women and children in South Africa contrasted with a spirit of constructive unionism in Ireland and the passing of the land acts. The Irish Parliamentary Party, which Seán's father supported, was undergoing a revival in fortunes. So too were the forces of cultural and revolutionary nationalism, the latter an underground tradition which Lemass's mother held dear. His transition from innocent childhood to an awareness of civic nationalism in adolescence was punctuated most obviously by a major labour dispute: the Dublin Lock-Out of 1913. A strike by tram workers led to strikes in solidarity by workers across the city. In retaliation over 20,000 workers in Dublin were locked out by the city's capitalists, who enjoyed the support of the state, the Church and the media.

The Lemass brothers grew up in the midst of such pivotal events in the Ireland of the Edwardian twilight. Because their father was a fairly prosperous businessman, their class allegiance was not as straightforward as many of their less well-off contemporaries. As products of a nationalistic Christian Brothers education, however, class and national issues intertwined, and their reaction to anti-nationalist outrages was hostile. One such event occurred very close to the family home. In July 1914 several unarmed civilians were massacred by British troops on Bachelor's Walk, just yards from the Lemasses' front door. In the same month, and just before the outbreak of the First World War, Noel left school. The timing of Noel's school-leaving was no coincidence: great events were unfolding which made the classroom seem a small world indeed. For the eldest boy the pressure to work was also greater than for Seán, who did not enter the world of work with the same alacrity as his brother. Whereas Seán was educated to 'seventh standard' at school, Noel reached just 'fourth standard'.[10]

Large numbers of young Irish men were joining the British Army around this time. Emmet Dalton enlisted in 1915 and at the age of seventeen was appointed to the rank of second lieutenant. He was to serve in nearly every theatre of war from France to Palestine.[11] Seán Lemass's path was different. After leaving school he briefly enrolled at a commercial training college, but when Noel joined the Irish Volunteers Seán followed him, still a schoolboy and aged just fifteen.

The body Noel introduced Seán to was a rump organisation, the smaller faction to emerge after the split in 1914 over whether or not the cause of Irish nationalism would be advanced by joining the British war effort. The adjutant of the battalion the Lemass brothers joined was a 32-year-old schoolteacher, Éamon de Valera. Lemass's recollection of his first glimpse of de Valera has been repeated with relish by his biographers. 'My impression of him was of a long, thin fellow with knee breeches and a tweed hat. But he had, of course, enormous personal magnetism . . . it impressed me enormously, notwithstanding what I thought was his rather queer-looking appearance.'[12] Lemass's description of de Valera's eccentric appearance squares with one witness's recollection of de Valera when com-mandant at Boland's Mills during the Easter Rising in 1916: 'a tall, gangling figure in green Volunteer uniform and red socks, running around day and night, without sleep, getting trenches dug, giving contradictory orders and forgetting the password so that he nearly got himself shot'.[13] The immaculately attired Lemass never possessed the same peculiar charisma as de Valera, but was to remain at his side for the rest of his life.

As rank-and-file recruits in 1915 the Lemass boys had little idea that the organisation they joined had been infiltrated by a radical clique within the Irish Republican Brotherhood (IRB) which was planning a heroic gesture. Eoin MacNeill, Professor of Early and Medieval History at University College Dublin and titular head of the Irish Volunteers, found himself outmanoeuvred by the radicals, who were plotting a symbolic armed insurrection against British rule in Ireland. When MacNeill learned of these preparations he cancelled manoeuvres due to take place on Easter Sunday, 23 April 1916. Despite MacNeill's countermanding order the insurrection went ahead the following day with the rebels seizing strategic buildings in Dublin, most prominently the General Post Office (GPO) on Sackville Street.

The decision of the young Lemass brothers to join what became the Easter Rising was, as Michael Laffan has described much of the conduct of that week, 'engagingly casual'.[14] Neither Noel nor Seán were close to the inner sanctum of the movement and, unaware that the Rising was taking place under the leadership of James Connolly and Patrick Pearse, they decided to head for a walk in the hills with their friends and neighbours, the O'Dea brothers. There they met Eoin MacNeill, out walking with his sons. There is something almost Olympian about this mountain-top meeting. MacNeill regretfully informed the boys that an insurrection had gone ahead.[15] Noel and Seán listened sympathetically, then, hubristically, jumped on the next tram to the city centre to take part in the fight.

That the Lemass brothers were unaware of what was taking place was not unusual – the Rising was planned in secrecy – though their ignorance does indicate that they were not close to the leadership in any way. For this reason they did not fight with their own battalion under de Valera at Boland's Mills. Instead they reported for duty at the GPO, were armed and then separated. Noel was stationed to the Imperial Hotel on the opposite side of the road while Seán was posted to the roof of the GPO.[16]

This posting was, as Lemass's grandson Seán Haughey concedes, 'very lucky' from the point of view of his later political career.[17] For young Seán the experience must have been a heady mix of terror and exhilaration, though hardly the gung-ho adventure some describe.[18] Tom Garvin claims he 'got up on top of the GPO with a shotgun and started blazing away', a statement which rather creates the impression of a strident Lemass clambering madly to the building's summit to take on the British.[19] Lemass in fact said: 'I fired a few shots from the GPO, but whether they hit anybody I don't know.'[20]

According to others who were on the roof during Easter week, the most trying experience was not the fighting but the discomfort from the heat of the burning buildings on the opposite side of the street.[21] There, among the flames, Noel was shot in the hand. Seán escaped the entire experience without wounds, instead recalling how the whole affair left him tired and hungry.[22] When the British started to shell the GPO he was moved off the roof and did not get to use any of the bombs he had been armed with.[23]

When the GPO itself became engulfed in flames the order was given to evacuate the building and Lemass emerged on to Moore Street. He was armed with a Martini rifle and, finding a bayonet discarded on the street, fixed it to his gun. As he recalled: 'this could have been my death warrant', because minutes later all volunteers with bayonets were ordered to assemble to charge the British barricade at the top of the street. But Lemass was spared the suicidal bayonet charge. He claimed, rather dubiously but not entirely implausibly, that this was because he fell asleep from sheer exhaustion. He explained: 'I ate a tin of preserved fruit from a shop through which we had passed, and while seated on the stairway into the yard watching the obstacles being removed I fell asleep for a few moments.'[24]

Bertie Ahern professes a romantic attachment to the story of Lemass carrying James Connolly from the GPO after the ceasefire.[25] But, as Lemass admitted, the process of carrying the fatally wounded Connolly from the building was less glorious, being 'so slow and so frequently interrupted that almost everyone in the GPO helped in it at some stage'.[26] After the surrender Lemass was taken with the other prisoners to Richmond Barracks, Inchicore. According to one source Lemass was allowed to leave custody by the intervention of a kindly constable of the Dublin Metropolitan Police who knew the Lemass family and drew attention to his youth.[27] *Time* magazine was to paraphrase the Dublin vernacular account of this incident in an inimitably American way in its 1963 profile of Lemass: 'The cops gave him a kick in the arse and told him to go home to his mom.'[28]

John the Apostle? Lemass and the War of Independence

For the young Lemass the experience of flames and bullets, followed by the execution of the leaders of the Rising, was life changing. Although he recalled that after the Rising his father, a constitutional nationalist, 'had come over to our side',[29] Seán's abrupt transition from youth to adulthood on the parapet of the GPO was hard for his father to accept. For his mother, a sympathiser with revolutionary Fenianism, it was somewhat easier. In his primary and secondary education, however, young Seán had proved a bright student. On his release from detention John Lemass encouraged his son to become a barrister and the teenage Seán returned to school to prepare to sit his exams. But 'you couldn't expect a young fellow who had been through the Rising to sit down seriously and study', as Lemass commented when interviewed in 1969.[30]

Lemass is celebrated by historians as the supreme pragmatist; but he did not subscribe to Michael Collins' damning, anti-aesthetic appraisal of the Rising as a failure which possessed 'the air of Greek tragedy'. Dublin was a drama-mad city in 1916 and there is evidence that Lemass subscribed to Patrick Pearse's faith in the symbolic power of drama. The man who would later become associated with the politics of the possible also shared the spirit of fatalism that pervaded the event:

> In the early days of Easter 1916 there were rumours that the German army was marching up from the South or that an enormous group of volunteers were marching on Dublin from the country. But by the Wednesday or Thursday we knew that these were only rumours, that we were on our own and that there was no one to save us ... [and yet he stayed on, explaining that] escape would have been contrary to the basic philosophy of the whole business. The idea was that we were ready to take up the fight in arms and were ready to be executed and that this would produce the reawakening.[31]

Garvin seeks to situate Lemass away from Pearse and the emotionality of doomed rebellion.[32] But Lemass – in his own words – described Pearse as 'a very impressive person, mainly because of his bearing and solemnity and, of course, his wonderful oratory ... in the GPO in 1916 he was terribly calm, very much in control of himself ...'[33]

In that same interview the seventy-year-old Lemass also contended that history had neglected the period after the Rising and before the Irish Volunteers were reorganised in late 1917. Aside from accounts from nationalists held in 'the university of revolution', the British internment camp at Frongoch in Wales, this period sits rather awkwardly in the canonical revolutionary years, 1916–23. Given his later ascent in republican politics it is remarkable that Lemass was absent from the central revolutionary caucus across the Irish Sea. Instead he resumed a workaday existence at the family business in Capel Street.

In his spare time he helped found an acting troupe, the Kilronan Players, with his friend and later Dublin music hall favourite Jimmy O'Dea. Lemass would play the straight man to O'Dea, who was to make his name as a comic actor. With the leading figures of the Volunteer movement imprisoned, he instead spent a lot of time with the boys and girls of Dublin's trendy artistic and literary set. On long summer Sundays the handsome young hatter's son would travel out to Skerries, north County Dublin, in a hackney car with an assortment of young actors and actresses. On one such occasion, in 1917, the young members of the Kilronan Players were relaxing on the beach in Skerries. Holidaying beside them were the widows of four of the executed signatories of the 1916 Proclamation, James Connolly, Joseph Plunkett, Éamonn Ceannt and Thomas MacDonagh.[34] Muriel MacDonagh, the widow of Thomas MacDonagh, was drowned accidentally that afternoon, leaving her two children as orphans. It was O'Dea and Lemass who ran for the police, ultimately to no avail, when it became obvious that the tragic MacDonagh had got into difficulty in the water.[35]

Lemass did not completely abandon his military activities at this time, and joined a private nationalist militia under Colonel Maurice Moore, an old but enlightened landed type who had done his soldiering in the Boer War.[36] From late 1917 those who had been interned since the Rising were released and the Volunteers proper started to reform. Lemass was appointed lieutenant in a north Dublin company of troops. In defiance of a British-imposed curfew a lot of training took place at night. Lemass explained that many of his men

> ... used to complain to me that their wives never believed that they were out training all night when they'd come back covered in mud. Their wives always thought they'd spent the night lying in some ditch sleeping off the pints they'd been drinking. So part of my job was to assure their wives that they had been on serious business, not sleeping it out.[37]

Such prosaic responsibilities belied the rapid escalation of political and militant nationalism in a very short space of time. By 1917 the British Army had sustained massive casualties in France and Prime Minister David Lloyd George was under pressure to introduce conscription in Ireland. Angered at the unfulfilled promise of Home Rule for Ireland and the passage of the Military Service Bill, the Irish Parliamentary Party withdrew from Westminster in April 1918. Shortly afterwards representatives of the various political shades of Irish nationalism convened at Dublin's Mansion House and produced an anti-conscription pledge which – crucially – was endorsed by Ireland's Catholic bishops.

Sinn Féin, the radical abstentionists in the nationalist communion, ballooned in size and popularity. In a few months the party superseded the century-old Irish Parliamentary Party, its support buoyed by the British decision to crack down on cultural and political nationalism in Ireland. In the general election of December 1918 Sinn Féin's separatist republicanism received a resounding endorsement from an enlarged Irish electorate. With this mandate the Irish Republic was declared in January 1919. The British government, however, refused to recognise it. Dáil Éireann, the revolutionary parliament of the new Republic, sat for the first time in April 1919 and the Democratic Programme was read out. At the same time two policemen were shot dead in County Tipperary by a group of volunteers. The War of Independence had begun and the Irish Republican Army was born.

Lemass was absent from all of these developments. But as violence surged in Dublin he was drawn into the conflict. The Dublin IRA battalion to which he belonged was involved in sporadic engagements with British troops and Lemass undoubtedly partook in some of these, although there is little evidence of his involvement. The specific biographical accounts of his activity during the hostilities are drawn chiefly from the writings of Liam Skinner which, in discussing this period of his life, are the stuff of a *Boy's Own* war story. According to Skinner, Lemass was reputedly involved in the recovery of £500 of stolen jewellery from a 'gang of robbers'.[38] It is more likely that Lemass was himself involved in a number of armed seizures of money and material: unglamorous, if financially vital, episodes in the national struggle, involving conflict with civilians rather than soldiers.[39]

Seán and Noel's former schoolfellow Dalton enjoyed a more meteoric ascent during this period, despite joining the fight late.

Stationed with the British Army in north Africa in early 1918 his war diary captures the boredom of camp life and an emerging yearning to return home to join the Irish struggle. While Lemass was drilling in Dublin, Dalton was a restless soldier in the desert heat. He broke an oil lamp while playing football,[40] drove to the pyramids with a nun,[41] danced with a countess,[42] played golf and billiards seemingly incessantly[43] and accidentally cut the padré's nose while playing 'stone bombs'.[44] But he also had more than one 'heated discussion' with fellow officers on the Irish question and, when talking to Arabs, compared their plight at the hands of the Turks to Ireland's at the hands of the British.[45] 'There is something radically wrong with me because I feel terribly fed up,' he wrote.[46] In summer 1919 he was discharged and found his purpose in the War of Independence. His military experience ensured he rose quickly within the ranks of the IRA and he became director of training in its General Headquarters staff. Ernie O'Malley had been sucked in too, quitting his medical studies to become a captain in the IRA; he was also attached to General Headquarters.

Seán Lemass's record in the conflict was less stellar than his schoolmates'. It is likely that he felt a little overshadowed by older brother Noel, who played a more prominent role despite balancing work as an engineer with military action. When asked about his brother's activities during the War of Independence Lemass's reply made much of Noel's engineering apprenticeship and little of his soldiering.[47] But there is evidence that Noel was engaged in illegal drilling in Derry early in the conflict.[48] He certainly made more column inches than his younger brother at the time. He was arrested in south County Dublin as part of a large group of IRA men and imprisoned in Mountjoy Prison in north Dublin.[49] At Noel's trial a lieutenant of the South Lancashire regiment claimed that Noel had been drilling volunteers. On seeing a lorry of troops and policemen approach, these men fled, and Noel had allegedly thrown a loaded revolver and holster over a hedge. Unrepentant in court, Noel challenged the evidence as unsound and in the best tradition of *Speeches from the Dock*, the Irish nationalist bible, questioned the legitimacy of a court 'constituted of an army of occupation'.[50] He was imprisoned at Mountjoy and later Derry.[51]

As a captain in the Dublin IRA's 3rd battalion Noel was remembered by one of the men under him as 'a flamboyant extrovert; a very tall, swashbuckling type. But a great company man; very keen, an attractive person.'[52] Noel heightened the battalion's activities considerably, displaying leadership skills befitting his tall frame and dashing good looks. He orchestrated a major ambush on Dublin's Mespil Road in February 1921 and in the following month was caught in a Black and Tan raid of IRA headquarters and interrogated (and in all likelihood tortured) by the notorious head constable, Eugene Igoe of British intelligence.[53] He was released but a further arrest warrant was issued for him in June 1921 as someone 'suspected of acting, having acted, and being about to act in a manner prejudicial to the restoration and maintenance of order in Ireland'.[54]

Seán Lemass's record during the War of Independence is clouded by a smokescreen of his own creation. There has been persistent speculation that he was a member of Michael Collins' 'Squad', the hitmen who executed eleven men suspected of being British intelligence agents on 'Bloody Sunday', 21 November 1920.[55] The elite British group was replaced by an intelligence unit headed by Noel's erstwhile interrogator, the infamous Igoe. When asked later in life if he was a member of Collins' Squad Lemass's reply was typically ambiguous: 'Firing squads,' he said, 'don't have reunions.'

Lemass was certainly not a member of the Squad though, and any evidence that he took part at all in the Bloody Sunday killings is dubious. Two years before the publication of his definitive biography *Enigmatic Patriot*, John Horgan claimed that Lemass shot dead a crippled British officer – a Captain G. T. Bagally – in a house on Lower Baggot Street.[56] Yet Horgan omitted mention of Bagally's disability when the book was published. Bagally, who had lost a leg in the First World War, was a courts martial officer who reputedly assisted Dublin Castle's 'Murder Gang' in hunting down the IRA.[57] One member of Collins' Squad, Patrick McCrea, recalled that Bagally was suspected of being one of the torturers of Kevin Barry, the teenage volunteer whose execution by Crown forces on 1 November 1920 aroused much popular resentment.[58]

According to Michael Foy, an IRA hit squad including Lemass called to Bagally's lodgings that morning with a sledgehammer to break into his bedroom. After being admitted through the front door by a maid, they discovered that the officer's bedroom was unlocked. Finding Bagally lying in bed in his pyjamas, they shot him twice in the heart.[59] According to McCrea, who does not mention Lemass in his account, Bagally made a pitiful attempt to jump out the window to escape, but before he reached it 'he was out of action'.[60]

Was Lemass party to this murder, and if so did he pull the trigger? The evidence Horgan gives for Lemass's involvement in the murder is based on fleeting references, omissions and gossip and, as such, is as unconvincing as his claim that Lemass's supposed getaway route that day was a harbinger of his cool political strategy later on.[61] Foy's claim that Lemass carried out the killing is based on the single testimony of a junior IRA man collected years later and a series of illegible notes scribbled by Ernie O'Malley in later life.[62] Tom Garvin admits his strong doubts about Lemass's involvement in Bloody Sunday, but cannot bring himself to unequivocally dismiss the heroic role ascribed to Lemass by civil service whispers.[63]

It is significant that Lemass is not listed anywhere as a member of Michael Collins' Squad.[64] Before their deaths a number of its members provided a list of protagonists. Lemass does not feature in any of them.[65] Although membership at the time of Bloody Sunday was somewhat fluid, flitting between twelve and nineteen named men, the Squad was by nature and necessity a small, tight-knit collective. The number of men in it was brought up to twenty-one only the year after the murders, 1921.[66] Later that year membership swelled to fifty and the Squad became known as 'the Guard'.[67] By the time of the Civil War in 1922 members of this group had become the core of the Free State's shadowy and thuggish Special Branch based at Oriel House just north of the Liffey. Special Branch would subsequently be involved in the abduction and murder of Noel Lemass in 1923 (discussed below), making Lemass's participation in the intimate gang which carried out the Bloody Sunday murders all the more unlikely.

The 3rd battalion of the Dublin IRA 'A' company, to which Lemass belonged, operated around Parliament Street, Dame Street, George's Street and Camden Street. Baggot Street was therefore near their turf and the unit is reputed to have been active on Bloody Sunday.[68] There is no reliable evidence that Lemass took part in the killing, however. A key piece of evidence against Lemass's involvement concerns gunmen and dinner parties. According to Lemass, firing squads do not meet for reunions but in fact Collins' Squad *did*, in the form of reunion dinners. According to a witness of several of these reunions, Lemass's name did not feature once in any of the frequent, macabre reminiscences about the Bloody Sunday murders across the dinner table.[69]

Given the absence of evidence that he pulled a trigger on Bloody Sunday, Lemass's curious half-admission about firing squads and reunions appears disingenuous. He did little to quell rumours of his shady past as part of the Squad and with one very good reason: they greatly increased his political standing. If Lemass was involved it was in a very minor capacity. What is certain is that two other young men shared Bagally's fate for their supposed involvement. Thomas Whelan and Paddy Moran, who both had alibis placing them elsewhere at the time of the killing, were hanged for the crippled captain's murder on 14 March 1921.[70] Lemass, an active but fringe member of the IRA at this time, was seized in Dublin in late 1920 by the Crown authorities, imprisoned and eventually interned in Ballykinlar Camp, County Down.

The Majority Has No Right To Do Wrong: The Civil War

A year later, Lemass was released along with the other internees at Ballykinlar after the Anglo-Irish Treaty was signed in December 1921. 'Its signing improved my personal circumstances and I welcomed it on that account,' he recalled.[71] On the train ride between Belfast and Dublin the 22-year-old Seán, never much of a drinker, became so inebriated that he required medical attention after the train pulled in to Dublin.[72] High spirits aside, Lemass was quiet during this truce period. He reportedly helped disrupt trade through the Irish provisional government's 'Belfast Boycott' of goods manufactured by unionist firms in 1922, but the records of that embargo contain no mention of him.[73] Neither did he play a part in the subsequent Treaty debate.

One of the most significant steps he took at this stage was a change in his personal habits. He swore off drink and took to smoking his iconic pipe. Another serious incident involving alcohol may have had something to do with this resolution. Charles Haughey claimed that during the boycott of unionist goods, an IRA group including Lemass raided a distillery.

> They were going along knocking out the bungs, emptying all the whiskey. He was the last in line and collapsed into the whiskey on the floor [after inhaling the fumes]. When the others got out they realised that he was missing and went back for him. If they hadn't done so he would have drowned in whiskey.[74]

Lemass cheated death in this instance, but the division of Civil War loomed. The Irish negotiating team had achieved a substantial, but limited, degree of independence. The men who returned from London were viewed by many as heroes, by many others as sell-outs. At a hastily arranged cabinet meeting Éamon de Valera suggested dismissing the signatories from the cabinet. Between the signing of the Treaty and its approval by the Dáil on 7 January 1922 Ireland's Catholic bishops and their clergy exerted a disproportionate influence on public opinion and political debate in favour of the deal.[75] After the Dáil narrowly ratified the Treaty, de Valera and his allies walked out of the chamber.

After the Treaty was signed Lemass took up a job as a training officer with the new Free State police at the Royal Dublin Society. He claimed to have switched to the anti-Treaty position after noting that his pay cheque came from the provisional government rather than the government of the Irish Republic.[76] Curiously, following his initial resignation he enlisted again as a training officer, this time at Beggar's Bush Barracks. Seán remained a peripheral figure at this point, party to the 'debating and arguing'[77] over the Treaty, but never a main player in the debate.

Soon he was to leave the employment of the Free State for a second time. In February 1922 the first volleys of the Civil War were exchanged in Limerick. The following month a large anti-Treaty section of the IRA removed itself from civil control. In April members of the Republican Army Council set up headquarters in the Four Courts, the courts of justice of the capital and just a short walk from the Lemass family home. Lemass took the decisive step of defecting with a handful of work colleagues to report to the Four Courts and to the leading dissident officer in the IRA, Rory O'Connor.[78]

As with Seán's decision to join the fight at the GPO in 1916 it is likely that Noel was influential in this move. Noel left work to join the Four Courts garrison and was probably responsible for getting his brother, who was always more 'reserved in manner', to take up arms again.[79] But by this action Seán really earned his militant republican spurs in his own right. O'Connor, who had mooted to the press the possibility of Ireland being guided under dictatorship by a virtuous minority, appointed him adjutant to the commander of the garrison, Paddy O'Brien. O'Brien was described by Ernie O'Malley, Lemass's school friend with whom he was now reacquainted, as 'straight, soldierly, beautifully proportioned ... blue-eyed, serious, good featured'.[80] The importance of Lemass's role in the Four Courts garrison is indicated by the survival of a republican soldier's pass, signed by Lemass as 'Barrack Adjt.', permitting the bearer entry to and exit from 'Oglaigh na hEireann G.H.Q., Four Courts Barrack'.[81]

Lemass's stance at this critical juncture is hard to fathom if viewed with hindsight coloured by a distorted conception of him as the pragmatic chairman of 'Ireland Inc.'. As his biographers have agreed, in the impassioned world of Irish politics he was the supreme pragmatist. So why could he not identify with Michael Collins' argument that the Treaty was a 'stepping stone' to independence and a 32-county Republic? For Garvin, Lemass's initial pay-cheque resignation indicates a legalism and a somewhat marginal republic-anism, a decision based on peer pressure rather than political conviction.[82] This underestimates the logic of the broader anti-Treaty position at the time. The Treaty had received backing from the Irish electorate under the duress of an external threat of war from Britain. Lemass was not alone in seeing the discontinuation of Dáil Éireann, the revolutionary parliament of the republic they had sworn to uphold, as an ominous sign. Around the time that the agreement was signed, Willie Gallacher, the renowned Scottish communist from 'Red Clydeside', presciently warned the top brass of the anti-Treaty IRA that if the signatories of the Treaty were not arrested when they stepped off the boat 'it will not be long before they're arresting you'.[83]

There were many impassioned speeches during the Treaty debate. The controversy centred on the Oath of Allegiance to the British Crown that deputies would be required to take, but another aspect of the exchange was the association of the anti-Treaty position with a workers' republic and the pro-Treaty with bourgeois and imperialist interests. This point was put forcefully by Countess Constance Markiewicz and others.[84] After some deliberation Lemass became a confirmed anti-Treatyite, making Garvin's assertion that he accepted implicitly the assumptions of private enterprise appear teleological.[85] Lemass certainly did not identify so wholeheartedly with common sense capitalist constitutionalism that he would accept the Treaty. Nor, for that matter, was his much-celebrated hard-headed business pragmatism much in evidence when he joined the poets and dreamers in the GPO in 1916. Neither can these formative decisions be put down to naive youthful loyalty[86] or quixotism[87] alone. Boys matured into men much sooner in those days and Lemass, by virtue of his active service in the Rising, did so quicker than most. He was a fully fledged twenty-two years old when he entered the Four Courts.

Like many others, Lemass welcomed the Treaty but objected on principle to what many saw as the death of Dáil Éireann.[88] So strong was his conviction that by the time he reported to the Four Courts in April 1922 Lemass, who five years later was to enter the Free State parliament as a member, believed negotiation was out of the question and that he would have to take up arms against his former comrades in order to achieve his political goals.[89] The Irish electorate endorsed the Treaty in June 1922. Like de Valera, Lemass subscribed to the high-handed belief that the majority had no right to do wrong.[90] Instead of adhering to the democratic decision of the Dáil and the Irish people, he would join the militarists led by Liam Lynch, chief of staff of the IRA, whose attitude to liberal democracy – like O'Connor's – was dismissive.[91]

After two and a half months and under increasing pressure from the British to end the occupation, the Free State Army prepared to attack the republicans. Illustrating the desperation which had now set in within the republican camp inside the building's walls, the normally composed Lemass fell into a sewer while scoping lines of communication out of the Four Courts, ruining his immaculate attire, on which he prided himself, and ensuring he 'smelled to heaven'.[92] On 28 June Major General Tom Ennis, who had been a senior IRA officer on Bloody Sunday and was now a commanding officer in the Free State Army, ordered immediate evacuation.

Inside the Four Courts trepidation set in. It was dark and the electricity had been cut off. The men and boys of the republican garrison knelt beneath the great dome of the building. Clutching their rifles and with heads bowed, they received absolution from Fr Albert, a Franciscan wearing sandals and a hooded brown habit. Underlining the hopelessness of their position, as Fr Albert moved among the men tears streamed down his cheeks.[93] Lemass, observing this ritual while smoking his pipe, turned to the socialist republican Peadar O'Donnell, who was standing beside him, and said:

> 'It's going to be tough out there with those Staters.' 'Yes', was the reply, 'we could all be killed.' After a short pause Lemass

turned to him with a quizzical look and pointing with his pipe to where Father Albert's queue was waiting: 'I wonder is there enough (religion) left in me to join the queue?' 'I shouldn't think so,' answered Peadar, and so they took their chance.[94]

Shortly after Lemass and O'Donnell had declined confession, the Free State began shelling the republican position from the opposite bank of the River Liffey with British artillery. Bullets whizzing past them and shells crashing into the building's walls, O'Brien, Lemass and O'Malley stoically looked over the hopeless situation from the roof of the Four Courts.[95] The republican stand was ended shortly thereafter.

Michael Collins' decision to attack was influenced by none other than Emmet Dalton, who had risen to director of military operations in the Free State Army. Dalton urged the use of artillery to shell the republican garrison, an assault which succeeded in securing the republican surrender. The responsibility for destroying Ireland's national records held in the Four Courts was not all Dalton's, however. Lemass was one of only three republican headquarters staff party to the frantic and fateful decision to store petrol and paraffin in the cellars of the old building. Before the assault and amid rumours that republican officers were entering into negotiations with the Free State, Ernie O'Malley, Paddy O'Brien and Lemass held a secret meeting. They agreed to 'blow up or burn the Four Courts rather than hand them over'.[96]

Following their surrender, Lemass and his comrades were rounded up by Free State troops and marched to the yard of the nearby Jameson's Distillery. When questioned about his detention after the Easter Rising, Lemass encapsulated the mentality of noble sacrifice that marked the event by recalling that the very thought of escape did not feature in his thoughts in 1916.[97] By 1922, however, things had changed. 'Lemass came over to me in a hurry,' recalled O'Malley.

> Normally he was very calm, but now he was excited, trying hard to keep his breath as he spoke. 'I think there's a chance of escape. The small gate here,' pointing towards the front corner of the yard, 'leads into the next house, the manager's house, and we can walk right through.'[98]

According to Garvin, the escape was carried out with 'suspicious ease'.[99] This hunch is accurate. In Lemass's private papers there is an extraordinary and hitherto undisclosed letter from a former Free State soldier named Hugh Murphy. Writing in early 1950 Murphy recalled how, unbeknown to Lemass and his comrades, he witnessed their escape. He remembered having a clear shot at Lemass and the rest of the party but did not open fire. With impeccable manners, Lemass wrote back to thank him 'for having refrained from shooting at me during the escape'.[100]

Lemass and O'Malley made it over to the south side of the river, where they passed an old woman who, according to O'Malley, began to cry.

> 'The poor boys, the poor boys, they were all killed inside, God help them.' 'No they weren't,' said Seán, 'and there are plenty more to take their place.' She looked at us in doubt, then sobbed as she tried to speak. 'God bless you and guard you for those words,' she said.[101]

Lemass's determined escape saw him join the republican effort outside the confines of Dublin city. With the wounded O'Brien he headed to Bray before finally regrouping with republicans at Blessington, County Wicklow.[102] The republican strategy was to capture towns to the south of Dublin that had been occupied by Free State troops and Lemass served as an officer in the sieges on Enniscorthy and Ferns, County Wexford, in late July 1922. Although a rag-tag army, the republican forces numbered between 300 and 400 men in this engagement.[103] Lemass again found himself alongside O'Malley. 'It's well worth our while to bring a few priests about with us,' O'Malley remarked during the siege of Enniscorthy, thinking of the favourable effect on local opinion and Free State opposition of having clerics on-side. Lemass, O'Malley claims, grinned at the suggestion.[104]

A short while later an exchange of fire with Free State troops beside the town barracks in Enniscorthy resulted in the deaths of two of Lemass's band, including O'Brien, who was shot through the lung. Lemass watched his once-mighty commanding officer die, pallid, weak and unable to speak because of the pain. O'Malley stooped to kiss the dying O'Brien before leaving with Lemass, remarking that the taking of Enniscorthy was never worth his loss. 'No,' agreed Lemass, 'I wish we had never come near the damn place.'[105]

The republicans were eventually repelled. Many fell back to the southwest to defend the fabled 'Munster Republic'. Lemass instead returned home.[106] On the way back to Dublin, O'Malley, Lemass and a number of other republican officers attended Mass in Baltinglass, County Wicklow.

> The sermon was about ourselves. We were looters, robbers, murderers. The Hand of God was against us . . . The people should have nothing to do with us, neither help, aid nor shelter us. We were outlaws, rebels against authority. It was good to get out in the fresh air again.[107]

Later that year the Irish bishops issued an infamous pastoral including a penal section denying republicans confession, communion or Christian burial.[108]

Back in Dublin, a former IRA man recalled Lemass's presence at a number of safe houses at the time.[109] It was when in one such safe house that Todd Andrews, a comrade and later political colleague, recalled a 'conversation . . . on George Moore and the Abbey Theatre . . . about the merits of [Thomas] Moore and [W. B.] Yeats'. What struck him was the strong anti-intellectualism of Lemass's reaction to the topic.[110] Perhaps after watching O'Brien's life ebb agonisingly away, Moore and Yeats seemed like trifling topics to the former thespian. O'Malley, on the other hand, provides a very different picture of the confined Lemass:

> He read aloud Carlyle's explosive sentences; quoted Kropotkin; sketched with enthusiasm the plots of Upton Sinclair's novels, and recited Kipling's spattered word rhymes, the latter possibly because he thought they would annoy me.[111]

At large in the city, O'Malley charged Lemass with establishing a communications network. But with the republicans' every move checked by the Free State police's brutally efficient Special Branch, or Criminal Investigation Department (CID), this endeavour was unsuccessful. Just before the year was out Lemass was arrested on the quays near O'Connell Bridge and interned once again, this time by the Irish Free State. He was detained at Hare Park Camp in the Curragh, entering the prison on 28 November 1922.[112] He was to remain there for nearly a year. After trying to escape from the

Curragh, Lemass was tortured by his Free State captors using physical and psychological punishments inherited from the British.

Unlike the majority of other prisoners, and despite his father owning a business, the young Lemass received no money by mail from his family during his long detention.[113] Conditions were harrowing in the camp and his lack of finance meant he had to learn the values of self-sufficiency the hard way. Winning money from fellow prisoners and guards at poker therefore became not merely a recreation, but a means of survival for him.

Unfinished Bitterness: The Death of Noel Lemass

Noel and Seán's first taste of battle had come when they joined the Rising, after meeting Eoin MacNeill during their mountain walk on Easter Monday 1916. On that walk they had passed a remote spot on the Featherbed Mountain.[114] Seven years later, and in stark contrast to the youthful energy and nationalist certainty that impelled the Lemass brothers in their descent from the hills that day, Noel's lifeless and mutilated body was found at that very spot.

Noel was the victim of what was an apparently sadistic murder. It had been carried out in the vicinity of the Hell Fire Club, a ruin in which the wayward sons of the Anglo-Irish gentry had once carried out barbaric rituals. According to *The Irish Times*:

> there was what appeared to be an entrance bullet wound on the left temple, and the top of the skull was broken, suggesting an exit wound. The body was clothed in a dark tweed suit, light shirt, silk socks, tan shoes, spats, and a knitted tie. The pockets contained Rosary beads, a watch-glass, a rimless glass, a tobacco pouch, and an empty cigarette case. The trouser pockets were turned inside out as if they had been rifled.[115]

It was from these aspects of his dress that Noel was identified by his father, John, since the body was so badly decomposed that there was no flesh left on the face.[116] He had also been tortured; his teeth pulled from his jaws one by one.[117] A later forensic examination showed that both his jaw and arm had been broken and he had been shot three times.[118] He was twenty-six years old.

Four months elapsed between Noel's disappearance, on 3 June 1923, and the discovery of his corpse. Noel was kidnapped by men in plain clothes as he walked with a friend, John Devine, along Exchequer Street in Dublin. At the inquest Devine recalled how he and Noel were caught by their collars from behind by men holding guns. They were bundled into a nearby alley where they were searched and interrogated.[119] Devine's captor was a 'well dressed man, wearing a grey cap and dark brown tweed suit'. All Devine could make out of Noel's captor was that he was a taller man because his glasses had been pulled off in the assault.[120] Noel was taken in the direction of Drury Street while Devine was marched up towards Oriel House, headquarters of the CID. Devine was released at Lincoln Place and made his way to the Lemass family's house to tell them what had happened. But he was deterred when he noticed two men similar to those who had abducted them 'standing against the Bank of Ireland opposite Lemass's house'. Clearly shaken by the whole experience, Devine instead returned home.[121]

At this point Seán Lemass was still interned. From behind bars he had little influence on events outside, which included the reformation of the Sinn Féin party taking place under de Valera and prominent County Kerry republican Austin Stack.[122] This was a cutthroat period in Irish history, with the Free State forces regularly executing prisoners and, in March 1923 in Stack's locale, blowing up landmines with prisoners shackled to them. Having been moved to Mountjoy Prison Lemass had, however, been reunited with Ernie O'Malley, who had since not only cheated death after being riddled with bullets but also been elected Sinn Féin TD for Dublin North from his prison cell. Lemass enjoyed literary conversations with O'Malley and rekindled his acting career in prisoners' hammy amateur dramatic efforts.[123]

Talking in 1969, Seán revealed that he had heard of Noel's disappearance before the discovery of the body, while imprisoned. He added, rather fatalistically: 'for some reason, my parents thought of advertising in the "missing persons" columns of the newspapers but it was quite obvious to all of us that he must have been killed.'[124] In this interview Lemass was rather disparaging of his parents' efforts, especially those of his father. Noel was an escaped prisoner and it seems that his arrest was not initially viewed with undue worry by friends or family. This changed when, after enquiries by John Lemass in early July, the authorities claimed to know nothing of his whereabouts.[125] John Lemass wrote to the Minister for Defence and to Oriel House enquiring of Noel. He also secured a question in the Dáil on the matter. Responding to it, Kevin O'Higgins, the Minister for Home Affairs, stated that he was unable to confirm a rumour that Noel's body had been found at Chapelizod, west Dublin.[126]

The Dáil discussion on the abduction excited outrage in *The Irish Times*: 'Dublin now has returned to virtually normal conditions and the kidnapping of a man in broad daylight in one of the city's busiest streets ought to be impossible.'[127] A Free State mouthpiece during the Civil War, the newspaper's tone reflected a shift towards a growing liberal anxiety for stability after the republican surrender in May 1923, one which ignored the fact that the ceasefire still left a lot of room for bitter, unfinished business to be concluded between the two sides. Noel's disappearance proved a high-profile embarrassment to a Free State government keen to wash its hands of blood and edge back towards the liberal centre. The government wanted to be seen to be acting under the rule of law, thus distancing itself from the guerillas in the hills and strengthening its own credibility.

This desire, coupled with the standing of the Lemasses as an established commercial family in Dublin and the tireless efforts of John to establish his son's fate, did much to secure the prominence of the case. Speaking almost two months after Noel's abduction, President W. T. Cosgrave condemned the 'interference with any citizen of the State, except in the manner prescribed by law'.[128] Responding to criticism, Kevin O'Higgins claimed that the authorities knew nothing of Noel's disappearance until a fortnight later.[129] O'Higgins also claimed that the Lemass family did not notify the authorities that their son had disappeared until 16 July 1923. In a letter to *The Irish Times* John corrected him, revealing he had in fact written to the Minister for Defence, Richard Mulcahy, a week before this date.

In September 1923 John Lemass was informed by two released republican prisoners, Richard Broderick and Christopher Tuite, that while held in custody they were told that Noel had been shot and thrown into the river at Blessington, County Wicklow. At John's urging the police dredged the Liffey in an effort to recover the body, but to no avail.[130] The police had just finished dredging the Liffey again in early October 1923 when Noel's body was found in a dry ditch on the side of the Featherbed Mountain, a high, isolated spot 6 miles from Rathfarnham, County Dublin.[131] John and Frances drove to the spot and identified their son's body. *The Irish Times* reported that 'John Lemass, a younger brother of the deceased man, was released from prison on parole for a week on the discovery of his brother's remains'.[132] It was with a heavy heart that Seán Lemass made his way back to his family home to help console his parents and his younger siblings.

An inquest into the death was held in Rathmines Town Hall and attracted much media attention. Having just secured temporary release, Seán Lemass appointed a solicitor to represent him. Appearing as a witness, Broderick (one of the republican prisoners who had contacted John Lemass) testified that a captain in the Free State police's Special Branch, James Murray, had confessed to killing Noel and dumping his body in the Liffey.[133] Broderick also claimed that a death threat had subsequently been issued to him signed 'Fifty Members of the old IRA'. It ordered Broderick to 'attend forthwith at Military Headquarters, Dublin, and deny absolutely that captain J. Murry [sic] ever stated to you that he shot the late lamented Mr. Lemass on pain of death', adding 'Lemass is gone, and the earlier he is forgotten the better.'[134] The same letter was delivered to the other former prisoner, Tuite. Both Broderick and Tuite gave evidence despite being threatened with assassination and having their families intimidated by armed men.

Captain Murray's involvement in Noel's death may be indicated by the sadistic nature of another killing for which he was later convicted, that of Joseph Bergin, a teenage military policeman from County Laois who was stationed in the Curragh. In December 1923 Bergin fell under suspicion for carrying messages to some of the 12,000 republican prisoners who were still being held in the Curragh Camp, eight months after the end of the Civil War. Just two months previously Seán Lemass had been one of their number. Bergin's bullet-riddled body was found floating in the canal at Milltown Bridge, County Kildare. Local schoolchildren had reported seeing blood spatters and brain matter on the road nearby. Bergin had been interrogated and tortured and, while still alive, tied to a car and dragged to the canal, where he was shot six times in the head and his body dumped.[135]

Letters read at Murray's trial for the murder of Bergin suggested that Colonel Michael Costello, the army's director of intelligence, had assisted Murray after this killing. It was alleged that Costello had secured Murray's passage to Argentina and had agreed to pay money to his wife and children during his long disappearance.[136] Murray, however, missed Ireland and returned prematurely. This was to prove an unwise decision.

Colonel Costello, like Dalton a protégé of Michael Collins and a member of the same Free State officer clique, alleged that Murray was a renegade. Costello claimed he had merely instructed Murray to intercept Bergin, whom they suspected of being a republican 'mole', and turn him into a Free State spy.[137] Murray denied killing Bergin and claimed he had been framed by Costello. Murray's brother, a commandant in the Free State army, testified that senior officers had suggested to Captain Murray that he take the blame for Noel Lemass's murder as well as Bergin's.[138] 'Such things were not unusual in the army at the time,' he said, adding, 'unofficial executions were taken for granted.'[139] The mention of Noel Lemass did Murray's case no good and he was sentenced to hang for the murder of Bergin. The sentence was commuted, but he died of tuberculosis in Portlaoise Prison in 1929. Later, Costello went on to manage the Irish Sugar Company and Seán Lemass corresponded regularly with him.

Lemass's cynicism about Noel's disappearance was borne of a familiarity with Free State brutality and collusion. Noel's body was not come upon accidentally by a walker or farmer, but was the result of an anonymous tip-off. This suggests that those involved in the killing also reported it. General Eoin O'Duffy, Garda chief commissioner and later leader of the fascistic Blueshirt movement, appeared at the Lemass inquest and was asked who had called the police to report the body. Before he could answer, the state solicitor claimed privilege over 'any communications that passed between the Government or any servant of the Government and any other person on the matter'.[140]

The timing of the discovery raises several possibilities. Perhaps, anxious that the political pressure to find Noel would lead to their arrest, his killers waited for four months before revealing the body's whereabouts. Maybe they returned to the spot where they shot him before telephoning the police to confirm the location. The time lapse between the killing and the body's discovery may have been because they could not remember where they had dumped the body. Finding the body again must have been complicated by the absence of landmarks (the body was found 20 yards from the Glencree road), the colour of Noel's clothing and the body's advanced state of decomposition.

The Lemass family believed that the body was found in the river by the police and moved to the mountains. This corroborates Broderick's story, and the discovery coincided with the renewed dredging of the river, which began on 10 October 1923.[141] This course of action appears unnecessarily complex, though. Neither, according to the Garda sergeant who examined the body, was there any rust on Noel's rosary beads or glasses,[142] indicating that the body had not been immersed in water.

The sluggishness of the Special Branch in investigating the case, a point raised by Labour deputy Tom Johnson in the Dáil a few months earlier, is unsurprising.[143] In August 1923 O'Higgins told the press that Special Branch had carried out 'exhaustive enquiries' into Noel's disappearance. This was an evidently false claim given the likely direct involvement of its members in his demise. The charge of 'laxity' was repeated by John Lemass at the inquest, and levelled against the government as a whole.[144] Seán Lemass's solicitor, probably at his instruction, highlighted the complicity of Special Branch and the police in the disappearance by pointing out the ease with which Devine, Noel Lemass's companion that day, was marched up to Oriel House by his abductor, through busy public streets and past policemen on the beat.[145]

The inquest concluded that armed forces of the state were involved in the abduction of Noel Lemass but there was not sufficient evidence as to a perpetrator. A judicial enquiry was demanded but nothing materialised.[146] It is evident that dark forces close to the centre of the nascent Irish state were complicit in Noel Lemass's horrific end. The Free State's Special Branch was a boys' club which frequently acted with a reckless abandon and enjoyed relative impunity. Alongside political murders, their swagger aroused uncomfortable parallels with the recent War of Independence, such as the brazen, drunken discharging of shots from speeding lorries in built-up areas.[147] At the very least, Kevin O'Higgins gave his agents in Oriel House the confidence to go out and be assured that there would be little outcry when they carried out extrajudicial killings. The worst excesses of the killing squads took place under his stewardship of the CID.[148]

Discussing Noel's death, John Horgan hints at the involvement of a government minister, Joe McGrath, Lemass's former commanding officer when both were held as prisoners in Ballykinlar during the War of Independence.[149] McGrath brought a libel action and won damages against a journalist who alleged his responsibility for Noel's death in 1927.[150] The offending passage in a book titled *The Real Ireland* read:

> Noel Lemass was known to have ambushed a Ford car containing three Free State officers and an N.C.O. near Leeson Street Bridge, a bomb being thrown which killed three of the occupants of the car and wounded the fourth. Responsibility for the murder of Lemass was brought home with reasonable certainty to Joe McGrath, then Free State Minister of Labour, and head of the Free State Military Secret Service.[151]

Frances, displaying a mother's loyalty to her firstborn, always stressed Noel's lack of political and military activity and denied his involvement in the Leeson Street Bridge ambush.[152] Seán Lemass, too, sought to downplay his brother's militant activity and emphasise his work as an engineer.[153] Nonetheless, there is no disguising the fact that Noel's actions during the Civil War were those of a committed republican.

Noel was a popular, 'laughing cavalier' type in the anti-Treaty camp, a status illustrated well by Francis Stuart, the famous writer and Nazi sympathiser. To the approval of his mother-in-law, W. B. Yeats' muse, Maude Gonne, Stuart fought with the IRA during the Civil War. In his heavily autobiographical work, *Black List, Section H*, Stuart's narrator – 'H' – is arrested by Free State troops after an IRA assault on a Dublin railway station. 'H', a member of Dublin's arty set, and more at home with a French novel in his hand than a gun,

> spent the night with a crowd of prisoners in a long barrack building where at first he was eyed doubtfully because, perhaps, of his foreign-looking suit . . . But he was soon noticed and spoken to by one of a group of captured soldiers at the end of the building, Noel Lemass, who himself had Continental connections, and who remembered H from visits to the house on St. Stephen's Green. He offered H a Gaullois cigarette, after which, on his return to his mattress, his immediate neighbours started talking to him too.[154]

Noel had been arrested a month after he, like Seán, had managed to flee the Four Courts. Captured in a round-up of 160 dissidents after an elaborate republican plan to isolate Dublin by destroying bridges, roads and railways, he was prominent enough to be described as a 'well-known Dublin irregular' in a report in *The Irish Times*.[155] His seniority is suggested by his arrest; it was along with four other officers and they had been travelling in a car.[156] The irrepressible Noel was imprisoned in Kilmainham Gaol on 14 August 1922. From there he was transferred to Gormanston Camp on 8 September 1922, from where it took him just six days to escape.[157] He was reputed to have fled to England or the Isle of Man before his fateful return to Dublin in June 1923.

A Grisly Whodunit

With the Civil War over by 24 May 1923, the timing of Noel's abduction and execution suggests that his martial activities were significant enough to have given rise to a vendetta. The exact nature of this, as Horgan notes, has never been disclosed.[158] Apart from his alleged responsibility for throwing a bomb in the Leeson Street Bridge ambush, there are two main monocausal explanations for Noel's abduction and murder.

The first lies with the assassination of Cork TD Seán Hales, who was gunned down as he left the Dáil in December 1922. This infamous murder was carried out under a general instruction issued by the IRA chief of staff Liam Lynch in late November 1922, sanctioning the killing of Free State TDs and senators. Lynch's order signalled a grim intensification of the conflict. It was issued after the Free State government had begun executing captured republicans, most notably the renowned author and anti-imperialist Erskine Childers.

The state's reaction to Hales' murder was characteristically brutal and swift.[159] Two days later leading republicans Joe McKelvey and Richard Barrett were executed, along with Rory O'Connor and Liam Mellows. Mellows was one of the most progressive social and anti-colonial minds in the country at the time, and Seán Lemass retained a long-lasting fondness for this republican martyr. O'Connor, who had appointed Lemass adjutant at the Four Courts, had his death warrant signed by Kevin O'Higgins. Before the Civil War O'Connor had been the best man at O'Higgins' wedding. At the time Dublin was a small city, claustrophobically shrouded in political tension. Whispers implicated the eldest Lemass brother in Hales' death and may have been all the evidence Noel's murderers needed to justify their revenge. Hales' killing was in fact carried out by a lone IRA gunman, a northside Dubliner named Owen Donnelly.[160]

The second explanation lies with Hazel Lavery, an American-born socialite and second wife of portrait artist Sir John Lavery. An intoxicating beauty who posed as the female personification of Ireland on the bank notes created after independence, it has been rumoured that Hazel had extra-marital affairs with both Michael Collins and Kevin O'Higgins. A letter she wrote to Emmet Dalton after Collins' assassination does little to dispel this accusation. At the time of his murder Dalton was Michael Collins' aide-de-camp. Dalton was alongside Collins when the 'Big Fella' was killed in the Béal na mBláth ambush on 22 August 1922 and cradled his lifeless body in his arms as the convoy made its sorrowful way back to Cork city after the shooting. After Collins was killed, Dalton wrote to Hazel informing her that a previous letter she had written to him had been found on the arrested republican leader Ernie O'Malley, alongside whom Seán Lemass fought at the Four Courts and in Wexford. Dalton stated: 'I cannot see what use it would be to them', but mentioned that the IRA had marked it 'a valuable document'.[161]

Hazel's reply spelled out the reason for her concern: apparently, she had been having an affair with Collins around the time of the Treaty negotiations.[162] This left Collins open to the charge that the seductive whims of a pro-Treaty, high-society harlot had interfered with the national interest when he signed the Anglo-Irish Treaty in December 1921. Hazel Lavery wrote to Dalton claiming to have been 'constantly threatened and blackmailed these past months by anonymous letters and telephone messages'. 'Three of my letters fell into the hands of the Irregulars,' she claimed, adding that 'Michael [Collins] was able to trace and recover' one letter but the rest were at large. She knew this

> because certain passages are quoted in the anonymous commu-nications . . . which offer to release these letters under certain conditions. Of course I have paid no attention – I am not the least afraid nor do I care what happens to me. But I could not bear to have Michael's memory ever touched by scandal. And of course my husband would be unhappy if he knew and he is so wonderfully good and kind to me. Keep in touch with Mr O'Higgins.[163]

In this letter Hazel thanked Dalton for replying to a previous letter. It is alleged that in *this* letter, written the week after Collins was killed, Hazel first informed Dalton that her letters had been tampered with and specifically accused Noel Lemass.[164] The mention of Noel's name in Lavery's letter to Dalton provides an indication of Noel's prominence as a republican and provides a compelling motive for Noel's death, apparently ordered as revenge for Collins' assassination by the bitter, faithful Dalton.

The publication of letters as propaganda pieces had been used earlier in the Civil War to sensational effect.[165] The frantic search for the offending letter, or letters, perhaps explains why Noel's trouser pockets had been rifled, as reported when the body was found. Tim Pat Coogan claims Dalton showed Hazel's initial letter to an RTÉ film crew who made a documentary on his life in 1978, but that the letter has since been 'mislaid' by Dalton's son.[166] Hazel Lavery's specific mention of Noel Lemass cannot, therefore, be validated. Even if it could, it would not provide definitive proof of Dalton ordering the murder of Lemass. Hazel Lavery was, in any case, something of a fantasist.

While any interaction between Seán Lemass and Michael Collins is uncertain, two of his brothers had experienced moments of closeness to the 'Big Fella'. Frank Lemass, the youngest sibling (born in 1911), recalled Collins using number 2 Capel Street as a safe house when on the run. As a child he would get into bed beside Collins, who would tell him ghost stories.[167] When Collins was killed on 22 August 1922 Noel Lemass was imprisoned with hundreds of republicans in Kilmainham Gaol. The famous west Cork republican Tom Barry, also detained in the prison at the time, recalled:

> There was a heavy silence throughout the jail, and ten minutes later from the corridor outside the top tier of cells I looked down on the extraordinary spectacle of about a thousand kneeling Republican prisoners spontaneously reciting the Rosary aloud for the repose of the soul of the dead Michael Collins.[168]

Rather than Noel's death being the result of one single action, his end is likely to have been a consequence of his standing as a republican activist during a period when intimidation and violence swirled with a grim frequency, as the Free State Army and their former comrades became locked in a bloody welter of reprisals and counter-reprisals. The formal end of the Civil War did little to quell unfinished bitterness, as the assassination of Kevin O'Higgins at the hands of the IRA in 1927 demonstrated.

Based on the available evidence, the most probable solution to the macabre whodunit is this: Captain James Murray killed Noel Lemass, but he was acting under orders and alongside others. Even in the killing of Bergin he had certainly been instructed to pick him up for questioning, perhaps even instructed to kill him. In disposing of Noel Lemass, Murray's actions were almost certainly unofficially sanctioned at a higher level.[169] After the Big Fella's assassination Collins' close associates – including Emmet Dalton and his blood-thirsty younger brother Charlie (who, unlike Seán Lemass, certainly was a 'Squad' killer on Bloody Sunday) – were in the mood for revenge.

According to widespread Dublin rumours, Noel Lemass had been involved in an abortive attempt to kill Collins in 1922.[170] It is unclear whether this was the same attack mentioned in the book *The Real Ireland*, from which Joe McGrath won damages. Another of Collins' men, Tom Ennis, the Free State officer who issued the ultimatum to Lemass and his comrades to evacuate the Four Courts in June 1922, is said to have commented later in life that he was still haunted by Noel Lemass's lifeless eyes looking up at him on the mountainside.[171] The evidence pointing to the 'Squad' clique's involvement in Noel's killing makes it all the more unlikely that Seán Lemass was prominent enough to have killed alongside them on Bloody Sunday.

Seán Lemass's daughter Sheila recalls that her father discovered the name of his brother's killer but revealed his identity only to his wife, Kathleen.[172] That name, which was closely guarded by members of the Lemass family, is Emmet Dalton, erstwhile classmate of the Lemass brothers.[173]

Dalton certainly wearied of war after the assassination of Collins, whom he adored, and resigned his commission in December 1922.[174] Of course this did not mean that he removed himself completely from his former circles, including Collins' thugs in the Free State's CID. It is unlikely that a boyhood dislike, intensified by the animosities of the Civil War, mutated into murderous intent. On the other hand, malicious whispers about Noel, mixed with Dalton's fondness for drink, an adulation for Collins which he expressed in fawning, almost homoerotic terms,[175] and the capacity to use the state to murder together provide a compelling argument that Dalton – perhaps encouraged by his callous younger brother and other, still active, members of the Free State military clique such as Ennis – was behind the killing. It is unlikely, however, that the unequivocal truth will ever surface.

Noel's younger brother Seán was not among the immediate opponents to the Treaty. But this was not unusual at a confused and panicked time in Irish history, full of curious twists of fate. Noel's likely killer, Captain James Murray, was born in the same place, in the same year, as Seán Lemass. He was to die aged just thirty in a prison cell, while Seán Lemass walked out of his and eventually went on to become Taoiseach. Noel's murder, for which Murray was made the fall guy by more powerful men, was not the first or last sanctioned in the higher reaches of the Free State.

Rather than a flirtation with allegiance to the Free State, Lemass's employment as a training officer reflected the fact that, at this point, the split in the army was not distinct. There was nothing flighty about Lemass's decision to join the republican side in the Civil War. On the other hand he owed his nascent political career almost entirely to Noel, who took all the hard knocks while his younger brother escaped them. Noel's fighting reputation and nasty end did much to enhance Seán's credibility in republican circles. Both rose to the rank of captain in the Volunteers, but there was a touch of vainglory in Seán's claim, later in life, that Noel was mistaken for him when abducted and murdered. This is highly unlikely. Firstly, the Free State authorities knew that they had Seán Lemass under lock and key at the time of Noel's abduction. Secondly, Noel's identity is bound to have been established in the time elapsed between his abduction, his detention and torture, and his death.

Throughout his life Seán Lemass repressed the memory of the death of Noel. In his political career this manifested itself in an admirable reluctance to glorify the Irish revolutionary period. In many ways Lemass made a 'pact of forgetting' with himself. This has been repeated in histories of his early life. Lemass's biographers have delved into this period looking for precocious signals of the path he steered in his later political career: cool-headed actions are interpreted as legitimate pointers, less rational actions are put down to the follies of youth. All such accounts are brief; all obscure the domineering presence of Noel Lemass.[176]

Seán Lemass experienced a thrilling and violent transition from childhood to early adulthood and it is natural for biographers to elevate the importance of their subjects. But he owed his early career in politics to Noel's prominence and his untimely death. In 1925 Seán wrote a number of articles in the Sinn Féin newspaper *An Phoblacht* criticising the movement's leadership. This broadside provoked a frank response from the chairman of a Dublin branch of the party. He claimed that many republicans were 'totally oblivious' to his existence 'until the murder of his late dear brother brought him on the horizon of the national movement'.[177]

For years afterwards the Lemass family travelled to that spot on the Featherbed, where a monument now stands, to commemorate Noel. Seán Lemass later displayed exceptional magnanimity to those implicated in Noel's murder. At the same time, the heartbreak of his brother's untimely demise imbued a rather cold and unsentimental streak in him. After a long spell of alcoholic self-immersion, Dalton decided on a career in film-making. In 1958, with the help of a state loan supplied by Lemass, he was able to establish the now-famous Ardmore Studios. McGrath, too, benefited financially from Lemass's extraordinary capacity to forgive and forget.[178] In his letter to Murphy, the soldier who had decided not to shoot Lemass after he escaped from the Four Courts, Lemass noted cheerily that Civil War animosity had 'disappeared altogether' and claimed to 'meet often some who were "on the other side" at that time for friendly discussions and the renewal of older friendships'.[179]

A carefully private man, Lemass declined to talk of his activities during this period and for that reason they have been subjected to little historical scrutiny. They reveal a young man who was not yet able to exert any decisive agency over the shaping of modern Ireland, a brave yet frequently subaltern character who owed much – and was to owe much more – to his tragic older brother.

2

Emerging from the Shadows

How Far a Martyred Brother Can Get You

The Civil War ended in miserable defeat for the republicans. As the Treatyites consolidated their power in the nascent Irish Free State, surviving anti-Treatyites who still had any fight left in them coalesced in the Sinn Féin party. This small but steadfast republican band would hold their heads high and aloofly, contesting elections but refusing to recognise the legitimacy of the Free State.[1]

Unlike Liam Mellows, most anti-Treatyite leaders of the Civil War set social aims aside because they did not want politics to encroach on militancy.[2] Nonetheless, during the Civil War republican violence was often intertwined with social radicalism – demonstrated through land seizures and the burning of large estate houses. A police intelligence report from 1923 sought to deny the anti-imperial politics driving the republican side in the conflict. At the same time, it noted that in the newly emerging Sinn Féin the '"torch and can" legions are being kept well in the background for the present, and no mention is made in propaganda of the futile twelve-months war'; 'the impression is gained that "Sinn Fein" ... is a thing apart from loot, destruction and "Irregularism" generally'.[3]

The post-Civil War Sinn Féin were not dogmatists devoid of social and economic policies.[4] Very soon after the end of the Civil War Sinn Féin had drawn up what a police report of July 1923 described as a 22-point blueprint for industrial and social development in Ireland.[5] A general election was held in August 1923, shortly after the end of the conflict. Benefiting greatly from episcopal support, the pro-Treaty Cumann na nGaedheal won sixty-three seats. Considering that nearly all republicans of any standing were either on the run or imprisoned (like Ernie O'Malley), Sinn Féin performed remarkably well, winning forty-four seats, which they refused to take.

At this point the influence of the young Lemass was still very limited. Behind bars, he had no role in the drafting of Sinn Féin's economic programme; he was only released from prison upon the discovery of Noel's body in October 1923.[6] In later life Lemass called the abstentionists within Sinn Féin a 'galaxy of cranks', a slick phrase which has stuck.[7] But pragmatism was not the sole preserve of those who would go on to form Fianna Fáil. Lemass, the archetypal Irish political pragmatist, had his political career kick-started by two emotionally charged leg-ups which he owed to Noel's memory: both his election to the party's Standing Committee in 1923 and his elevation to candidacy in a 1924 by-election were announced without his knowledge.[8]

The first of these emotional appointments took place on the day of Noel Lemass's funeral in October 1923, an impressive public display of republican funeral ritual. Thousands of people thronged Dublin's streets as part of the elegiac procession. In this sentimental atmosphere, Sinn Féin's hierarchy raised Seán Lemass up from intelligence work to political decision-making. The second promotion occurred after the death of a brother as well, this time premier W. T. Cosgrave's brother Philip, a Cumann na nGaedheal TD whose death shortly after Noel's funeral prompted a by-election in Dublin South.[9] In large part owing to Noel's standing, an oblivious Lemass was announced as Sinn Féin's candidate. Although he was to work hard in both roles, the nature of his appointment to them demonstrated just how far a republican martyr in the family could get you. Until this point he had no experience of democratic politics.

Lemass's main opponent in the by-election was Cumann na nGaedheal's James O'Mara. O'Mara was a millionaire who came from a more affluent business background, based around his father's bacon-curing empire. Lemass was still referring to him as 'the bacon man' in 1969.[10] Lemass's manifesto for the March 1924 election was resoundingly republican, anti-partitionist and socialist. He told a meeting that the republican government would be 'ruled by the worker'.[11]

At the turn of the new year there had been a mutiny within the Free State Army, orchestrated by men close to the late Michael Collins and driven, as an IRA intelligence report put it, by 'personal jealousies and ambitions'.[12] Following the mutiny's suppression, the conservative wing of Cumann na nGaedheal, headed by Cosgrave, cemented its dominance in the party.[13] Lemass's position on this crisis demonstrates his adherence to Sinn Féin's steadfast and righteous brand of republicanism. He regarded 'both sides' in the crisis as his 'enemies'. At a later campaign rally he displayed his hatred for the new institutions of state, demanding that both the Dáil and Seanad 'clear out of Ireland'.[14]

When it came to the vote, Lemass polled better than the previous anti-Treaty candidate (Michael O'Mullane, more of whom later), but was beaten soundly by O'Mara. Charlotte Despard, a feminist republican and suffragette, wrote in her diary on 13 March 1924 that she had 'heard this evening that Lemass was defeated', but noted that the republican vote had increased by 2,000 votes.[15] Another prominent republican woman, Sighle Humphreys, recorded the result in her diary entry for 14 March: O'Mara 17,193; Lemass 13,942; O'Neill 2,928.[16] Humphreys' diary shows that the month after this by-election defeat Lemass gave the oration at a republican procession to Glasnevin Cemetery in memory of the dead men of the Dublin brigade.[17] This was careful political positioning: those commemorated, of course, included Noel Lemass.

It was around this time that Lemass married Kathleen Hughes. The young lovers were both aged twenty-four. They had met while holidaying in Skerries, the spot where Lemass and Jimmy O'Dea went to enjoy the company of young women. A honeymoon in London gave the newly-weds a chance to get away from Dublin. While there, unwilling to let romantic escape encroach on his republican principles, Lemass dragged Kathleen out of a theatre when the band struck up 'God Save The King'.[18]

Kathleen's father, a buyer at the famous Dublin department store Arnott's, disapproved of the union. If it was not his new son-in-law's militancy that provoked dislike it might have been his ostensibly staunch radicalism. And if marriage 'steadied him up'[19] it did not show in his political rhetoric, which remained a trenchant mix of republicanism, socialism and anti-partitionism. Lemass unapologetically viewed his politics as following in the noble and coherent cause of Tone, Davis, Pearse and Connolly, not to mention the many republican martyrs of the Civil War.

During his second by-election campaign, which took place shortly after the marriage, Lemass declared that he 'cared nothing for the old catch-cries about the rights of private property and the sacredness of interests'. A republican government, he promised, would act 'in the interests of the whole Irish people and not in the interests of a privileged class'.[20] At another campaign rally he warned that anyone who voted for him 'must accept the whole anti-Treaty policy or none of it'. His principles, he claimed, were 'not for sale no matter how high the price offered'; the day he accepted '99 per cent, one per cent less than the whole Irish nation' he would cease to be their representative.[21]

Civil War divisions, then, were a central part of Lemass's campaign. A notable feature of the 1922–3 conflict was that the girls and women of Cumann na mBan, the female IRA auxiliary, became integral to the struggle as never before. 'During the Tan war,' Ernie O'Malley recalled, 'the girls had always helped but they had never sufficient status. Now they were our comrades. Indefatigable, they put the men to shame with their individual zeal and initiative.'[22] Garvin has criticised the emotionalism of women republicans in this period as irresponsible; he places Lemass closer to the Parnellite constitutionalism of his father.[23] However, the young Lemass, who often misspelled his middle name 'Frances' after his mother, was evidently in thrall to matrilineal revolutionary Fenianism as well.

As a Sinn Féin candidate, women were paramount in Lemass's campaign. The party enjoyed a vociferous female following, as Charlotte Despard conveys in her diary. At the hustings he could rely on crowds of female republicans to 'hiss and boo' at his opponents[24] or interrupt them with 'shrill cries and interjections'.[25] It was not until months after his election that the Cumann na mBan leadership started to discipline its members for impersonating voters. This illegal tactic provided Lemass with plenty of extra votes.[26]

Female republicans were also to the forefront in stressing the need for politicians to address 'bread and butter' issues like urban economic deprivation as well as abstract political ideas, an attitude that Lemass would later make his own. One of the ferocious women of 1916, Countess Constance Markiewicz took on the role of mentor to Lemass during his early political career. Lemass later referred to Markiewicz's 'great intellectual qualities and personal integrity'; she was, he said, 'one of the most remarkable, intelligent, talented and dedicated women that this country has ever known'.[27]

During his second by-election campaign Lemass's opponent, Séamus Hughes, made jibes about Sinn Féin's female backing. Attacking the wild women who backed Lemass, he urged that 'there must be some appreciation that this country is not simply a stage or a platform on which certain foolish and neurotic young men and old women might cut capers'. His crowd met these remarks with cheers and laughter.[28] Lemass was to have the last laugh on Hughes, however. A week later he beat him narrowly and was elected with 17,297 votes. On 19 November 1924 the main entry in Charlotte Despard's diary read, simply yet decisively, 'S. Dublin victory. S. Lemass is in.'[29]

Minister for Defence in the Ghost Government

By-election victory in Dublin South propelled Lemass into the national limelight on the back of what was a massive vote. The win confirmed the start of his political career and entitled him to a place in the Dáil. Instead he joined the republican government set up by de Valera to rival Dáil Éireann, the Comhairle na dTeachtaí (Council of Deputies). This shadowy period in Lemass's early career has been skirted over by his biographers and before now Lemass's term as titular head of the IRA in 1925 has not been detailed.

De Valera's Council of Deputies was something like a government in exile: it possessed plenty of self-importance but relatively little clout. Nonetheless, this shadow cabinet could count on the cooperation of the bruised but bullish IRA. At this point the positions of IRA chief of staff and Minister for Defence in Comhairle na dTeachtaí were held by one man, Frank Aiken. Aiken, a native of Armagh, had earned distinction as an IRA commander during the War of Independence and Civil War. He succeeded Liam Lynch as IRA chief of staff in March 1923 and issued the ceasefire order of May 1923, bringing the Civil War to an end.

In February 1925 Aiken suggested to de Valera that the two offices he occupied be separated and that a 'temporary appointment' be made to the latter.[30] Accepting Aiken's resignation, de Valera appointed Lemass 'Minister for Defence'. The promotion reflected Noel and Seán's fighting record. For Lemass it marked an abrupt transition from the shrill cries and cut and thrust of electioneering to a shadowy, and overwhelmingly male, world.

In their capacity as 'ministers' in Comhairle na dTeachtaí de Valera, Aiken and Austin Stack regularly attended Executive meetings with commandants of the 'legion of the rearguard', as de Valera had termed the IRA. These bodies converged but at the same time were kept distinct. De Valera and Aiken came to the agreement that the 'government' would be the controlling authority for the IRA but that at meetings political matters were to be discussed 'only after the formal "dismiss" is given – when the volunteers revert to groups of citizens'.[31] Military procedure, then, still characterised political republicanism.

Due to the danger of infiltration by Free State intelligence, Lemass's first 'ministerial' position was pervaded by an air of boyish secrecy. His name was kept a secret and when de Valera wrote to Aiken to confirm the name of the man who had been appointed to his erstwhile position Aiken neatly cut the words 'Seán Lemass' out of the letter with a pair of scissors, leaving a hole.[32] When Lemass signed 'ministerial' communiqués it was with an indecipherable squiggle rather than his trademark signature.

All this disguised the fact that for the last year Lemass had swapped the gun for politics and was less in touch with the IRA leadership than he would have liked to think.[33] He had been 'out' in both 1916 and 1922 and yet in the eyes of the men of the gun the credibility of his appointment was largely based on his brother's standing as a republican martyr. His first real taste of responsibility as a 'minister' underlined this: he had the unenviable task of bridging the gap between the military and political camps in Sinn Féin, an emerging gulf which was repeatedly emphasised by Free State spies. A police report noted that the militants, 'under Ernie O'Malley', 'do not take kindly to electioneering stunts'.[34] On the political side, however, it was reported that abstentionism was on the wane and that 'a number of the TDs are in favour of taking their seats in the Dáil now'.[35]

With these tensions weighing on him, the young Lemass wrote hesitantly to Aiken, the chief of staff of the IRA, admitting: 'I am not quite sure as to what my duties and powers are to be.'[36] He received a letter back from Aiken congratulating him on his appointment as Minister for Defence. 'I am delighted that you have accepted it, as is every member of General Headquarters Staff. I would like to have a chat with you as soon as possible . . . you can come to my diggs if you wish.'[37]

Aiken's avuncular tone belied a fearsome reputation. Shortly before Lemass took up his post the British tabloid *The People* reported on a 'Plot Against the Irish Free State'. 'The mastermind behind this plot is a republican leader named Frank Aitken, who works independently of de Valera,' it claimed; 'Aitken is a law unto himself. He has as much consideration for the mandates of de Valera as he had for those of the British Government.'[38]

In fact, Aiken had little appetite for a major escalation of violence and wanted a return to the October 1922 decision of the Army

Executive that the IRA would give allegiance to the republican 'government'. Aiken envisaged a symbiotic relationship between the civil and military wings of republicanism and informed Lemass that he was obliged to consult with IRA GHQ and the Army Council on all decisions. Significantly though, he also instructed Lemass that fundamentally the 'Government' represented the controlling authority over the IRA.[39]

Lemass's 'ministry' operated on a budget of £800 a month. He was not restricted to purely military matters, as demonstrated in a long letter he wrote to the editor of the *Irish Independent* supporting a proposed strike by Dublin council workers in October 1925.[40] In a 'cabinet' meeting of June 1925 Lemass signalled his closeness to de Valera by seconding his motion that a committee should be appointed to monitor the content of the Sinn Féin newspaper *An Phoblacht* and report back to Comhairle na dTeachtaí. Significantly, at this early stage he also indicated a willingness to enter the Free State parliament.[41]

His desire to use his first 'ministerial' appointment to wield personal authority over the republican army soon became evident. On 14 March 1925 he wrote to Aiken instructing him to improve the IRA's accounting methods using a new system through which he would receive money for his ministry from a newly created IRA finance and accounts officer, who would keep regular books. He requested statements of expenditure for the previous month, asking Aiken to 'please hurry them up'. Finally he instructed the IRA to liaise with the shadow Minister for Finance to settle a dispute over some money owed.[42] He wrote to Aiken again on 18 March regarding appeals to America for money by IRA units, and on 22 March asking for a report on an action in County Wexford.[43] On 24 March he wrote yet again to Aiken, once more impressing on him the importance of 'correct procedure' regarding accounts.[44] Aiken wrote back complaining that he had 'already acknowledged verbally' many of Lemass's queries and seems to have been slightly irked by the young Dubliner's fastidious approach to his new 'ministerial' role.[45]

Lemass proved much more unpopular with senior army figures. At an IRA Army Council meeting on 19 March 1925 Peadar O'Donnell, the left-wing IRA commandant alongside whom Lemass fought in the Four Courts, came out against Aiken's designs for the controlling position of the 'Minister for Defence'. O'Donnell, whose seminal 1929 novel *Adrigoole* depicted a horrific real-life case of starvation in his native Donegal, sought to steer the republican movement towards socialism but shared many of his comrades' distrust for politicians. He took particular exception to the clause making the IRA responsible to a 'minister'.[46] It was clear that in reaction to Aiken's reorganisation drive a struggle was emer-ging in which the officers of the IRA wanted power concentrated in their hands, not Lemass's.

The tensions between the republican movement's civil and military wings came to a head at the IRA General Army Convention of November 1925 when the IRA decided to abandon its allegiance to de Valera's shadow government. Instead, an Army Council with dictatorial powers was set up.[47] Horgan states that both Lemass and Frank Aiken were expelled from the IRA at this time.[48] In fact records of the election to the IRA's Executive, which took place at the convention, show that Aiken was elected with twenty votes.[49] Lemass ran, but gathered just fifteen votes and was not elected.[50]

The day after his humiliating defeat in this private ballot, Lemass reported to Comhairle na dTeachtaí that the convention had resolved that the 'supreme governing body of the army was to be the army council'.[51] Lemass informed those present that this 'settled' the issue of control: the IRA would answer to itself, not Sinn Féin. In a desperate attempt to rescue his brief from this devastating blow, he proposed to seek coordination of the activities of the IRA and the party. Lemass believed that the IRA could supplant the standing army of the Free State, acting as a sort of revolutionary militia, which would cooperate with the revolutionary party.

The writing, however, was on the wall. While Lemass faffed over the possibility of 'coordination' it was de Valera who spelled it out. The republicans had fought the Civil War as an armed, anti-democratic vanguard. Without the IRA, the legitimacy of the 'cabinet' was now lost. 'You can only have a government on two grounds, either by the express will of the popular and democratic government, or a revolutionary military government,' he announced. 'If the army withdraws its allegiance, then there is no government ... since it was established by the army.' The redoubtable republican Mary MacSwiney agreed. Comhairle na dTeachtaí could afford to ignore the Dáil, the 'popular and democratic government', because it was itself a 'military revolutionary government'. 'Where is the government if the army does this?' she asked.[52]

Lemass was trying to salvage his ministerial credibility, but the fact remained that the IRA had walked out on his watch. Faced with this uncomfortable truth, he tried to cover his back. As the meeting progressed he claimed that 'certain suspicions were raised amongst different sections of the army through the indiscreet utterances of people whose names I am aware of'. In reality, his poor vote at the Army Convention represented the IRA elite's rejection of the 'Minister for Defence' and his titular control over them.

It was a rejection which undoubtedly motivated Lemass to redouble his efforts to achieve greater political prominence. Aiken, who enjoyed greater standing than Lemass, remained in the IRA, claiming he had a right to carry out 'any honourable political policy for strengthening the nation'.[53] Defying its ban on the participation of members in parliamentary politics, he ran as a Fianna Fáil candidate in late 1926 while still a member.[54]

Lemass used to boast that he had kept the IRA in check to civil authority. There is some evidence to support this assertion. For instance in March 1925 he prohibited the use of IRA units in unsanctioned 'shooting and intimidatory tactics' in County Wexford, instead preferring to 'keep the agitation within bounds'.[55] But in reality the inflated 'Minister for Defence' role was largely ascribed to him by Aiken, a more senior figure who realised that 'unless some one body [a civil authority] was directing the activities of all organisations working for the Republic, overlapping and confusion would be bound to occur'.[56]

Lemass was arrested by Garda Special Branch in mid–1925 because he was regarded as a member of the IRA leadership. He was not, and had little influence on the IRA's activity at local level. During his brief term as its nominal head, a man was shot dead by IRA members in Claremorris, County Mayo, mistaken for someone else.[57] This was a tragically common gaffe by an undisciplined guerilla army. Raiding operations increased after Lemass's departure from his position in November 1925.[58] In that month the IRA carried off the spectacular jailbreak of nineteen republicans from Mountjoy Prison.[59] The rescuers disguised themselves as policemen to gain entry to the prison and when inside tied up the warders. The plan bears uncannily close resemblance to a jailbreak orchestrated by Emmet Dalton on the same prison during the War of Independence in 1921, described by Todd Andrews as 'the most spectacularly daring event in the Tan war'.[60] The IRA obviously drew inspiration from Lemass's erstwhile schoolmate in designing the 1925 raid. Like much IRA activity during his brief 'ministerial' term, this action was carried out under Lemass's authority; his influence on it, however, was minimal. According to Peadar O'Donnell: 'Nobody took Lemass's position of Minister for Defence very seriously, and since apart from that role he would be looked on as very junior, he was little noticed.'[61]

Starting to Play Internal Politics

If the IRA were generally hostile to him, Lemass found more room to manoeuvre within the party. Back in March 1925 Sinn Féin held forty-eight unoccupied seats in the Dáil and was under pressure internally and externally to take them up. The Labour Party's newspaper *Voice of Labour* summarised the logic of dumping abstentionism in an 'Open Letter to Éamon de Valera' in early 1925. It welcomed Sinn Féin's allegiance to the Democratic Programme of Dáil Éireann but protested 'it would be impossible to give practical effect to your economic policy except through the medium of Constitutional channels'. The sincerity of Lemass's social goals was questioned: 'If it were the *first* duty of the government to see that no child in Ireland would be hungry, then disputes and contentions about forms of government would give place to an endeavour to find the first means of fulfilling that duty.'[62]

Police informants continued to emphasise the 'big split' in the republican movement over the issue of abstentionism.[63] Reports from different counties demonstrate that this tension within Sinn Féin was felt across the country.[64] In these circumstances Lemass might have been expected to plump for the pragmatic policy of dumping abstentionism. Instead he disregarded the bigger picture and focused on consolidating his power by undermining a rival in the party, a schoolteacher named Michael O'Mullane.

The passionate appointment of Lemass as a candidate for the March 1924 by-election meant that O'Mullane, the former anti-Treaty candidate, was replaced. O'Mullane overcame his disappointment and threw his weight behind the Lemass campaign. He was a key member of his campaign team in both by-elections and spoke in support of his candidature at a number of meetings.[65] Charlotte Despard recalls O'Mullane and Lemass speaking together at a large republican meeting at Foster Place, Dublin.[66] At the by-election count on 19 November 1924 O'Mullane reportedly 'rushed out to announce that Mr Lemass had won'.[67]

Compared to the young Lemass's rather shrill language, O'Mullane's was more level-headed. He embraced a more moderate republicanism, a position it would take Lemass much longer to reach. Speaking in the run-up to the November 1924 by-election O'Mullane stated that he recognised the Remembrance Day poppy as a symbol of the bravery of Irishmen who had fought in the First World War.[68] After assuming responsibility for law and order in 1932 Fianna Fáil dropped their active support for anti-poppy day rallies, which often turned into riots. But as late as 1930 Lemass was writing to IRA leader Seán MacBride claiming that the party had circulated all cumainn (branches) in Dublin city to attend the anarchic annual demonstration and 'to do everything possible to ensure its success'.[69]

By contrast, as early as 1924 O'Mullane had come to the realisation that Sinn Féin needed to change if it was to establish hegemony over Irish politics, prefiguring Lemass's later conversion to this viewpoint. O'Mullane signalled this by an attack on Fr Michael O'Flanagan, a prominent, radical Roscommon priest. O'Flanagan had been the vice-president of Sinn Féin from 1917 and was at this point a member of the party's Standing Committee. During several by-election campaigns in 1925 O'Flanagan heaped abuse on Ireland's bishops for their extreme political partisanship. He denounced attempts to turn 'churches into political meeting places by making stupid, ill-informed political speeches from the altar'.[70]

O'Mullane reacted by publicly criticising O'Flanagan, claiming that his outspoken opposition to Ireland's bishops was harming the party's chances.[71] O'Mullane was also known to be sceptical about abstentionism. According to intelligence reports, members of the Sinn Féin leadership 'felt that O'Mullane's comments were perfectly correct, but that he should not have made them in public'.[72] A year later Lemass would adopt logic very similar to O'Mullane's. At this point, however, he eyed the political capital which defending O'Flanagan would bring. Displaying a cold ruthlessness towards his former campaigner, he worked hard to defend O'Flanagan, undermining O'Mullane and eventually securing his expulsion from Sinn Féin.[73]

Lemass next came to prominence through a series of articles on Sinn Féin policy written in *An Phoblacht* between late 1925 and early 1926. At this time Lemass was still clinging to his non-existent 'ministerial' brief and added his signature on behalf of Comhairle na dTeachtaí to a document pledging cooperation between that body, Sinn Féin, the IRA and Cumann na mBan.[74] The IRA's decision to remove itself from his control had left him impotent, though. His frustration is evident in the *An Phoblacht* articles, in which he criticised Sinn Féin's tendency to 'sit at the roadside and debate abstruse points'. Lemass placed the blame squarely on those who had 'outlived their utility' and urged their replacement by 'young and active' people.[75] At the unveiling of a memorial in County Tipperary in late 1925 he repeated the main theme of the articles: a battle cry rallying 'the young men who have yet to test their faith in the freedom of battle' and criticising older men who had 'abandoned active participation in the struggle'.[76]

Although caustic, Lemass's *An Phoblacht* articles lacked thorough-going analysis, were overwhelmingly rhetorical, and echoed the common refrain of any revolutionary party: the need for action. Their significance, however, lies in the fact that the gamble paid off. His articles exploited the financial and organisational decline of Sinn Féin between 1924 and 1926, identifying these tensions adroitly and attacking them head-on. To take the same route of public criticism as O'Mullane so soon after heaping scorn on him exhibited cunning but also courage. It was risky to take on the old order of the revolutionary period. To a great extent, Lemass was aping O'Mullane and hoping he would survive a counter-attack similar to that by which he had sunk O'Mullane's political career.

When this counter-attack came, Lemass must have been stung by the resounding truth of the retort that politically he was a relative nobody until 'the brutal murder of his late dear brother'.[77] This was an uncomfortable truth. At rallies during his election campaign the little-known Lemass was billed as 'Brother of murdered Capt. Noel Lemass, IRA'.[78] Unlike O'Mullane, though, Lemass was able to ride out the criticism. The difference was that O'Mullane had moved too early. Lemass exhibited better timing, moving later when the target was weaker.

The articles befitted Lemass's unashamedly pugnacious public persona at this point. This explains why intelligence reports from this period by the Free State's secret agents located Lemass within the 'extreme element' of Sinn Féin who opposed entry into the Dáil.[79] On the contrary, Lemass was aligned to de Valera, the one real statesman among the 'cranks' who had helped to establish his political career. As the two sides of Sinn Féin increasingly edged away from one another, Lemass largely stayed out of discussions on the rights and wrongs of Dáil entry.[80] With a gambler's poise, he was waiting to see whether changing horses would pay off.

In March 1926 he had a chance to find out when Sinn Féin held its Ard-Fheis. Since New Year a split had been firmly on the cards, with intelligence reports claiming that 'a number of Irregulars are in favour of entry to the Dáil'.[81] The pretence that the Republic still existed was wearing thin. De Valera proposed a motion that if the Oath of Allegiance to the British Crown was abolished, Sinn Féin would take up their seats in the Dáil. He was prepared to 'take the risks and go after the people'; he would take 'the bog road' instead of 'the High road'.[82] Fr O'Flanagan challenged de Valera's motion, proposing an amendment rejecting entry to the hated Free State parliament at all costs.

After a close vote the majority of members present decided that they would follow O'Flanagan on 'the High road'. This time around Lemass dropped his loyalty to O'Flanagan. He later dismissed him in tones that suggested he viewed him as an arch-crank in the Sinn Féin galaxy. He was, according to Lemass, 'under the impression that he was a kind of spiritual chaplain, and Pope to the Sinn Féin organisation'.[83] Fundamentally, though, having lost the army, Lemass had little option but to plump for de Valera's new departure. His allegiance had shifted from the spiritual chaplain to the higher priest of the republican communion.

The gamble appeared to have failed when de Valera's attempts to dump abstentionism were defeated and he resigned as president of Sinn Féin. Intelligence reports recorded the seismic impact of de Valera's departure on local Sinn Féin cumainn and IRA groupings around the country. In west Cork, for instance, the majority of members voted in favour of 'Dev'; in Cork city the split 'had a serious effect' in Sinn Féin clubs.[84] De Valera's popularity disguised the fact that although he still held the post of president of the Republic, he was without a political party. Nonetheless, as with the Treaty split of 1922, de Valera would plough on with only minority support. Once again, Lemass would follow him.

The Warriors of Destiny

According to de Valera it was Lemass who, after a conversation outside Rathmines Town Hall, convinced him to stay on in politics after the hopelessness of his Ard-Fheis defeat.[85] De Valera's threat to leave politics was empty, though: in the republican movement his political charisma and statesmanlike standing were unrivalled.[86] As early as November 1925, at the meeting of the republican cabinet to discuss the army's departure, de Valera had urged his 'ministers' to 'practically face this, that a certain phase of our struggle has come to a natural close, or an unnatural close as you please. We will have to close that chapter finally and firmly, and face the whole position as if we were beginning anew.'[87] At this meeting de Valera had said he did not want to wait 'three or four or six months' for a vote on the new departure. But he agreed to the postponement because in the meantime it would give him an opportunity to see who would rally to his call for Sinn Féin to enter the Dáil.[88] To all intents and purposes, his mind was made up. His Ard-Fheis defeat merely provided that final, firm closing of the chapter.

Lemass is credited with setting up the initial meeting of de Valera's supporters from Sinn Féin. He was certainly present at a meeting that took place at the party's old headquarters on Dublin's Suffolk Street on Good Friday (2 April) 1926 at which he disputed the new name, Fianna Fáil.[89] Intriguingly, Free State intelligence reports reveal that an initial meeting of de Valera's supporters was held the previous month, at the Wicklow Hotel in Dublin. Listing prominent participants, the report mentioned his future cabinet rival Seán MacEntee and his erstwhile rival O'Mullane, but not Lemass himself.[90]

Lemass had, nevertheless, taken a decisive political step. Fianna Fáil was inaugurated at the La Scala Theatre off O'Connell Street in May 1926. The transition enabled him to accumulate the political power he craved. At the inaugural Ard-Fheis in November 1926 he was elected honorary secretary of the party. The following year he was appointed director of elections.

What changed, then? According to Richard Dunphy the break from Sinn Féin constituted much more than swapping abstentionism for resistance within accommodation. He argues that early Fianna Fáil was a fundamentally different organisation.[91] Firstly, Dunphy asserts, the membership and organisation of Fianna Fáil *cumainn* were more extensive. Secondly, its political ideology altered markedly.

Fianna Fáil certainly put a lot more energy into recruitment than Sinn Féin. The prospect of meaningful electoral victory galvanised the party, which absorbed a lot of local IRA officers who had been inactive since the Civil War. Fianna Fáil grew from 460 cumainn in November 1926 to over 1,000 by the summer of 1927.[92] Lemass played a leading role in this recruitment drive, initially in Dublin and then later around Ireland, travelling in his car to rural parishes where retired IRA big men resided.

Herein lay another significant and overlooked transition in Lemass's political development: it was *men*, not women, whom Lemass sought to recruit. His fellow honorary secretary Gerry Boland claimed that in the early stages of his political career Lemass got on better with women than many of his comrades. This recollection clashes with Todd Andrews' claim that Lemass was sexist.[93] As a Sinn Féiner, Lemass relied on women, but as an architect of Fianna Fáil his political disregard for women began to show for the first time. It is apparent that the young married man, already a father and with another child on the way, now had little time for the radical women who had played such a key role in bringing him to prominence.

To Lemass, in any case, the tenacity of recruitment work made it a male preserve: roads were bad and the transport available was worse; it often took a number of visits involving all-night arguments to convince one man to join.[94] Fianna Fáil account books reveal that Lemass travelled far and wide. He was one of the most frequent claimants of travel expenses; larger amounts were justified by inserting the location ('West Cork', 'Tipp.', 'Clare') next to the figures.[95] According to Kevin Boland, the son of Gerry Boland: 'Lemass had an abrupt manner: he did not have the balance that was required for country people. He came to realise that he could not deal with the country mind.'[96] This impatient disregard for rural Ireland was never to desert him.

While Boland was the more confident operator in the field, the job of honorary secretary comprised much more, especially at election time. Lemass and Boland placed great value on publicity, encouraging party members to write letters to local newspapers – 'a very useful method of propaganda'.[97] They instructed members to boycott the *Irish Independent* and the *Evening Herald*, two anti-republican papers, recommending that they read *The Irish Times* or the *Evening Mail* instead.[98] Lemass and Boland also encouraged candidates to get their hands on 'every car that can be borrowed or hired' to transport aged or disabled voters to the polling station.[99]

While Lemass and Boland have been credited with much of this vital groundwork, the pedantic attention to detail of the party pamphlets *Córas Bua* and *Bealach Bua* issued to each member belonged to de Valera.[100] Lemass followed his chief's lead, most notably in the emphasis he placed on economic nationalism and social justice. The party's founding documents declared that the resources of Ireland belonged to its people and that it favoured a minimum wage, land redistribution and improvement in working conditions.[101] After all, de Valera contended, without industrial development and improved social conditions Irish reunification would remain an aspiration.[102]

However, the extent to which Lemass and his colleagues ditched the ardent militarism of the "'torch and can" legions' for the politics of the possible with the formation of Fianna Fáil in May 1926 should not be overstated. At officer level there was joint membership of the IRA and Fianna Fáil until the clampdown of 1927 but among the rank and file there were cases of dual membership up until 1932.[103] Neither were the members of the IRA and Sinn Féin who refused to make the transition to Fianna Fáil merely impractical dogmatists. After the foundation of Fianna Fáil, elements within the IRA leadership criticised the party for its abandonment of revolutionary politics rather than its abandonment of abstentionism; indeed IRA chief of staff Moss Twomey regarded the latter principle as 'futile and wrong'.[104]

When it came to ideology, the break from Sinn Féin was not immediately apparent either. Lemass was evidently keen to sacrifice high-minded principles on the altar of parliamentary politics, but his willingness to drop social radicalism was less obvious. Cumann na nGaedheal followed a conservative social and economic strategy – produce and capital were overwhelmingly directed towards export to Britain and the rural and urban poor were neglected. Republicans found employment hard to come by and many were forced to emigrate. The conditions excited a keen sense of social justice in the young Lemass.

Seán MacBride, later Minister for External Affairs and co-founder of Amnesty International, recalled Lemass writing to him shortly after Fianna Fáil was founded. He wanted MacBride to give evidence in an internal investigation into allegations of financial corruption against potential party candidate and future lord mayor of Dublin Bob Briscoe.[105] Briscoe was alleged to have made a personal fortune while gun-running during the War of Independence and Civil War. Lemass's own financial rectitude would later be called into question, but at this stage he was evidently determined to weed out any corruption within the party.

Fianna Fáil remained opposed to the Free State and its docile ratification of the Boundary Agreement in 1925. The party also retained the custom of attending the Bodenstown Commemoration, the annual republican pilgrimage to the grave of United Irishmen leader Theobald Wolfe Tone, in County Kildare. Commenting on police surveillance of the event in July 1926, Lemass told 'those Ministers and job-hunters, horse, foot, and artillery to keep away. The dignity of the occasion will be safe in the hands of those who are honestly endeavouring to put the principles which Wolfe Tone taught into practice in our time.'[106]

Events were to intervene to force Lemass into the parliament he denounced, however. In the June 1927 election the Irish electorate rejected abstentionist Sinn Féin, which won just five seats. Cumann na nGaedheal did badly as well, losing sixteen seats. Lemass retained his seat in Dublin South and Fianna Fáil won forty-four seats. Its representatives were refused admission to the Dáil because they would not take the Oath of Allegiance to the British Crown. After Fianna Fáil deputies were denied entry to the chamber Lemass presided over a stormy meeting at the party's committee rooms on Abbey Street. The platform that had been denied them that day would be found at every crossroads in the country, claimed de Valera.[107] Lemass headed an unsuccessful legal challenge to the obligation to take the oath.[108]

Soon, though, the power of the gun was once again to dictate the course of Lemass's political life. Fianna Fáil's decision to finally enter the parliamentary fray was forced on them by the assassination of Kevin O'Higgins the following month. O'Higgins, whose name was tainted with the Free State's policy of executing republican prisoners during the Civil War, held the positions of Minister for Justice, vice-president of the Executive Council, and Minister for External Relations. A consummate pietist who, like Collins, is alleged to have succumbed to Lady Lavery's charms, O'Higgins was gunned down by the IRA on 10 July 1927 as he walked to Mass.

Given his lack of action over Noel's disappearance, it is unlikely that Lemass shed any tears for the murdered minister. But it was this event, much more than the pragmatism of Fianna Fáil, which forced

the party's embrace of parliamentary politics. Lemass later dismissed
the assassination as the actions of 'a head case'.[109] The government
reacted by introducing the Electoral Amendment Act, the draconian
Public Safety Act, and – most importantly – a bill declaring that
deputies who failed to take the oath would lose their seats.

Performing a quite spectacular U-turn, Fianna Fáil now entered
the Dáil. Before O'Higgins' assassination Lemass had said that taking
the oath would be politically immoral. Now, as party whip, he was
among the first to sign the Dáil book binding deputies to the Oath
of Allegiance to the British Crown. Lemass signed the book at 11
a.m. on 11 August 1927.[110] At 1.30 p.m. de Valera arrived at the Dáil.
He signed beneath the oath after insisting in Irish that he was not
doing so, removing the Bible from beside the book, and covering
the wording of the oath with a piece of paper.[111] His actions proved
that cutting a spurious minister's name out of a letter with a pair of
scissors was by no means the only juvenile display of which the
leadership of the warriors of destiny were capable.

Looking After the 'Plain, Good, Honest-to-God, Working Men'

There was another general election in September 1927, in which
Lemass easily met the quota and was elected again.[112] He was keenly
aware that if Fianna Fáil were to be judged as representing a new
direction in politics they needed to answer Cumann na nGaedheal's
accusation that republicans were irresponsible, destructive dreamers.
He insisted that the party would deliver 'real concrete advantages
for the common people and not merely an idealist's paradise'.[113]

Lemass was by this point regarded as one of the party's best
speakers; after the election he was appointed to Fianna Fáil's Industry
and Commerce Committee. The position also established his
seniority over future cabinet rival Seán MacEntee, who served
under him on this body. MacEntee was a Belfast republican who,
like Lemass, came from a prosperous, middle class, commercial,
nationalist background. While his youthful socialism was more
pronounced than that of his Capel Street contemporary, MacEntee
soon established himself to the right of Lemass and the party in
general. The rivalry between the two men was to run and run for
decades to come.

At this time fastidiousness was key to Lemass's further ascent
within the party. He soon set about establishing himself as the
disciplinarian of the Fianna Fáil parliamentary party. He volunteered

himself onto the party's Disciplinary Committee and frequently complained about unexplained absences. He pushed hard for centralised coordination, complaining that some deputies were not voting on party lines, particularly his lines.[114]

Inside and outside the Dáil chamber Lemass was establishing the efficiency which would become his trademark; but he was also lucky in his chief parliamentary rival. Up against Finance Minister Ernest Blythe – an Ulster Protestant nationalist whose main passion was Irish language revival – Lemass was afforded room to make the position his niche. He became a trenchant advocate of the protection of Irish business from foreign competition. Tariff protection was a well-established nationalist policy, championed by such illustrious nineteenth-century nationalists as Thomas Davis, Daniel O'Connell and Charles Stewart Parnell.[115]

It was also the policy of Arthur Griffith, the original founder of Sinn Féin. Griffith had signed the Anglo-Irish Treaty, but died shortly thereafter. In power the pro-Treaty party, Cumann na nGaedheal, was less influenced by Griffith than by large Irish-based businesses which favoured free trade and easy access to the British market. By contrast Lemass and Fianna Fáil stuck more faithfully to the original Sinn Féin economic formula. In line with this policy Lemass proposed replacing the Tariff Commission. This body investigated applications for the protection of industries referred to it by the Minister for Finance. Lemass wanted a more interventionist alternative. He envisaged a body which would be able to impose wholesale protection on sectors of the economy that required it. If businesses objected they could be overruled.[116] This radical idea dismissed the selfish vested interests of large so-called manufacturers who were in fact importers who stood to gain from the absence of tariffs.[117] It also went against the strong anti-tariff lobbying of companies like Guinness and Jacob's. Instead, the national interest would come first.

Lemass said that his primary objective was to curtail emigration. Somewhat naively, he did not think that the imposition of tariffs would lead to retaliatory action from Britain. Speaking in a 1927 Dáil debate he confidently predicted that Britain would not impose tariffs if Ireland did so, citing the well-worn example of Denmark and its protectionist policies. If Ireland industrialised behind tariff walls, 'not three millions of people, but ten or twelve millions' would stay at home instead of emigrating.[118]

If Lemass's policy of native control of industry was essentially Griffithian, he departed from the script by couching it in explicitly class terms. Protectionism would be favourable to the worker. In December 1928 he claimed that this policy would result in 'an adequate wage to all able-bodied workers'.[119] Whereas the government supported big farmers and encouraged agricultural export, Lemass and Fianna Fáil championed the small farmer and worker. In the 1930 budget debate he spoke to defend 'the men who build up the wealth of this country, and they are not dukes, earls or millionaires. They are plain, good, honest-to-God, working men.' Already formulating his brand of interventionist state capitalism at the expense of a timid Labour Party, he backed his colleague James Ryan's proposals to centralise imports and control pricing[120] and made the case for a break with sterling.[121]

Lemass, like Ryan, recognised that agricultural prosperity was integral to the nation's prosperity, but he argued that unemployment was 'the most urgent national problem' and that industrialisation was the 'solution'.[122] He often repeated his belief in the material causes of Ireland's sorry record of emigration and unemployment.[123] Although taken for granted today, Lemass had to denounce spurious ethnological arguments to the contrary. These included the charges that Ireland was 'doomed by Providence to poverty' and that the Irish had 'an extraordinary urge to go adventuring abroad'. These were examples, said Lemass, of an oppressed colonial mentality.[124]

In attacking the government's policy of low taxation and its social consequences of poverty and deprivation, Lemass asserted his preference for greater state spending. This was to form the crux of his rivalry with MacEntee. Fianna Fáil's achievement of power in 1932 marked the beginning of a long interdepartmental conflict between Lemass's Department of Industry and Commerce and the conservative policies of the Department of Finance. This recurrent clash was rehearsed between Lemass and Finance Minister Ernest Blythe in the late 1920s.

Lemass's economic pronouncements at this time cannot be taken as seamlessly coherent, however, and his populist propensity to speak out of both sides of his mouth is quite evident. A good example is an address he made to the Fianna Fáil Ard-Fheis in 1929. Lemass is not identified with the policy of compulsory Irish and never bothered to become proficient in the language. But as a career politician he had acutely populist faculties. With only a *cúpla focail* and preferring golf to Gaelic games he nonetheless instructed the 1929 Ard-Fheis on the quintessential importance to national recovery of the Irish language, games and customs.[125]

This is not to call into question his awareness of the cultural and political factors affecting economic performance. Most notably, he railed against the lack of confidence he detected in his fellow countrymen. In a draft document he composed around 1929 entitled 'Notes for a Specimen Speech', he wrote:

> Definitely link up the oath with the economic position. Point out that the depression in trade is due to the feeling of insecurity that exists, which in turn is due to the fact that a large portion of the people are debarred from having a voice in the framing of legislation. State that the oath is the biggest factor, preventing a return of a sense of confidence in the future, and consequent prosperity.[126]

In the same document Lemass went on to stress 'the need for economy' in government, arguing that 'every unnecessary government service should be closed down and the money saved'.[127] This was to prove the novelty of Fianna Fáil's radicalism. The demand for cheap government was a common theme among radicals from the time of the French Revolution, but Lemass and the party hierarchy deliberately linked it with the legacy of imperialism in the country. De Valera claimed that no man was worth over £1,000 a year and the party mocked the top hats worn by government ministers as relics of the Ascendancy.

There were contradictions here, however, contradictions typical of populist politicking. In 1928 the Minister for Agriculture, Patrick Hogan, wrote to his confidant, the Bishop of Killaloe Michael Fogarty, reporting that Fianna Fáil were beginning to make the right noises at their 1928 Ard-Fheis. The once-radical Lemass, he said, was 'learning sense'. When a delegate pressed for greater spending on unemployment relief Lemass replied that the people could 'not afford' the extra taxation necessary.[128] And despite his regular attacks on the meagre social spending under what he referred to as Cumann na nGaedheal's 'Imperial policy', Lemass also made contradictory protestations about how taxation was too high.[129]

The Shannon Scheme is a case in point. The centrepiece of technocratic modernisation in the Irish Free State, depictions of its engineers would later adorn Lemass's ministerial balcony on

Kildare Street. At the time, the monumental scale of the project was captured in the paintings of Seán Keating, the artist who was commissioned by the Electricity Supply Board to record the work in progress at Ardnacrusha. The heroic depiction of its engineers and workers by Keating, and later by his pupil Gabriel Hayes, captured the frightening scale of the project, which promised to change the patterns of rural Irish social and economic life by harnessing hydro-power for electrification. Shannon was the sort of grand develop-mentalist plan Lemass was later to become associated with. Symbolically, it subjected Pegeen Mike to dynamite.

Yet Lemass opposed the scheme. He came out against the monopolisation of electricity supply through Shannon, arguing that the Irish market was not big enough and the cost was too high.[130] In his 1929 draft speech, in which he sought to link political objectives with economic development, he derided what he called the govern-ment's 'spectacular schemes'. Instead, he claimed: 'A Republican government would have devoted this money to more immediate use: such as drainage schemes, etc.'[131] This rather myopic criticism of Shannon clearly placed party political goals before the national interest. When in power, of course, he would prove quite willing to undertake 'spectacular schemes'.

In the same year Lemass produced an unpublished economic memorandum for the party. In it, he spoke with some admiration for the idea of a 'United States of Europe', a 'European Customs Union' and of the possibilities of 'unlimited freedom of trade'.[132] Garvin, mired in hindsight, regards this document as an expression of Lemass's fundamental belief in free trade and European federalism.[133] Horgan takes a more realistic view. He points out that his advocacy for 'economic self-sufficiency' and 'Economic Nationalism' (expressed later in the paper) indicates that in any conflict between the economic and the political, the political had to be the victor for Lemass.[134]

For its time the memorandum was exceptionally comprehensive, ranging from fairly detailed employment statistics for different sectors of industry[135] and agriculture[136] to a critique of the standard of technical education in Ireland.[137] But Lemass's discussion of free trade does not suggest conversion to this philosophy. Far from it, he initially mentioned the ideal of untrammelled free trade in the same way in which politicians often mention the ideal of communism, in order to contrast it with reality and, ultimately, to debunk it.[138]

The fundamental purpose of the memorandum was to state the case for protectionism as a policy which would reduce emigration. Thus the Irish economy would be reorganised to challenge the profit-driven notion that 'the interests of a class should be fostered to the detriment of the interests of the whole people' and regardless of the rise in the cost of living that this would entail.[139] Lemass was attacking the conservative capitalist hegemony of the Free State Department of Finance, claiming that in the future 'the utility of the methods we adopt must be judged, not by the number of very rich individuals or Corporations they create, but by the average standard of living of all the people'.[140]

It was a battle Lemass sensed he was winning. He was fortunate that economic circumstances favoured the broad thrust of his economic policy: in 1920s Ireland wages and prices fell after wartime inflation; agriculture was depressed; unemployment and technical change were destabilising industry; the British economy (to which Ireland was still closely tied) was in decline; and the ideology of laissez-faireism was being challenged globally.[141] In keeping with the prevailing economic current and the British reaction to the 1929 crash, Cumann na nGaedheal had already started to increase protective tariffs. Indicating the new respectability that global economic trends had given to his economic views, Lemass delivered the memorandum in lecture form at University College Cork in January 1930.[142]

As the one surviving example of the several memoranda he composed at this time, the centrality of this memo to Lemass's thinking is overstated.[143] The 1929 memorandum does not stand as an articulation of an overriding philosophy of free trade, but rather a long rumination on the different approaches open to Ireland in response to the international economic crisis sparked by the 1929 crash. Put simply, and allowing for the disparity between public populism and private conviction, Lemass's pronouncements on economic and social planning in this period were ideologically more diverse than has been acknowledged. The unifying theme was the need for tariff protection in the national interest, which meant more state interventionism and greater centralisation. Stripped of the populist rhetoric Lemass cloaked it in, this meant greater power concentrated in the Executive and, frequently, in him.

A Social Radical?

Lemass's economic brief has obscured the fact that the majority of contributions he made to public debate in this era concerned justice. Lemass, like other Fianna Fáil TDs, continued to defend IRA prisoners on humanitarian grounds and accused Cumann na nGaedheal of political bias in policing and justice. In early 1928 he urged the government to consign fratricidal tension to the past, accusing it of 'ruthlessly pursuing the Civil War' since 1922.[144] He called the 1927 Public Safety Act 'a menace to the peace of the country' and stated he would not give its powers 'to a Fianna Fáil government or a government of archangels' because it was an instrument of political prejudice.[145]

In 1928 he wrote to ask every Fianna Fáil TD to raise 'objectionable activities by members of the Civic Guards and particularly the Detective Force' in the Dáil.[146] He repeatedly criticised the government for treating political prisoners in the same way as criminals. The detention of certain prisoners was politically, rather than criminally, motivated, he claimed.[147] The IRA prisoners who he had helped spring from Mountjoy in 1925 were being 'spitefully pursued' by the state. Instead, he insisted, everything making for bitterness and division should be removed from national life.[148]

Lemass's personal loss during the conflict was well known and he appeared magnanimous in declaring publicly his unwillingness to talk about the Civil War. Nonetheless, his solution to Civil War tensions was articulated from an unbending republican standpoint. He may have publicly clamoured for peace but was unwilling to disavow republican militancy in doing so. When heckled at a Fianna Fáil meeting in Mullingar over the threat of renewed civil conflict presented by IRA arms dumps he replied, with a rather blinkered logic: 'All danger from the dumps will be removed when the causes of ill-feeling between Irishmen are removed.'[149]

As the party's leading disciplinarian Lemass was instrumental in constructing the adversarial rules of the tribe. He urged members of the Fianna Fáil party to abstain from all fraternisation with Cumann na nGaedheal deputies in the Dáil bar or at the restaurant. These were, after all, the men who had ordered the cold-blooded execution of their comrades. In this, his first period as an opposition TD, Lemass regularly raised the idea that government policy was at the whim of plots orchestrated by fifth columnists and their English media allies.

Lemass's detection of political partisanship and the roles of agents provocateurs[150] in Cumann na nGaedheal's administration of justice was not entirely illusory. With Noel's death he had witnessed the collusion of the state in political murder. He remained critical of the Garda Special Branch, whose members had facilitated Noel's death. In July 1928 he accused the Gardaí of victimising Peadar O'Donnell, stating that the office of the prominent IRA leader had been raided fifteen times in four weeks.[151] In a lengthy speech in 1929 he asserted that 'the machinery of the Department of Justice has been operated to make political propaganda for one party in this State'. As an example he claimed that employees of a Dublin bus company had faced imprisonment and harassment just because the firm's directors were republicans.[152]

In pursuing this critical line on justice Lemass had to put up with the counter-accusation that Fianna Fáil were involved in the intimidation of juries.[153] This accusation had more foundation than some of his own wilder conspiracy theories. But in this period Lemass's keen sense of social justice obscured any appreciation that his own language often verged on intolerance. Speaking at a rally in Athlone during the second general election campaign in 1927 Lemass referred to a Cumann na nGaedheal candidate as a 'true blue imperialist'.[154] Speaking a week later in Longford he implied that the British Conservative Party was funding the government's election campaign.[155] He also dismissed the Seanad wholesale as a 'bulwark of imperialism'.[156]

Lemass's rhetoric throughout the decade very closely resembled that of the socialist republicanism of O'Donnell, who had come out against his 'ministerial' influence over the IRA in 1925, but whom Lemass admired nonetheless. Lemass also remained fond of another prominent left republican, his old friend Ernie O'Malley.[157] 'The most outstanding characteristic of the Labour Party is that it is the most respectable party in the state ... So long as they cannot be accused of being even pale pink in politics they seem to think they have fulfilled their function towards the Irish people,' Lemass told the Dáil in a famous put-down in 1930.[158] The following year, when the government attacked Saor Éire, a group founded by the left wing of the IRA leadership in 1931, Lemass stated that while 78,000 Dubiners lived in rooms unfit for habitation, the government was creating a communist bogey.[159] That same year, when the government banned the Bodenstown ritual, Fianna Fáil publicly sided with the IRA and defied the ban with them.

Lemass borrowed from the same left-wing republicans the idea of withholding the periodic payments Irish farmers were required to make to Britain – the land annuities.[160] And yet, according to O'Donnell, Lemass made it clear that Fianna Fáil would only adopt the policy as long as it did not involve a derogation of property rights.[161] Despite his socialist rhetoric, Lemass's emerging stance on social radicalism is indicated by his 'departmental' secretary George Gilmore's recollection that in his capacity as 'Minister for Defence' Lemass had Mick Price, a republican prisoner of socialist convictions, transferred to another section of Mountjoy Prison 'in case he might affect the other prisoners with Larkinism'.[162] This illustrates the rapidly emerging gulf between the Sinn Féin and Fianna Fáil attitude to social radicalism. While Lemass was busy segregating socialists, Fr O'Flanagan was sharing a platform with James Larkin on O'Connell Street.[163]

Although Fianna Fáil relied on its old IRA links, Lemass privately resisted approaches from it at this point. In the run-up to the general election of June 1927 the IRA leadership approached 'Republican Bodies' (Sinn Féin and Fianna Fáil) with proposals for cooperation. Pointedly, the former 'Minister for Defence' was not included on the IRA's list of Fianna Fáil TDs it was to summon to a meeting on the proposals.[164] Lemass attended anyway, and refused to give the IRA a guarantee that Fianna Fáil would never enter the Dáil. A deadlock ensued and the negotiations broke down.[165] As an uninvited delegate who had experience of dealing with the IRA Army Council, it is likely that Lemass's presence was decisive.

A major difference between mainstream republicanism and its left-wing variants emerged most clearly in the late 1920s and early 1930s, when Fianna Fáil's former comrades moved more firmly to the left of the new party. Post-Treaty Sinn Féin was an ideologically republican, revolutionary movement averse to Westminster-style party politics. Fianna Fáil, on the other hand, wary of being tainted by the red brush, became ever more cautious. In late 1927 Fianna Fáil launched a popular campaign against Dáil salaries, which they claimed were too high. But the party as a whole, like Lemass, was more petit bourgeois and individualist than Sinn Féin, and while criticising salaries courted wealthy contacts for substantial cash donations.[166] De Valera departed Ireland for America in 1927, to get control of the funds pledged to the republic during his first fund-raising trip in 1919–20. And Lemass was increasingly turning to business contacts in Ireland in search of electoral funds.

Lemass's attitude to the Church in his early career has received little attention. He may have grinned at Ernie O'Malley's suggestion that the republicans used priests during the siege of Enniscorthy in 1922, but he was soon to discover its value at political level. His biographers have recorded an agnostic sentiment he frequently expressed as a republican prisoner during the Civil War to tease his more devout comrades: 'Oh God, if there is a God, save my soul, if I have a soul.'[167] Lemass's Catholic faith amounted to more than just conforming to 'the rituals of the tribe', however.[168] In the 1920s an increasingly confident Catholic hierarchy pressed for the state's adoption of Church morality on issues relating to public health, sex and the family. Desperate to attain power, Lemass and Fianna Fáil gradually discarded the healthy anti-hierarchy radicalism of the republican cause during the Civil War, when republicans were excommunicated en masse.

A republican propaganda leaflet from 1922 written by Fr O'Flanagan aimed at recruiting parish priests to defy their bishops and join the cause, declaring 'a parallel of the treachery of the Bishops of Erin is difficult to find in the history of any nation'.[169] O'Flanagan returned in February 1925 after three years promoting the Irish republic in America and marked his homecoming with an equally incendiary speech at a rally alongside de Valera in Roscommon.[170] The next day Lemass, as a Sinn Féin TD, presided over a rally held beneath the Parnell monument at the top of O'Connell Street in which O'Flanagan delighted the crowd and caused outrage in the press by referring to the Irish as a 'bishop-ridden' people.[171] A week later, at a meeting in Sligo, Flanagan was heckled by some of the crowd, who told him to take off his collar. A mass brawl subsequently broke out below the podium.[172]

On 11 March 1925 Countess Markiewicz defended O'Flanagan, comparing him to Joan of Arc.[173] Three days later Lemass had a letter published in the *Irish Independent* which endorsed O'Flanagan's crusade against the bishops. The bishops had identified themselves with the Free State; Lemass pitted himself as a radical opponent of Church and state. He wrote:

> The question of the political influence of the Catholic clergy, an influence that throughout our history has been used with uncanny consistency to defeat the aspiration of Irish nationality, has to be faced sooner or later.[174]

The anti-clerical content of Lemass's letter was transplanted into a Free State intelligence report dated four days later. In it, the agent claimed that Fr O'Flanagan enjoyed widespread support from the republican rank and file, among whom a mood existed that 'the Bishops will have to be fought some time or other as to whether they have a right to dictate what politics a Catholic should have'.[175]

Lemass, though, was soon to drop his identification with the radicalism of Fr O'Flanagan. Even before the formation of Fianna Fáil an intelligence report claimed that de Valera's faction 'intend communicating with all the Bishops throughout the Free State and Northern area' to ask them to support the abolition of the oath and therefore Sinn Féin's entry to the Dáil.[176] By March 1926 de Valera had patched things up with the bishops and could count on the support of several influential senior Churchmen.[177] Although many parish priests continued to shower Fianna Fáil's marginal constitutionalism with opprobrium, the Irish bishops generally refrained from public comment on the oath controversy in 1926 and 1927.[178]

The bishops' silence on the oath issue was a significant development and symptomatic of the rapid rapprochement that had taken place between Fianna Fáil and the Irish hierarchy. Lemass's anti-clericalism had fizzled out as well. In 1927 he wrote to Edward Byrne, the Catholic archbishop of Dublin, looking for moral guidance. 'Am I morally justified in taking the oath ... seeing that I am publicly pledged ... to nullify ... the authority of the British Crown and Cabinet in Irish Affairs?'[179]

Archbishop Byrne was a supporter of Cumann na nGaedheal and, suspicious of Lemass's political motivations in writing to him, never gave him a straight answer. Lemass, undeterred, continued to make use of the Catholic clergy in building up Fianna Fáil. The idea of bringing a few priests along now raised an eyebrow rather than a grin. Fr Eugene Coyle, a member of the Fianna Fáil National Executive and a parish priest in County Fermanagh, was used as an intermediary in discussions between northern nationalists and Lemass in February 1928.[180] Lemass was courting the National League of the North, a body intimately associated with ecclesiastical structures,[181] and he could count on the help of the bishop of Clogher, Dr Patrick McKenna, in these negotiations.

Politicians' attitudes towards morality in this era had as much to do with fears over population decline, public health and the stability of the state as much as prudishness. For a man with a reputation as a far-sighted progressive, though, Lemass conformed very neatly to the teaching of the Vatican on issues such as these. For an economic pragmatist, he seems not to have made the link (or found it politically beneficial to ignore it) between the suffocating social influence of the Church and the limits to national growth. Lemass possessed a well-tuned awareness of the social and cultural dimensions to economic expansion. In his 1929 memorandum, for example, he cited what he considered an Irish national 'inferiority complex' as economically pertinent.[182] Given that the memo was composed in a mindset marked by the postcolonial hang-ups of a young nation, his implication that Ireland's history complex had to be overcome was impressively forward-looking.[183] His failure to address subservience to the Catholic Church as a key factor in this complex was not.

Horgan argues that Lemass displayed moral courage in the Dáil debate over the Censorship of Publications Bill in 1928 by saying 'sexual passion in itself is neither indecent nor immoral'.[184] This act appointed a board to decide what the Irish public would be allowed to read and banned the publication of material advocating 'the unnatural prevention of conception'.[185] Lemass's comments on 'sexual passion' formed a small part of his address, though the rest of his contribution plunged into the moral hysteria discourse typical of the debate. He said the government had been 'too slow and too cautious' in introducing a bill against 'indecent and evil literature',[186] and went on:

> I was under the impression that the evil which was stated to exist was very largely exaggerated. Since, however, the Bill was introduced in the last session, I have made it my duty to make inquiries, and I find that the evil has been by no means exaggerated, and that there is in circulation in this country a number of newspapers in particular which make it a practice week after week to scour the police courts, to sweep the underworld of great cities, for the purpose of getting a supply of filth with which to feed the debased appetites of their readers.[187]

His most constructive contribution to the debate was his contention that the board should be larger than proposed to prevent 'unwise decisions'.[188] With a larger membership (which would have had enough time to read books submitted to them thoroughly) some of the board's more bizarre decisions may not have occurred.[189]

Neither was there much moral courage in evidence a few months later when Lemass spoke in favour of a motion that the Dáil should not sit on Catholic holidays of obligation. The motion was a shameless attempt headed by Fianna Fáil's Seán T. O'Kelly, the party's Catholic standard-bearer, to curry favour with the Church. It was couched in the anti-colonial rhetoric of replacing English-imposed customs with native ones but, as Labour's Richard Anthony pointed out, the proposal fell short of extending holidays to the general public.[190] Dismissed as 'cant, humbug and hypocrisy', the motion was roundly defeated. Unsurprisingly, Lemass voted with his tribe. But he also clumsily intervened in the debate, asserting that the pope observed Church holidays. If the Holy Father was resting, he implied, so should deputies. A curt reply informed him that the pope still carried out work on those days.[191]

Interestingly, Lemass's ostensibly pious concerns at this point chimed with the more conservative of his former colleagues within Sinn Féin, who were perturbed by the growing radicalism of the IRA. Mary MacSwiney, for instance, had similar hang-ups about the 'floods of immorality poured into this country from England'.[192] Nonetheless, what really distinguished Fianna Fáil from their erstwhile comrades was the party's determined effort to foster strong links with the Catholic establishment. Archbishop of Melbourne Daniel Mannix was a key ally of the Fianna Fáil elite in these early years and Monsignor John Hagan, rector of the Irish College in Rome, regularly weighed in on issues of party policy.[193] In the 1931 controversy over the sacking of a Mayo librarian, where the party exploited clerical feeling for political purposes, Lemass's silence was deafening. Increasingly, then, political expediency demanded that Lemass – the Christian Brothers' boy – would adopt much the same uncritical attitude to the hierarchy as the Clongowes-educated Cumann na nGaedhealites whom he apparently reviled.

If Lemass's attitude to the Church warmed in this decade, his attitude to the state was at best lukewarm. He later dismissed as 'nonsense' the rumour[194] that he had entered the Dáil in 1927 with a gun bulging out of his pocket. But in this era he repeatedly emphasised the party's extra-constitutional status. As Brian Farrell recognised in his short biography of Lemass, the rehashing of the story of Lemass as the man who refused to mention the Civil War (despite suffering more than most in it) is highly misleading.[195] When speaking on security and justice, he claimed the Free State's standing army was an imperialist invention. Instead of it, he favoured a republican citizens' militia.[196] Lemass and Fianna Fáil attended the annual commemoration of the dead of the national struggle at Bodenstown, not the annual state ceremony in Dublin. Although he could marshal the language of conciliation in the Dáil if and when politics demanded it, Civil War divisions died hard. Lemass's regrets that he would not be able to attend the state's 1928 commemoration were, pointedly, typed in green ink.[197]

The 1928 Dáil speech in which Lemass described Fianna Fáil as 'a slightly constitutional party' is well known. 'We have adopted the method of political agitation to achieve our ends because we believe, in the present circumstances, that method is best in the interests of the nation and of the republican movement,' he added. Labour deputy T. J. O'Connell's reply is less documented, but highly incisive: 'It took you five years to make up your mind.'[198] O'Connell's remark illustrated that it was not just those on the opposite side of the Civil War divide who regarded Fianna Fáil's embrace of liberal democracy with suspicion: for many deputies Fianna Fáil's constitutional somersault provided evidence of the original pragmatism of the pro-Treaty position.

The 'slightly constitutional' remark highlights an ambivalence about the use of force and a willingness, even, to bask in its glamour. A founder member of Fianna Fáil said that Lemass 'brought military matters into politics'; 'everything was in the nature of a disciplinary task which had to be done and not complained about'.[199] In breaking from Sinn Féin Lemass shed the uncomfortable task of simultaneously representing and appeasing its military wing. He realised that his hunger for power could not be fulfilled within Sinn Féin, where he faced distrust from the IRA. Yet in shaping early Fianna Fáil his impatience with democracy was not dumped along with the abstentionist principle. Informed of a candidate's refusal to run on a Fianna Fáil ticket in the 1927 election campaign Lemass instructed his cumann to register him anyway. 'If he's elected he can resign, but he won't,' he commented.[200]

Despite entering the Free State parliament, Lemass was initially unwilling to recognise its borders. In discussing the Boundary Commission he referred to the half a million Catholics who required 'emancipation from the bigot rule of the Orange clique in Belfast'.[201] In 1928 Lemass travelled to London to explore the 'possibility' of building Fianna Fáil in England. He evidently thought it a good idea, including in his report to that year's Ard-Fheis that he 'hoped to start a number of strong cumainn there during the present

winter'.[202] Lemass also recommended the organisation of Fianna
Fáil in Scotland; subsequently a branch sprang up in Glasgow. He
was a member of a committee formed to investigate the possibility
of the party's extension to Northern Ireland as well. Lemass noted
the propaganda value to the party of de Valera's arrest by the Royal
Ulster Constabulary the following year when on a trip to Belfast
and urged that 'closest attention' be paid to Northern Ireland.[203]
However, Lemass and Boland concluded that 'an essential step to
the realisation of national unity will be a political victory by
Republicans in the South, and that it will be wise policy not to
divert our energies from that object until it has been attained'.[204]
Northern nationalists would have to wait.

Garvin, Horgan and O'Sullivan play down the 'slightly constitutional' remark. They claim that it was not an attempt by Lemass to
restore his standing with the IRA. It is not feasible, however, that
this objective did not cross Lemass's mind when composing his
speech. Early Fianna Fáil leaned heavily on the IRA's muscle to
help it secure political power. Before the 1932 election Lemass met
with the IRA's top brass in Dublin to pore over electoral lists, in
order to facilitate electoral fraud.[205] On the other hand, Charles
Lysaght's description of Lemass as a 'ruthless young terrorist' is
unfair.[206] A more accurate observation is that, along with a lust for
power, Lemass brought with him to Fianna Fáil the gunman's
disregard for such lofty notions as the democratisation of the Irish
State apparatus. Lemass had taken up arms against both British and
Free State rule. After release from prison he came to occupy the post
of Minister for Defence in the shadow republican government. The
refusal to recognise the democratic mandate of Dáil Éireann that
this position entailed was encapsulated in Seán T. O'Kelly's reference
to Minister for Defence Desmond Fitzgerald in a 1929 debate as
'the so-called Minister for Defence'.[207]

Fitzgerald responded to Lemass in a 1929 speech on the political
bias of the Department of Justice by accusing Fianna Fáil of lacking
'the ethical side of citizenship'.[208] The party's antipathy to the state
ran much deeper than that, though. Earlier in the day Éamon de
Valera declared 'this House itself is faulty' and founded on 'a coup
d'état in the summer of 1922'.[209] The Sinn Féin party from which
Fianna Fáil had developed was founded on the assumption that the
republican majority was justified in ignoring the majority will on
the Treaty issue, that they were the partisans in a struggle between

historic truth and fundamental error, and that their sub-state alone held legitimacy.[210] The break with Sinn Féin may have been pronounced in terms of social ideals, but was certainly less clear in the area of constitutional legitimacy.

Years later Lemass commented that his political transformation 'was a recognition that if we did not get organised on a political basis we were going to disappear like the Jacobins, exercising no influence at all on the course of events in Ireland'.[211] This identification with French revolutionary politics was pejorative but is nonetheless intriguing. On a practical level Lemass was criticising the movement's transition from revolutionary leadership to obsolescence. At the same time he was invoking a name synonymous with radical, illiberal centralised interventionism in the name of the common good, a dynamic with which he sympathised. In his election literature as a Sinn Féin candidate he pledged 'the rebuilding of Ireland, not from the top down but from the bottom up'. But 'bottom up' was never his style of politics as a leading figure in Fianna Fáil. His praise of the 'vigour and enthusiasm' of Stalin's Five-Year Plan in 1930 should not be blown out of proportion, but provides a more accurate indication of his attitude towards getting things done.[212]

His biographers have stressed the evolution of Lemass's political ideology in the 1920s. In this period Lemass, the 'good, if perhaps unconscious Parnellite',[213] is said to have turned a corner, in 1926 abandoning the 'absurdity'[214] of Sinn Féin's abstentionism for the pragmatism of Fianna Fáil's conditioned constitutionalism. But Lemass's was a slow journey to liberal constitutionalism, replete with opportunism as much as enlightenment.

As a representative of the shadow government and therefore a politician first, and a soldier second, Lemass was viewed with suspicion by the IRA. The euphoria of his election success had subsided, and almost as soon as he was appointed 'Minister for Defence' his standing had started to decline and he began to lose the IRA. It was at this point that his serious political manoeuvring began. If Lemass shed some of his principles along the way to parliamentarism, he retained many too, most pointedly a sceptical attitude towards democracy. Two events outside his control – the assassination of Kevin O'Higgins in 1927 and the global crash of 1929 – shaped his political and economic direction in this period. He mulled over free trade but stuck to traditional republican protectionism; and he continued to pay lip service to republican dogma. Perhaps the greatest transition Lemass underwent, however, was the jettisoning of some of the social radicalism and anti-clericalism of his early political career for the bourgeois respectability of parliamentary politics.

Tom Garvin talks of the two poles of Irish Catholic political culture to emerge from the revolutionary period.

> The vision of the Republic as a moral community, as a community of equals submerging individual identity and self interest for the common good on the one hand, and a non-magical, lawyers' pragmatic nationalism on the other, which saw Irish independence as a means to the construction of a commercialised, mechanically representative democracy.[215]

Lemass, if we are to entertain this dichotomy, belonged to the former political culture. As Fianna Fáil's popular support grew on the back of the global economic crisis, the dream of political power was rapidly emerging as a reality for Lemass and his colleagues. But with political power now tangible, could the ideas of the Awkward Squad – viewed by respectable opinion as communistic – translate into practical expression? Lemass, the young outlaw, was now a 32-year-old father of three. As polls closed across the country after the 1932 election campaign he once again waited to see if the gamble would pay off; this time the stakes were higher than ever before.

3

Free State Minister

Setting Up Shop

In March 1932, just six years after Lemass had helped found the party, Fianna Fáil entered power with a fifteen-seat majority over Cumann na nGaedheal. Lemass's first biographer, Liam Skinner, recalled 'the astonishment occasioned even amongst party supporters when the name of Seán Lemass was included in the first Fianna Fáil Ministry by Mr de Valera – and in the all-important post of Minister for Industry and Commerce'.[1] Lemass was only thirty-three years old and virtually unknown to the greater Irish public.

His party's appeal was based around the assertion of greater sovereignty; radical agrarianism and self-sufficiency; industrial development and employment; and the revival of Irish culture. Its ticket was one of constitutional and socio-economic radicalism. As well as seeking to sever Ireland's links with the British Crown, Fianna Fáil rejected the old economic order of the liberal market economy.

Much of the party's popular appeal was founded on the policy Lemass and company had borrowed from the socialist republican Peadar O'Donnell in the mid-1920s – encouraging Irish farmers to withhold annuity payments due to the British Crown. This, along with the redistribution of land to small farmers, tied in neatly with the popular cultural celebration of the Irish smallholder. The second major policy, that of industrialisation, would be Lemass's responsibility. This, on the other hand, sat less easily with Irish rural essentialism. The juxtaposition of rural Ireland and industrial England was heightened during the 1930s, by which point Irish emigration had become directed almost entirely to Britain. While employment was a priority, factories evoked grim, smoggy Albion, a vision far removed from Gaelic dreams.

Lemass soon resigned his post as honorary secretary of Fianna Fáil to give his new department his passionate attention.[2] As he set to work, he contented himself with the certainty that he was standing on the 'right' side of a historical struggle. Dan Breen, a gun-toting hero of the revolutionary period and now a fellow Fianna Fáiler, articulated the essence of this struggle in his account, *My Fight For Irish Freedom*. Breen recalled standing on top of the Hill of Tara:

My eyes wandered over the plains beneath my feet. Here and there I saw a stately mansion or a castle; but I knew that these were not the homes of the clansmen of our kings. They were the fortresses of those who had deprived Irishmen of their heritage. Of farm homes there were none. Here and there a labourer's cottage marked the home of the Gael who had survived to be hewer of wood and drawer of water for the conqueror. I searched the countryside for the men whom this fair land should have raised, but the roads were deserted; the bullocks had replaced the King and the peasant.[3]

In broad terms, Lemass subscribed to the same national view. At the same time, he did not identify with the medievalism of this social vision. His challenge, like that of James Connolly, whom he had helped carry from the GPO, was to bring modernity to the nationalist idiom. His task was to replace the crumbling stately mansions and castles of Breen's description with busy factories, and without compromising national integrity along the way. Lemass viewed industrialisation as a matter of necessity to stymie emigration. But he also subscribed to de Valera's drive to redirect agriculture towards subsistence. This, they hoped, would reverse the process continued by Cumann na nGaedheal whereby, to quote de Valera, 'the bullock replaced the human being'.[4]

From the start, it was clear to Lemass that his would be an uphill struggle. When he took over at Industry and Commerce the department was not 'all important' in the sense of the great department of state: Finance. De Valera had given the critical Finance portfolio to Lemass's rival, Seán MacEntee. Historians have charted the internal power game which emerged within the Fianna Fáil cabinet between Lemass and MacEntee. This intense personal rivalry operated on many levels, but rested on one persistent difference: Lemass wanted to stimulate growth by spending money whereas, frequently, MacEntee wanted to save it.

There was another highly significant and overlooked factor in this relationship, however. It rested on the architecture of ministerial empire. As Lemass pointed out when interviewed in 1969, his department's umbrella title covered responsibilities that are today carried out by a number of departments.[5] Industry and Commerce was the only government ministry without a counterpart in the preceding British administration because since the Act of Union,

A satire on Fianna Fáil's rustic image. *Dublin Opinion,* January 1937.
Lemass, seated on the far right, does not seem to be listening very intently.

effective since 1801, matters of Irish enterprise and development
had been largely determined in London.

Consequently, in the post-independence period the department
was without a home. When Lemass was made minister he found a
department occupying 75,000 square feet of office space strewn
across a number of dispersed locations in Dublin city. Lemass's office
was in Government Buildings on Upper Merrion Street. The
department's Trade and Industries branch and Employment branch
were located in separate offices on Lord Edward Street; its Statistics
branch was housed in Ship Street Barracks; and the Finance and
Establishment branches were on St Stephen's Green. Other Industry
and Commerce offices were to be found up a number of cramped
staircases around Dublin, mostly on Palace Street, Cathal Brugha
Street, Earlsfort Terrace, Griffith Barracks, and in Dublin Castle.[6]
This meant that if Lemass wanted to see any senior officer in his
department that officer had to be given twenty-four hours notice so
that he had enough time to arrange cover and travel over to his
minister.[7] By contrast MacEntee's Department of Finance occupied
the plum spot – a single, prominent location on Merrion Square,
right next to the Dáil chamber.

Shortly after assuming office in March 1932 Lemass complained to his new departmental secretary John Leydon about this disabling situation. Leydon was a quiet man who has consistently been overlooked by the Lemassiography, which instead concentrates on the later influence upon Lemass of another top civil servant, T. K. Whitaker. Leydon, who replaced Lord Glenavy as departmental secretary at Industry and Commerce in May 1932, was small in stature but had a big influence on decision-making. He was a pious man who had considered entering the priesthood. As a young civil servant in the early 1950s, Seán MacEntee's son-in-law, Conor Cruise O'Brien, accompanied Leydon on a trip to the United States. He remembered Leydon's determination that the first thing they would do after the gruelling transatlantic journey was attend Mass.[8] The departmental secretary's deep Catholicism has added to the impression that he was 'rigid and puritanical'.[9] But he was also the dedicated civil servant, a product of the careful Whitehall tradition. Characteristically, on his appointment as departmental secretary he wrote to the government to 'express my appreciation of the honour conferred on me'.[10] Tellingly reverting to military terminology, Lemass said of Leydon: 'no minister could ever have a better chief of staff'.[11]

One of Lemass's first actions as minister was to push, through Leydon, for a centralised HQ. Already anticipating MacEntee's opposition to his request, Lemass told Leydon to impress on his equivalent in Finance that the building work 'would afford very substantial employment'.[12] Leydon pressed, but Finance worried about the cost and passed on the matter to the Office of Public Works (OPW), thus sweeping the matter under the carpet for the time being. Ruing his department's serious physical disadvantage, Lemass was already starting to feel handicapped by MacEntee before any major disagreements on policy surfaced.

Lemass's rapidly emerging MacEntee nausea was assuaged in the following months when he saw his staunchly protectionist 1929 document realised in a landmark piece of legislation. The Control of Manufactures Act passed on 8 June 1932. It sought to ensure home ownership of industry by tightening the licensing requirements for foreign capitalists looking to set up in Ireland. The following month, fulfilling his promise of the previous decade, Lemass successfully subverted the Tariff Commission. In July 1932 the Emergency Imposition of Duties Bill was passed, asserting *his* power to impose tariffs by order over the commission's. Having discounted free trade, Lemass was increasingly placing his faith in the state as the principal agent of progress.

But unlike James Connolly, Lemass envisioned Irish development through a capitalist economy, albeit one nurtured closely by the state. He wanted the central role in this revolution-of-sorts. His control, however, was not as absolute as he would have liked. He wanted wide-ranging powers over Irish capitalists under the Control of Manufactures Act. MacEntee, though, was wary of the state encroaching too much on the market and vetoed Lemass's plans.[13]

Lemass was absent from the Dáil on the day his second big piece of legislation – the Emergency Imposition of Duties Bill – was passed. On the same day Britain imposed tariffs on Irish produce in retaliation for the Irish refusal to pay the land annuities.[14] At the time Lemass was en route to an imperial trade conference in Ottawa, Canada, alongside the Tánaiste and Minister for Local Government and Public Health, Seán T. O'Kelly, and Minister for Agriculture, James Ryan. Agonisingly for Lemass, the Economic War had begun without him.

Aboard the steam ship *Laurentic*, somewhere in the Atlantic Ocean, Lemass strode up and down the deck ruminating on the breaking news. Puffing away on his pipe, several issues became crystallised in his head. Retaliatory duties on British imports would only hurt Irish consumers. Instead the Irish state should exercise 'wide powers' on a larger scale. The way to hurt Britain was to withhold agricultural produce. The state should bring exports and imports under central control – *his* control. He hurriedly composed a letter to de Valera:

> A Uachtaráin a chara,
> We received by wireless the news of the 20% ad valorem duties to be imposed on Free State produce exported to Britain ...
> I think that the present situation, if rightly handled, can prove of *permanent* benefit to the Free State if our people are prepared to stick out the transition stage ... The situation calls for wide powers of action and movement in the hands of the Government and, in this connection, you should consider whether any special action is necessary to secure that decisions will not be delayed by keeping to the usual formal procedure in the Department of Finance ...

I do not know what situation we are likely to be faced with at
Ottawa, but I have a strong feeling that we will waste a lot of
time and achieve nothing . . . Personally, I would much prefer
to be at home in the present circumstances.[15]

His excitement at the outbreak of economic conflict was tempered
only by a familiar concern over the influence of MacEntee on de
Valera. Lemass could content himself that with the change of
government had come an unprecedented diminution in the
influence of the Department of Finance. Amazingly, de Valera
omitted MacEntee, his Minister for Finance, from the government's
Economic Committee, formed in May 1932. Lemass was a member
of this body and also had a large say in the April 1932 budget.
Previously, the budget had been an area where the Minister for
Finance reigned supreme.[16]

Neither was MacEntee named in the Irish delegation to Ottawa.
Many historians have viewed this as signifying de Valera's recognition
of Lemass above his rival. However, Lemass's frustration at being cut
off from the unfolding events at home was palpable. He knew
MacEntee would present robust opposition to his plans to expand
the state's role, hiding behind 'the usual formal procedure' of Finance.
And with Lemass, O'Kelly and Ryan in Ottawa, MacEntee (back
home in Dublin) had de Valera's ear.

Horgan claims that it was not until the autumn of 1932 that
Lemass became convinced of the need for 'drastic action' in the
economic sphere.[17] The letter from the *Laurentic* demonstrates that
his mind was made up by the summer. Lemass became increasingly
more draconian on his return to Ireland. His proposal that he
centralise export through a special board was, predictably, punctured
by MacEntee. Wounded, he surveyed the devastating effect that the
Economic War was having on Ireland's agricultural economy. Rather
than calling for an end to the trade hostilities, Lemass decided that
in order to pursue the war successfully the government would have
to ditch its agrarian vision.

By November 1932 he had composed an alternative economic
'transition stage' which he intended Irish agriculture to stick out.
Moreover, he outlined the frightening consequences if it did not.
He unfurled his views to his cabinet colleagues in a highly significant
memorandum advocating sweeping changes to Ireland's economic
organisation. Lemass predicted a return to mass starvation if Ireland
did not restructure the agricultural sector. But to rid itself of the

peasant the government would need the tyrannical powers of a king. He proposed 'drastic remedies' which 'would certainly require dictatorial powers for their execution'.[18] These included the state evicting unproductive farmers and employing the redundant farmers and farm workers on public works schemes.[19] The alternative, he claimed, was famine.

Lemass hoped that mentioning the 'F' word would at least merit consideration of his plans for eviction. The collective memory of starvation, however, hung over Ireland at this time like a dimly remembered but disquieting nightmare. Alarmism about a return to famine conditions was a well-worn tune in the 1930s. His advocacy of evictions, on the other hand, was a quite stunning departure from the party line. Given the historical memory of evictions during the Famine and the Land War, it was similarly ill-judged.

Above all, these ideas were politically suicidal, betraying Lemass's lack of identification with the rural smallholders on whom the party based its support. His concerns were understandable. The problem was his impatient, authoritarian delivery of them. The plans were defeated by a hostile cabinet led, of course, by MacEntee. In one of the earliest examples of Finance taking a wrecking ball to Industry and Commerce's grand plans, he successfully ruined Lemass's proposals to alleviate unemployment and restructure the agrarian economy.[20]

This defeat reflected the fact that his ministerial colleagues were increasingly coming to view their youngest colleague as motivated by a consistent and thinly veiled aspiration to concentrate greater control under his powers. Unfortunately, an illiberal, 'dictatorial' attitude was to emerge as a constant theme of Lemass's big ideas for national resurgence, many of which were not only worthwhile but necessary. His biographers have relayed how Lemass, the progressive, was hamstrung by the conservative consensus spearheaded by the obstructionist MacEntee. While often true, the juxtaposition of the two men has become reductive in leaning towards the Dublin man[21] when it is evident that Lemass was a regular victim of his own impatience.

Tensions Internal and External

To Lemass's political opponents, this anti-democratic attitude tarnished Fianna Fáil as a collective. Cumann na nGaedheal painted their defeat in the 1932 election as a triumph of republican violence and left-wing subversion. Lemass, when asked about the IRA's role in the 1932 election, downplayed its significance, claiming 'they were involved in various activities of a fairly confused kind at that time'.[22] In reality Fianna Fáil's successful campaign owed much to the support of the paramilitary force Lemass had once belonged to. For the 1932 election the IRA leadership suspended its orders forbidding members to work for political parties and assisted Fianna Fáil in canvassing, postering and organising meetings.[23] This was a significant transition from the talks Lemass had held with the IRA in 1927, when the differences between the main political and military camps of republicanism could not be reconciled.

Lemass was complicit in the mass rigging of votes that took place in Dublin during the 1932 election.[24] According to one source, IRA volunteers were handed lists from the electoral register and dispatched around the city to vote, some as many as fifty times each.[25] One of the first and most symbolic steps the new government took after the election was to unconditionally release IRA prisoners, a move Lemass had vigorously endorsed throughout the previous decade. The IRA re-emerged proudly in public at a subsequent rally at Stephen's Green in Dublin.

The jubilant scenes masked the fact that the organisation had effectively placed itself at the bidding of Fianna Fáil's Executive. And, if necessary, the government could trump the IRA by appealing to the rule of law. According to Lemass, there was never any significant challenge from the IRA during the 1930s. He claimed to have trusted the organisation's leadership because it consisted of 'those we had worked during the civil war'.[26] It is clear that he now regarded the IRA as safely in his pocket once again, having lost the republican army when 'Minister for Defence' in the previous decade. Like then, he was not on quite so cosy terms with the IRA as he described. The difference was he now knew he could rely on its members to carry out Fianna Fáil's street fighting.

It is somewhat ironic, therefore, that it was the cut and thrust of democracy – about which Lemass was at times ambiguous – which provided the rambunctious young minister with the rehabilitation within the Fianna Fáil cabinet he needed. De Valera's government relied on the Labour Party's backing to maintain office. But just one year into its term, Labour's support for Fianna Fáil was showing signs of strain. In January 1933 de Valera decided to go to the country. The party appointed Lemass chief organiser of the election campaign;

he responded by turning in a bravura performance to restore his battered standing in the party hierarchy.

Reverting to his electioneering tactics of the 1920s, the conspirator in Lemass came bobbing to the surface once again. He publicly ratcheted up the tension between Britain and Ireland, seeking to enhance Fianna Fáil's populist nationalist appeal. The 1933 election campaign provided an outlet for his pent-up frustration at being marooned at the Imperial Conference at Ottawa with Ryan and O'Kelly, a period of exile that had given MacEntee the opportunity to work on de Valera. Lemass claimed that when in Canada the British Secretary of State for Dominion Affairs, James H. Thomas, had sidled up to him and told him that he expected civil war to break out afresh in Ireland. Lemass inferred that the British were engineering a coup and accused Thomas of 'economic Black-and-Tannery'.[27] Cumann na nGaedheal, he claimed, were doing the work of the British for them and were ultimately responsible for the Economic War.[28]

Lemass's claim is contradicted by James Ryan, a Wexford farmer, medical doctor and de Valera's Minister for Agriculture. According to him Thomas 'wouldn't talk' to the Irish delegation at Ottawa.[29] Lemass may have been bluffing, then, but there is evidence elsewhere that the British were attempting agent provocateur tactics in Ireland. Thomas had anticipated Fianna Fáil's 1932 election victory and viewed their election promises with alarm. He was determined to let de Valera make the first move in souring relations and precipitating economic warfare.[30] When it came, with the default on the land annuities, Thomas recommended to the British cabinet that their response be 'no less emphatic'.[31] He encouraged the imposition of duties because he expected them to improve W. T. Cosgrave's electoral chances over de Valera's.[32] Britain's subsequent tariffs on Irish agricultural exports were crippling, prompting Lemass's 'drastic' proposals for economic reorganisation. Throughout the Economic War, Thomas's communications with the British cabinet left them in no doubt that the Dominions Office regarded Cumann na nGaedheal as 'loyalists' and Fianna Fáil as dangerous radicals.[33]

Running a hostile eye over the Irish cabinet, Thomas discerned a united front under de Valera and did not perceive Lemass to be worthy of much mention in his reports to his superiors in Westminster. This was surprising as Lemass's criticism of Thomas was pretty wild, diverging sharply from the clever discourtesy aimed at the British-appointed governor general by Frank Aiken and de Valera a few months previously when they ignored him at an official function.[34] More importantly, Lemass's muck-and-bullets language did little to dampen the enmity rapidly developing along old Civil War lines.

On the streets this was played out in clashes between the 'Blueshirts', a fascistic mass movement which sought to protect Cumann na nGaedheal rallies, and the IRA, which sought to break them up. Coming to prominence on a wave of anti-communist hysteria in Ireland, the Blueshirts claimed to be protecting freedom of speech. The 1933 election was one of violence between the IRA and the Blueshirts beneath the hustings, at election booths, cattle marts and rallies. Privately, Lemass discouraged Fianna Fáil party members from going near Blueshirt rallies.[35] Fianna Fáil would benefit from the IRA's elimination of the Blueshirt threat; there was always time to clamp down on the IRA in the calm that would follow the storm.

In stoking up Civil War tensions Lemass's language was certainly irresponsible, doing little to aid the development of a culture of political compromise in Ireland. In the political atmosphere, however, such barricades rhetoric was resoundingly effective. The 1933 election, during which Lemass resumed his central organisational role as director of elections, resulted in an overall majority for Fianna Fáil of twenty-nine seats and an increased vote for Lemass in his constituency.

After the election, his language was no less adversarial. When Cumann na nGaedheal and the Blueshirts merged with the National Centre Party in September 1933 to become 'Fine Gael – the United Ireland Party' Lemass dismissed this triple alliance as a 'cripple alliance'.[36] Lemass and MacEntee, the two cabinet rivals, now presented a united front. Together, they were the most vociferous deriders of Fine Gael on the government front bench. Lemass attacked the influence of unionists in the Seanad as well; he wanted it 'under our thumb', asserting that it was 'about time the Irish people become masters in this country'.[37]

Taunts between Lemass and Fine Gael's Eoin O'Duffy, another former favourite of Michael Collins who had appeared at the tribunal into Noel's death, are illustrative of the strong undercurrent of Irish-Ireland cultural nationalism in Irish politics in this period. Lemass liked to caricature the opposition as toffs in top hats, a class

A parody of the young Minister's oratorical style.
Dublin Opinion, July 1932.

criticism with Anglophobic undercurrents. In 1934 O'Duffy responded by claiming that Lemass and other cabinet members enjoyed 'foreign' jazz music and went dancing at Dublin's Metropole Hotel.[38] Lemass, like de Valera, suffered xenophobic rhetoric on the basis of his sallow complexion and exotic surname.

But Fianna Fáil's firm stance against the fascist threat masked internal tensions. Publicly, the party radiated impressive unity. Privately, Lemass's personality was again rankling with his colleagues. Safely ensconced in power over a heavily regulated domestic market, Lemass began to establish patronage links with Ireland's business elites. His socialist rhetoric of the previous decade beginning to pale, he sought to cultivate fund-raising committees for the party. According to prominent party man Todd Andrews, these were composed of vacuous businessmen, whose habitat was the bar-lounges of

Dublin hotels, and who displayed 'the moral flabbiness born of the exclusive worship of the bitch goddess success'.[39] Andrews recalled that Lemass did not take easily to people in general, but he had few problems courting businessmen.[40] In many ways Lemass was laying the foundations for Taca, the brazen boys' club for businessmen and politicos that future son-in-law Charles Haughey and his young political colleagues were later to develop.

Lemass's determination to consolidate Fianna Fáil's grip on power by building up the party's financial muscle led to his sanctioning a substantial, and very controversial, donation. Joe McGrath, the former Cumann na nGaedheal politician, had been heavily implicated in Noel Lemass's murder, as mentioned in the first chapter. Now proprietor of the major lottery racket, the Irish Hospitals' Sweepstake, McGrath was keen to establish good relations with the country's new political masters, despite his erstwhile allegiances. It was McGrath who offered the republican party its first big donation. Remarkably, Lemass accepted. His old partner as honorary secretary of the party, Gerald Boland, viewed the acceptance of this money as the beginning of the degeneration of Fianna Fáil, as his son Kevin explains:

> The third aim of the party constitution was 'To make the resources and wealth of Ireland subservient to the needs and welfare of all the people of Ireland', and, while the party never regarded itself as socialist, this was seriously intended and generally accepted as the underlying principle of its economic policy . . . when, in the early thirties, a subscription of the undreamed-of amount of £500 from Mr Joe McGrath arrived without warning at the party headquarters, the general secretary realised that, apart from the fact that Mr McGrath was a well known supporter and financial backer of Cumann na nGaedheal, this would run counter to the Fianna Fáil ethos. He showed the letter to my father . . . He asked 'What am I going to do about this?' The reply was immediate and as he expected, 'Send it back to him of course.' It was sent back by return of post, with the polite explanation that it was party policy not to accept subscriptions of this nature. Mr Lemass, who was the other joint honorary secretary, raised the matter at a subsequent meeting either of the National Executive or the Officer Board and the result of the discussion was the decision to accept the subscription.[41]

Lemass's business dealings with former adversaries are cited as evidence of his willingness to patch up Civil War tensions.[42] Back-slapping bonhomie notwithstanding, the fact remains that the donations to Fianna Fáil from McGrath and other members of the Irish bourgeoisie were also motivated by faith that Lemass would look kindly on their business empires. In the 1930s Lemass established close contact between businessmen such as Arthur Cox and Vincent Crowley and middlemen such as the Industrial Credit Corporation's J. J. Beddy.[43] Cox and Crowley, in particular, were close to John Leydon and if they wanted applications 'hurried up' never had a problem.[44]

Boland's disdain for what he perceived as a certain lack of ethics in Lemass's approach was a sentiment broadly shared by the majority of de Valera's cabinet ministers. Of them, MacEntee continued to prove Lemass's bête noir. After the 1933 election Leydon held talks with the chairman of the Office of Public Works during which it was proposed that the new departmental HQ Lemass craved be located in the Dublin Castle area. The next day Leydon discussed the proposal with his minister.[45] Lemass, however, would settle for nothing less than being at the centre of operations. In the months that followed he lobbied hard for his department to occupy a single, prime location close to the Dáil. In 1934 MacEntee's Department of Finance finally agreed, authorising the building of a HQ for the department on Kildare Street, on the opposite side of the road to the Dáil.[46]

From this point on the project became subject to some serious delaying tactics, most of which emanated from MacEntee. In August 1934 Finance took the highly unusual decision to hold a competition to find an architect to design the new department building. Usually, the OPW's architects prepared designs for public buildings. But Finance officials, with a rather puzzling relish, insisted on holding a competition. The motivations behind the department's uncommon zeal soon became clear. The selection and adjudication of entries was scheduled to take five months.[47] In fact, to MacEntee's content-ment, this phase delayed the project to provide Lemass with a new HQ by a total of one and a half years.[48] In October 1934, Finance received the draft conditions of the project but sent them back to the OPW, demanding revision. The revised conditions were received in January 1935. Finance demanded amendments to these as well and it was not until August 1935 that the terms were finally settled. MacEntee was quietly stunting the growth of Lemass's empire.

Checked at every turn by MacEntee, unpopular within cabinet, and amid the domestic and global upheavals of the 1930s, Lemass came to appreciate that his best prospects lay in following his chief's lead. He remained quiet but loyal to de Valera in his condemnation of Benito Mussolini's invasion of Ethiopia in 1935. It has been said that in broad terms Lemass was pro-republic during the Spanish Civil War. Holding his cards close to his chest, he conformed to de Valera's policy of non-intervention and refused to be drawn into the anti-communist crusade backed by the Irish bishops. In early 1937 he was accused of being pro-communist by the leader of the pro-Franco Irish Christian Front, Patrick Belton, for permitting exports to Spain. This was an absurd charge: Spain was just one of a number of countries used as an export market by Lemass to reduce Ireland's dependence on Britain. But, careful not to rise to Belton's bait and thus alienate sections of Catholic opinion, *The Irish Press* trod more carefully than usual. Instead of providing Lemass with the last word, the newspaper urged moderation.[49] As the most obvious representative of Ireland's urban working class in cabinet, Lemass was careful to tread a line close to his leader's.

In July 1936 the government took the decisive step of proscribing Lemass's old tool, the IRA. For the next three years the IRA's offshoots and the broader Irish left were preoccupied with the anti-fascist fight for the Spanish Republic, but marginalised by popular anti-communist vitriol at home. Again, Lemass followed de Valera's line throughout this period of tension between left and right, assuming the middle ground and reaping the rhetorical benefits as he did so. In the early 1930s he famously derided Eoin O'Duffy's fascism as acquired 'during a fortnight's cruise in the Mediterranean'. In sending up the Monaghan man as an exotica-seeking rural twit, Lemass succeeded in undermining not only Irish fascism but also the earnestness of the socialist opposition to it.

Fianna Fáil's electoral performance in the 1930s stands as a testament to this strategy and also to Lemass's efficacy as the party's director of elections. Fianna Fáil gained power with the support of the Labour Party in 1937 and an absolute majority in 1938. As a mark of his resounding popularity on home turf Lemass was consistently returned comfortably as a TD for Dublin South in the elections of 1932, 1933, 1937 and 1938. His triumph in the 1937 election was particularly impressive. Lemass topped a large field of sixteen candidates, his share of the vote almost 30 per cent.

Meanwhile, behind the scenes, the conflict between Finance and Industry and Commerce rumbled on. This interdepartmental rivalry was nothing new. It had existed under Cumann na nGaedheal's administration, most notably in disagreements over the cost and scale of the Shannon Scheme. But under Fianna Fáil it took on a new intensity. MacEntee may have sunk many of Lemass's progressive proposals, but he was less successful than his Cumann na nGaedheal predecessor Ernest Blythe in vetoing spending. This was in large part due to Lemass and Leydon's energy and ruthlessness. This ambitious duo and their officials were more active than their predecessors in meeting with capitalists keen to start up factories and frequently outmanoeuvred Finance. Industry and Commerce used the Emergency Imposition of Duties Act to its own interest. To Finance's chagrin, the department often commissioned the parliamentary draftsman to draft a new order before referring the proposal to Finance, which could be left with only one day to respond.[50]

In this rapidly escalating great game, Leydon's influence on blunting Finance was decisive. Leydon was very fond of Lemass and only ever signed himself off as 'Seán' when writing to his minister. The feeling was mutual. Lemass recognised that Leydon's talents would have earned greater financial rewards in the private sector and in 1934 he tried to secure him a special personal allowance of £300 to ensure his retention. MacEntee, however, vetoed the proposal.[51] Cementing the rivalry was another steadfast character: MacEntee's secretary and Leydon's opposite number, J. J. McElligott. McElligott was trained in the British system and shared its values of integrity. In line with the laissez-faireism of the British system McElligott opposed state intervention, believed that the budget should be balanced, and wanted to keep taxation as low as possible so as to favour exporting farmers and industrialists.

While Leydon and Lemass proved a dynamic duo, Finance prevailed over Industry and Commerce in the 1930s in one crucial and neglected regard. The unconventional and long-winded architectural competition instigated by Finance saw James Rupert Boyd-Barrett, a Cork architect, win the contract to build Lemass's palace. The stripped classicism of his design was the favoured architectural style of 1930s' fascism, and seems to have been to Lemass's taste as well. Lemass showed considerable interest in Boyd-Barrett's plan. A civil servant in the OPW noted how in January 1936 he was repeatedly instructed to bring the plans to Government Buildings for his inspection.[52] In another example of his determination to plant his department at the centre of power in the Irish state, at the planning stage the Minister for Industry and Commerce requested an underground tunnel linking the department to Government Buildings opposite. This design feature was politely refused by Boyd-Barrett.[53]

By 1937 Lemass was growing tired and frustrated with the many delays to the process. As deadlines came and went, he repeatedly got Leydon to press Finance and the OPW for a revised timetable for the building's completion.[54] Mulling over the delays, Lemass evidently smelled the rat in Finance. In July 1937 he wrote personally to Hugo Flinn, MacEntee's parliamentary secretary, complaining that:

> The actual arrangements are already 12 months behind the time table. I do not know what is the explanation for this delay, but I should be glad if you would be good enough to give the matter your personal attention with a view to ensuring that further progress shall be expedited.[55]

Flinn insisted that other factors, such as a building strike, the modification of designs and the supply of steel, were at play.[56] In line with Lemass's own protectionist policies, the steel for the mainframe of the building was fabricated in Ireland instead of being imported; this delayed construction by ten months.[57] The implications of the 1938 Anglo-Irish trade agreement, which are discussed later in this chapter, also resulted in further delay to Lemass's palace.

The youngest minister was becoming increasingly truculent about the slow pace of progress, though. An interdepartmental meeting in July 1935 anticipated that the building would be completed by June 1938.[58] In the event, construction did not begin until January 1939. All this exasperated the famous Lemassian impatience. In March 1939 he told Finance that he was 'very seriously concerned at the delay that has taken place', pointing out that five years had by this point passed by without any visible progress on the building.[59] Lemass had always stressed the employment that work on his new HQ would bring, and when construction eventually began in 1939 *The Irish Press* proudly printed pictures of the men who found employment on the project hard at work clearing the site.[60] Nonetheless, Lemass's physical disadvantage over MacEntee persisted for the entire decade, with his officers and clerks dispersed around the city. Viewed in this context, the macroeconomic changes Lemass was able to secure in this decade appear all the more remarkable.

Economic Puritanism Diluted

Politically, Lemass stuck very closely to de Valera throughout the decade, out of both necessity and loyalty. Nonetheless, in Dáil debates he was increasingly singled out by the opposition for the manner in which he was exercising his unprecedented ministerial power over the economy. Lemass frequently overrode parliament by relying on statutory measures to implement his plans. At the drop of a hat he would often revert to the emergency imposition of duties. Fine Gael's James Dillon, who would become a long-term opponent of Lemass, resented what he regarded as arbitrary and authoritarian methods. Dillon accused Lemass of bypassing parliament and of creating a bourgeois cronyism that prejudiced the consumer. He attacked his insistence on keeping policy details secret and awarding import licences at his own discretion. Dillon contended that, 'bad as socialism is, it is better than a monopoly in the hands of private capitalists'.[61]

In retort, Lemass challenged the social irresponsibility of the laissez-faire approach to government that characterised Cumann na nGaedheal. But rattling the sabre was less easy in power than in opposition. Lemass's populist noises of the 1920s about reducing the size of government were not kept and his department swelled. Socially, Lemass enjoyed rounds of golf and poker schools with the men he perceived to be Ireland's movers and shakers. He created openings both for people who moved in his circles and for other aspiring businessmen, particularly in clothing and footwear, industries which required relatively little initial capital.

Mary Daly has shown that there was very little coherent planning in this broad process. Most decisions about which industries were to be encouraged, and which were not, were taken on an ad hoc basis.[62] A slick city type, the ruddy-faced gombeenism of rural political patronage was foreign to Lemass. Nonetheless at the very least it can be said that the system he set up in the 1930s facilitated patronage of this kind. Location was not just determined by national and social needs; industries appeared in areas where Fianna Fáil needed votes too.

Lemass trod a rather fine line between pragmatism and patronage at this time. The protected national bourgeoisie grew in numbers and in political and economic clout. Garvin's description of Lemass as a 'puritan among clientelists'[63] appears somewhat contradictory in light of his earlier acknowledgement that under Lemass's new regime 'a lot of well-connected people became rich'.[64] If Lemass's

Lemass at a factory opening in his early career. Courtesy *The Irish Press.*

earlier acceptance of the donation from McGrath changed Boland's personal opinion of him, the party's collective turn away from its socialistic leanings is demonstrated by the decision of its Finance Committee to purchase a leather upholstered car priced at £145 in 1934.[65] To the founders of the Irish Republican Congress – a radical republican group formed in the same year – Fianna Fáil had firmly signalled its coalescence with Ireland's capitalists and turned its back on its early radicalism. Lemass, the congress's leadership argued, had paved the way for 'the entrance of Irish industrialist capital organising its field for exploitation'.[66]

Over in London, the British Board of Trade looked over these developments with a colder economic eye. Across the world manufacturing production and agricultural prices were falling.[67] Surveying the early tariffs that Lemass had placed on clothes, confectionery, car bodies and machinery, its officials concluded that some were 'very high' and 'probably prohibitive', others were not 'altogether unreasonable'. They concluded, however, 'it is very unlikely that the Irish Free State will be able to satisfy all her needs by internal production'.[68] Lemass's colleague Gerald Boland agreed. He viewed many of the industries developed behind a tariff wall as 'nonsense' because they could never hope to compete in quality or price with the British products they were copying.[69] In turn, Lemass viewed Boland's objections as those of 'a myopic Sinn Féiner who did not appreciate the difference between opposition and government'.[70]

The juxtaposition of his pragmatism against the whims of the 'cranks' was a favourite Lemass tactic. But Boland's point was a sound one. Isolation from the British market meant Industry and Commerce had to urgently scour the world for export markets. Ireland's import dependence continued as her exports declined. With tensions in Europe heightening, the British warily noted Lemass's attempts to exchange agricultural produce for machinery from Germany.[71] The following year James H. Thomas drew up a memo on Ireland for the British cabinet. Thomas, the senior British official whose economic tactics Lemass had likened to those of the Black and Tans, claimed that Fianna Fáil's 'ideal of a self-sufficing community' had become complicated by the Economic War. Although Irish ownership was the goal, 'the Irish Free State Ministry of Industry and Commerce do all they can to influence private concerns to place contracts for *foreign* rather than with *British* firms'.[72] Thomas noted the opposition of Irish manufacturers to foreign 'businesses which, in effect, are under external control though complying with the provisions of the [Control of Manufactures] act'.[73]

Thomas correctly identified the hostility of sections of the nascent Irish bourgeoisie to outside competition, but overstated Lemass's Anglophobic prejudice. In the climate of Irish–Irelandism and insular economics, it is refreshing to note that Lemass did not adhere wholesale to the almost hysterical antipathy towards 'aliens' in 1930s' Ireland. In 1933, for example, Lemass granted a licence to manufacture clothes to Hyman Jacobovitch. Not only was Jacobovitch a British Jew, but Lemass's sources had also placed a large question mark over whether he had the capital to make a success of the business.[74]

In fact, Lemass would informally enquire about British firms that wanted to set up business in Ireland through the Irish High Commission in London.[75] He let big British companies set up operations with a few Irish directors on them, aware that the real decisions were made at the company's headquarters in Britain. These included the confectionary firms Cadbury and Fry, the flour-milling business Rank, and the rubber manufacturers Dunlop. Lemass addressed native manufacturers' concerns by his subjection of foreign firms to his instruction in key areas such as size, location and labour force.

The Minister for Industry and Commerce at the opening of the Mallow Beet Factory with manager Alfred Navratil, 3 December 1934.

In this regard, and in line with party policy, Lemass was committed to the geographical dispersal of factories. Contrary to popular opinion, de Valera was 'all for industrialisation' and Gerald Boland was the most robust opponent of this policy within cabinet.[76] But despite the efforts to locate new industries in the west of Ireland, where Fianna Fáil enjoyed strong electoral support, most firms proved unwilling to locate west of the River Shannon. Pressure from firms unwilling to decentralise production ensured gains in manufacturing employment were concentrated close to Lemass's home turf, in the Dublin area and Leinster.[77] Sometimes compromises were reached, as was the case with Dunlop. The firm's insistence on locating in Dublin overrode Lemass's choice, driven by political imperatives, of Tralee, County Kerry. A compromise was reached, with the firm locating to Cork city.[78]

His Anglocentrism aside, James H. Thomas had come close to hitting on the raw nerve of protectionism: the lack of Irish capital, economies of scale, and know-how. As Lemass later conceded, the biggest obstacle to national industrial development was a lack of technical expertise in the country.[79] It is evident that Lemass was at times outflanked by foreign firms, which manipulated shareholding patterns in order to get around the restrictions of the Control of

Manufactures Act. At times, too, the Minister for Industry and Commerce was sometimes *willingly* outflanked to overcome the headaches of home production.

The petroleum industry serves as a good example of how the policy of native control of industry was in practice diluted. Lemass and Leydon sought to protect small Irish oil companies like Munster Simms from big multinationals like Shell. Harold Simms, the heir to the Munster Simms petroleum empire, reveals how Lemass granted the company a modest monopoly in the 1930s. One of the conditions Lemass attached to Munster Simms' licence was that the company employ Irish workers.[80] Lemass kept a close watch on the firm and Munster Simms was obliged on several occasions to request exemptions from its licence for the purchase of materials that were only available from abroad.[81] But despite help from the state, small Irish firms like Munster Simms could never compete with the 'big boys'. As Simms states, even during the height of protectionism it was large foreign concerns like Unilever which held real clout with governments. Soon after tariff protection was dismantled, Munster Simms was gobbled up by Shell.[82]

In 1937 Lemass defended his policies:

> Industrial progress has been so rapid in the last few years that mistakes were nearly inevitable, but I do not admit they were either numerous or serious. During that time, I acted on the principle that the only way to avert mistakes was to do nothing. As I did not intend to do nothing, I discounted the mistakes in advance.[83]

The 'Hobson's Choice'[84] that Lemass conveyed displayed the zero-sum mentality of a gambler. Yes, Ireland needed to industrialise. But mistakes could have been avoided through dialogue with a more diverse range of local interest groups and specialists and through a pragmatic acceptance that Ireland should not have been manufacturing certain goods because they were simply too high in price and too poor in quality.

What was noticeably missing from Lemass's efforts was any clear economic strategy beyond industrialisation and employment under native ownership. There were no plans, for example, to substantially improve the road network. There was no fertiliser plant in what remained an agricultural country. The lack of a national shipping

Lemass, still opening factories, '40 years on'.
Dublin Opinion, April 1935.

line, leaving Irish exports at the mercy of the British when the Second World War came, would prove a major oversight. It is hard to escape the conclusion that in the 1930s Ireland's scant resources were frequently distributed according to connections rather than consistent planning. Where state control encroached it was more effective in blocking certain patterns of resource distribution than in fairly distributing resources in the hands of producers and consumers and, occasionally, it created white elephants at public expense. Lemass repeatedly cited employment creation as an overriding consideration but there is little evidence that tariffs were evaluated on that basis. Neither was the impact of tariffs on consumers or other industries sufficiently examined.

The hardest truth of the Economic War was that a cessation in trade between Ireland and her largest market was causing living standards to decline and aggravating emigration. Lemass responded to the British imposition of export duties on Irish agricultural exports by offering compensation to farmers in the form of bounties. The bounties offered for calf skins led to the fabled mass destruction of Irish calves.[85]

Again, something had to give. Quietly, the government sought out negotiations with the British. In 1935 the two countries agreed a series of Coal–Cattle pacts. The tariff war began to ease thereafter. Under this agreement Britain increased the quota for Irish cattle by 50 per cent. In return, Ireland would import coal only from British sources. Tellingly, the Coal–Cattle pacts of 1935 defied Fianna Fáil's agrarian vision. They were good for graziers and cattle exporters, not self-sufficient small farmers.

With European war looming, the imperative to normalise trade relations with Britain became even more pressing. On 15 January 1938 Lemass and Leydon left Dun Laoghaire for talks with their British opposite numbers in London. They were accompanied by de Valera, Ryan, MacEntee, and their departmental secretaries. The Irish delegation held several meetings with British Prime Minister Neville Chamberlain and a handful of British ministers. In addition to these meetings Lemass held private discussions with the president of the British Board of Trade, Oliver Stanley. The delegation returned home by boat on 20 January, but were back in London a month later. This time the delegation were entertained at London's exclusive Piccadilly Hotel and enjoyed a lavish lunch at the residence of the high commissioner for Ireland. Lemass again held separate discussions at the British Board of Trade and the Dominions Office as well as taking part in full meetings. When the delegation returned for a third time in March 1938, the pattern continued, with meetings in the House of Commons running into the early hours. On 23 April 1938 the trade delegation left Dun Laoghaire for the final time. Two days later the Anglo-Irish Agreement was signed.

Lemass had missed the start of the Economic War, but he was ever-present for its lengthy denouement. In all, he attended no fewer than twenty-one meetings in a three-week period protracted over three months.[86] After the agreement was signed relations between the two neighbours returned to a happier plane and signalled the end of a costly conflict. Leydon's contacts at Whitehall proved invaluable in this process; he took the lead role afterwards in discussions with officials from Britain and Northern Ireland. Late that year he shuttled back and forth to London, receiving assurances from the British Board of Trade that Ireland would receive a 'square deal' on British shipments of food and fuel if, as expected, hostilities were to break out suddenly on the continent.

Sex, Factories and Faith

In the 1930s Lemass played a leading role in meeting what he called the 'dual purpose' of providing housing and employment during the economic slump.[87] The Economic War actually brought prosperity

to Ireland's urban centres, where cheaper food and better job prospects won Fianna Fáil much working-class support.[88] The meanness
of social spending under W. T. Cosgrave's governments meant Fianna
Fáil was almost obliged to expand welfare legislation when in power.
During the 1930s Lemass championed old age pensions, unemployment assistance, widows' and orphans' pensions, and a mass house-
building programme. In his own words, 'no housing had been built
at all by the Cumann na nGaedheal government and the slum
situation in Dublin and all over the country was appalling'.[89] The
house-building programme of Fianna Fáil in the 1930s was closely
linked with the establishment of what would become a long-standing
patronage network between the party and building merchants.
Nonetheless it represented a marked change from conservative
inaction to social provision.

When it came to rural constituencies, the writer Aodh de Blacam,
a member of Fianna Fáil's National Executive, was one of the leading
literary cheerleaders of protectionism. He saw the policy Lemass had
been charged with implementing as promising the revitalisation of
Catholic-agrarian Ireland. In 1932, the year the party assumed
power, de Blacam wrote on the subject of 'Ideal Industrialism' in
Ireland. He described the knitting industry in Dungloe, County
Donegal, where 'over 100 girls' worked in the local factory. On first
glance this vision of rural employment seems progressive for its time.
But de Blacam was quick to qualify it by emphasising the young
women's lack of social and financial independence. 'The girls live in
their fathers' houses and it is to these homes that the profits of their
work go.'[90] In de Blacam's conceptualisation of national progress,
industrialisation would not threaten the sanctity of the Irish family.

How did de Blacam's vision compare with the Ireland Lemass
was building? As we have seen, early in his ministerial career Lemass
abandoned the rural idyll for the pragmatism of restructuring the
economy to cope better with the realities of the Economic War. The
flip side of this admirable pragmatism, already glimpsed in his
advocacy for evictions, was a certain disregard for human dignity
when it did not fit with his plans. In a 1935 memorandum Lemass
is to be found at his impatient worst again, this time when offering
a drastic solution to underdevelopment and unemployment in areas
such as the one de Blacam described in County Donegal.

The protected industries Lemass established in the 1930s were
almost entirely located outside Gaeltacht areas. Throughout the

decade the Department of Lands and Fisheries had proposed locating a number of textile industries to the Gaeltacht in order to improve economic conditions there. Lemass vetoed all of these proposals because he thought that increasing agricultural or industrial productivity in such areas was a waste of time.[91] Instead Gaeltacht dwellers should be induced to look for work in factories elsewhere. To this end, Lemass's solution was labour camps and the forced channelling of people he evidently regarded as peasants into industry, the army and the Gardaí. Lemass envisaged gender-segregated labour camps.

> It is proposed that special labour camps be established in the Gaeltacht where unskilled men would be taught various trades, plumbing, carpentering, painting, brick-laying, etc . . . The men in camp would not be paid while undergoing training but would be fed, clothed and housed.[92]

Women would not be subjected to camp labour, but would attend special schools where they would be trained for domestic service in the towns and cities. While the inhabitants of the Gaeltacht were being shunted out of their villages, Lemass wanted to encourage workers from other parts of Ireland to holiday in them, urging 'state-owned hotels be established' in the emptying villages.[93]

There is an evident dichotomy here between the conservative developmentalism of de Blacam's vision and the more radical, near authoritarian, developmentalism of Lemass. The latter had a contemptuous eye for colleagues whom he felt were affected by *aboulia* – a Greek word describing a lack of will or initiative, of which he was particularly fond.[94] The 1935 memo demonstrates that by the middle of the decade Lemass was still clinging dear to his brand of authoritarianism as a radical alternative to *aboulia*. However, when it came to the sort of checks on female employment de Blacam envisaged, Lemass was much more willing to conform to the conservative social ideals of his contemporaries.

In 1936, Lemass's Conditions of Employment Act was passed. This piece of legislation accompanied the government's housing and welfare provisions. Once again, Lemass's realistic approach to the changes needed to cope with industrialisation shines through. The act stands as a genuinely progressive piece of legislation for its time. It regulated working hours for adults and adolescents, restricted overtime, and opened up dialogue between the state and the country's unions. On its back Lemass was elected president of the

International Labour Office (ILO) Conference in 1937.[95] He trumpeted the act as having created 'an industrial code far ahead of that in force for any other country'.[96]

Yet Lemass's new industrial code was not 'far ahead' in appreciating the liberating potential of female participation in the labour market. Section 16 of the act enabled the Minister for Industry and Commerce to prohibit the employment of women in some areas and to fix the proportion of men to women.[97] Lemass also brought in restrictions on the use of modern machinery on the grounds that it facilitated the employment of women.[98] These restrictions came on the heel of the ban on female schoolteachers getting married introduced by Fianna Fáil shortly after assuming power.

Horgan contextualises Lemass's bill against the widespread support at the time for restrictions on women's work, citing a 1932 speech by Louie Bennett, the prominent feminist trade unionist, blaming increased female employment for the deterioration in family life.[99] He fails to mention, however, the substantial opposition to the bill at the time of its introduction. This opposition was headed by the Irish Women Workers' Union (IWWU), which included Bennett, and a number of Lemass's former comrades who were now members of the Republican Congress.[100] Lemass repeatedly refused the IWWU consultative status in framing the legislation.

Lemass's reservations about female employment were not unusual for the era and should not be overstated; but they demonstrate the limits to his dynamism when it came to the social sphere, something which the Lemassiography largely ignores. Contrary to the impression gained from Lemass's biographers, the Minister for Industry and Commerce shared many of the habits, qualities and prejudices of Irishmen and women of the time as well as baulking against some of them. For example, the work stoppages caused by the attendance of both employers and workers at race meetings have been cited as indicating the absence of modern industrial values in 1930s Ireland.[101] Lemass, of course, was an avid gambler, and race meetings, to him, signified a rare legitimate reason to halt work temporarily.[102] Part of the *enigma* of Lemass – to borrow John Horgan's summation of the man – is his ambiguity. In the 1938 Anglo-Irish trade talks it was Lemass, whom Garvin claims disagreed with the application to Ireland of Max Weber's concept of the Protestant ethic and the spirit of capitalism,[103] who came out with the distinctly Weberian assertion that folk in the northeast corner of Ireland had 'a greater *aptitude* for industrial pursuits' than had the rest of the island's people.[104]

Lemass's conformity to the social values of his peers is illustrated most forcefully in his lack of input into the 1937 Constitution. The document, masterminded by de Valera, is commonly criticised for being 'too Catholic'. Brian Girvin describes the Constitution as 'illiberal, nationalistic and denominational'.[105] When de Valera was drafting it Lemass is reputed to have told him: 'we can't very well make the Constitution a manifesto of Fianna Fáil policy'.[106] This retrospective attempt to divorce the document from its political context should not be swallowed whole. The Constitution was drawn up with one eye firmly trained on the maintenance of power in the election accompanying the referendum on its adoption. Therefore a key consideration for the Fianna Fáil hierarchy was the growing prominence of Catholic social thought and anti-communism as a political force. In this regard, it would be facile to look to Lemass – a shrewd political operator – in the vain hope of finding a liberal bulwark to the excesses of de Valeran Catholicism.

Catholic social doctrine, based on the papal encyclicals *Rerum Novarum* (1891) and *Quadragesimo Anno* (1931), was in political vogue in 1930s Ireland. The latter encyclical elaborated papal doctrine on twentieth-century social and economic questions and reduced the state's role to 'subsidiary function'.[107] In other words, the modern state should not encroach on the just freedom of individuals and families. It should respect the rights of private property, and should not 'discharge its duty arbitrarily'.[108] Ostensibly, these dictates ran contrary to Lemass's rather impatient exercise of power. In practice, he recognised the political value in assimilating them. In 1939 Lemass demonstrated this by describing the Constitution as 'possibly the first attempt to translate into practical law the principles of social justice as laid down by Pope Leo XIII'.[109]

But if the political imperative helps to explain Lemass's support for the Constitution, it does not fully explain his lack of input at the drafting stage. Privately, de Valera encouraged criticism from his cabinet and most ministers submitted pages of proposed alterations to the first draft. MacEntee, Minister for Finance, sent de Valera a 43-page memo suggesting changes. From the Department of Agriculture, James Ryan's alterations ran to nineteen pages. Minister for Defence Frank Aiken's suggested changes took up nine A4 pages. By contrast 'no observations were received from the Department of Industry and Commerce'.[110]

If the populist political imperatives underlying the Constitution are placed to one side, a niggling conservatism in Lemass's social and religious outlook is brought to the fore. As Horgan points out, as Lemass went through the penultimate draft of the Constitution his 'Victorian moral values' crept into play.[111] He suggested Article 45.2.i, which pledged the state to make 'reasonable provision' for citizens' 'domestic needs', be changed to sharpen the distinction between the deserving and undeserving poor; Lemass proposed it apply to 'able and willing' citizens.[112] De Valera, contrary to the roles ascribed the pair in the popular imagination, did not consent to these proposed alterations.

Lemass's stance on the Constitution represented a clear departure from the egalitarian discourses of Irish republicanism in the previous decade, which he had passionately invoked and which envisioned a society based on secular principles of citizenship and equality. Once again, however, it is important to stress that Lemass's acquiescence in the Constitution's Catholicism is only surprising if his exceptionality as a radical modernising force is overstated.

As he did his rounds as minister, opening new factories across Ireland, Lemass was invariably flanked by the local bishop. He would open the factory, the bishop would bless it. Whatever his personal religious beliefs, informal links with the bishops remained vital to the party's political success. As Dermot Keogh has pointed out, none of de Valera's cabinet members lived up to Fianna Fáil's revolutionary image when it came to their engagement with Catholicism.[113] The plump, bespectacled Seán T. O'Kelly, Minister for Local Government and de Valera's number two, was a Knight of Columbanus and good friend of papal nuncio Paschal Robinson. MacEntee had three brothers-in-law who were members of the clergy. De Valera, of course, was strongly pro-Church, and Tom Derrig (Education) and James Ryan (Agriculture) were respectful of Church interests. Keogh lists Frank Aiken and Lemass as 'somewhat cooler in their personal attitude towards the Catholic Church, but neither was particularly anticlerical, or laic, in political outlook'.[114]

As with other aspects of his private life, there is some uncertainty surrounding Lemass's relationship with the Knights of Columbanus, the shady body to which O'Kelly belonged. This Catholic order was founded in 1915 in Belfast. After partition, the organisation transferred its headquarters to Dublin.[115] The order, which still exists today, denies that it is a secret society, but has all the trappings of one.[116] As in Lemass's day, there is a hierarchy culminating in the supreme knight. Membership is closed to the general public, and

Lemass opens Dickens' Leather factory, Dungarvan, 1937.
Courtesy Waterford County Museum.

knights-elect promise to preserve the secrets of the order. Its membership is composed chiefly of businessmen and professionals and it remains the most influential lay group within the Irish Church. Its principal goals are to promote Catholic social principles as laid out in the papal encyclicals.[117]

When in opposition Lemass, like other Fianna Fáil TDs, had made much political capital out of suggestions that the Cumann na nGaedheal government was in thrall to the Freemasons and their largely Protestant membership. In 1927, for instance, Lemass declared that Cosgrave was 'not a free agent' and that 'some secret power, some secret influence, some secret society behind his government' was determining government policy.[118] Now allegations of secret society membership were levelled at him. In a high-profile legal case of 1934 it was alleged that the knights had engineered nominations to a public position through its patronage network. Lemass, MacEntee and O'Kelly were all named as belonging to the secretive order by the head of the knights in Connacht.[119] According to the order's official history, not only was Lemass a member at this time, but he was able to reach the top of the political ladder years later (as Taoiseach) without ever leaving its ranks.[120]

De Valera disliked secret societies in general and the Knights of Columbanus in particular. Quite reasonably, he thought simultaneously holding positions in public office and the order conflicted with the public interest.[121] For Catholics to seek the protection of the order, contended de Valera, was 'absurd' in a country where '93 per cent of the population are Catholics'.[122] This demographic consideration obscures the economic goals of the order at the time. Interestingly, these tied in closely with Lemass's priorities for national economic regeneration. As the 1927 report of the Catholic Truth Society of Ireland (CTSI) put it: 'The Catholic is substantially in control of Government, the Civil Service, the Judiciary, the Army and the Police.' However, 'the Catholic still suffers as a result of the Penal Laws – in industrial and commercial life he is still suffering from the poverty under which he started a century ago'.[123] The way forward, the report concluded, was for national lay organisations (like the Knights of Columbanus) to develop a sort of counter-Ascendancy boys' club.

Despite the official history of the Knights of Columbanus, it is uncertain whether Lemass was a member of the knights and, if so, how far this particular patronage network extended into his public duties.[124] It is certain, however, that he had discarded the secular, anti-clerical ethos of his early republicanism for a closer adherence to de Valera's moral community.

If his 1935 plans for Gaeilgeoirí display a Dubliner's disregard for rural Ireland, the coercive aspect also demonstrates that Lemass had also dropped another egalitarian staple of his early political rhetoric – a citizens' militia to replace Ireland's standing army. Instead, in power, he sought to build up the Free State police and army, the very bodies he had opposed so vociferously in the previous decade. A crucial consideration for Lemass was that with industrialisation had come greater worker militancy. His grim plans for the Gaeltacht were drawn up around the same time that he was using the Irish Army to break a Dublin transport strike.[125] A provincial newspaper criticised Lemass for doing so, claiming he had made a local issue a national one 'by putting State forces, to which the man in Dingle contributes as much as the man in Dartry, on the Dublin transport service'.[126] The IRA, it seems, concurred and intervened in the dispute. The government responded by arresting forty-seven republicans and detaining them in the Curragh. During these disturbances Lemass was protected from the IRA and strikers by the Free State 'horse, foot, and artillery' he had derided a few years previously. *The Independent* noted, not without irony, that during the strike Lemass had to be given an escort to Mass at the Pro-Cathedral 'by cavalry in their saffron and blue uniforms'.[127]

Lemass's actions during the strike were a harbinger of the government's crackdown on the IRA a year later. By this stage Fianna Fáil had firmly reconciled itself with the institutions of state and the IRA had outlived its usefulness to the party. In that year, 1936, Lemass launched his Conditions of Employment Act by returning to a lingering theme of his public pronouncements – the totalitarian alternative. He boasted that the act had been achieved 'by a government that is still a democratic government dependent entirely upon a parliamentary institution for its power'.[128] The mention of totalitarianism in defending his achievements was not unique in the age of the competitive national tyrannies of Mussolini, Hitler and Stalin. However, it was a theme that Lemass was to invoke throughout his career, right up to the mid-1960s. Lemass used it not only to cast Fianna Fáil as progressive but to conjure up the possibilities of sweeping controls unhindered by the checks of the democratic system.

Lemass's grip on the devastating realities of the Economic War meant he was willing to substitute folksiness with coercion. He also recognised that industrialisation necessitated welfare and housing reform. Simultaneously, he was more social conservative than 'cultural revolutionary'. Lemass detested misty-eyed sentimentality, seeing it as a barrier to progress. By the end of the decade, however, it was not just the sentimentalism of de Blacam's vision of 'ideal industrialism' which lay in tatters. Poring over trends in migration, officials from the Gaeltacht Industries section of the Department of Lands noted the high proportion of young women on emigrant boats. They concluded that what made England so attractive to these girls and women was that over there more work was available for women, and their money was not appropriated by the family. Unlike in Ireland, 'what they earn is their own'.[129]

The Radical Interventionist

One of the lessons Lemass took from the economist John Maynard Keynes, a man whose writings he greatly admired, was that in the age of cartels and monopolies laissez-faireism had ceased to be a libertarian concept. But as an island nation with few national resources, Ireland's insular trade position was proving untenable. Quite simply, as Lemass had argued from the outset, Ireland was not ready to fight the Economic War without major structural changes.

The relief provided by the 1935 and 1938 trade deals aside, closing Ireland off from its largest market consistently demanded original thinking on ways to improve domestic productivity.

Lemass was responsible for the creation of a plethora of state-promoted companies in the 1930s. Through these bodies he sought to secure development in the national interest. Cumann na Gaedheal had already created three such agencies – the Electricity Supply Board (ESB), the Dairy Disposal Company (DDC), and the Agricultural Credit Company (ACC). Lemass was to add many more state-sponsored ventures to the list, constructing a semi-state archipelago that sprawled far and wide. Some – such as Bord na Móna, Córas Iompair Éireann (CIÉ) and Aer Lingus – survive today.

Lemass had his doubts about protectionism, the argument goes, but had to plug the gaps which Irish private enterprise could not or would not fill.[130] But Lemass's logic was not solely to develop state enterprise to build up infrastructure for private capital. Irish businesses certainly made oligarchic demands of Lemass,[131] but the Minister for Industry and Commerce used the power of the state not only in a nurturing capacity but also, as he saw it, as a radical interventionist force. Certain sectors, such as public transport, should be extended and linked up to combat 'cut throat competition', he argued.[132] While identifying new markets, he was also keen to control them.

When the final draft of the Constitution was being prepared Lemass proposed that Article 45.2.iii, which guards against the concentration of ownership by 'a few individuals to the common detriment', be changed. 'Few individuals' should instead read 'a particular class', he argued.[133] The suggested amendment reflected the fact that a 'few individuals' effectively did run Irish industry, namely Lemass, his top civil servants and the heads of the semi-state companies. Lemass wanted to sharpen the distinction between this situation, which he saw as operating in the 'common good', and inequitable monopoly in the interests of a small class of businessmen.

This is an important point. While Lemass courted certain businessmen and managers he had little time for those who fell outside his patronage network. A senior employee of Bord na Móna recalled that 'the Irish equivalent of nepotism worked to a very large extent in the early days of the board', with 'more than the usual number of connections with what is called the Fight for Freedom'.[134] An insight into this attitude, albeit on a smaller scale, is provided by Lemass's employment policy when it came to improvements on his

'Strongman' Lemass faces
down the Irish taxpayer.
Dublin Opinion,
December 1939.

own home. If ever an odd job needed doing he would only employ old IRA men, 'for everything, from mending and papering to gardening'.[135]

Lemass's term at Industry and Commerce was not merely an incubation period for private enterprise; it was also a period of marked expansion for state ownership and ministerial prerogative. As mentioned, Lemass wanted even greater powers of control over all industry, whether native or foreign. Fianna Fáil's first decade in power saw the emergence of Lemass's use of the institutions of state to carry out the bureaucratic bullying of certain firms. When some firms sought to diversify and expand their ranges they found they were required to obtain licence after licence.[136] It is notable that others did not face such obstacles. Generally speaking, companies that were suspected of breaching the terms of their licences were given the opportunity to defend themselves at the department. If still dissatisfied, Lemass instructed the state solicitor to start proceedings.[137]

Significantly, alongside his 1932 proposals for large-scale public works and the removal of surplus population from the land, Lemass also wanted currency reform. When Britain abandoned the gold standard in 1931 the sterling area emerged. It described those countries which tied the value of their currency to sterling because Britain was their major market, and included most Commonwealth countries and a few more in the Middle East, the Baltic, and Scandinavia. This collective effort contributed to a greater degree of stability on international money markets. In his radical 1932 memo Lemass, by contrast, proposed a state bank and a break with sterling.

He dismissed the benefits of the sterling area, claiming that the tie with sterling made Irish goods less competitive and therefore cost jobs. For Ireland to break with sterling would have confirmed the divorce from the British market attempted through the Economic War. Practically, it would have spelled even greater isolation for Ireland.

Lemass remained sceptical about whether banking was a productive sector of the economy at all. In 1938 he confirmed his allegiances by aligning himself with the dissenting minority report of the Irish Banking Commission. This commission was chaired by the former Finance secretary Joseph Brennan and prepared a majority report attacking Lemass's interventionism and calling for limits on the borrowing powers of the state-sponsored bodies. It attacked Lemass by highlighting the fact that he had established many semi-state ventures without legislative authority.[138] By contrast, the minority report, which Lemass favoured, proposed bringing the country's banks and currency under governmental control. As usual, Lemass's reformist approach to banking was vetoed at an early stage by the Department of Finance.[139]

The Irish tobacco industry provides another case in point in Lemass's growing penchant for state control. In January 1934 several ministers and civil servants met to discuss proposals for setting up a tobacco industry in Ireland. Lemass, a pipe smoker, argued that the less palatable Irish leaf could be mixed with foreign leaf to mask the taste. This was a more viable proposition for pipe tobacco, which made up just 28 per cent of the market, than for cigarettes.[140] Manufacturers complained that the public would be likely to complain about the taste of the Irish tobacco leaf because smokers were used to high-grade American tobacco.[141] A question therefore arose as to the best way to ensure the blend of home and foreign tobacco leaves were mixed to the right percentages – enough Irish leaf to boost home production, enough foreign leaf to ensure taste. Lemass made it clear that he favoured state compulsion in this process rather than self-regulation. He proposed appointing inspectors to enter plantations and factories to oversee the mixing of the blends, examine the plants, scrutinise farmers' financial records, and issue summary fines if necessary.[142] Irish tobacco farmers instead pleaded for 'inducements, but not compulsion'.[143] These calls were in vain.

Authoritarianism was becoming Lemass's favourite productive control. He would wield it increasingly in the coming years, and not merely at Ireland's large tobacco companies.[144] In the 1930s Lemass exercised an extensive and at times idiosyncratic influence on industrial policy. Where necessary, forthright and uncompromising compulsion, rather than benign incubation, was to be the norm. To defuse mounting allegations of a dictatorial personal influence on national economic policy, Lemass elevated a number of colleagues to prime positions in the management of state enterprise. In particular, the persistent physical disadvantage of not having a single departmental building in the 1930s had the effect of drawing him closer to Leydon as he came to rely increasingly on his able and unsung lieutenant. He strategically placed Leydon on a number of boards in the 1930s. His departmental secretary proved more than a mere mouthpiece for Lemass, however, and was instrumental in many of the key ventures of the protectionist era.

One prominent example is the Irish aviation industry. In recent years, in recognition of Lemass's passion for air travel, there have been calls for Dublin Airport to be renamed 'Lemass Airport'.[145] In 1936 Lemass approved the use of Foynes as a base for flying boats and in 1938 he famously gave the go-ahead for the construction of Dublin Airport.[146] Leydon deserves more credit for his central role in this process. Lemass appointed Leydon chairman of Aer Rianta and Aer Lingus in 1937, where he exercised a decisive agency. Leydon headed liaisons with the Department of Industry and Commerce's Aviation Branch. It was he who wrote the instructions for Irish representatives in their discussions with the British and Canadian governments over transatlantic air services in 1935, including the key clause that an Irish airport should be 'the first port of call for all eastbound traffic and the last port of call for all westbound traffic'.[147] It was also Leydon who spearheaded talks in Dublin in early 1938 between representatives of the British and American air forces, the US Department of Commerce, and Imperial and Pan-American Airways.[148]

Another example is turf, where Lemass owed much to Frank Aiken. Lemass's establishment of the Turf Development Board in 1934 provided Ireland with a much-needed alternative source of fuel. But at this time any association with the bog was to imply a peasant backwardness and the urbane Lemass initially had little time for turf development. He was constantly reminded of its potential as a fuel by Aiken, who was prolific in his efforts to develop scientific answers to Ireland's resource problems.[149] Leydon, too, was a strong supporter of the use of turf as fuel. According to Todd Andrews, whom Lemass appointed to head the turf scheme, Lemass only consented to turf development because he wanted to get Aiken off his back.[150] When he had finally plumped for turf, Lemass ditched the snobbish criticism of the new scheme, which he had previously held, for the zeal of the convert. By 1935 he was so enthused about turf that he launched the national turf-cutting competition by excitedly relaying an anecdote about a house in a Baltic state made entirely of turf, including the furniture and the carpets.[151]

Lemass was also happy to let his lieutenants lead in areas he considered less strategically important. Unlike his flamboyant son-in-law, Charles Haughey, Lemass was not an ostentatious patron of the arts. But, as with other aspects of his life and career, the energy with which Lemass went about the primary tasks of his office has obscured the extent to which he engaged the arts world. Although Lemass did not care much for the arts, he was by no means a philistine and realised that art provided a means of articulating national modernisation.[152] In this decade he began a friendship with a Catholic priest, Fr Senan Moynihan, the founder of the *Capuchin Annual*, a beautifully produced magazine which discussed Irish history, art and literature. Moynihan's editorial office, a regular meeting place for writers and artists, was situated above the Lemass family home and business in Capel Street.[153] Lemass invested his own money into the magazine,[154] and men of the arts now began to appear on the horizon of his rapidly expanding patronage network.

In 1937 he agreed to appoint a Committee on Design in Industry. This body was charged with advising his department on the design of Irish-made goods. The fourteen-member committee included Seán Keating, the painter the ESB had commissioned to depict the Shannon Scheme. Industry and Commerce was also involved in the Irish entry for the World's Fair, a showpiece exalting 'The World of Tomorrow' at which different countries constructed pavilions asserting their place in the brave new world. As Ireland's first appearance at an international trade fair, Lemass was interested in the opportunities it presented for boosting the export market. He entrusted his parliamentary secretary, Seán Moylan, to deal with the up-and-coming young architect chosen to design the Irish pavilion, Michael Scott.

A snappy dresser, raconteur and womaniser, Scott was part of Dublin's elite post-independence coterie of successful men and liked to entertain boozily from his millionaire's pad in Sandycove. Lemass got to know certain members of this group over the poker table, but tact demanded he keep them at arm's length. Scott, too, would remain on the fringes of Lemass's world; however, he was never too far away to be ignored.[155] In designing the pavilion, Moylan allowed Scott a long leash. The result was an art deco effort in the shape of a shamrock. Inside the building a massive modernist mural by Keating depicting the Shannon Scheme looked down on soil, water and stones transported in from the old country.

Scott's pavilion, the first of his landmark state-sponsored architectural projects, encapsulated the economic tensions between the old world and the new that Lemass encountered in the 1930s. Industrial modernisation was carried out against the backdrop of the Economic War and the desperate search for alternative export markets. Despite Lemass's efforts to boost diverse native industries in products such as soap, candles and tyres during his first decade in power, the pavilion bowed to the hackneyed staples of Irish identity, exhibiting whiskey, stout, racehorses and religious iconography.[156]

Here lay the rub. The headstrong young Dubliner's confidence imbued his projects with a dynamism and energy that helped overcome conservative opposition. This managerial style was also, by its very nature, sometimes overambitious in seeking out alternative markets, or 'slapdash' as Lemass termed it himself. The attempt to produce industrial alcohol from potatoes is one example. Leydon warned Lemass against setting up industrial alcohol factories, but he pressed ahead regardless. Distilleries sprang up in counties Louth, Donegal, Mayo and Monaghan. Unfortunately, farmers often broke their contracts to supply the factories with potatoes, favouring instead the attraction of the open market.[157] The patterns of rural productivity once again proved a source of frustration to Lemass and the project proved a costly failure. Again, Lemass's autocratic tendencies undermined the scheme – he made no effort to include the expertise of the Department of Agriculture in the project.

Conditions on the turf camps in the 1930s provide a darker example of the negative consequences of his anti-*aboulia*. Like Lemass, Todd Andrews, his man at the Turf Development Board, saw camp labour as a good way to ensure productivity and reduce unemployment. He argued that, in their innovative character, camp labour schemes were preferable to the 'trite old objection of administrative impracticability trotted out by elderly boy clerks'.[158] But the human

Yet another factory opening parody appears in *Dublin Opinion*, May 1938.

cost of the authoritarian radicalism of these two developmentalist allies was already clear by the mid-1930s.

Lemass's 1935 plans for the Gaeltacht may have been quashed by his displeased colleagues, but in the same year the Turf Development Board took over a turf-harvesting operation at Turraun Bog in County Offaly. The management style at Turraun Camp was coercive and the working conditions appalling. Labour disputes and strikes were commonplace and after a short while it was clear that, aside from any other considerations, the scheme was ultimately un-economic. After a short time the Turf Board fell on its sword and advised that Turraun be closed. Lemass, however, insisted it stay open.[159] He would stick doggedly to the idea of the Irish labour camp over the next decade or so. It should be noted that the labour camp was only a bit part of his Keynesian drive for full employment; neither was the organised labour camp unique to Ireland at this time. But in his plans for camp labour Lemass's reversion to the militarism of his dissident early years is noticeable.

In a memo composed in 1938 Lemass envisioned the Irish labour camp, free from the frustrations of labour disruption. It would be an essentially militaristic experience. He wrote that participants would be 'subject to regulations as a soldier is subject to army regulations'.

Harsh discipline would be imposed and recourse to ordinary courts denied.[160] In a clause obviously intended to add a favourable slant to the forcible enlistment of recruits to these miserable workplaces, Lemass advised that the '*voluntary* enrolment of members would be assisted by withholding the dole from applicants'.[161]

Lemass's desire to institute an experimental camp for coerced labourers was finally realised in 1939 at Clonsast Bog, near Portarlington, County Laois. It proved an abject failure. As Lemass intended, the '*voluntary* enrolment of members' had been carried out by withholding the dole from the inner-city unemployed. Recruitment was dispersed between the Office of Public Works, the Turf Development Board, employment exchange officials and Gardaí. Working in conjunction, officials from these state bodies forced unemployed men to leave home and take up work on the bog.[162] Some 80 per cent of recruits either failed to attend or dropped out within the first week.[163] Those who stayed complained of the poor pay and conditions, and the monotony of camp life.[164] Clearly, most non-participants viewed the devastating cessation of unemployment assistance payments as a less daunting prospect than employment and accommodation on a remote bog. The Clonsast scheme bore all the hallmarks of Lemassian enthusiasm for grand schemes but also his willingness to erode liberties and regiment labour in the pursuit of economic targets.

These designs reflected the increasingly desperate situation in Europe. As early as 1935, Minister for Defence Frank Aiken pressed for the establishment of a cabinet committee to investigate the anticipated problems of supply if war broke out on the continent.[165] An interdepartmental committee was established at the end of October 1935 and charged with preparing lists of material needed for food, clothing, transport and other essentials in time of war. It consisted of civil servants from five departments and was headed by T. J. Flynn, Lemass's assistant secretary at Industry and Commerce.[166] The following year, against the backdrop of general European militarisation and major civil conflict in Spain, it set about drawing up plans for the economic survival of the country as a neutral state.[167]

In November 1937 Lemass, other ministers, and high-ranking civil servants were informed by the British Food Department that 'complete economic control' would be exercised by the British government in the event of the outbreak of war, which would lead to the 'absence of a free market in the UK'.[168] This was an early indication that, if war broke out, there would be a disruption in normal trading conditions between Ireland and Britain and the latter would exercise severe market restrictions. It prompted the establishment of the Emergency Supplies Branch of the Department of Industry and Commerce in 1938. This body was described as 'the nucleus of an organisation for central purchasing and selling'.[169]

From its inception Lemass's Emergency Supplies Branch clashed with Irish manufacturers and banks. Anticipating that war on the continent would result in a severe restriction in supplies, Lemass instructed Irish manufacturers and importers to lay in at least six months' reserve stock of supplies.[170] However, he steadfastly refused their requests to guarantee any loss incurred. To Lemass it came down to a matter of patriotic duty; to provide a guarantee to the businesses he had helped nurture was unconscionable. A stand-off ensued. The upshot was that, with war nearing, Ireland did not have adequate reserve supplies of essential materials.

Meanwhile, the Supply Committee established in 1936 did not report to the government until the summer of 1939, by which time war was only months away.[171] It prepared three reports, which fairly accurately outlined the deficiencies in essential materials that Ireland would face during the Second World War. But despite Industry and Commerce's leading role, Lemass had no input into the committee and seems to have maintained a devil-may-care attitude towards it. After all, it was Aiken's baby, not his – it could remain in his lap.

Despite MacEntee's efforts, Lemass had been trying to centralise economic control over the course of the 1930s, and by 1938 he had a vehicle for doing so – the Emergency Supplies Branch of his department. Moreover, trading relations with Britain were by this stage more congenial. But at this critical juncture in world history, his attempts to streamline the economy under centralised control were encountering difficulties largely borne of his exercise of ministerial power over the previous years. He was confronted by a cocky native bourgeoisie unwilling to lay in reserve stocks of supplies without financial guarantees from the state. Additionally, Lemass was hamstrung by the highly significant oversight of having failed to establish a national merchant marine. Neither had the young minister's blunt managerial style over the last decade done much to endear him to the opposition he now faced as he tried to reorganise the Irish economy to cope with the coming wartime disruption.

Emergency Imminent

In December 1939 Fianna Fáil held its fourteenth Ard-Fheis. The honorary secretaries' report noted contentedly that since coming to power the party had fulfilled a number of the points in its initial constitution of 1926. It pointed to the ruralisation of industry, the settling of as many families as possible on the land, and the achievement of economic self-sufficiency.[172] As we have seen, by 1932 Lemass had signalled his dissidence from party orthodoxy on each of these points. But he had also outwardly signalled his allegiance to de Valera, overseeing the weakening of the cattle export sector in favour of tillage, and pursuing a messy amalgam of economic policies combining the party line with his own designs. This contributed to what Mary Daly describes as Fianna Fáil's mixture of quasi-socialism, Catholic social teaching and Gaelic antiquarianism.[173]

Lemass emerged onto the national policy-making scene as something of a control freak in the 1930s. During this period the rivalry between Lemass and MacEntee was cooled by de Valera's unifying influence over the cabinet. Similarly, it was exacerbated by de Valera's lengthy absences from Ireland towards the end of the decade.[174] Despite the power Lemass wielded, the balance sheet of Fianna Fáil's performance during the Economic War years is not dominated by his successes. On the credit side the party had successfully removed the Crown from Irish affairs, achieving a Republic in all but name and reclaiming strategic ports. But as the party figurehead, these were really de Valera's successes. Lemass's real achievement was the significant growth in industrial employment and the establishment of state enterprise. On the debit side the economic failures were all too clear. Emigration, trade dependency and the flight from the land continued.

Lemass knew that the political and economic 'break' signified by Fianna Fáil's coming to power in 1932 was somewhat illusory.[175] By the end of the decade unemployment and net migration statistics still made for depressing reading. Between 1935 and 1938 there was a yearly average of 100,000 people on the unemployment live register.[176] Between 1933 and 1938 around 20,000 more people left Ireland every year than came into the country.[177] Most discouragingly, emigration rose consistently between 1932, when around 60,000 left the state annually, and 1939, when the figure was over 90,000.[178] The Irish economy limped rather than strode out of the Economic War, scarred by the outflow of young people, meagre growth, and industrial stagnation.[179] Lemass's determination to 'solve' these problems through shovel-ready camp schemes ultimately proved naïve.

From opposition, Lemass espoused an anti-corruption agenda. When in power he played a pre-eminent role in associating the party, which purported to represent the plain people of Ireland, with the country's business elites. His biographers have not been kind to him on this score. John Horgan concedes that some of the forms of protection that Lemass spearheaded were 'disastrously scattergun in nature'.[180] Garvin acknowledges that under Lemass's regime of the 1930s 'a lot of well-connected people became rich'.[181] Lemass pursued native industrialisation with a patriotic desire to develop the Irish nation, and to right historical wrongs through headstrong dynamism. Industrial Ireland emerged, a state capitalist system under the disproportionate political influence of two groups: a single minister and his bureaucrats on the one hand and, on the other, the local monopolies they had put in place. Critically, despite gaining his long-desired remit to centralise the distribution of resources in 1938, Lemass did not take strident steps to organise the Irish economy on a war footing. Alarmingly, Ireland would enter the Second World War still precariously reliant on British goodwill.

4

The Great Dictator

Minister for Supplies

When Britain and France declared war on Germany on 3 September 1939, the Fianna Fáil government hurriedly enacted an Emergency Powers Act. Addressing the Dáil on the previous afternoon, de Valera told the house that the situation necessitated a 'rearrangement of the functions which are carried out by the members of the Government'. It would be imperative, he added, 'to put a Minister in charge of supplies so that he will be able to give his whole time to that very important service'.[1] Shortly thereafter the Emergency Supplies Branch of Industry and Commerce was upgraded to a department of state and Lemass was appointed Minister for Supplies.

With the coming of European war, Lemass finally acquired the dictatorial economic powers he had craved since the 1920s. His new department was equipped with what was to become an extraordinarily interventionist *raison d'être*: to secure effective and equitable distribution for as long as Emergency conditions prevailed. Lemass was empowered to control the prices, import and export of all commodities, dictating the methods of 'treatment, keeping, storage, movement, distribution, sale, purchase, use and consumption' of all goods.[2]

The new minister had the power to control all prices and profits in Ireland through the issue of Emergency Powers orders. Lemass could now exercise an unprecedented measure of control over a wide range of industries and effectively policed the domestic market as well. The Minister for Supplies gradually came to assume almost unadulterated control over Irish economic life. Lemass, to quote Ronan Fanning, 'assumed the role and status of an economic overlord'.[3] Skinner writes that Lemass was endowed with the powers of 'a dictator over the individual citizen, the employer, the worker, and shopkeeper'.[4] The former IRA gunman was now spearheading what John Horgan describes as 'the high-water mark' of Irish state interventionism.[5] Powers that had eluded him in the 1930s now fell into his lap. Effectively, Lemass would control Irish economic life by decree for a number of years. The Ministers and Secretaries Act

(1924), which defined ministers and departments of state, was even amended in 1939 to allow the Minister for Supplies to act as a 'corporation sole'.[6]

Meanwhile Lemass's big rival, Seán MacEntee, was moved from Finance to Industry and Commerce. Simultaneously, Lemass was promoted to a hastily formed Cabinet Emergency Committee headed by de Valera and composed of himself, Seán T. O'Kelly and Frank Aiken. There was now little doubt about Lemass's superiority over MacEntee. In January 1941 Lemass's bulging brief expanded even further. The Cabinet Committee on Emergency Problems, of which he was a member, agreed that the Minister for Supplies would undertake the campaign to grow more food.[7] This represented an expansion of the already exceptional powers Lemass enjoyed. On hearing of the decision, the Minister for Agriculture, James Ryan, complained angrily to de Valera of the overlapping of ministerial responsibilities that this entailed.[8] Ryan often maintained a central position in cabinet between the extremes of Lemass and MacEntee. His uncharacteristic response was symptomatic of the resentment among other ministers at the autocratic control that Lemass was accumulating.

Lemass was to accrue yet more power, though. In a cabinet reshuffle of August 1941 necessitated by the resignation of the Minister for Local Government and Public Health, P. J. Ruttledge, Lemass gained control of his old department, Industry and Commerce, while retaining the Supplies portfolio. This development was to the further chagrin of MacEntee, who was relegated to fill Ruttledge's vacancy. Lemass's ascendancy over MacEntee was confirmed in November 1942 when a new Cabinet Committee on Economic Planning was established. This elite body was composed of de Valera, Seán T. O'Kelly and Lemass. To cap it all, Lemass was often excused from the drudgery of parliamentary party meetings in the early 1940s due to his large workload.[9]

Work on Lemass's ministerial palace on Kildare Street began in January 1939. From a vertiginous scaffold Gabriel Hayes, a female sculptor, crafted the figures still visible on the outside of the building, which depict men at work in various poses reminiscent of Soviet realism. Lemass did his best to fast-track materials specified in the architect's plans but now unobtainable due to wartime trade disruption. These included blinds for the windows and extra petrol for the building contractor. The building's massive bronze doors were the only ones in Ireland at the time, but the Australian walnut, earmarked for the wood panelling in the ministerial corridor, proved impossible to procure.[10]

With MacEntee appointed Minister for Industry and Commerce in 1939, Lemass fretted less over delays to the building project on Kildare Street. Instead he set about expanding his new Department of Supplies. Within the new department, Lemass and Leydon led by example in creating an infectious buzz of efficiency. Unshackled from the usual opposition to his grand plans from across the cabinet table by MacEntee, Lemass thrived in this atmosphere of independence and creativity and revolutionised civil service working practices. He made a point of streamlining action by enabling all officials concerned with decision-making to attend departmental conferences at which decisions were taken.[11] His staff prided themselves on the department's 'greater promptitude' than other arms of state,[12] and were encouraged to deal with all matters quickly by using the telephone and keeping a minimum of paperwork.[13] Civil servants in Supplies were said to regularly work long after hours without any remuneration.[14]

Lemass possessed a distinctly expansionist desire to subsume other departments, and the Department of Supplies soon confirmed its status as the pre-eminent department in the management of Ireland's Emergency. Departmental posts were filled by officers parachuted in from other departments as the capacity of Supplies rose dramatically. There were 169 people working for the department in 1940. This figure had reached 1,069 by 1944.[15] Supplies gobbled up the Turf Development Board in 1943,[16] took on the responsibility for the drafting of the Irish contingency plan for invasion,[17] and counted the Emergency Supplies Research Bureau as yet another organisation that came under its aegis.[18] In its youth and freneticism, Lemass's department resembled a restless, precocious child. It even changed address at a rapid speed, moving from Ballsbridge to Earlsfort Terrace, then back to Ballsbridge, leaving sections of its rapidly expanding operation in Kildare Street and O'Connell Street as it did so.[19]

Skinner claims that at one period during the war the Department of Supplies was receiving 20,000 letters a day from members of the public.[20] This is an exaggeration, but it conveys the size of the bureaucracy Lemass established. Expansion was signalled most clearly by the emergence of the department's Inspection Branch. It was established in March 1941 when Leydon head-hunted twenty customs officers.[21] Lemass charged these men with visiting traders to ensure they were complying with their 'statutory obligations of equitable distribution at fair price'.[22] By October 1943 there were 106 Department of Supplies inspectors, six senior inspectors, and a full clerical staff. There were now 'Inspection Stations' in Cork, Waterford, Limerick, Galway, Sligo, Dundalk, Fenit, Westport, Mullingar and Letterkenny.[23] The Dublin operation had grown so large that it was divided into seven sub-areas.[24]

When Lemass regained control of Industry and Commerce in the cabinet reshuffle of August 1941, his annoyance over the delays to his HQ returned with venom. He demanded a 'detailed statement' from the OPW on the 'exact nature of the causes of the delay', pressed for the building's completion 'at the earliest possible date', and insisted that more men be employed on the project as plasterers and carpenters to speed up its completion.[25] However, the architect, Boyd-Barrett, would have the finishing touches completed only by expert tradesmen.[26] In December 1941 Lemass found time to inspect sculptor Gabriel Hayes' drawings, which would adorn the building's panels. These impressive designs depicted vast numbers of men and machinery at work in various industries. The two large panels on Lemass's ministerial balcony would show muscular, high-cheekboned men at work on the Shannon Scheme and at a cement plant. The small panels of the balcony would depict the spinning, pottery, shoemaking and tobacco industries. Over the main entrance Hayes would carve Lugh, god of light in Irish mythology, releasing a flight of aeroplanes. These splendid ornaments presented a striking mix of social realism and mythology. Lemass liked the plans but, still bitter about the overall delay, was not gushing in his praise. He told Hayes that 'the designs would form a suitable basis from which the carvings might be produced'.[27]

The building was completed in October 1942. With it, the long-standing physical advantage MacEntee had over Lemass had come to an end. In that same bitterly cold month, Lemass and Leydon, along with the throngs of staff comprising his two departments, finally moved in to his newly completed winter palace: the Department of Industry and Commerce on Kildare Street. With characteristic Lemassian efficiency, 600 staff were whisked through the bronze gates, through the ornate entrance hall and marble floors, and into their new offices in just four days. Lemass boasted that no individual civil servant suffered more than a half day's disturbance to his or her work.[28]

Shortly after moving in to his new HQ Lemass, in his haste, slipped on the shiny Galway marble floor of the main landing after coming down the staircase. His mandarins soon ensured that Boyd-Barrett's marble made way for more practical rubber flooring.[29] He was also annoyed by *The Irish Times'* coverage of his palatial new surroundings in an article entitled 'Eighty Feet High But No Lift', which exposed how wartime shortages had left the six-storey building without an elevator.[30]

The main thing, though, was that after a decade of waiting he had finally moved in to his new home. His imposing new surroundings were particularly impressive because nearly all building work had ground to a standstill during the Emergency due to shortages. Above all, these new surroundings radiated power. Lemass did not get the underground tunnel to Leinster House he wanted, but the building's basement became an air-conditioned bunker for the cabinet in case of bombing raids. Rooms in the ministerial suite were furnished with Axminster carpets and French polished mahogany.[31] Behind his enormous new desk he could bask in the warmth of his marble fireplace as he cleaned out his pipe into his aeroplane-shaped ashtray, crafted from an aircraft piston. More importantly, he could comfortably set to work on expanding his empire.

At the Mercy of the British

For all its audacity, Lemass's new department was perilously reliant on British goodwill. Lemass introduced the first of his long-desired export controls in September 1939. Under this, the Emergency Powers (Control of Export) Order, he decreed that any commodity intended for export had first to obtain a licence.[32] The detail of the order exposed the good faith Lemass placed in Britain in the wake of the 1938 trade deal. It was put in place only after Britain had enacted similar legislation and was at the mercy of these British controls.[33] Lemass drew up a list of vital commodities exempted from export restriction including such necessities as crops, meat, metals, clothing, chemicals, petrol, wool and fruit and vegetables.[34] Fundamentally, this list of vital commodities was drawn up with the intention of honouring trade agreements with Britain and appeasing the British Board of Trade rather than safeguarding essential supplies for the home market.[35]

Despite anticipated supply shortages, Lemass decided not to introduce a rationing system in Ireland when war broke out. Instead,

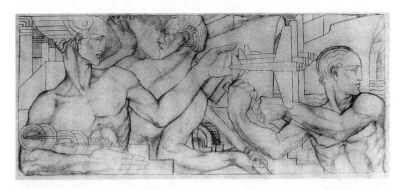

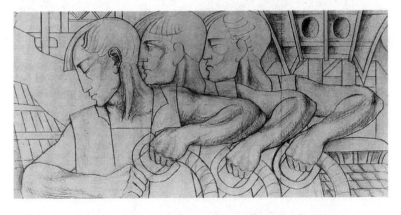

Clockwise from top left: the Celtic god Lugh, set in stone on the Department of Industry and Commerce building, Kildare Street; Gabriel Hayes' depictions of Irish aviation; of the Shannon Scheme; of the Irish shipbuilding industry; of the steel industry; shipbuilding in stone on the Department of Industry and Commerce building, Kildare Street; the Shannon Scheme in stone on the Department of Industry and Commerce building, Kildare Street. Courtesy Fionnbharr Ó Riordán.

British complaints that the availability of a certain Irish export was compromising *their* rationing system frequently led to the appearance of the offending article on the list of goods prohibited for Irish export by Supplies.[36] This made for a 'haphazard' list that contained what senior Department of Supplies officials described as 'quaint and often ridiculous items such as lanterns, sunshades, vacuum flasks, book ends and fancy blotters', all included on the whim of the British authorities.[37] These obscure items were joined by musical instruments, lipsticks and fountain pens,[38] in November 1941 by horseflesh 'and offals thereof' and, in April 1943, badger hair.[39] The papers of Frank Aiken even contain a censored newspaper article claiming that 'abnormal demands from Britain for goat meat for human consumption are behind the drying up of the supply of goats for the carnivora of Dublin zoo'.[40]

In April 1940, while the conflict was still a 'phoney war', Lemass and Ryan travelled to London for talks with Anthony Eden, Prime Minister Neville Chamberlain's Secretary of State for Dominion Affairs. In line with controls the British had been hinting at since the mid-1930s, Eden warned Lemass that the 'elimination of competition' on shipping was in the pipeline.[41] With Britain's war economy operating on a highly centralised basis, the 'absence of a free market' the British had anticipated a few years earlier was becoming a reality.[42] Lemass pressed Eden for a clearer picture of the 'nature and degree' of trade restrictions to follow. Significantly, however, he declared himself happy with the prospective restrictions on shipping.

Overall, Eden and Lemass enjoyed a warm exchange. Before talks, the delegates lunched at the Savoy and discussions were described as 'extremely friendly'. At their conclusion, Lemass 'thanked Mr. Eden most cordially for the welcome extended to his colleagues and himself', 'expressed pleasure' at the outcome of the meetings, and heaped praise on Eden for Britain's 'help and cooperation'. Eden, in return, expressed a desire to end partition.[43]

Reflecting on the decadence of the talks J. P. Walshe, a senior civil servant at the Department of External Affairs, wrote to de Valera, characterising the British as 'too soft, too class-prejudiced (they are almost all of the wealthy Tory family type) to be able to win a war against men of steel like Hitler, Stalin'.[44] Days later, a pivotal geopolitical event took place, the consequences of which would illustrate just how far Walshe had misjudged the British and just how far Lemass's new ministerial powers were a chimera. In May 1940

German tanks rolled into France and the Low Countries. France fell to Nazi Germany in early June 1940.

Lemass claimed to have been 'not so much involved' on the issue of neutrality during the war, claiming 'I wouldn't have known all the details of what was going on'.[45] This was pure bluff. Shortly after the catastrophic fall of France, Malcolm MacDonald, the former British Dominions Secretary, presented de Valera with an enticing proposal. If independent Ireland would join the Allied war effort and let the Royal Navy use its ports, Britain would accept the principle of a united Ireland. At a meeting of the government the following day the atmosphere was tense. It was decided that de Valera, along with Lemass and Frank Aiken, would meet MacDonald over lunch to discuss the proposal.

Later that day de Valera, Lemass and Aiken dined with MacDonald. MacDonald's report of the meeting noted that while Aiken 'was extremely rigid in his opposition to our plan', Lemass was 'far more prepared to discuss our plan in a reasonable way'. Lemass knew better than anyone else how dependent on British 'help and co-operation' Ireland was. At the same time, like Aiken, he was wary of the vague promise of 'the principle of a United Ireland'.[46] Lemass was, then, more involved in the neutrality issue than he later admitted, having taken part in what must rank as one of the most decisive luncheons in modern Irish history.

In light of this inconclusive meeting, the British presented de Valera with an amended proposal. Northern Ireland and Éire would cooperate as a joint body assisted by Britain, and the British would gain use of Irish ports. In return, Irish unification would be viewed as an 'accomplished fact'. When it comes to this more lucrative bargain Lemass's claim to ignorance holds more weight. Desmond Ryan recorded that the 'small industrialists behind Fianna Fáil' could be accused of acquiring a 'vested interest in maintaining partition, since tariffs blunt the competition of the powerful and long-established Ulster industrialists'.[47] Emergency conditions, however, heightened tensions between Lemass and a considerable number of Ireland's capitalists. It is reasonable to assume then that, had it been up to Lemass, he may very well have plumped for this deal, given the rapidly deteriorating trade situation. De Valera, however, never submitted these improved terms for discussion at cabinet. Instead he rejected the proposal because it gave 'no guarantee that in the end we would have a united Ireland'.[48]

Developments on the continent had seriously wrong-footed Lemass's economic strategy. By this point he was really sweating under the increasing pressure of British export controls. Ireland was beginning to experience the first agonising pangs of what would become a full economic squeeze by Britain. The following month, August 1940, British Ministry of Food officials raised the tantalising prospect of reviving Ireland's agricultural economy, which was seriously faltering, by liberalising restrictions on Irish cattle imports. As a quid pro quo they requested that the Irish allow British merchant vessels to leave cargo in Irish ports for export to Britain later.[49] At an interdepartmental meeting of senior Irish civil servants it was agreed that there was a 'strong economic argument' in favour of granting the British these facilities.[50] This latest deal was turned down at an Irish cabinet meeting, however, which noted the recent extension of German bombing on the Thames Estuary, the Bristol Channel, the Mersey and the Clyde.[51]

Lemass found himself impaled on a veritable Morton's Fork. The country was precariously reliant on its nearest neighbour for supplies. But alleviating the pain of British trade restrictions by granting Britain shipping facilities was likely to alter the character of neutrality in German eyes. The cabinet anticipated mass civilian deaths through Luftwaffe bombing raids as a result.

Frustrated by what they saw as selfish assertions of neutrality, the British attitude darkened. Winston Churchill had replaced Chamberlain as British Prime Minister and in the following months Britain's stance hardened considerably. Germany's occupation of Norway and France had given her bases on the Atlantic which increased the range of U-boats in the war against British merchant shipping. As a nudge to neutral Ireland to join the war effort, the British imposed much stricter trade restrictions in late 1940. By early 1941 the relationship between the two countries had become very strained. To the British government, headed by Churchill – the embodiment of the 'wealthy Tory family type' – the price of Irish neutrality would be a crippling and remorseless supply squeeze.

During the cordial talks with Eden before the storm clouds broke, Lemass had agreed to the British Ministry of Shipping's request that it handle the charters for Ireland's neutral shipping. This was because, the British claimed, competition from Ireland for neutral tonnage was proving 'embarrassing'.[52] By July Britain had overcome its 'embarrassment' by securing all the neutral tonnage to

Ireland's detriment. This left Ireland 'high and dry', as officials from Supplies put it.[53] According to Sir John Maffey, the top British diplomatic representative in Ireland, the British supply squeeze left Leydon feeling 'badly let down by his opposite numbers in the [British] Board of Trade with whom he had negotiated in better days'. The desperation of the situation enraged the normally reserved Leydon whom, Maffey recalled, 'spoke to me with considerable violence about our policy and added that he hoped to "never go to London again"'.[54] Lemass shared his lieutenant's anger. He stormily described the shipping development as a 'double cross'.[55]

But if Lemass's anger was understandable, it also illustrated his failure to establish a vital economic arm in Ireland's industrial expansion during the 1930s. Sinn Féin had placed the establishment of an Irish merchant navy high on its list of priorities during the War of Independence. But as Minister for Industry and Commerce Lemass did not add a mercantile marine to the collection of semi-state companies he formed. This major oversight ensured that, as well as being at the mercy of British naval might, the venture was ramshackle and small in scale.[56] When questioned about building up Ireland's shipping service during the Emergency Lemass described it as 'an exciting business – buying any ships that you could get your hands on, anything that would float, patching them up and keeping them in operation'.[57] Liam Skinner, in discussing Lemass's wartime record, notes with pride the reappearance of the Irish flag on the high seas in the summer of 1941.[58] But the hazardous conditions of naval warfare during the war were far removed from the jaunty seafaring image that both men evoked.

Leydon and his counterpart at Finance, J. J. McElligott, hastily drew up the provisions for the founding of Irish Shipping Ltd, which was launched in March 1941. The company was able to secure fifteen ships in total, most of these foreign vessels laid up in Irish ports and requisitioned by Supplies.[59] The bulk of what little shipping Ireland possessed was concentrated on importing grain from the USA and the Lisbon trade route.[60] Mary Daly's claim that Irish Shipping was 'highly successful' is contentious.[61] Irish Shipping was reduced to acquiring decrepit ships that were (as Lemass's comment suggests) dangerous to sail in, so much so that a stock joke developed among Irish sailors that torpedoes from U-boats were much less hazardous than their own ships. Ireland's dependence on Britain was most vividly illustrated by Lemass's reliance on shipped imports at a time of fierce marine warfare. With better planning and procurement in this area in the pre-war period, the sacrifice of 138 Irish sailors and 20 ships during the Second World War would surely have been balanced by greater material rewards for the Irish public.

Lemass's macroeconomic impotence was demonstrated between Christmas Eve 1940 and New Year 1941, when petrol pumps across the state ran dry, leaving members of the public, keen to return to Dublin after their Christmas holidays, stranded. It was the overriding issue of shipping and not, as one history of the Emergency contends, a capricious Irish U-turn on trade agreements 'at the last minute' that scuppered trade between Britain and Ireland and provided the 'rude shock for the Irish government and people' at the turn of the new year in 1941, when the petrol ran out.[62]

Facing questions about the trade position after the petrol drought, Lemass was forced to illustrate frankly how he was at the mercy of the British petrol distribution companies and their masters in Westminster.[63] He admitted that the message from Britain accompanying the squeeze, much like one tied to a brick thrown at a window, had been to 'tighten up the ration system drastically'.[64] His pitiful position was aggravated in January 1941 when the British government tore up the previous year's shipping chartering arrangements, citing the 'exigencies of war'.[65]

Later in 1941 Supplies again came under heavy criticism from the British Board of Trade for allowing Irish enterprise too much independence. Irish firms continued to place orders with British suppliers without first obtaining the necessary licences from the Irish government. Where there existed a number of importers for a certain commodity, rather than a monopoly, British authorities either strongly urged or forced Supplies to establish itself as the central importing agent for that commodity, effectively controlling the entry of all goods.[66] Even in instances where departmental papers claim that Lemass set up central importing bodies under his own initiative – such as Tea Importers (Éire) Ltd, established in July 1941[67] – the timing is suggestive of British pressure. With some Irish firms continuing to export with scant regard to British restrictions, the British Board of Trade flexed its muscles and for the remainder of the war periodically forced Supplies, against the department's wishes, to add new export restrictions to the raft of public pronouncements it was already issuing.[68]

The British 'double cross' caught Lemass out, but it also taught him to take a firmer attitude with both Ireland's capitalists and

Britain's trade officials. In this regard Ireland's beer proved a rare but reliable trump card. In 1938 and 1939 Ireland exported around 800,000 barrels of beer annually. In 1940 and 1941 this figure leapt to the 900,000 mark.[69] This increase was due to the rise in demand for beer from the rapidly expanding number of men enlisted in the British military and in British war work. By the end of 1941, however, wheat was becoming seriously scarce in Ireland and consequently Lemass banned its export in March 1942.[70] Faced with a thirsty garrison of American and British troops in Northern Ireland, the British agreed to release stocks of wheat and coal in return for beer and, in 1943, Lemass was able to secure agricultural machinery in exchange for beer.[71]

This was barter at its best for Lemass. Foreign Affairs records indicate that, unsurprisingly, such agreements were reached only after stormy exchanges between the two sides. After the British complained of the 'acute' beer shortage in Belfast following Lemass's restrictions,[72] a hasty agreement was drawn up whereby Britain would exchange badly needed stocks of wheat in exchange for Irish alcohol.[73] The export ban was lifted only temporarily, however. A short time later Guinness complained that they did not have sufficient coal to produce enough beer for both the home and export markets.[74] British officials agreed to release more coal to Ireland if Leydon would give them the assurance that the extra coal would be used exclusively by Guinness to produce more beer.[75] Leydon, displaying a scrupulous honesty Lemass would have disapproved of, cited the desperate need for coal among the Irish general public and refused to give his assurance. The deal collapsed.

Later attempts to secure fertilisers and machinery were met with the British Ministry of Food's high-handed insistence that 'barter arrangements were not looked upon with favour' and that they preferred a 'gentleman's agreement'.[76] Leydon, quite reasonably, replied that experience had proven such agreements were 'useless'.[77] Barter proved a highly volatile business, and when Ireland did succeed in securing fertilisers and machinery in return for beer it was in the face of strong opposition from the United States Combined Raw Materials Board and the British Ministry of Agriculture. Consequently, the quantities received were described as 'most disappointing'.[78]

Whereas other departments, desperate for imported British goods, urged a conciliatory approach to the British,[79] Leydon and

Lemass often maintained a hard line. While uncomfortably at the mercy of British trade for much of the period, Lemass and Leydon's poker-faced demeanour worked more effectively as the Emergency drew to a close. 'For heaven's sake make it clear that you are not trying to force our hand,' urged a friendly official from the British Dominions Office to Leydon in trade talks in 1943.[80] Refusing to heed such advice in this and other instances, Lemass favoured presenting the British with the fait accompli of halting beer exports and testing their response.[81] It was a risky strategy with very high stakes, but barter arrangements resumed shortly after the threat of export suspension and reached a stable footing by 1944. For Lemass, the teetotaller, beer had provided a rare quenching of the state's general supplies drought.

Tackling 'Moral Flabbiness': The State and Private Capital

In 1945 the functions of Lemass's Department of Supplies were transferred back to the Department of Industry and Commerce. Subsequently, the latter produced several documents assessing the Department of Supplies and its role during the war. Industry and Commerce's observations on price control, contributed to the Committee of Inquiry into Taxation on Industry in the early 1950s, provide evidence that the authors viewed the Emergency as an exceptional period in which social interests took priority over conventional economic objectives.

The committee's report explained that a system of price control in ordinary conditions 'sought, where practicable, to provide incentives to manufacturers to increase output. If output was increased, profits increased proportionately and the manufacturer benefited accordingly.'[82] This, the normal situation, contrasted markedly with wartime conditions, which 'necessitate the limitation of profits to levels considered reasonable'.[83] Herein lay a crucial distinction not only between alternative ways in which the economy was regulated, but in terms of in what direction, and for whom, the economy was geared. As the committee noted in the early pages of its report, 'during the war the social advantages of relieving unemployment and developing natural resources took priority over productivity'.[84]

These remarks demonstrate that officials in the Department of Supplies viewed their role, in a time of material deprivation, as a moral one. This moral economic attitude was infused in them by

After an uncharacteristically friendly editorial, Lemass gets a piggyback from *The Irish Times'* larger-than-life editor R. M. Smyllie. *Dublin Opinion*, June 1942.

Lemass and occasionally pitted the department against the greed of Ireland's protected capitalists. Domestically, the amount of elbow room that Supplies took on during these years was bound to rankle with some of those seated at the head table of the Irish economy. In large part, the department's interventionism was influenced by British pressure to centralise economic control. But, as mentioned, from its inception as the Emergency Supplies Branch of Industry and Commerce in late 1938, the department clashed with Irish manufacturers and banks. Large businesses were frequently uncooperative with Lemass's efforts to compile statistics and conserve reserve stocks. The minister was consistently irritated by the willingness of prominent Irish industrialists to enter into private negotiations in Britain, where they made commitments with long-term consequences for the nation's trade without consulting the government.[85]

In 1940 these tensions came to a head when Lemass accused the Federation of Irish Manufacturers of 'dictating' to his department.[86] But, in a number of cases, these roles were reversed. Supplies, donning the armour of moral economy, exhibited an aggressive tendency to centralise economic control. Generally, when a company found itself at loggerheads with Supplies the directors were summoned to the department's offices in Ballsbridge and differences were 'discussed'. Such was the case with Ireland's largest manufacturer of floor polish, a Dublin firm which in early 1944 announced that it was limiting its output for the remainder of the Emergency due to a lack of ingredients. Lemass told the firm's directors that it was their 'patriotic duty' to continue production. The number of consumer complaints concerning inferior-quality floor polish rose steeply thereafter, but the product stayed on the shelves.[87] Gerald Boland, Minister for Defence at the time, derided these 'nack-lane factories' producing inferior goods; his son Kevin recalled with dread trying to shave with Irish-manufactured razor blades during the Emergency.[88]

Lemass, nonetheless, was laying down the law to Irish commerce as never before. His ultimatums were backed up by his powers over export. He was wholly intolerant of native capitalists he perceived as disingenuous. He refused to grant extra export licences to Ireland's industrial mammoth Guinness in 1943 despite the trade benefits that this would deliver because he was convinced that the company had been dishonest in listing their supplies.[89] His department also lobbied hard in 1944 for new legislation that would give the Minister for Supplies the 'fullest discretion' in deciding the penalties imposed on firms who had wavered from the percentage rate of gross profit, a 'relatively small minority who are deliberately evading control' and with whom Lemass and Leydon were clearly determined to settle old scores.[90]

Under the new legislation proposed by Supplies, Lemass would be able to demand the payment to the exchequer of profits which he considered excess. Until the sum was recovered Supplies would appoint a receiver. The trader would be given the right of appeal at a special tribunal, but recourse to ordinary courts would be denied and the tribunal could increase the penalties threefold.[91] These proposals were clearly influenced by tough British measures to prevent profiteering through an excess profits tax.[92] Under this legislation, wartime and pre-war profits were compared and the difference taxed at a high percentage. The proposals exhibit the vigour with which Lemass was prepared to deal with businesses he considered had deliberately deviated from his department's moral economic line.

Once again, his colleagues' distaste for Lemass's empire-building scuppered some of his bolder moves in regulating enterprise. Supplies' power-hungry expansion of its functions was viewed as obnoxious by other departments; this characteristic of the department is aptly termed 'cannibalism' by John Horgan.[93] Unsurprisingly, other departments – particularly the Department of Finance – pointed to the disproportionately large amount of power that the prospective excess profits legislation conferred on Supplies and the state in general.[94] Despite acceptance at a cabinet meeting of September 1944, the Unlawful Profits Bill was never introduced.[95]

Two years later Lemass unsuccessfully proposed that he assume the power of compulsory acquisition of companies on behalf of the state. The tension between Supplies' moral interventionism and trade expertise was encapsulated in a Dáil debate of 1947 over Lemass's Industrial Efficiency and Prices Bill, another never-realised piece of legislation that aimed to punish what the minister saw as profiteering in the protected industries. Defending the bill, Lemass argued that 'where an industry receives help in that form from the community it must be prepared to give to the community reasonable safeguards that it is not unduly exploiting that position for the private benefit of individuals'.[96]

If this demonstrated that Lemass was at times willing to put a gun to the head of Ireland's businessmen, the practical relationship between the state and private capital was often based on joint purchase, Lemass's favourite method of organising supply during the war. Under this scheme a business trading in essential goods was established by Lemass with a board nominated by the trade. These included Grain Importers (Éire), Animal Feeding Stuffs (Éire), Fuel Importers (Éire) and Irish Shipping.[97] While these bodies were not exclusively state-run, they were still subject to a hefty degree of central intervention. Either Leydon or a high-ranking official from Supplies sat on the board and all meetings were held at the department's offices in Ballsbridge.[98] Under joint purchase, companies were run on a strictly not-for-profit basis, as a monopoly, and with board membership subject to Lemass's approval.[99] As an example, the joint purchase company Tea Importers Ltd had only four shareholders – the tea merchants who sat on its board. Each had only a £1 share of its nominal £100 capital.[100]

Although joint purchase arrangements relied on the participation of Irish capitalists, these captains of industry were effectively sidelined in several instances. After the Emergency, the president of the Federation of Irish Manufacturers, P. L. McEvoy, commented on the changes to the Irish economy which Lemass had introduced. 'State socialism by any other name smells as bad, and we view with deep concern the practice which has sprung up here of establishing nominally private limited companies, the capital of which is provided out of State funds, and the directors of which are persons nominated by the Minister.' He went on to say: 'I think I would prefer an open policy of nationalisation to this back-door method of achieving the same object.'[101] In contrast to a socialist system, McEvoy claimed,

The gargantuan bureaucracy of Lemass's new department, as captured by *Dublin Opinion*, March 1941

Lemass's system was 'free from responsibility to the representatives of the people'; it was directed by a small clique, a 'narrow panel from which the directors of these companies and boards are chosen'.[102]

In defending himself and his 'narrow panel' of managers, Lemass raised the moral economic standard, citing the imperative of equitable supply and distribution in a time of shortages. But this could not fully shield his department's relative indolence in the initial stages of the Emergency. With the British economic squeeze taking hold in early 1941, W. T. Cosgrave implied that Lemass had misled the house on the issue of supplies. 'For the better part of some 12 months now,' he claimed, 'the public has been informed, principally by the Minister for Supplies, that the situation with regard to supplies of essential commodities . . . was quite comfortable.'[103] Defending himself against these accusations, Lemass claimed that Ireland had entered the war period better prepared than many other European countries. He had never promoted a false impression simply to reassure the Irish people, he insisted.

A large body of evidence suggests otherwise. For instance, Lemass pursued a short-sighted policy of allowing the export of machinery and plant to Britain in the first fourteen months of the Emergency.[104] Somewhat predictably, when Ireland was desperate to obtain machinery and plant after the fall of France, Britain refused. Such short-sightedness had at least one obviously negative consequence: the absence, in some cases, of mechanical diggers to enable the quicker burial of infected carcasses during the major foot-and-mouth outbreak of 1941, which compounded the spread of the disease to neighbouring herds.[105]

Similarly, shortly after the outbreak of war Lemass announced strict supervision on the usage of timber.[106] He continued, however, to grant export licences for timber freely up to the end of 1940.[107] By this point it should have been obvious, both from the rigid control introduced by the British authorities over domestic timber and their frantic efforts to acquire future shipments from overseas, that timber would be extremely scarce. In June 1940 British officials contacted Supplies with a view to procuring as much Irish timber as possible and had no problems in securing it. The chief concern of senior civil servants in Supplies seems to have been that the Department of Lands, and not themselves, would carry out the negotiations.[108] As late as October 1941, officials from Supplies agreed that advertisements for the sale of large amounts of timber would not be censored from the press.[109] The following two years would witness a dearth of fuel in the country. According to Robert Fisk, in 1942 it took a train three hours to make the seven-mile journey from Dublin to Dun Laoghaire, the passengers collecting timber beside the track to fuel the locomotive.[110] This was despite the fact that Lemass had established three joint purchase companies to manage supplies of wood.[111]

Another example concerns the desperate shortage of wheat in Ireland during the war, which led to the roundly detested 'black loaf'. In the 1930s the Irish government had carried out tests with a seed dressing called 'Golden Grain', a preservative that protected cereal crops from disease and increased yields considerably.[112] Ireland's dependence on cereals and grains was intensifying due to the supply situation,[113] but by 1941 Ireland was importing 1,000 tons of grain a week while consumption was 1,000 tons a day.[114] Nonetheless, Lemass 'was not aware of the seriousness of the supply position until approached by some of the importing firms in late 1941'.[115] With Britain ceasing its export in 1941 as part of the supply squeeze, Lemass had to grub around desperately for alternative supplies of 'Golden Grain', eventually procuring them from Spain.[116] These supplies were adequate for only one season. By mid-1943 Lemass was obliged to concede to the Dáil that the country did not have sufficient chemical supplies.[117] The department's failure to secure supplies at an earlier stage resulted in poorer yields at a time when the British supply squeeze necessitated a significant increase in Irish self-sufficiency.

In other instances, Lemass's interventionism proved maladroit. For example, rubber from torpedoed British ships was often salvaged off the west coast. The government was desperate to retain all salvaged rubber for domestic industrial use and Lemass appointed Dunlop, operating from the marina in Cork city, as their agents for the collection, processing and distribution of scrap rubber from the sea.[118] If this implied the state's recognition of the private trade expertise that Dunlop possessed, it was soured by the official process involved in the recovery of salvaged rubber. All scrap recovered had first to be delivered by the salvor to the receiver of wreck, along with their claim, a report of the circumstances in which the recovery took place and a certificate from the commanding officer of the military forces in the area.[119] This process was designed with the intention that 'every possible aid is given to vessels in danger', to guard against the eerie prospect of deliberate wrecking.[120] However, to quote a member of the Marine and Coast Watching Service, the process was 'tangled in red tape'.[121] Eventually, necessity trumped procedure. Against official protocol, coast watchers and Dunlop pioneered a fast-track scheme in defiance of Lemass's scheme whereby salvors simply wrote their names and addresses on rubber bales and sent them to Cork to be weighed; Dunlop then repaid the salvors per lb.[122]

To McEvoy, the overstepping of the normal boundaries of state interference with trade was always, as with the previous example, clunky and undynamic. But Supplies did not manage to secure the legislation that would have given Lemass, the 'economic overlord', full autocratic powers over business. And when it came to the role of the state, Lemass was not the left-leaning radical some of his contemporaries reckoned.[123] In 1944 he reassured manufacturers and retailers that 'this state is based firmly on the principle of private commercial enterprise . . . and the sooner we can allow private enterprise to have free play again, the more rapid will be our return to better conditions'.[124] Lemass's tone in this speech does not go so far as to suggest that these assembled businessmen were collectively the grey eminence directing Emergency economic policy from behind the scenes, but it does highlight the fact that for all the aggrandisement of his functions Lemass could not rule out collaboration with private enterprise.

Writing after the Emergency, Lemass's senior civil servants acknowledged that they had tried and failed to do things all on their own. Cooperation with trade groups was an 'essential feature' of import arrangements and in some cases the equitable distribution of essential supplies was left entirely to private businesses.[125] The department also noted pessimistically that, despite Lemass's powers, 'traders will have learned that even when they do nothing to secure supplies they still share in the benefits of supplies obtained through official action' and that 'in a period of shortage money can be made almost without effort'.[126] As Jonathan Swift wrote: 'Laws are like cobwebs, which may catch small flies but let wasps and hornets break through.'[127] Although he was not afraid to pursue wasps and hornets, the expansion of Lemass's bureaucratic apparatus meant that it soon came to bear down disproportionately on the small flies.

An Inspector Calls: Policing the Domestic Economy

In Ireland, the effect of Britain's declaration of war on Germany on 3 September 1939 was immediate. Increased numbers of Irish people resident in Britain returned home to escape the anticipated carnage.[128] There was also a rapid increase in the cost of living. The outbreak of war caused a surge of panic-buying. This, in turn, forced prices up considerably. On 5 September 1939 Dublin coal merchants' offices shut their doors at 1 p.m. in an attempt to stall the rush.[129] On 7 September Lemass wielded his new powers by issuing a Prices Standstill Order for coal, fixing prices at their 26 August levels.[130] By 11 September, however, the price of coal had shot up by 50 per cent.[131]

As the month progressed and prices continued to rise, Lemass's lack of control became clearer. On 20 September 1939 *The Irish Press* told its readers that coal prices would rise even further. This, it explained, was because the coal importers had informed the Minister for Supplies that the rates decreed in his Prices Standstill Order were inadequate given the war risk attached to freights.[132] This revelation was an early indication that prices would be dictated by Britain and the large importers rather than by Lemass. Media coverage of the nation's supply issue thereafter was less revelatory and suggests that from this early stage Lemass instructed the press to be less open on supply issues.[133] Possessing scant stockpiles of essential goods, Lemass reacted to a similar rush on sugar later in the month with the introduction of partial rationing on sugar, tea and fuel. Defending these regulatory measures, Lemass insisted it would be 'folly' not to prepare for a lengthy war.[134]

From these, the earliest stages of the Emergency, Lemass established a theme of moral economy as central to the national supply situation. The insistence that the state would be the main, but not the only, economic actor during the Emergency was central to this message. Frequently asserting the need for the public to practise frugality, Lemass stated that the government had neither the resources nor the organisation to overcome the supply crisis without the cooperation of individual citizens.[135] In their market practices the people of Ireland were responsible, he claimed, for the economic well-being of the country. Lemass criticised both hoarders and profiteering shopkeepers, but stressed individual consumer ethics as well.[136] In radio announcements on the supply position he urged people to exercise self-restraint in their consumption of key goods.

Crucially, Lemass publicly stated that he did not want to introduce a full rationing system.[137] 'Voluntary measures of economy' were preferable to full rationing, he asserted, asking for the 'voluntary assistance of every housewife' in reducing consumption.[138] Instead of a comprehensive rationing system, goods were subject to price orders dictated by Lemass. This system required constant powers of market supervision that were quite beyond the capabilities of a single minister. The frequent addition and removal of price orders and regulatory measures on certain goods led to accusations of complacency on Lemass's part. He was 'chopping and changing' on the food supply, to the people's detriment, it was claimed in the Dáil.[139] It was stated elsewhere that he was incompetent in the face of the 'soaring prices of the very essentials of existence'.[140]

To instil a moral economic ethic in the public without the accompaniment of a comprehensive rationing system and coherent price structure was a mighty task, even for a man of Lemass's tenacity and work ethic. To return to the price of coal, on 20 September 1939 Lemass decreed that coal could not be sold at any price over an extra 2 shillings per ton on the price he had outlined in his latest

Prices Standstill Order.[141] The following day, 21 September, he announced that coal could not be sold at any price over an extra 5 shillings per ton on the price as outlined in the aforementioned order.[142]

The rapidity and variability of such announcements exposed Ireland's reliance on British-controlled imports. More importantly, it did little to dispel the cloud of confusion surrounding what constituted the legal price for commodities as determined by the government. In practice, the public learned to negotiate black-market prices rather than adhere to ministerial price orders. A theological debate raged in the *Irish Ecclesiastical Record* on the issue.[143] Many readers wrote in to the journal to rubbish Lemass's price orders, claiming that the *just* price of goods bore no relation to the constantly changing *legal* price. In other words, it was not a sin to buy and sell goods at their black-market price, provided these prices were not extortionate. One theologian wrote that it was not sinful for sellers to 'charge something more' than the controlled price for goods 'provided that the excess is within reasonable limits'; charging *20* shillings for 1 lb of tea was wrong, therefore, but charging *a shilling or two* over the controlled price was justified.[144] After all, he reasoned, 'there's nothing like a nice cup of tea'.[145]

This sort of attitude infuriated Lemass. He insisted that the government could not suppress the black market unless the public helped 'and the public aren't helping'. This situation, he claimed, was jeopardising the very 'institutions of state'.[146] Lemass's determination was redoubled by material adversity. In marked contrast to the 1930s, conditions for workers during the Emergency were exacerbated by the Wages Standstill Order, in effect from May 1941, which outlawed strikes for greater pay. Wartime inflation compounded these hard times. According to a conservative estimate of price inflation at the time, wages increased by one third during the Emergency while the cost of living rose by two thirds.[147] According to a less conservative estimate, these proportions were a staggering 13 per cent and 70 per cent respectively.[148]

In early 1941 Lemass informed the Irish public that they had been 'lucky' on the economic front for the past fifteen months and that the effects of the war were now going to become worse.[149] In 1941 most forms of fuel became rationed goods.[150] It was not long before Lemass announced that a full rationing system would be implemented. A mini-census was undertaken by the statistics branch of the Department of Industry and Commerce. On 'Registration Night', 16 November 1941, ration books were issued to 3 million people.[151] A complete system of rationing was finally in place in Ireland by May 1942.

Lemass's introduction of full rationing came after he misjudged the petrol supply situation when the pumps ran dry in early 1941. He recalled going to bed relieved on 23 December 1941 after hearing that a tanker shipment of petrol was due into Dublin Port on Christmas Eve. Brian Farrell details how the next morning he awoke to news that the tanker had in fact been sunk by a U-boat after leaving Liverpool, forcing him to reduce the petrol ration from two gallons to a quarter of a gallon per week.[152] This story is somewhat misleading. After desperate appeals to Britain, 1 million gallons of petrol were supplied to Ireland on 1 January 1941. Consequently, Lemass announced that one coupon could be exchanged for a gallon of petrol.[153] This was a serious underestimation of demand and an overestimation of the extent to which people adhered to his orders. *The Irish Press* reported that garages were openly defying the order by offering one and a half gallons per coupon.[154] Three days later stocks were exhausted.[155] It was not until 9 January that Lemass announced the ration would be reduced to a quarter of a gallon per coupon.[156]

Significantly, the Irish Housewives Association, a pressure group formed in 1941, had publicly highlighted the ineffectiveness of the partial rationing system exposed in this and other episodes. The organisation questioned whether 'a voluntary curtailment of consumption' was working and called instead for a comprehensive system of rationing.[157] It pointed to Britain's comprehensive rationing as a model and contended that the poorest and largest families could not survive on the government's meagre food and clothing allowances. The influence of this extraordinary pressure group on Lemass was undoubtedly greater than has been acknowledged. The submission of the famous 'Housewives' Petition', in which this argument was made, coincided neatly with Lemass's introduction of full rationing and, although he did not admit it, definitely informed his decision.

Whereas the collective regulation of a host of commodities under the comprehensive rationing system of 1942 did not eradicate the black market, it at least provided a readily intelligible system based on a ration book. Backed up by a mature bureaucratic operation, this system made the regulation of trade more comprehensible for the public and ensured abuses could be checked and policed more easily. Full rationing was accompanied by an increase in the penalties for engaging in black-market activity.[158]

And yet Lemass's full rationing system was instituted so late that the cultural and economic practice of black-market trade was already well established in Ireland. In contrast to Britain, where comprehensive rationing was introduced early in the war, Lemass moved from 'voluntary curtailment of consumption' between late 1939 and early 1942, to full rationing and heavy regulation from 1942 onwards. The Irish public was confused by the transition. Lemass's pronouncements on the flour supply provide a good example of why. In a June 1941 radio address he urged 'all citizens who can afford to purchase flour' to do so, assuring listeners that 'some people may have been reluctant to do so for fear that they might leave short other less fortunately circumstanced people' but that 'supplies are more than adequate'.[159] By early 1942 flour was so scarce that it was only available in very small rations. 'The poor are like hunted rats looking for bread,' remarked Fine Gael front bencher Richard Mulcahy of the bread queues which had developed as flour dwindled.[160]

Hugely inflated prices were paid for most goods bought on the Emergency black market. Common prices for tea, for example, were between 20 and 25 shillings per lb, seventy-five to eighty times higher than Lemass's fixed minimum price of 3 or 4 pence per lb.[161] To illustrate the extent of this illegal inflation, at the time weekly unemployment benefit for a married man with children in a rural area was just 25 shillings.[162] Turf, it was claimed in a 1941 article, was 'sold by the sackful at the canalside by merchants at anything they dare' above Lemass's controlled price of 45 shillings per ton and fetching as much as £3 per ton.[163]

In early 1943 Minister for Justice Gerald Boland expressed concern at the increase in theft linked to black-market activity. Lamenting the rise in convictions, he went on to explain: 'People are short of commodities and I am afraid our morality is not as deep-seated as it ought to be.'[164] *The Statistical Abstract* for 1945 noted that 'criminal proceedings have shown a very serious increase generally since the outbreak of war'.[165] Convictions for theft in neutral Ireland trebled from 1,160 in 1939 to 3,395 by 1943.[166]

Backed up by the combined bureaucratic capacity of his departments, Lemass declared war on the black market. With full rationing in 1942 came harsher penalties for black-market behaviour and more scrupulous checks by Lemass's inspectors. Inspectors visited shops on a regular basis and proved meticulous in pursuing prose-cutions against *every* member of staff involved in any indiscretion. Fines for 'aiding and abetting' were issued to shop owners, their spouses, and even shop boys or girls. Defending the stringency of his department's approach in the Dáil, Lemass argued that 'failure to keep records or the keeping of inaccurate records is not and should not be regarded as a trivial offence' as it undermined 'the aim of rationing'. This aim was articulated in unequivocally moral economic language: 'to ensure that every person in the community will get an equal right to a fair share of the available supplies'.[167]

The number of ministerial orders (which were effectively economic diktats) issued by Lemass rose steeply from 56 in 1939 to 160 in 1943.[168] Cases against middle- to large-scale black marketeers were commonly heard at the Special Criminal Court. Frequently, these individuals received large fines or prison sentences. For example in late 1942 a Dublin man who attempted to sell an inspector a large quantity of tyres, candles and flour was sentenced to three years' imprisonment.[169] Those accused of black-market activity on a smaller scale appeared at District Court hearings. There, instead of a pliant judiciary willing to impose harsh penalties for infringement of the moral economy, the department was frustrated by judges' 'uneven applications of justice'.[170] Frequently, the imposition of mandatory prison sentences, which Lemass insisted was a necessary deterrent to black-market activity, was refused. Throwing out a prosecution for the overcharging of tea in 1943 a Dublin justice declared that he did not pretend to keep track of price orders and that there were so many of them that he felt 'baffled' by them.[171]

Ruminating on the matter, Lemass's senior civil servants proposed that 'judicial functions be usurped by officials' with Supplies acting as 'prosecutor, judge and jury'.[172] Anticipating legal challenges, the department would mitigate sentences on its terms, rather than the court's, and 'only if it saw fit'.[173] They recommended that seized documents be held 'indefinitely' by the department.[174] This self-righteous approach to the sentencing of black marketeers provides a fine example of the 'cannibalism' which distinguished the department and illustrates the extent to which the assault on the black market was becoming a dirty war.

Outside the walls of Lemass's Kildare Street base there was a growing realisation (even in the censored wartime press, where editors were forced to bite their tongues) that a sense of proportion was being lost in the severe sentences the department was pressing for. The *Irish Independent* sagely warned that 'officials should not delude themselves that they are in this way getting after the real culprits – the people behind the scenes who manipulate the black market on the grand scale'.[175] The wisdom of this sentiment is borne out by the large number of women who appeared in court for using coupons from ration books that were not their own but who claimed that they had a large number of children to feed and were not aware that they were committing an offence by using a friend or relative's coupons.[176]

A populist sentiment that demonised the profiteering middleman and the hoarding middle class typified the political discourse surrounding supply shortages: 'The criminals who deal in the black market . . . are not of the Bill Sykes type,' declared Lemass in late 1941, 'they are pompous and respectable looking citizens robbing others of their fair share.'[177] But in the department's war on the black market, the pursuit of social justice was increasingly becoming an elusive end justifying sometimes dubious means. The full force of Lemass's obese department often bore down disproportionately on small shopkeepers because they administered food and clothing coupons and were at the forefront of black-market involvement. Bigger businesses, on the other hand, often evaded censure.

Petty prosecutions pursued in Lemass's name included the fining of a sixteen-year-old Limerick girl for overcharging for a packet of cigarettes[178] and a £10 fine on a Dublin woman for selling eight cigarettes to an inspector at the price of ten.[179] In another case a Dundalk trader was entrapped by two inspectors posing as husband and wife into selling a lady's cardigan to them without coupons.[180] The department was accused of entrapment in confiscating the petrol ration from six doctors after recruiting another doctor to offer them black-market petrol at work.[181] In an example of how Lemass's enthusiastic offensive against the black market could lead to disproportionate punishment, the department successfully pressed for the imprisonment of Nora Barnes, a Waterford shopkeeper who was sentenced to two months in July 1944 for receiving a stolen coat.[182]

In a 1941 Dáil debate on pricing, Fianna Fáil TD Cornelius Meaney encapsulated a growing anti-apparatchik sentiment by contending:'You will require an inspector at every cross-roads, probably a committee inspecting him, and even an inspector inspecting the

The hopelessness of Lemass's war on the black market.
Dublin Opinion, February 1942.

inspectors.'[183] In Britain, Churchill had indicated his disdain for excessive wartime bureaucracy by telling his Minister of Food: 'You will gain much credit by stamping on these trashy little prosecutions, and also by purging the regulations from petty, meticulous arrogant officialism.'[184] The negative popular image of stiff-necked officialdom was not dispelled by the well-intentioned but rather sudden measures Lemass introduced. In 1941 he unexpectedly discontinued the sale of cooking appliances and announced that electricity and gas were to be rationed. Prior to this move, the government introduced that embodiment of Emergency petty officialdom, the 'glimmer man', an inspector who regulated gas and electricity use and who was the subject of much derision.[185]

The department's strident interventionism was as much the product of its own monstrous growth as of its success in establishing a moral economy based on meaningful interaction with the nation's citizens. In Northern Ireland the Ministry of Food's administrative structure was less punitive than Lemass's. Regionally, there were divisional food offices rather than inspection centres, and organisation extended to the parish level where vocational committees met regularly to compile lists of licensed retailers and suspend or revoke licences for black-market activity.[186]

Supplies' organisation was, by contrast, authoritarian, and in this regard, as James Dillon claimed, Lemass was 'the father and mother of the black market'.[187] While a hardline approach was sometimes necessary with British officials when conducting volatile trade talks, it was less suited to the domestic sphere. In a post-war Dáil debate Lemass even argued that rationing and price control offences should have been scheduled for the military court, which had the power to hand down the death sentence.[188] But even in occupied Europe the threat of death if found trading on the black market did not result in a reduction of the black trade but rather an increase in prices due to the high risks involved.[189]

Ultimately, Lemass's bureaucratic and disciplinary approach to the Irish black market was not very successful. A localised, consultative approach may have been more effective and certainly would have proved more popular. Instead, the department's zeal for its own version of moral economy was not matched by traders, the general public or judges and justices, all of whom the department regarded as guilty of treating serious rationing and price offences 'rather lightly'.[190] While not quite resembling Keystone Kops in their efforts to apprehend black marketeers, the Department of Supplies, for all its bluster, proved less successful than it later claimed in policing Ireland's domestic moral economy.

Lemassian Coercion

In 1940 Lemass stated:

> If democracy is to work, however, particularly in time of war, it can do so only by getting through voluntary co-operation with the central authority the same effective combination of all efforts to the same objective that in a totalitarian state is secured by regulation and control.[191]

As demonstrated by his stance on the wartime black market, Lemass did not think that 'voluntary co-operation with the central authority' was as forthcoming from the Irish public as it should have been during this testing period. Instead, he repeatedly signalled his willingness to revert to 'regulation and control'.

Food supply is a case in point. By virtue of neutrality, Ireland did not receive Allied help in the form of food shipments. This intensified the pressure on Ireland's farmers to grow more food by reverting to tillage rather than dairy farming.[192] During the Emergency the government introduced a raft of controls on agricultural production, including making tillage compulsory. James Ryan's Department of Agriculture oversaw the majority of these controls, while Lemass's Department of Supplies dealt with the pricing of agricultural goods, the drive to grow more food, and complaints alleging overcharging.[193]

Under the Emergency Powers Order covering it, farmers who did not comply with compulsory tillage regulations could face eviction and the dispossession of their land by the state. Inspectors had the power to enter onto holdings, repeatedly if necessary, and to provide the evidence that could result in prison, fines, dispossession or all three.[194] The issue of land repossession was a particularly sensitive one in Ireland. If historical memory of the Great Famine was powerful during the Emergency, that of the land agitation of the late nineteenth century exerted a similarly compelling presence in the collective mindset. Lemass, though, was still strongly in favour of dispossessing unproductive farmers and declared himself in favour of this hard-headed, top-down approach. The officers of the Department of Agriculture who enforced tillage regulations constituted an obvious – if less 'cannibalistic' – parallel to Supplies' Inspectorate. Predictably, within the cabinet it was Lemass who favoured extending their role in land dispossession most strongly.

Between 1941 and 1945 an average of 305 farmers were convicted every year for failing to comply with tillage regulations.[195] In this period the state dispossessed and cultivated some 7,365 acres of farmland.[196] The amount of land confiscated was not as large as Lemass would have liked but, as with rationing restrictions, the regulations impacted the small man disproportionately. By 1944 even farmers with smallholdings of just 5 acres were compelled to till their land. Compulsory tillage was avoided by large farmers who simply sold their land to avoid coming under regulations.[197] A culture of resistance grew up around compulsory tillage and an 'agin the government' mentality surfaced conspicuously. In several court cases the government was frustrated by the judiciary who, in several cases, found that the state had prosecuted prematurely and let farmers off. De Valera stormily claimed that judges who acquitted farmers on such grounds 'did not realise the seriousness of the situation'.[198]

The government had the moral economic imperative of preventing starvation on its side. On the other hand, farmers' disdain for outside interference was exacerbated by the lack of modern aids to production available to them. Although many farmers toiled hard to meet tillage quotas, the absence of machinery, fertiliser and lime made cultivation much harder and in some cases almost impossible. Many would have concurred with James Dillon's contention that 'tillage without manure is not farming. It is mining – e.g. taking the fertility out of the soil without putting anything back.'[199] As mentioned, Lemass's early record in securing these productive aids was unimpressive. He was able to secure the exchange of agricultural machinery for beer in the closing stages of the war.[200] But even this barter arrangement only resulted in Ireland receiving 100 tractors and 20 threshing sets.[201] By contrast, the number of tractors in Northern Ireland had risen from 550 (1939) to 7,000 (1944).[202] Despite their seemingly insatiable quest for greater productivity in this sector, Seán Lemass and his developmentalist allies did not antagonise Catholic sensitivity to the family and the home to the extent of advocating a Women's Land Army (as existed in Britain) to aid the tillage drive.

Even without mass mechanisation and the deployment of female labour, compulsory tillage signalled an important departure in Fianna Fáil's broad approach to rural productivity. Significant market and social disruption resulted. This led to a bad-tempered exchange of views on the broader question of agricultural productivity between the two ministers responsible in 1944.

Inspired by the British economist John Maynard Keynes and the 1944 British White Paper on Employment Policy, Lemass sat down to draft a memorandum on full employment. In it, he claimed that a full employment policy was 'in line with modern economic thought'.[203] His desire to expand his powers was expressed impatiently, rashly even, and with little regard for liberal constraints. In the memo he returned to a familiar theme, ruing democracy itself for its disruptive effect on long-term planning.[204]

When it came to labour, Lemass did not foresee a significant post-war easing of the Emergency controls on workers introduced in 1941. He declared himself against 'the introduction of new techniques which might operate to defeat the expansion of output capacity'.[205] Full employment would mean jobs but also coercive regulation over the trade unions, leading to the effective removal of collective bargaining. Wage rises would be linked to increases in production.[206] His ideas followed on from his 1942 proposal of a wide-ranging Ministry of Labour to deal with the expected tide of returning workers, an idea vetoed by de Valera.[207] Lemass was aiming for greater state control over the unions and argued that 'the general scheme of control of labour should be retained after the Emergency has passed'.[208]

What irked Ryan were Lemass's observations on Ireland's agricultural economy. Lemass declared himself for 'the improvement, reorganisation and mechanisation' of agriculture.[209] Citing the high number of uneconomic holdings in the country, he argued that 'land policy must be geared towards ownership based on ability to work the land'.[210] Most significantly, Lemass wanted the dispossession of farmland by the state to continue after the Emergency. The state must complete the 'elimination of incompetent or lazy farmers', he argued.[211]

Lemass's enthusiasm for widespread dispossessions was probably only matched by that of James Larkin, the trade union leader and socialist deputy, who urged that any farmer who 'will not farm scientifically' be dispossessed by the state.[212] The enthusiasm for dispossession was challenged, however, by the man responsible for the enforcement of the tillage orders: Ryan. He had mounted a robust public defence of the necessity for such expropriations when informed of tales of hardship in the Dáil, but he privately quelled Lemass's enthusiasm for a more stringent enforcement of compulsory tillage.[213]

On receiving Lemass's memo he questioned his enthusiasm for land dispossession as a means of improving efficiency. Ryan undoubtedly realised that a deep-seated resentment existed against the more coercive measures used by the department to increase the wheat yield and warned his fellow minister against the idea.[214] During the Emergency such displacements had proved 'a delicate and difficult matter', he claimed.[215] He went on to warn that if displacement was pursued on the same scale post-war there would be 'a danger of serious agitation and public disturbance'.[216] Ryan, who possessed a greater understanding of farming than either Lemass or Larkin, recognised that the threat of dispossession was viewed by the farming community as hostile encroachment rather than a means of ensuring the fair operation of the market.

Ryan went further, implying that Lemass's proposals fundament-ally misunderstood the nature of agricultural productivity. Farmers, unlike coal miners, did not 'slack' after having attained a certain income, he told him.[217] This was clearly an attack on Lemass's downplaying of the distinctions between agricultural and industrial economies.[218] He argued that if compulsory tillage was extended to include the mandatory requisition of all unproductive farm units it would see the state take over holdings where a good farmer was merely going through a lull in productivity, due to the time involved in raising a young family, for instance.[219] 'In cases where the farms are practically derelict for reasons such as complete lack of capital, or the incapacity of the owner because of senility or mental trouble, there would be a good case for the state taking over and arranging new ownership,' Ryan asserted. But in these cases a young family member 'would in time pull the place together and become a first-class farmer'. It would, therefore, be 'unthinkable to disturb the family in such cases no matter how much below the desired standard the farm might be'.[220]

This clash between Lemass and Ryan is typically juxtaposed by Garvin as pitting Lemass's progressive, developmentalist agenda against the backward and conservative ideals of his peers.[221] John Horgan, too, sees Ryan's 'fatalism' as 'deeply disturbing'.[222] However, both neglect to mention the crucial backdrop of disruption that Fianna Fáil's pursuit of compulsory tillage had wrought. Ryan was right to point out the social disruption that the continuation of the scheme would cause, not to mention its political unpopularity. He had also highlighted the misconceptions underlying Lemass's view of farmers as 'lazy'. While perhaps not the Stakhanovite effort desired by Lemass, the country's farmers nonetheless raised the amount of land under corn crops from a five-year average of just under 1 million (between 1935 and 1939) to 1.5 million acres (between 1940 and 1944).[223]

Yet again, Lemass had been faced down on evictions, but his use of 'regulation and control' was evident elsewhere, most notably in the state's efforts to increase fuel productivity. According to Garvin, the young Lemass enjoyed the generous periods of isolation and leisure when detained in prison camps.[224] These luxuries were not afforded the workers in the miserable Emergency turf labour camps he championed. Under the 1941 Emergency Powers Order (No. 79) the restrictions on the length of the working week contained in Lemass's 1936 Conditions of Employment Act were removed so that turf production would increase.[225] This legislative change was closely linked to Lemass's camp labour designs, which he was now at greater liberty to implement.

One of Lemass's many schemes for camp labour in Ireland, brashly implemented with the illiberal testing-ground mentality which the Emergency engendered in him, was the Construction Corps.[226] Lemass's Construction Corps operated as an army battalion into which adolescent working-class urban youths were coerced. Its members – teenagers and young men – lived and worked in squalid conditions, under army discipline, frequently stationed to remote bogs. As well as being characterised by widespread sexual abuse, bullying and depression, living conditions were compared to a 'concentration camp' by the father of one member who had com-plained of mistreatment.[227] In 1943 it was alleged by Labour Party deputies that some 5,000 able-bodied young men had been refused unemployment assistance because they had refused to join the corps. 'Why should the state maintain a man who refuses to join the Construction Corps?' replied Lemass.[228]

During the Emergency, Lemass regularly adopted a similarly unbending attitude to the negative effects of compulsory tillage, turf camps and other forms of state compulsion. Camp labour involved the housing of labourers in camps in which conditions, as Todd Andrews conceded, were 'more typical of refugee camps'.[229] The Gardaí kept a file on workers employed by the Turf Development Board on their scheme at Glencree Bog, County Wicklow,[230] and policemen were present at the camp.[231] Police surveillance of the personnel employed on state turf schemes underlines the seriousness of the nation's fuel situation but also the sinisterly authoritarian aspect to these ventures.

In Lemass's defence, such labour camps cannot be divorced from the overriding context of employment and emigration, productivity and material survival at what was a desperate juncture in modern Irish history. In 1941 the British and Irish governments agreed that Britain would effectively control emigration by the issuing of permit cards in Ireland and work visas in Britain. This trend continued throughout the Emergency, with Irish employment exchanges effectively transformed into offshore branches of the British Ministry of Labour, which paid the travel costs of migrant workers.[232] The state also prohibited the movement of people in an effort to improve rural productivity.

Lemass's cabinet adversary Seán MacEntee favoured the extension of emigration embargoes, particularly in the 'congested districts' (areas of western counties where the land was poor and unemploy-ment high).[233] Lemass, assuming his familiar place in the opposite corner to MacEntee, instead proposed labour camps staffed by a 'reserve pool of labour' to be drawn from these rural areas.[234] The reserve pool would feature 'a class of worker' that would partake of employment instead of remaining at home idle, the victim of 'inequitable' embargoes.[235]

Lemass's liberal language disguised his penchant for coercion, which again reared its head in the conditions he proposed to attach

Lemass, by now highest in the party pecking order behind Dev, but closely followed by MacEntee. *Dublin Opinion*, February 1944.

to the labour camps of 'reserve pool' workers. In Lemass's design, a worker in the reserve pool would be placed on a register and 'sign an undertaking to hold himself available for employment on the production of food and fuel in any place in Éire to which at any time he may be directed to go'.[236] For this he would receive a small weekly retainer but would be automatically disqualified from emigrating. 'Failure or refusal' to work at a particular camp would be 'punishable by fine or imprisonment or both' and – irrespective of mitigating circumstances – the individual would be deprived of his unemployment assistance and retainer.[237] The authoritarian nature of Lemass's scheme ensured that it was unsuccessful: not enough men proved willing to sign up to the conditions of the reserve pool. For example, of 400 unemployment assistance recipients in Mayo offered employment in the reserve pool only four took up the offer.[238]

Demonstrating how far from the liberal centre Lemass had strayed, the coerciveness of his scheme was significantly diluted by cabinet. It would apply to men over the age of twenty-two, not eighteen-year-olds as Lemass had envisaged; refusal to work at a camp would not be met with fines or imprisonment but with the means-tested cessation of unemployment assistance for a short period; and participants would be allowed to apply for removal from the register at any time.[239] At the end of the Emergency the unsuccessfulness of Lemass's camp labour schemes were attacked by MacEntee, who smugly highlighted 'the difficulties inherent in the problem of labour mobility on an extensive scale as proved in connection with the turf development scheme'.[240] These remarks were telling of the divisions in cabinet between Lemass, who clearly relished the role of 'economic overlord', and his more cautious colleagues.

Between Beveridge and the Encyclicals

As the Emergency wound to an end, Lemass found himself navigating a course between the conservative dictates of Catholic social theory and the post-war development of the welfare state. Unlike McEvoy, president of the Federation of Irish Manufacturers, Lemass saw the problem as not too much state influence but too little. Full employment – synonymous with the goal of self-sufficiency – was only practicable under dictatorship, he argued, and had not been accomplished in any state where democratic rights were fully preserved. He also gruffly reiterated his belief that the freedom of land ownership from state interference was dependent on its efficient use.[241]

His ideas were certainly radical in terms of the scope of interventionism, but they were formulated against an emerging backdrop of welfare improvement in Northern Ireland, signalling the growth of a more compassionate role for the state than he envisaged during the Emergency. There were signs, nonetheless, that his authoritarian attitude towards the exercise of state power was easing. Lemass engaged in yet another spat with MacEntee over the applicability of the British Beveridge Report to Ireland, defending the groundbreaking 1942 proposals, which were to lay the foundations of the welfare state.

This pitted him against the quite formidable Irish conservative block of the time. Opposition to what Beveridge represented was conveyed by Archbishop John Charles McQuaid in his opposition to the Public Health Bill of 1945 when he wrote to de Valera to express his concern at the 'unusual and absolute power of medical inspection of children and adults by compulsory regulation'.[242] As Dick Walsh has argued, the views Lemass expressed in favour of Beveridge were 'quite at odds with his personal convictions'.[243] His Beveridgeism was certainly not all-encompassing. Recognising that the government's freeze on wages necessitated a welfare cushion, he secured children's allowances in 1943. He insisted, in line with his Catholic faith, that the father receive the allowance, thus dispelling the spectre of the single mother.

Nonetheless, Lemass appeared to be a stout defender of state prerogative against agenda-driven outside interference when he squared up to the vocationalist lobby in the same year. He dismissed the 1943 report of the Commission on Vocational Organisation as a 'slovenly document'. As Lemass later admitted, 'every centrally-controlled organisation tends towards the concentration of production units rather than the preservation of small units'.[244] The Commission on Vocational Organisation's report reflected the public antipathy towards this attitude. It favoured instead the replacement of 'the state's despotic control of production and labour' with 'voluntary collaboration for the good of the nation at a critical time'.[245] The commission's chairman, Bishop Michael Browne of Galway, chided Lemass for calling it a 'slovenly document', claiming this was a 'gratuitous insult'.[246]

This was not the Church–state clash it appeared to be, however. It represented Lemass's rejection of bottom-up, decentralised initiatives in time of war as much as his disdain for Church interference in the secular realm. Neither should a minor dispute between Lemass and Archbishop of Dublin John Charles McQuaid in 1944 be viewed as signalling a clash between Church and state. McQuaid wrote to Lemass in his capacity of chairman of the Commission on Youth Unemployment, which Lemass had launched in 1943, informing him that he would not accept answers to a questionnaire the commission had sent to Irish voluntary organisations if they came from non-Catholics. Lemass proposed the compromise solution that the questionnaire should exclude questions about people's spiritual and religious welfare. In the end, it was left to de Valera to defy McQuaid and assert the right of the civil authority in the matter.[247]

In fact, relations between Lemass and McQuaid were warmer than is conveyed in the Lemassiography. Leydon issued a 'warning to clergymen' in January 1943, reminding clergymen that due to fuel shortages the use of their cars was confined to 'immediate spiritual consolation'. McQuaid was astonished by what he regarded as Leydon's impertinence. He wrote to him in scolding tones, complaining that the warning had been addressed to him 'without even a covering note' and that he required an 'immediate explanation'.[248] Leydon, whose deep religious convictions were matched only by his scrupulousness as a civil servant, was not going to be bullied and ignored McQuaid.[249]

On this occasion and many others throughout the Emergency, McQuaid's indignation was indulged by Lemass, who pursued a strategy of appeasing the formidable archbishop. During a period of pronounced shortages McQuaid had little trouble securing building materials for the construction of a new church in Crumlin.[250] Similarly, despite clothing shortages, Lemass granted McQuaid's request that members of religious orders be accommodated with 'special arrangements' for the supply of clothing for ordination.[251] Whereas others experienced great difficulty in securing permits for their vehicles, Lemass immediately issued McQuaid with a permit when the archbishop decided that he wanted a new car.[252] Most notably, Lemass regularly granted the archbishop an ample supplementary allowance of petrol.[253] Later in the Emergency McQuaid wrote to Lemass to express his gratitude for these extra petrol coupons.[254]

In contrast to his minister, Leydon granted McQuaid his supplementary petrol allowance grudgingly. His attitude was understandable. By November 1941 McQuaid was receiving an allowance of an incredible fifty-one gallons per month on Lemass's nod. As discussed earlier, at the start of that year the ration for the general public had reached a low of one gallon per month. 'I assume there is some exceptional reason,' Leydon enquired when writing to McQuaid to authorise his massive monthly allowance in late 1941.[255] McQuaid composed a reply listing his reasons for needing so much petrol but, angered by Leydon's attitude, the letter was furiously crossed out and never sent.[256]

For Lemass, having the archbishop onside meant he could rely on McQuaid to aid the government's propaganda campaigns during the Emergency. Post-war, his pay-off from McQuaid came in the form of a papal recognition of his work in securing relief supplies to

Air travel opens up Ireland to John Bull and Uncle Sam. *Dublin Opinion*, November 1945.

war-ravaged Europe.[257] Lemass was pursuing what he regarded as a pragmatic strategy towards the Church. To others, this approach signalled coalescence with the power of the bishops. The future British poet laureate John Betjeman, who was working in Dublin as press attaché to Sir John Maffey, asserted that 'the key to Ireland' was 'the Church, its pontiffs, the Nuncio, MacRory and McQuaid and I think we should bother less about relations, good or bad, with the Government and more about relations with the Irish Roman Catholic Church'.[258]

Surveying the bigger picture of the rapidly emerging post-war power blocs in Europe, Lemass insisted that his world view was essentially democratic. In 1945 he described Ireland as a democratic nation which naturally gravitated towards the democratic West.[259] He was obviously frustrated that Ireland had been frozen out of the work of shaping the new world because she had been neutral during the Second World War and yearned for the missed opportunity of being part of economic planning alongside the major powers. The biggest obstacle to Ireland's participation in post-war international organisation was evidently her refusal to join the Allied war effort. Unable to admit this publicly, he instead reverted to blaming the obstacle of partition, 'a dark shadow over our hopes to put our relations with all states on a basis of complete cordiality and co-operation', without which Ireland would be free to play an 'unbiased part in international affairs'.[260]

Domestic pressures were increasingly over-clouding Lemass's concerns at Ireland's isolation, however. Workers pressed for the removal of the Wages Standstill Order which had removed the right to strike and artificially pegged back earnings for six years. With the termination of the order, Lemass set up the Labour Court in September 1946, a much milder system of worker–employer regulation than he had envisaged during the Emergency. His Industrial Efficiency and Prices Bill of 1947, a casualty of Fianna Fáil's political unpopularity, was perceived by Irish manufacturers as a significant concession to the unions because it proposed 'development councils' in industry, which gave unions a more direct voice in industrial relations.

As Farrell has argued, these measures were a mix of 'carrot and stick' – they allowed labour its voice but also removed the obstacles to direct ministerial intervention.[261] Evidently, Lemass's broader social and economic approach combined coercion as well as conciliation. Fianna Fáil won the 1943 and 1944 elections but soon had to deal with inflation, mounting labour unrest and political agitation. The party's fears about post-war radicalism were partly realised in the teachers' strike of 1946 and the growing popularity of two new parties, Clann na Talmhan and Clann na Poblachta. Eyeing these developments, Lemass remained intolerant of industrial action he perceived as tantamount to treason. When mill workers rejected a Labour Court recommendation in favour of strike action in early 1947 he presented the cabinet with a far-reaching proposal to ban strike action altogether.[262] In certain spheres, he still possessed the Emergency mindset in terms of the extraordinary checks to liberty he thought justifiable.

In the run-up to the 1948 election Lemass swung sharply to the right, as Fianna Fáil desperately tried to stymie the mood of change in the country. His focus was mainly on Fianna Fáil's sixteen-year record, the economy, and the threat of communism. He took a sideswipe at the radicalism of Clann na Poblachta, declaring Ireland was 'on the hit list for attack in the campaign now being waged to destroy Christian democracy in Europe'.[263] Going against his earlier stance on the Beveridge Report, he warned against the 'potential revolution in rising expectations' that it threatened.[264]

Lemass's real opinions on Beveridge probably lay somewhere between his praise for the plan in 1944 and his denunciation of it in 1948. But by 1948 he had, like de Valera, taken fright at the emer-

Lemass eyes the
Tánaiste's seat.
Dublin Opinion,
June 1945.

gence of Clann na Poblachta as a more authentic republican party
than Fianna Fáil. The government had imprisoned a number of its
members during the Emergency, meting out the same punishment
that Lemass and most of his colleagues had faced from the Free State
during the Civil War. In 1947 de Valera introduced the Electoral
Amendment Bill, a naked attempt at gerrymandering in a desperate
attempt to stem the rise of the Clann. It did not work. Neither did
the Minister for Industry and Commerce's red-baiting. Lemass's
stance was unusual: he was the appeaser of labour within Fianna Fáil;
it was MacEntee who usually attacked the left. Nonetheless, there is
little evidence to suggest that Lemass engaged in 'violent anti-
partitionist rhetoric', as Garvin puts it, in a bid to outdo the
republicanism of the Clann during the 1948 election. By this stage,
as discussed below, his rhetoric had shifted from the green to the red.

Decline and Fall

When de Valera expanded the economic planning committee to
include the whole cabinet in April 1945 it signalled the end of
Lemass's spell as economic dictator. Thus began a barren spell for the

The noble cabinet, in Roman robes, pictured in *Dublin Opinion*, March 1944, after Lemass criticised the publication for 'easy laughs' at the expense of parliament.

man credited with saving Ireland from starvation. In the presidential campaign of that year he reverted to mudslinging against Seán T. O'Kelly's opponent, General Seán MacEoin, calling him a Blueshirt and claiming that the foreign press were behind his campaign. When O'Kelly was elected president, de Valera moved Frank Aiken to Finance. Aiken, like MacEntee, was a consistent opponent of Lemass's bolder plans. Lemass was appointed Tánaiste, but this disguised the fact that with the easing of Emergency restrictions his power had waned. In January 1947 he also suffered personal loss when John, his father, died at the age of seventy-eight.[265]

The Emergency was a watershed in Lemass's political career. Despite his mistakes, he had overseen Ireland's material survival. And yet, for the first time, his popularity had started to suffer as a consequence of Emergency controls. The cartoons of Charles Edward Kelly (C.E.K.) in the satirical magazine *Dublin Opinion* had made Lemass instantly recognisable to the general public. And in popular discourse the perceived unfairness of rationing had earned him the unfavourable sobriquet 'Half Ounce' during the Emergency.

Of more concern to his political standing was his embroilment in two successive corruption scandals in this period. Firstly, in 1944 it was alleged that he had been involved in insider trading in selling railway shares before the Transport Bill, which he had authored, was passed. The bill amalgamated railway companies under the state monopoly CIÉ. Labour's William Norton speculated in the Dáil that 'many "get-rich-quick merchants" have been trafficking in railway shares and are going to be handsomely compensated under the provisions of this Bill'.[266]

Lemass is restrained by cabinet colleagues after threatening to reduce the tea ration. *Dublin Opinion*, April 1943

Lemass was visibly annoyed by these accusations. He was placed under tribunal investigation and suffered innuendo in the Dáil. At the tribunal the judges implied that he had passed on to associates knowledge that the share price would shortly improve due to amalgamation, enabling them to purchase shares cheaply. Meanwhile it was alleged that Lemass had made misleading and illusory comments to the Dáil in May and November 1943, in an effort to keep the share price down.[267] The tribunal heard that when rumours eventually broke that the Great Southern Railway was to be included in the bill the company's stock exchange value rocketed by over £2.5 million.[268] Lemass said that neither he nor members of his family had bought railway stock and denied having casually leaked the information to friends over golf or poker drives.[269] Later he claimed to have never owned a single share in any company.[270]

It is evident, nonetheless, that people close to Lemass benefited professionally and financially from the Transport Bill. Lemass's younger brother Frank, for instance, was appointed general manager of CIÉ. Previously he had been secretary of the United Transport Company, one of the firms whose fortunes were transformed by the merger.[271] While it is important to note that Lemass was cleared of any wrongdoing by the tribunal, some mud inevitably stuck. And in 1946 rumours of stock manipulation, this time much less well-founded, again became attached to the Minister for Industry and Commerce over the sale of Locke's Distillery in Kilbeggan, County Westmeath.

Moreover, rumours that Lemass had a serious gambling problem started to circulate. It was claimed that he had divulged sensitive

information because he needed to cover his debts. A cabinet colleague is said to have referred to Lemass as 'that crook'.[272] Brian
Farrell claims that Lemass was the victim of a smear campaign, in
part engineered from within his own party.[273] This is credible, given
the jealousy of Lemass's cabinet colleagues at the extension of his
powers during the Emergency. In any case, the sheer scale of those
powers imbued these allegations of corruption with a certain inevit-
ability. Just as those employed by Lemass to carry out odd jobs on his
home were exclusively old IRA comrades, there was an element of
'jobs for the boys' on the boards of the semi-state companies he
established. The names of certain 'captains of industry' recurred on
state boards. For instance Henry Kennedy (president of the Irish
Agricultural Organisation Society) was also on the board of the
Industrial Research and Standards Council and the ESB. By 1947
Lemass's lieutenant Leydon (who had substantial family wealth) was
chairman of Aer Lingus and Aer Rianta and was a board member of
Aerlínte Éireann, the ESB, Irish Shipping, and the Irish Assurance
Company.[274]

But the revolving doors to positions of power overseen by Lemass
were just one aspect of a wider discontent. The crisis of the Second
World War had not only provided the acid test of Ireland's fledgling
independence but also resulted in the post-independence apogee of
centralised state intervention in Ireland. The Emergency Powers Act
enabled the Fianna Fáil cabinet to pass orders without the need for
specific legislation or detailed scrutiny in Dáil Éireann.[275] This
marked a significant transfer of power and authority from local
government to the Executive.[276] The powers Lemass accrued under
the act ensured broad ministerial power was accompanied by broad
unpopularity.

During the Emergency Lemass was very much at the mercy of
geopolitical and economic currents that placed a high premium on
Ireland's steadfast maintenance of neutrality. Both Lemass and his
right-hand man Leydon displayed an understandable wariness of
British 'gentleman's agreements' and their suspicious stance was
justified in certain cases. Supplies' dealings with British trade officials
illustrated Ireland's dependence on Britain, but the department's
officials did not adopt the obedient and submissive role of the good
subject. Yet it seems that neither Lemass nor Leydon foresaw the
extent of the British trade squeeze of early 1941. In a volatile trading
environment it is surprising that Lemass did not oversee greater

CONFIDENTIAL

Mr S.P. Lemass, Deputy Prime Minister (Tanaiste) and Minister for Industry and Commerce. He took part in the Easter rebellion of 1916 and was subsequently Chief of Staff of the I.R.A. He has been a leading member of the Fianna Fail Party for a considerable time and was its Secretary from 1927-32. He has held a number of important posts in Mr de Valera's Government. He was elected President of the International Labour Conference at Geneva in 1937, and was present at the 1938 Treaty Talks in this country. Mr Lemass is a lucid speaker and probably the ablest member of the Eire Government. Throughout his career he has fostered the industrial development of his country somewhat on protectionist, self-sufficiency lines. He was over here recently for discussions with Sir Stafford Cripps and Mr Shinwell. Lord Rugby describes Mr Lemass as "a man of sound practical sense, not swayed by political emotions". On present showing

Confidential British file on Fianna Fáil cabinet members, 1947. NAUK, PREM 8,824.

stockpiling of chemicals and machinery vital to Ireland's agricultural economy. Although Lemass was keen to take on the role and status of an 'economic overlord', he was reluctant to admit to the mistakes that necessarily arose when charged with such huge responsibility. This reluctance, if unsurprising, makes his more significant errors in managing Ireland's supplies all the more glaring.

Domestically, Lemass was tied to the moral imperative of protecting the consumer from black-market profiteers, but faced huge fluctuations in price and supply which were outside of his control. It is obvious that Lemass often took an unbending stance with business interests, despite the patronage that had built up under the protectionist policies of the 1930s. Although Lemass's priority was always a material one, his remit as Minister for Supplies became, as a matter of necessity as much as of choice, strongly influenced by moral considerations of equitable distribution and fair price. Civil servants at Lemass's department possessed a somewhat haughty self-image as the policemen of a moral economy. In this period Lemass spearheaded a brief lurch in Irish economic direction towards a planned, state capitalist economy, with the emphasis firmly on the *state*. His department came to view private commercial spirit in time of war as fundamentally profit-driven and anti-communitarian.[277] The relationship between the department and native capitalists was clearly tempestuous and the former defined itself as upholding a moral economic standard against the avarice of the latter.

However, Lemass's decisive, left-leaning approach was not all-encompassing. Many of his most decisive productive measures were taken two years too late. He failed to establish an early and comprehensive scheme of centralised purchase and distribution despite early indications that Britain was moving in this direction and that Ireland would, to a great extent, have to follow suit. Confronted with what he saw as unpatriotic business activity, Lemass did not hesitate to roll up his sleeves. But in his uneven rationing, regulation of trade and rash expansionism, he caught more small flies than hornets. Supplies failed to stymie the worst excesses of profiteering, and small shopkeepers received by far the greatest number of convictions for unfair pricing.

Naturally enough, the minister's mistakes are rarely conveyed in the Department of Supplies' Historical Survey, a glowing departmental self-appraisal of its wartime activities which Brian Farrell has concisely repeated.[278] Likewise, Lemass's splendid new Kildare Street HQ masked the grim reality of Irish economic life. Like hundreds of thousands of other Irish men and women at the time, most of the stonecutters who fashioned its imposing edifice emigrated to England after its construction because there was no work available in Ireland. Within the cabinet, Lemass was the harshest critic of the decentralised impulse of the broad vocationalist movement.[279] In general terms he argued that the Irish needed a strong central government to counteract what he called their 'fissiparous tendencies'.[280] However, the emergence of bottom-up political agitation as a reaction to what was perceived as state authoritarianism demonstrates that the party, and Lemass in particular, had undermined its natural constituency – the plain people of Ireland – during the war years. This would be forcefully conveyed in the result of the 1948 election.

5

Mischief-Maker

Dáil Reporter

Reflecting the rebellious mood in the country at large, there was dissent from within the Fianna Fáil party on the eve of the 1948 general election. Party members were dissatisfied at the extent to which decision-making was concentrated within the Executive and criticised ministers for neglecting party meetings. Like the general public, the party rank and file had grown uncomfortable with rule by fiat.[1]

Other than de Valera, no one embodied this leadership style as much as Lemass. But, aloof to these concerns and facing into the 1948 election, the 'economic dictator' and party disciplinarian was in rambunctious form and in no mood for change. Lemass certainly did not expect to lose the election that year. When it was called, the government still had fifteen months to run. Despite Fianna Fáil's relatively poor showing at the polls, he thought he could count on the support of the National Labour Party, one of the two Labour groupings to have emerged from the split in the party in 1944.[2] On a personal basis, he was counting on the close links he had cultivated with the leaders of the Irish Transport and General Workers' Union and was confident that these men would steer National Labour into coalition with Fianna Fáil.[3] But the rug was pulled from under Lemass's feet when National Labour's members instead opted to form the first coalition (or inter-party) government along with Fine Gael, Clann na Poblachta, the Labour Party, Clann na Talmhan and a few independents.[4]

In the wake of defeat Lemass was in no mood for ponderous reflection. At forty-eight years of age, the loss of ministerial power after sixteen years was hard to stomach. He reacted by turning the screw internally. At a party meeting shortly after the election defeat he proposed that no motions be tabled in the Dáil without the consent of the party hierarchy. More importantly, he ruled that all questions 'other than those of a purely local nature' had to be submitted to a special party committee before being tabled.[5]

These moves demonstrated Lemass's conviction that a lack of party discipline had caused the defeat. While his lieutenant was busy

Mr. Seán Lemass,
Occupation: Watching Mr. Morrissey.
Pastime: Rubbing soap on the stone outside Dan Morrissey's door.
Ambition: To be there when it happens.
Secret Regret: That in a fallible world it is not possible to have absolute truth in the news.

C.E.K.'s 'portrait' of Lemass,
Dublin Opinion,
November 1951.

housekeeping, de Valera reacted to the loss of power by resuming the role of world statesman and announced his departure on a worldwide 'anti-partition crusade'. At a party meeting the following week Lemass was elected vice-chairman and deputy leader of Fianna Fáil.[6] In de Valera's stead, he would chair party meetings. He soon established an internal 'Discipline Committee'[7] and chaired a new Central Committee composed of ten members to operate as a shadow cabinet, steering party direction.[8]

Like a sacked breadwinner trying to cope with his lack of status by asserting his patriarchal authority at home, Lemass busied himself in the role of stern father figure to the party in de Valera's absence. However, he was still evidently in shock that the natural order of things had been disturbed. Just as the polished walnut New York-style elevators were being installed in his Kildare Street palace, Lemass had to pack up his personal belongings and vacate his office.[9] In his eyes, Fianna Fáil, the sole guarantors of Irish national resurgence, had been displaced by an ideologically contradictory dolly mix of parties. And regardless of his apotheosis within Fianna Fáil, the party's defeat abruptly applied the brakes to his ambition to succeed the 65-year-old de Valera as leader of party and nation.

Lemass had polled well in his constituency, maintaining his seat with just under 30 per cent of the vote. But the loss of his ministerial salary suddenly placed him in financial trouble. Unlike the majority of his peers he did not drink, but he gambled heavily. At Lemass's poker schools the stakes were very high. One could not enter these exclusive gambling events without being prepared to part with a lot of cash.[10] He regularly travelled to the Curragh for big card games with horse trainers and owners[11] and there were persistent rumours in the Irish Army of his gambling excesses.[12] He also enjoyed games of poker with political colleagues such as James Ryan and Ben Briscoe, but for more modest stakes.[13]

Neither was his lifestyle lavish, but he liked to look the part and bought up to ten suits a year. For the time, this sort of sartorial expenditure was extraordinary. He had enrolled his children in private schools and, to add to his financial woes, shortly after losing the election his favourite daughter Peggy fell ill with tuberculosis, necessitating expensive private medical treatment. He was forced to take out a substantial loan from the bank, offering the deeds of his house as security.[14]

Fortunately for Lemass, de Valera saw he was in trouble and handed him the reins of *The Irish Press*, Fianna Fáil's press mouthpiece, before commencing his global tour. Lemass's appointment as managing director of the newspaper was announced in February 1948.[15] Businessmen he had supported through his protectionist policies also came to his rescue. He was handed a number of directorships with firms keen to establish favourable links with the former minister.[16] These back-slapping appointments soon eased his money troubles completely.

Lemass's biographers have agreed that his time in opposition between 1948 and 1951 was not a distinguished period in his career and this three-year period has received relatively little attention.[17] As a consequence, his journalistic contributions to *The Irish Press* have largely escaped scrutiny. As well as occupying the post of managing director Lemass also authored the 'Political Commentary' section of the newspaper. Written under the nom de plume 'Dáil Reporter', the weekly column displayed an intimate, and at times bitchy, account of parliamentary proceedings. This, combined with the piece's sharp commentary, the detailed attention it gave to his kingdom at Industry and Commerce, and the rather clumsy third-person references to himself, marked it out as Lemass's work. Lemass had been saved from financial oblivion, but relative to his wartime power he now found himself impotent. So he took on the role of mischief-maker.

His articles often conveyed his conviction that the Irish body politic was ailing under unnatural conditions. One party government was 'normal', he informed readers, but coalition produced 'general paralysis'.[18] He increasingly turned to the recent past – the Emergency – in an attempt to bolster his point. This involved much scare-mongering over the possibility of a third world war. The 'government's honeymoon days' had been brought to an end by the threat of another global conflict, he wrote in mid-1948. A coalition government was simply 'not designed for crisis administration'.[19] Telling readers that this threat could no longer be written off as a 'Fianna Fáil bogey', he revealed that de Valera had instructed every department of state to compile a record of events, to be stored in the strong room in Leinster House. These records would only be consulted if another war broke out. 'This war record is being referred to now,'[20] he added sombrely.

Lemass had agreed to the removal of a number of Emergency controls post-war. But from the wilderness of opposition, he seemed to be yearning for the re-imposition of the streamlined powers he enjoyed during that crisis period. One by one, he lamented the dismantling of his pet projects of the Emergency era, accusing Fine Gael of being 'prejudiced against every project initiated by Fianna Fáil'.[21] He attacked the government's decision to disband the Construction Corps without consulting Archbishop McQuaid.[22] When the first inter-party government scrapped compulsory tillage, Lemass warned that the Americans were displeased because they believed 'heaven helps those who help themselves'.[23] In early 1949 he attacked the coalition's plans for a partial lifting of rationing. This would only benefit the 'white flour classes', he claimed.[24]

Lemass also continued to employ the red scare rhetoric that was such a negative feature of the 1948 election. He repeatedly linked the strength of the Communist Party in Italy with the precipitation of global conflict. 'If Italy goes left it means Crisis not only for that country but for the world,' he wrote in April 1948, emphasising the need to build up the army and fuel supplies.[25] Enmeshed in the red-baiting of these articles was a growing scepticism over neutrality. 'If the War-Clouds Break', Ireland would have to reconsider her neutrality, he wrote. It was the intention of the Italian Communist Party to stay neutral in any West–East conflict and Ireland could not be seen to be aligned with them.[26] The coming war, which he was predicting with a gloomy regularity, would be one which would arouse 'important moral as well as material issues for this country'.[27]

In his almost obsessive warnings about war, Lemass's determination to manage the crisis better the second time than he had the first is clearly perceptible. But his comments were also based on an older belief in the broader strategic benefits to Ireland of single-party government. De Valera had expressed this in 1932 when he claimed that the British would never negotiate with any government they expected to fall.[28]

Lemass clearly thought that coalition rule was harming Ireland's standing in the post-war world. In Anglo-Irish talks in 1947 he had demurred over British enthusiasm that Ireland join the International Monetary Fund (IMF).[29] On the other hand, he questioned why Seán MacBride, the Minister for External Affairs, had not been more publicly enthusiastic about the embryonic development of a western European economic community.[30] Lemass and de Valera had attended the preliminary meeting of the Convention for European Economic Cooperation in Paris in 1947. The cooperation promised then was being realised by mid-1948.[31] The prospect of MacBride now taking the credit for the benefits of the American European Recovery Programme infuriated Lemass, and he speculated that the coalition would scupper Ireland's chances of receiving Marshall Aid.[32]

If Lemass's vocal anti-communism was a relatively new theme in his political rhetoric, his geopolitical stance was also tempered with more traditional concerns. Commenting on moves to reduce tariffs, his mood was protectionist. This was fine for 'highly developed industrial states', but for Ireland 'the power to assist new forms of production by tariffs and quotas is essential'.[33] Neither was he silent on partition, and in mid-1948 criticised the implications of the British Nationality Bill for nationalists in Northern Ireland.[34]

These ruminations on Ireland's place in the world were idle talk until the rude shock administered by Taoiseach John A. Costello's declaration of the Republic in September 1948. Earlier that year Labour leader William Norton had raised the prospect of the abolition of the External Relations Act, which asserted the British Crown's authority over Ireland's external affairs. The 'Dáil Reporter' played his part in the mounting pressure on the government to repeal the act. Lemass smugly claimed that the act's repeal would be the 'crowning achievement' of Fianna Fáil's efforts to release Ireland from 'the Treaty and dictated constitution of 1923'.[35] He even raised the prospect of 'unanimous' Dáil support for the act's repeal. The following week he attempted to simultaneously force the pace of the bill and outflank Clann na Poblachta's republicanism, pointing to 'the dilemma' posed for the coalition by Fine Gael's attachment to the British Commonwealth as a bulwark against 'Russian imperialism'.[36]

At this stage Lemass had the comfort of discussing an abstract situation. Two weeks later, however, Costello's unexpected actions would force him to return to the more specific issue of Ireland's constitutional position – one on which he and de Valera held a subtle yet significant difference of opinion. Speaking in Ottawa, Canada, on 7 September 1948 Costello surprised everyone by declaring the abolition of the External Relations Act and the establishment of the Irish Republic. The declaration of the Republic was, to quote historian Joseph Lee, 'the most inept diplomatic exhibition in the history of the state'.[37] Yet Lemass had to react immediately to the announcement as 'Dáil Reporter' the following day.

Sticking to his guns, he welcomed the move as a rationalisation of Ireland's constitutional position.[38] Lemass's columns of 8 and 15 September were tempered by an emphasis on the contradictions within the coalition towards neutrality[39] and the Civil War fought a generation ago.[40] Nonetheless, the tone was one of shoulder-shrugging acceptance of Costello's action.

The problem was that this attitude was out of kilter with the majority view of the Fianna Fáil party and de Valera, who saw the move as detrimental to the resolution of partition. If anything, Lemass had forced the pace of repeal of the act too hard. As the contradictions between his opinion and de Valera's became clearer, he decided not to pursue it any further. Instead, he returned to playing up differences within the coalition on Ireland's position vis-à-vis the Commonwealth.

The appearance of cracks in Fianna Fáil on this issue would have undermined the paramount objective of protecting the republican mantle from Cumann na Poblachta. The need for party unity meant that Lemass was forced to fall in line behind de Valera. Gagging his enthusiasm for the 'rationalisation' that the declaration of the Republic delivered, Lemass dutifully conformed to the trenchant anti-partitionism that was a staple of de Valera's global crusade.

Once again, he was following his chief. Instead of welcoming what he obviously regarded as a constitutional progression, Lemass used the Dáil debate over the Republic of Ireland Bill to stoke up old Civil War tensions. As the Dáil reassembled in April 1949 he remarked:

> Fine Gael deputies are in somewhat higher spirits than usual. They believe that their political stock has been enhanced by the Easter celebrations which, they consider, served the dual purpose of throwing a veil round the party's rather troublesome past and of distracting public attention from pressing material

problems. Naturally, their new role of upholders of the Republican constitution, the enactment of which their party opposed, has found most Fine Gael members a little self-conscious and even embarrassed when they contact those whose Republican faith is deep-rooted and long established.[41]

A month later Seán MacBride, the leader of Clann na Poblachta, circulated a letter to all Fianna Fáil deputies questioning the party's leadership. Lemass sprang into action, affirming his closeness to de Valera on foreign affairs. MacBride, he implied, only got a ministerial post at External Affairs because he could speak French. The head of the government should also hold the External Affairs portfolio, he claimed, and the only man for either job was Éamon de Valera.[42]

For Lemass, party unity had to prevail, and he would not let his ambitions to succeed the ageing de Valera imperil it. In order to mask internal tensions, he devoted most of his energy (and his column inches) to the 'yah, boo' of adversarial politics. The main message was that in coalition governments ministerial initiative was blunted by the need to achieve consensus.[43] 'In every coalition predominant considerations relate more to party advantage than to the dignity of democratic institutions,' he wrote.[44]

A favourite ploy was playing up the ideological differences between Fine Gael and Labour.[45] Lemass also teased the smaller parties – Clann na Talmhan and National Labour – warning them that they were being swallowed up in the jaws of Fine Gael.[46] He claimed that the silk hat worn by ministers, which had disappeared under Fianna Fáil, had returned under the coalition.[47] An insubstantial swing to Fianna Fáil in a west Cork by-election was blamed on the 'ex-Unionist' vote there.[48] Raidió Éireann was politically biased, it should change its name to 'CBS' or 'Coalition Broadcasting Service'.[49] Lemass even claimed that political preference was being shown in appointments to state boards, a charge which was very close to home.[50]

All of these themes were unimaginative enough, but Lemass also used his column to pursue ad hominem arguments and settle old scores. He was still sore about the 'searching judicial inquiry' that he was subjected to in 1944.[51] Still protesting his innocence, he wrote that 'the general body of opinion favours the theory of one Minister having told his friends what was intended, whether or not he realised that they could use the knowledge to their financial advantage'.[52]

Shortly after Fine Gael's James Dillon promised to 'drown' Britain in eggs, C.E.K. pictures Lemass ordering rashers. *Dublin Opinion*, July 1948.

Reading between the lines, this looked suspiciously like an admission that he had been loose-tongued in discussing the Transport Bill socially, not realising its full implications.

In June 1949 the second of the major corruption scandals of the 1940s involving Lemass was resolved when he and others were acquitted of charges of corruption by the Locke Tribunal. The tribunal had investigated allegations that Lemass and others had gained financially from the sale of a distillery in County Westmeath. Minister for Finance Paddy McGilligan reacted to the ruling by criticising the tribunal judges. Lemass harboured a strong dislike for McGilligan. Shortly after losing power in 1948 he had warned progressives within the new administration that with McGilligan as Minister for Finance their plans for development would be 'lost, and lost forever, in the dim recesses of the Department of Finance'.[53] His anger at McGilligan's remarks was palpable; he termed it 'the most disgraceful episode in recent Irish political history' and accused several Fine Gael deputies of 'dirty tactics' and a 'mean role' in the affair.[54]

The most biting criticism of Lemass's mischievous phase was reserved for James Dillon, his long-term Dáil enemy and Minister for Agriculture. During trade talks in June 1948 Dillon, who opted for more colourful turns of phrase than Lemass, promised to 'drown' British representatives in eggs. Lemass dismissed this as a 'flamboyancy'.[55] Dillon was by this point firmly in Lemass's sights as one of the Fine Gael deputies who had pushed for the Locke Tribunal. He retaliated by calling for a judicial tribunal into allegations of corruption Dillon had levelled at a Fianna Fáil deputy, Martin Corry. Leaving the matter to a Dáil committee would lead to 'grave abuse' motivated by party political loyalties, Lemass claimed.[56]

Another regular target was Minister for Industry and Commerce Dan Morrissey. Lemass regarded Morrissey, his successor, as less able than he had been to stand up to the Department of Finance and its power of veto.[57] But the zenith of Lemass's mischief-making period was to come in 1949 when the Labour Party leader William Norton successfully sued *The Irish Press* for damage to his reputation arising out of Lemass's claim that he neglected his departmental duties.[58]

Lemass had made similar claims against James Dillon, but the accusation was the last straw for Norton, whom Lemass loved to taunt as an inauthentic left winger.[59] In January 1949, for instance, Lemass wrote:

> He knows all the things that a Labour leader is expected to say and usually says them, but on the rare occasions on which he leaves the general for the particular he discloses an unexpectedly conservative outlook . . . He is far closer to his Fine Gael colleagues than a cursory reading of his public utterances would suggest.[60]

The real offence was caused at the resumption of the Dáil in February 1949 when Lemass stirred things up by composing acerbic pen portraits of the government. Norton 'occupies most of his time with party matters and leaves his Department to run itself', Lemass stated.[61] Taoiseach John A. Costello had done 'better in office than was expected'. MacBride 'speaks well' but has an 'easy' job at External Affairs. McGilligan, at Finance, was 'effective' and 'lucid'. James Dillon was 'a spectacular failure, with emphasis on the spectacular, in contrast with Mr Morrissey'.[62] He dismissed Noël Browne as not 'of Ministerial calibre'. Future Taoiseach Liam Cosgrave, according to Lemass, 'lacks personal colour and carries little weight'.[63]

Norton was only awarded a token libel, but the episode forced Lemass to tone down the mischief-making. He now turned his attention to helping establish *The Sunday Press*. As part of his market research he visited London on a fact-finding mission about newspaper production methods at the *Daily Mail*, Britain's leading right-wing newspaper.[64] When it emerged in September 1949, *The Sunday Press* was a less vulgar version of the *Sunday Independent*, but tried to

Lemass and Dillon's mutual New Year's Resolution to cease
bickering about one another, as imagined by C.E.K.,
Dublin Opinion, January 1952

rival it by being similarly light and populist, like the *News of the World*.

Lemass had obviously taken in much of the British tabloid style; the newspaper contained plenty of human interest stories, sport, and fashion pieces. Twenty years earlier he had instructed party members to boycott the *Independent* and his dislike of the paper showed no signs of abating. Reacting to the increasingly obvious charge that he was 'Dáil Reporter', Lemass accused Minister for Agriculture James Dillon of penning editorials in the *Sunday Independent*.[65] The *Sunday Press* was a determined challenge not only to that paper's circulation, but also its political bent.

Meanwhile, Lemass was still busy imposing strict discipline on party members. He and Frank Aiken secured the custom of party whips preparing a record of each party member's absences from meetings and Dáil sessions. Each absent member was now written to, notifying him of his absence and requesting an explanation.[66] He was determined to have his own house in order despite being preoccupied with sniping at the government.

Lemass's status as mischief-maker at this point of his career is illustrated by an anecdote told by a fellow mischief-maker, the writer Ulick O'Connor. O'Connor was a student at University College Dublin at the time and a critic of Michael Tierney, president of UCD and a man of Fine Gael allegiance. In 1950 Tierney banned

Lemass, as a 'St Leinstrinian' girl, administers a Chinese burn to Norton, *Dublin Opinion*, December 1954.

the outspoken O'Connor from attending debates of the university's Literary and Historical Society (L&H). O'Connor, who regarded Tierney as 'a monster, a bully, and a Nazi', was determined to have his revenge.[67]

With Lemass due to address the society as a high-profile speaker, Tierney warned O'Connor that if he attended, the Gardaí would be called and he would be arrested. O'Connor decided to defy Tierney and gained admittance to the debate disguised as a woman, complete with make-up and female attire applied to him by a make-up artist in the Abbey Theatre. Before Lemass spoke he turned to the society's auditor and asked him what would happen if Ulick O'Connor turned up. The auditor replied that the police would be called. At this, O'Connor stood up and shouted 'I second that!' in a female voice before removing his wig and handcuffing himself to a desk. Due to the ensuing commotion the debate was cancelled. O'Connor recalls looking up at Lemass, who 'got a tremendous kick out of it' and was struggling to suppress his laughter. O'Connor later wrote to Lemass to apologise and received 'a very generous, sweet letter' in return.[68]

Back in the political arena, it was around this time, displaying a starkly adversarial attitude, that Lemass embarked on what Garvin ranks as 'possibly his greatest and most dangerous mistake'.[69] In 1950 he launched a vicious attack on the Industrial Development Authority (IDA). Set up by the inter-party government in early 1949, the IDA was a semi-state body composed of industry experts whose task was to research export markets available for Irish produce and survey the state of Irish trade.

An overlooked aspect of Lemass's criticism of the IDA is that it was couched in terms of the public interest; he raised the import issue of the Dáil's accountability for the appointment of outside 'experts' to positions of public responsibility. The IDA was headed by a four-man board of businessmen. It was unfair, Lemass reasoned, that these men had been appointed for a fixed number of years. Lemass regarded this as a 'fait accompli' by the government. It would encroach on the Dáil's democratic mandate by preventing a newly elected government from removing the board.[70]

Unfortunately for Lemass, this argument was weakened by his own way of exercising ministerial power, which was hardly democratic. Patronage was at the heart of Lemass's political career and his opposition to the IDA provides a rare instance where this was displayed publicly. In the Dáil debate over the creation of the IDA, personal enmities flared. Lemass was accused of having described one of its founding members as a 'pompous ass'.[71] His stance was dismissed by Fine Gael's T. F. O'Higgins as 'petulant'.[72]

Lemass's outlook was coloured by what he regarded as the inexperience of the new man at Industry and Commerce, Daniel Morrissey, and the opposition to the IDA of his old lieutenant Leydon, who was still departmental secretary over at the old kingdom. For the most part, though, he opposed the authority because he viewed it as an attempt to emasculate his old empire.[73] As Bew and Patterson note, the IDA actually represented something of a victory for Lemass's way of doing things at Industry and Commerce over the traditionalists at the Department of Finance.[74] Indeed, the Keynesian policies of the first inter-party government represented a shift from the traditional, conservative Finance approach embodied by MacEntee. But Lemass despised any encroachment by those outside the Fianna Fáil communion and stoutly believed that the national interest and his personal exercise of power were synonymous.

Lemass's opposition to the IDA raises the question of his broader political direction during what is generally acknowledged as his fallow period. According to Horgan, in 1948 Lemass was still resolutely in favour of state intervention. By late 1949 and 1950 he was less sure, Horgan claims, as his attitude became more conservative.[75] But this 'shift to the right' was less pronounced than Horgan suggests. Lemass continued to bask in the role of mischief-maker. In 1949/50 he gave out mixed signals about the nature and degree of state interventionism. If he leaned regularly to the right at all, it was on the theme of thrift in public office. This was a very common political charge to lay from opposition, as Lemass's rhetoric of the 1920s proves. He criticised the budget of 1949 as delivering 'no sense of economy in the true sense of the term' because the cost of government had risen.[76] The coalition had brought bloated administrative costs and greater taxation, he claimed.[77]

Some things *had* changed. By 1949 Lemass had finally waved goodbye to the Second World War and was referring back to the Emergency less and less. Significantly, though, he was still piqued by the selfish attitude of native enterprise during the war. In May 1950 he declared himself in favour of 'full socialism', where the government controlled economic activity, investment and the consequences rather than what he called the 'cock-eyed socialism' of the inter-party government.[78] Horgan contends the remark is not to be taken entirely seriously.[79] Undoubtedly, it was yet another attempt to ratchet up the ideological tensions between Fine Gael and Labour. On the other hand, a preference for top-down state management, rather than democratic socialism, was consistent with Lemass's views at this juncture.

Ultimately, any evidence of Lemass's evolving policy views between 1948 and 1951 is clouded by the fact that he was intent on exploiting tensions within the coalition at this time, engaging in populist point-scoring at every opportunity. He consistently tried to outflank Labour, particularly over the slow pace of welfare reform, which he saw as the price of getting into bed with the conservative Fine Gael.[80] Commenting on agricultural markets, the theme of a larger historical struggle returned. He cited the historically rooted hostility of the Irish people to export-driven policy. 'This idea inspired the landlords and in the past century led to the depopulation of the Irish countryside and to wholesale emigration.' 'Increasing exports can conceal increasing misery and poverty at home,' he warned. 'The phrase "wealth accumulating and men decaying" told the story of Irish trade before Fianna Fáil gave a new direction and a new impetus to national endeavour.'[81] Soon, the opportunity would arise for Lemass to renew this 'impetus to national endeavour'.

'All the Slickness of a Greyhound-Switching Peasant'

The coalition government had lasted much longer than Lemass predicted, but it was fatally wounded by the Mother and Child controversy. Noël Browne, the crusading Minister for Health, introduced a scheme to provide free maternity care for all mothers and free medical care for children, which elicited the worst in clerical reaction and precipitated a general election.

Fianna Fáil's National Executive ratified the appointment of Lemass as director of elections after the 1951 election was called.[82] Back in his familiar role, he set about directing behind the scenes and speaking publicly nearly every day for the next three weeks. As managing director of *The Sunday Press*, Lemass had a decisive influence on the media spin during the campaign. He may have held a dim view of Browne's ministerial capability, but he ensured that Fianna Fáil capitalised on the crisis by trumpeting the party's hospital- and house-building record in the *The Irish Press*.[83] The newspaper also provided Browne, now an independent TD, with plenty of column space.

Lemass rallied all hands to the pump. *The Irish Press* splashed across its front page lengthy notices of Fianna Fáil conventions, meetings and lists of candidates.[84] On Lemass's instruction, celebrations planned for Fianna Fáil's jubilee were cancelled.[85] Addressing crowds throughout May 1951 Lemass returned to what he had chosen as the central theme of the election campaign: coalition governments were unnatural.[86] He had repeatedly stressed this point in his 'Dáil Reporter' pieces and with the election in full swing he reiterated it incessantly. A typical Lemass address during the campaign closely resembled this reminder to a Drogheda crowd: 'A Fine Gael government would have been bad enough. A Labour Party government might have been tolerable. A government that was one thing one day and another the next could produce and has produced only confusion and ineffectiveness.'[87]

Rather than return to the red scare, Lemass positioned himself to the left during the 1951 election campaign – despite the anti-communist sentiment accompanying the Korean War, which was raging at the time. While Seán MacEntee attacked the excessive spending of the first inter-party government and de Valera assumed whatever pose the role of populist father figure demanded, Lemass resumed his traditional role as the champion of the Irish working class. Whereas he had defended his wartime record at the start of his period in opposition, he now played it down. The times demanded conciliation, not coercion. He reminded a Dublin crowd how he had lifted wage restrictions post-war and established the Labour Court.[88] Although *The Irish Press* continued to churn out pious, red-baiting pieces, Lemass stressed the need to expand public transport and dismissed claims he would regulate workers' wages in the private sector.[89]

In terms of stressing that he wanted to 'minimise government interference' relative to Emergency controls,[90] Lemass was moving to the right. But he couched this outcome as distinctly favourable to the organised worker. This had been called a 'bread and butter' election, he said, and only Fianna Fáil would reduce the cost of living; under the coalition it was 'up with bread, up with butter'.[91] On the eve of the election Lemass reiterated Fianna Fáil's social achievements and affirmed that Fianna Fáil remained the party of the worker.[92]

Lemass sought to associate Fianna Fáil's record with protected national industrial development. Ireland's Marshall Aid money had been spent profligately, he claimed.[93] This waste would continue in the run-up to the election in order to secure the coalition favour at the polls.[94] Previously, Lemass had warned that the coalition was imperilling Ireland's chances of receiving Marshall Aid. Now he attacked 'the folly of borrowing dollars from America' itself and emphasised the need for greater home production.[95]

This sort of political manoeuvring was classic Lemass and the 1951 election campaign in general bore his indelible mark. He may have postponed the party's jubilee celebrations, but under his instruction a sixpenny history of the party went on sale the week before the polls opened. On its front cover, the image chosen to symbolise the party at this pivotal political juncture did not depict cosy homesteads, athletic youths or comely maidens. It pictured factories, chimneys and pylons: industry would sound loudest.[96]

Lemass's tactics proved shrewd. A balance of payments problem had arisen largely because Irish industry was coming up against the limits of his own protectionist strategy. And yet his juxtaposition of post-war boom with Ireland's stagnation was couched in left-leaning terms. Fianna Fáil was the party of dynamism, Fine Gael the party of decadence. Had Lemass known about Daniel Morrisey's attempts at this time to secure a ministerial set of china for the purposes of entertaining at Kildare Street, he would undoubtedly have made much out of it.[97]

The public proved receptive to the Lemass line. So too did Noël Browne and Peadar Cowan, two socialist TDs on whom Fianna Fáil relied to gain power. Fianna Fáil triumphed at the polls, ending three

Lemass, with toy
plane in hand,
enjoying the
Dáil holidays,
Dublin Opinion,
September 1952.

years in opposition by heading a minority government. The party's
return to power saw Lemass resume his old post at Industry and
Commerce. Todd Andrews thought that his greatest achievement on
taking up his old job again was forcing two of the leviathan state
companies, ESB and Bord na Móna, to overcome their frequent
conflicts and cooperate.[98]

Lemass's triumphant return as Minister for Industry and
Commerce and Tánaiste was marred by ill health, however. Shortly
after the party resumed power he had to undergo a gall bladder
operation and his influence in the cabinet declined. Lemass, who
seldom missed the party's monthly National Executive meetings,
was absent from every single meeting between October 1951 and
April 1952.[99] He did attend parliamentary party meetings in early
1952 where, again, his impatience came across; he wanted all questions
that did not concern general policy streamlined to ministers rather
than face discussion at party meetings.[100] But, owing to his health,
Lemass was forced to miss all party meetings between late March
and early June 1952.[101]

A short time after Lemass returned to action in mid-1952, de
Valera departed for the Netherlands for treatment to improve his
eyesight. Lemass wrote to his chief, who was largely consigned to his
hotel room in Utrecht, with a few 'cracks' to cheer him up.[102] Lemass
would have baulked at the thought of being part of a physically frail

old elite, but his own ailments came increasingly into play in the 1950s. In Seán MacEntee, who resumed the Finance portfolio in 1951, the purse strings were clasped by a conservative deflationist who disliked Lemass's Keynesian economic approach. Had he been in better physical form, Lemass might have mounted a more robust challenge to his old antagonist's ultra-conservative budget of April 1952.[103]

But while Lemass may have challenged MacEntee's economic conservatism, his social conservatism was displayed more clearly than ever. Getting back to attacking the Labour Party in the Dáil at every opportunity, he dismissed calls for equal pay for women performing work of equal value to men. This would lead, Lemass claimed, to married women entering paid employment. While this was the case 'in the United States and in most of the Scandinavian countries', in Ireland, he argued, it was 'contrary to our way of life'. 'It has been contended,' Lemass went on, 'that the married woman's place, the mother of the family, is in the home. Personally, I am a strong advocate of that argument.'[104]

At the same time, Lemass was throwing off a few traditionalist green robes and starting to go further towards securing trade co-operation with Northern Ireland than de Valera ever had. Crucially, during this period he established good relations with Northern Ireland's Minister for Commerce, William McCreevey.[105] This gave him an unprecedented working knowledge of the Belfast government. Speaking abroad, however, Lemass aped de Valera's anti-partitionism. On a visit to West Germany in 1952, he spoke about how Ireland's partition had prevented the industrial north and agricultural south from becoming an 'excellent economy'.[106] Playing to the North American gallery the following year, he described partition as an 'absurdity'.[107]

A member of Ireland's disgruntled literati provided a singular portrait of Lemass on his return to ministerial power. The writer Patrick Kavanagh viewed Lemass as economically reductive and conveyed this in his short-lived 1952 journal on literature and politics, *Kavanagh's Weekly*. 'The question of why the people are leaving the land,' he argued 'is not unconnected with the denigration of the intellect.'[108] The Fianna Fáil government that had replaced the coalition were, according to Kavanagh, 'dreary fellows with all the slickness of a greyhound-switching peasant' and in thrall to the bourgeoisie.[109]

Lemass and cabinet as de Valera's ballerinas.
Dublin Opinion, August 1953.

Take for instance Mr. Lemass, who is being groomed to wear the non-existent emperor's robe of Fianna Fáil leadership in the near future. Mr. Lemass is at best mediocre. He is Minister for Industry but we cannot remember any advantage his work has been. Some time recently we saw in the *Sunday Press* a series of profiles of Mr. Lemass holding his spectacles in various poses of profundity. We had to laugh. The lighting only exposed the man's shallowness.[110]

Kavanagh was seriously ill at the time and the portrait bore all the bitterness of a sick man. But it conveys a growing popular frustration with the contented protected national bourgeoisie at a time of economic stagnation. Kavanagh viewed Lemass's 1952 Tourism Bill as of no national benefit except to this narrow cross-section of society. Through the act, Bord Fáilte was awarded more money to 'encourage and develop tourist traffic'.[111] Lemass had faced questions in a similar vein to Kavanagh's in the Dáil; these touched on the fact that the primary beneficiaries of the act would be hotel owners.[112]

Kavanagh lamented Ireland's 'prostitution' to the 'Yank, who should be tolerated for a few months, robbed and sent back for more money', claiming Lemass was content to 'lie back with his pipe in his mouth to await their arrival, each carrying a wad of twenty dollar bills in his hip pocket'.[113] The depiction of the Minister for Industry and Commerce as an idle, dishonest peasant was probably calculated to rankle with Lemass, who despised this type of Irish identity and energetically fought to dispel it. In doing so, however, Kavanagh regarded Lemass as offering trade-centric cultural philistinism as a substitute. He argued that Lemass was 'exactly the reverse' of Indian Prime Minister Jawaharlal Nehru, who was reported as saying that he would rather be an outcast among the mountains than a member of a stock exchange.[114]

Curiously, Lemass and Kavanagh agreed on one thing at least: a hatred of Superman. Lemass detested the popular Superman comic strip (as did the Knights of Columbanus)[115] and made a point of removing it from *The Sunday Press*.[116] Superman was also disliked by Kavanagh, who saw it as an example of the newspaper's indulgence of American celebrities with 'genitals that hardly conformed to the Greek canon and Nietzschean heroes who have a pane of glass for a diaphragm'.[117]

Nonetheless, Kavanagh's caustic comments about Lemass were – according to the Monaghan poet – the death of *Kavanagh's Weekly*. The magazine folded, unable to secure advertising revenue. This was because, as a businessman friend of Kavanagh's reportedly told him, 'that kind of outspoken stuff was too dangerous. We had been critical of Lemass and he had to meet Lemass regularly.'[118] Although jaundiced, this illustrates Lemass's tsar-like status in the world of Irish enterprise. In January 1953 *The Irish Times* reported that Lemass was thinking of leaving politics for a high-flying job with a private company.[119] The rumour proved unfounded, but highlighted the close professional and personal ties that existed between Lemass and Ireland's business leaders – the plump cushion that had softened the loss of his ministerial salary.

And yet Lemass was, by this point, having grave doubts about the worth of protectionism. These tensions had come to the fore during the Emergency. It had taken Lemass some time to come to terms with the fact that he would have to discard some of the more substantial powers he enjoyed during this period. But his frustrations with sections of the Irish capitalist class lingered. As 1952 became 1953 he was ruminating more and more about the usefulness of the protection this Irish business coterie enjoyed. He signalled his discontent through the 1953 Restrictive Practices Act, which sought to eliminate price fixing in the protected industries.

According to Lemass Ireland needed 'external investment in industry' and any foreign business should set up in Ireland with the

Lemass returns from his trade mission to Canada with a moose.
Dublin Opinion, November 1953.

'reasonable prospect' that the markets of the world would be open to it.[120] On a trade mission to the United States and Canada in 1953, Lemass made it clear that he was after North American money. As if to reinforce the point, he took $300 from a Canadian diplomat at a late-night poker school on the Ottawa leg of the journey.[121]

Lemass had been making noises about abandoning protectionism and allowing foreign capital into Ireland for some time. While this would mean confrontation with some sections of the Irish bourgeoisie, Lemass knew he could count on other wealthy industrialist friends, such as Kevin McCourt and Aodogán O'Rahilly, who welcomed the prospect of 'opening Ireland up' to foreign investment.

The real significance of Lemass's political career between the years 1951 and 1954 lay in the application of this growing sentiment as political will. This was never going to be an easy task, as it went against a central thesis of the republicanism he had helped mould in the previous three decades. By 1954 Lemass was making it increasingly obvious that protectionism was under review. To many people, whether bourgeois or working class, this shift was little short of economic treason. It was an abandonment of protectionism for the liberal economics favoured by the 'silk hats' of Cumann na nGaedheal – the likes of the hated Kevin O'Higgins who had viewed Arthur Griffith's protectionism as the one blemish on his record.

This emerging new departure would not be matched by a liberalisation of internal party discipline. Neither would Lemass allow any personal agonising over economic policy taint Fianna Fáil unity. By this point he had slipped behind MacEntee in the party hierarchy, but at parliamentary party meetings in this period Lemass remained the consummate disciplinarian. He consistently blunted initiative by correcting deputies on how they should vote in the Dáil.

In March 1954, after the party suffered by-election defeats in Louth and Cork, de Valera announced a general election for mid-May. This was a cue for Lemass to return once more to the regurgitation of Fianna Fáil's past glories. Again, he played up the party's record in fostering industrialisation, appealing to old loyalties. He also headed a committee to prepare a set of rules to bind deputies more tightly to the party line.[122] Fianna Fáil TDs would not be permitted to defy party whips and could not take part in radio broadcasts without the consent of the Central Committee. Lemass meant business. The public's mood, however, was less easy to control.

Back to the Parish Pump

Despite Lemass's efforts, Fianna Fáil lost power for the second time in six years in July 1954. After the defeat he took over as the party's director of organisation, a role he occupied until March 1957. Previously, his reorganisation role in these years has received no detailed scrutiny. But this three-year period is perhaps the most romantic episode in Lemass's later career: he resumed the job he had occupied alongside Gerald Boland in the 1920s, setting out in his car to survey the position of Fianna Fáil around the country, armed for long journeys with his pipe, tobacco and several chocolate bars.

The bulging correspondence relating to his task provides a fascinating glimpse of Lemass's interaction with the party's rural base and his evolving policy views. As early as 1948, when the party found itself in opposition for the first time in sixteen years, Lemass had written of the necessity of involving 'younger members' in public meetings.[123] 'Dáil Reporter' had compared the spirit of the party's 1949 Ard-Fheis to that of early Fianna Fáil: 'The party leaders are older and perhaps more cautious, but the spirit of the organisation is that of vigorous youth. Now, as in 1927, there is the same exuberant desire to get things done quickly and completely.'[124]

Back in opposition in 1954, Lemass swapped writing about the importance of youth for putting the contention into practice. He was fifty-six at this stage and facing an energetic task, so he appointed an organisation committee composed of young men in a hurry. These included Charles Haughey, Brian Lenihan, Kevin Boland, Matt Cullen, Eoin Ryan and Lemass's son Noel (who was named after his deceased brother). Under Lemass's stewardship bonds were forged between the men who would come to form what journalist John Healy was later to term the 'inner cabinet' of Lenihan, Haughey and O'Malley. It also provided a unique space where future party leaders, such as Haughey and Albert Reynolds, met one another for the first time. Lemass also instructed another young party man and future Taoiseach, Jack Lynch, to set up a separate organisation committee in County Cork to relieve the workload of HQ in the south of the country.[125]

'Youth' was the watchword for Lemass between 1954 and 1957. He did not want Fianna Fáil candidates who had been taken 'off the shelf'[126] or 'out of the attic'.[127] He wanted a party 'virile in personnel and spirit', not composed of cobwebbed relics.[128] In practical terms, however, the huge outflux of young people to England harmed this particular thrust and, as he confessed, getting young people involved was 'very uphill work'.[129] Lemass was evidently frustrated by instances where, for instance, he had devoted time to building up a local cumann only for the branch secretary to promptly leave for work in England.[130] Neither was the cull of the old guard as pronounced as Lemass conveyed. Efforts to recruit the young were accompanied by the necessity of keeping the boys of the old brigade on board 'so long as they themselves want to keep going'.[131]

If the drive for youth was only a partial success, at least the new role gave Lemass the opportunity to impose discipline on the party's troublesome rank and file. In taking the post, the former minister was in fact moving to a post he had created himself in November 1953. Displaying a calculating foresight, he had ensured that in his new role he would have 'full executive powers in matters concerning organisation, publicity, and propaganda including power to control the activities of all officers engaged in these branches of work'.[132] He secured £500 expenses a year for himself in this role.[133] For colleagues like Gerald Boland, who clung dear to the party's original anti-materialism, this £500 was nothing but a gambling slush fund for the former minister.

Meanwhile, Lemass set about establishing his broader hegemony over the party. He was reappointed joint honorary secretary and for much of this period also enjoyed the power that came with chair-manship of the Fianna Fáil parliamentary party, a role which the increasingly frail de Valera relinquished in 1955. Lemass also used his post as director of organisation to bolster his internal power nexus. Individual members of his team attended local party meetings around the country. Then they reported back to Lemass on the strengths and weaknesses of local organisation, naming individuals whom they viewed as either beneficial or harmful to the party. Lemass established regular contact between party headquarters and local cumainn nationwide; dialogue would no longer merely take place around election time. This process was a double-edged sword whereby local party organisations received more support from headquarters, but were also whipped into line. If a 'critical tone' was reported at a cumann meeting, a member of the organisation committee was sent to investigate and 'close attention' would be paid to it by Lemass.[134]

This surveillance network acted as an early warning system for internal disquiet. In turning down dissenting resolutions submitted by cumainn for consideration at the party's Ard-Fheis on topics such as 'the undue influence of the National Executive in the selection of candidates for Bye and General Elections' his hand is evident.[135] In overruling local decisions, Lemass often deployed his practised lip service to democracy while acting against that very spirit. He told a disgruntled Galway Fianna Fáiler in 1955: 'In a democratic organi-sation such as ours it is sometimes necessary to accept decisions with which one may not be in agreement, and continue to work loyally for the organisation's interests nonetheless.'[136]

There was much grass roots resentment at the increasingly authoritarian role of the party Executive under this reorganisation drive.[137] In late 1956, when candidates were being decided for the forthcoming general election, Lemass upheld the decision of the Fianna Fáil National Executive in its refusal to ratify a female candidate, a Mrs Drennan. Drennan had been democratically elected by her cumann in Borris, County Carlow. In outlining the decision Lemass offered no clear reason as to why she had been debarred.[138] He was accused by one angry cumann member of turning Fianna Fáil into 'a dictatorship'.[139] Such insubordination reflected a palpable dislike of Dublin-centrism at grass roots level. Responding to one particular effort to bend local branches into shape, Mayo TD Michael Moran was to tell Lemass frankly that 'the people of south Mayo do not take very kindly to Organizers of the Dublin variety'.[140]

Back in the capital, Lemass established 'Comh Chomhairle Átha Cliath' in 1954, an elite new branch concerned exclusively with higher matters of policy. It drew criticism from the party organisation. Some party members thought that Lemass's new organisation committee and 'Comh Chomhairle' were the same thing and Lemass had to elaborate that the new body was 'a unit for lectures, debates, etc'.[141] At a meeting of Dublin South East cumann it was noted that the new initiative

> was causing a great amount of uneasiness. It appeared to be a new Head Quarters organisation, which could be joined directly by people without reference to the Cumainn. There were a number of people who would prefer to be in the Headquarters organisation rather than in the Cumainn where the work had to be done.[142]

For other party members, Lemass's disciplinary drive threatened the flower of grass roots democracy while leaving state bureaucracies unaccountable.

> This cumann feels that CIÉ must be a new form of government, but they did not present themselves to the people for election. If that is the position whereby government Ministers have their powers transferred to other bodies it is high time that the plain working class people woke up since FF cumanns serve no useful purpose and TDs are mere 'yes men' to party whips.[143]

The process of reorganisation was not all one-way traffic, however. In his new role Lemass gave up his ministerial desk for the grubby work of Irish local politics. This necessarily involved dirtying his hands on the parish pump. More familiar with dictating national economic policy, Lemass was instead forced to take an active interest in humdrum issues such as potholes, particularly around the local elections of July 1955, the by-elections of 1956, and the general election of 1957.

He became embroiled in issues such as the need for two new water pumps in a Westmeath parish[144] and the failure of *The Irish Press* to report the victory of the Tralee Roger Casement cumann in the Kerry Amateur Snooker Championship.[145] Lemass found himself trying to acquire a second-hand billiards table for the Ardee cumann[146] and chasing up memos on boreens in County Longford.[147] In an ironic role reversal from his previous position as Supplies Tsar, Lemass composed a begging letter to his old department, Industry and Commerce, to request an increased petrol allowance for a party man from Louth.[148]

What is more, in some cases it proved impossible for the National Executive to disturb local tradition.[149] When it came to vote management, Lemass discouraged the practice of dividing constituencies into separate spheres of influence for individual candidates, a particularly common practice in counties Cork, Donegal and Kerry. 'It is much better that our candidates should go as a team making it clear that the voters are entitled to record their preference in the order of their own choice,' he argued.[150] Nonetheless a Cork East TD complained to Lemass in 1956 of an 'Iron Curtain across this constituency below which I may not go', overseen by firebrand fellow Fianna Fáil TD Martin Corry.[151]

Lemass obviously found these sorts of local rivalries most tiresome. In the process of selecting a candidate for the Laois–Offaly by-election in March 1956 an organiser from Offaly had expressed his hope that an Offaly man would be selected. Lemass wrote to him confessing he was 'perturbed' at the comment: 'a good candidate from Leix would be better than a bad candidate from Offaly and vice versa. Urge the cumainn delegates to support the candidate most likely to win.'[152] After a meeting to decide on a candidate in Kilkenny in December 1956 he admitted to leaving 'not very happy' and 'much perturbed' by the squabbles that broke out.[153] Lemass responded to a long-winded letter from a party man in Bandon, County Cork, who cited physical fights and devious intrigue among party members in the town by thanking him, in his wry manner, for expressing his views so 'fully and frankly'.[154] His exasperation was obvious.

Lemass's attitude towards local political bickering was informed by his conviction that Ireland needed voting reform. At the level of local politics he favoured single-member electoral areas over the list system.[155] He described the latter as giving 'all the disadvantages of proportional representation without the advantages' because it threatened 'the emergence of a number of small parties' and left 'the selection of members largely to party organisation without the public having a voice in it'.[156] Lemass was a leading proponent of electoral reform and had pushed the issue at cabinet and committee

Lemass, at the forefront of the cavalry charge to abolish
proportional representation, *Dublin Opinion*, April 1959.

level within the party.[157] He favoured the straight vote, viewing proportional representation as slowing national progress by necessitating
coalition governments.

In general, the rhythms of parish life frustrated him. On more
than one occasion reorganisation meetings were postponed due to
clashes with local GAA fixtures. Lemass's annoyance was subtle but
perceptible. 'Once again, we have been informed that arrangements
have been cancelled owing to GAA fixtures.', he wrote to a party
man in Offaly. Through gritted teeth, he remarked: 'I am regarding
the rest of the programme as provisional until it is confirmed.'[158]

Fianna Fáil's electoral defeat in 1954 meant that a lot of his
energy had to be prioritised into indulging parochial politics. Lemass
could count on business friends in companies such as Clery's, the
Hospital Trust, Unidare and Sunbeam to provide the major capital
for Fianna Fáil's election campaigns in the 1950s.[159] But, as the old
adage goes, 'all politics is local' and Lemass devoted a considerable
amount of time to cultivating existing rural patronage networks to
secure the party's return to power.

He secured opportunities for a lot of small businessmen, provided
they were good party men. A Drogheda businessman who wanted to
open a newsagent's shop in the town wrote to Lemass complaining
that 'were the other applicant to get the agency it would be a shame
as his family have ever been opposed to Fianna Fáil'. He asked

Lemass to 'use whatever influence you have on my behalf'.[160] Lemass wrote to Vivion de Valera, son of the Taoiseach and managing director of *The Irish Press*, to request he take 'a personal interest in this matter' because it 'could have serious repercussions'.[161]

After meeting local party people and the odd gombeen man Lemass would often be asked to make representations for jobs on behalf of their sons, daughters, friends, nephews and nieces and he mostly obliged in pulling various strings. Lemass carried out many favours, for example finding work for men connected with the old IRA or helping a farmer to get his son into the Gardaí.[162] In securing a job at *The Irish Press* for a Donegal man Lemass assured Vivion de Valera that his 'reformation is complete as far as drink is concerned'.[163] Connections, of course, were crucial. In December 1955 Lemass agreed to a request by Christy Cowen of Clara, County Offaly (the grandfather of future Taoiseach Brian Cowen) that he use his influence to secure a job for a relative in the Dublin department store Guineys.[164] In May 1956 Cowen again sought Lemass's help in finding the same relative a job with CIÉ.[165]

In fact, in travelling around the country Lemass dealt with a disproportionately high volume of appeals for jobs in CIÉ, the firm at which Frank, Lemass's younger brother, was appointed general manager in 1946. But in opposition, there were limits to Lemass's generosity and his powers.[166] The architect Michael Scott is a high-profile example of patronage counting for less without political power. Scott, the architect of the World's Fair shamrock back in 1939, did not have strong patronage links with either of the coalition governments and work dried up somewhat. But after Fianna Fáil were returned to power, he continued to benefit from his closeness to Frank Lemass, who was instrumental in Scott winning contracts to design modernist leviathans in Dublin such as Donnybrook bus garage (1951) and Busáras (1953).[167]

Employment and the location of industry were tied up with intense political factionalism, which Lemass entertained. In 1954 he alerted Donegal TDs Cormac Breslin and Joe Brennan that his old IRA associate Peadar O'Donnell was attempting to 'cash in' on plans for a seaweed-processing factory on the Donegal coast and warned that 'the coalition will try to take all the credit' for the development of the fishery industry there.[168] Just before the change of government in 1957 Lemass received an angry letter from Fianna Fáil party members in Ennis headed 'The Stolen Factory' about a factory that was 'promised' to the County Clare town after the Dutch investors met with de Valera. The factory had subsequently been 'stolen' by a County Wicklow town after the intervention of Labour Senator Luke Duffy and Labour Ministers James Everett and William Norton. The letter beseeched Lemass to get the 'Dutchman' back to Clare.[169] Lemass promised to do what he could.

It was Norton, Tánaiste in the second coalition government, who made the first sustained attempt to bring greater foreign investment to Ireland. Lemass might have been expected to support this initiative. Instead, the tribalism of Irish politics dictated that his public pronouncements on the issue were characterised by ambiguity as Fianna Fáil in opposition reverted to its traditionalist line of economic nationalism.[170] Lemass passionately believed in Irish national development, but it just was not natural if Fianna Fáil were not dictating it.

At the level of local politics there are several examples of this stiflingly partisan outlook. One was Lemass's efforts to get party members in Clogherhead, County Louth, to infiltrate the town development association because he thought it was dominated by Fine Gael supporters.[171] Future president of Ireland Patrick Hillery wrote to Lemass in 1954 asking what he could do to get industry started in Kilrush, County Clare.[172] Lemass replied enthusiastically: 'almost any industry is possible, if someone with the "know-how" is associated with it. The job of a development association is primarily to contact such a person.'[173] But when confronted in Louth with an example of a development body operating on its initiative Lemass eyed it as politically suspect. He had a keen nose for any whiff of political bias in the allocation of positions[174] and was outraged at the perceived preference given to Clann na Talmhan supporters in the allocation of jobs on a drainage scheme in Corrib, County Galway.[175] At the same time he sustained the rot by displaying a narrowly tribalistic attitude towards national development.

When it came to the social and cultural factors underlying Ireland's lack of development, there were limits to Lemass's reforming approach. For example, he had no foibles about the awkward interplay of Church and state in the practice of political fund-raising after Sunday Mass. He wrote to a candidate in South Tipperary on the matter, advising him to deal with parish priests before bishops. 'The reasonable ones will not press their objections provided assurances are given that the manner of taking the collection will not embarrass people attending mass.' Those priests who objected could be effectively bullied, Lemass advised. 'The others will hesitate in pressing their objections if they are given to understand that the collection will be taken nevertheless.'[176] If any priests still objected to the party fund-raising outside Mass, Lemass promised to set up a party deputation to go over the head of the priest to the relevant bishop.[177]

Maureen, his daughter, described Lemass as conventionally patriarchal at home, a disciplinarian at times. She modelled her role as wife of Charles Haughey on her mother's role as wife of Seán Lemass. Like Lemass, 'poor Charlie' never learned how to change a nappy, boil an egg or make a cup of tea.[178] It is also evident that Lemass's encouragement of a new dynamic in the party did not involve the active engagement with women in Fianna Fáil. While he encouraged Fianna Fáil ladies' committees, the minutes of these bodies reveal that they were restricted to fund-raising activities – raffles, outings, fancy dress parties, dances and suppers.[179] Unlike regular cumainn, Lemass did not chase up ladies' cumainn to ensure they were registered with party HQ or liaise with them.[180] The men dealt with the politics, the ladies could make the fairy cakes.

Lemass's opinions on artistic expression remained nationalistic and mainstream as well. Patrick Kavanagh was not the only literary figure to get on his wrong side. In 1926 riots broke out at the Abbey Theatre over a scene in Seán O'Casey's *The Plough and the Stars* where a prostitute and a tricolour appear at the same time in a pub. Thirty years later, in 1956, the 1916 Jubilee Committee, which was chaired by Lemass, replicated the Abbey protesters' intolerance for what they regarded as O'Casey's besmirching of republicanism. In considering a play to mark the celebration, the committee turned down O'Casey's realism for the idealised Gaelic Ireland of Lady Gregory's *Devorgilla*, claiming: 'O'Casey's heroes do not show the past in the proper light.'[181]

Politically, Lemass could be less than proper himself. In the summer of 1954, still smarting from the party's electoral defeat, he revived his mischievous ways of a few years previously. In July he wrote to a Fianna Fáil TD in County Meath attempting (in vain) to get him to launch allegations against a political rival in order to 'work up a lively row'.[182] The following month he wrote to Vivion de Valera in an effort (which was also refused) to get *The Irish Press* to publish a disparaging story about his latest replacement as

Minister for Industry and Commerce, Labour's James Flanagan.[183] In September of that year he instructed Lord Mayor of Cork, Pa McGrath, TD, to carry out 'a well-timed explosion' to smear Fine Gael.[184]

In 1955 Lemass began a short correspondence with a County Cork woman which raises questions about his political convictions at a time when he is generally regarded as moving to the right. The woman, a Fianna Fáil supporter named Fan McCracken, wrote to Lemass requesting

> some information on this organization known as 'ASHIREE' ... in political conversations in which I find myself sometimes this name 'ASHIREE' is quoted and I don't know what to say ... what are FF views on 'ASHIREE'?[185]

'Ashiree' referred to Ailtirí na hAiséirghe (Architects of the Resurrection), a small fascist political party formed in 1942 which had gained nine seats in the 1945 local elections. The party aimed to create a one-party, totalitarian corporatist state; to rid Ireland of Jews; to criminalise the use of the English language; to move the Irish capital to the Hill of Tara; and to carry out a reconquest of Northern Ireland.[186] Lemass replied:

> I cannot give you much information about the Asheiri Organisation. Its programme is so vague as to be almost meaningless but appears to have Fascist characteristics. It is not of political importance, but its activities in some directions, particularly in respect to the encouragement of Irish, are not without merit.[187]

Lemass's faint praise for aspects of Ailtirí na hAiséirghe's bizarre programme are disturbing. At the same time it is evident that Lemass viewed Ireland's far right as unimportant and thus undeserving of the robust condemnations he reserved for Fine Gael or, for that matter, the IRA. This is confirmed by his response to a letter Mrs McCracken wrote to him shortly afterwards in which she enclosed an anti-semitic magazine entitled *Gothic Ripples* that had been put through her letterbox by supporters of Maria Duce, a small right-wing Catholic group.[188] By this point Lemass had obviously decided that she was a crank.[189] He drily thanked McCracken for enclosing the 'extraordinary publication' and promised to put it in his 'Museum of Curiosities'.[190]

This episode illustrates how during this period Lemass, who was an impatient man at the best of times, found time to indulge queries which strayed from the point of his work. In 1956 he received a letter from an excited shopkeeper from Stradbally, County Laois, who thought he had struck oil while digging the bog. Lemass responded in lengthy geological detail, explaining that the find only indicated surface oil.[191] Tom Garvin describes Lemass's leisure-time reading tastes as 'low brow'.[192] A cursory glance over the bookshelf at his Rathfarnham home suggests otherwise; the volumes on economics are interspersed with biographies of Lenin and Edward VII, books by Trotsky and Churchill, various Irish histories, and James Plunkett's *Strumpet City*.[193]

Although he had a taste for literature, the bulk of Lemass's correspondence was to local deputies. It displayed a good working knowledge of political conditions outside Dublin. As well as advising on tactics, he flagged articles in local newspapers (usually concerning unemployment) that he felt merited reply, and even wrote draft press releases and speeches for TDs and councillors. He authored all the correspondence for a Fianna Fáil deputy in County Louth in a lengthy and bad-tempered local newspaper dispute between him and Fine Gael's Patrick Donegan, a government minister.[194] He provided support and encouragement to younger candidates such as Brian Lenihan in Roscommon, whom he advised 'not to tangle with [Jack] McQuillan' (a fiery independent) but to concentrate on winning a seat from Fine Gael.[195]

Lemass instructed local cumainn on minutiae such as the best methods of leafleting and canvassing.[196] He spoke at a considerable number of local party meetings during this period. While he usually turned down invitations to social events, he ensured that a younger member of the central organisation committee attended instead. Lemass encouraged local Fianna Fáil activists to set up new cumainn and carried out the tedious work of writing to each one with a cumann registration form, requesting monthly reports, encouraging all members and friends to attend the annual Bodenstown Commemoration in June, and congratulating them on meetings. He identified parishes and townlands where he felt thumb-twiddling and disorganisation was handing Fine Gael what he termed 'walk-overs'.[197]

Although his work symbolised a reassertion of executive power, he was quick to reprimand fellow big men in the organisation. He wrote to senior figures in the Fianna Fáil hierarchy such as Frank Aiken and Bob Briscoe to complain of lack of organisation in areas that lay on their turf. In 1957 he reprimanded rising star Donogh O'Malley for the 'irresponsible disclosure of party business to outsiders'.[198] This was not the first time that Lemass had rapped the wayward O'Malley over the knuckles. At a meeting of the Central Committee the previous year it was decided that Lemass would 'interview him and finally warn him that if he again is seen under the influence of drink he will be expelled from the party'.[199]

He was no less a stickler for the rules when it came to money. In late 1956 the party's National Executive instructed Fianna Fáil in Limerick to either let or sell their headquarters building because of debts the branch had built up. The branch protested, citing monies recently settled and the arrangement of a 'Monster Raffle' to clear the debts.[200] No favours were forthcoming from Lemass, though.[201] Dashing the hopes of the Limerick cumann, he insisted that the sale of the premises would go ahead and instructed Des O'Malley, then a leading member of the party in Limerick, to arrange it. Those who had built up debts should live with the consequences. Similarly, Lemass turned down the request of the party in Cork West that the National Executive cover some of the personal costs incurred by 'an impetuous young man' with a wife and three children who had borrowed recklessly to fund his election campaign as a Fianna Fáil candidate. 'I know that something like it has been done before,' wrote Lemass, 'but even those precedents have caused nothing but trouble.'[202]

Out With the Old, In With the New?

As well as his organisational work, this period also witnessed Lemass's assertion of policy on a range of issues outside his immediate brief. In doing so, he was stepping out of de Valera's shadow and into the limelight.

The issue of Northern Ireland provides an insight into the art of Lemassian consensus-building at party level. Significantly, whereas de Valera maintained that Britain had put the border there and therefore it was their responsibility to remove it, Lemass was beginning to see partition as something that could be resolved by Belfast and Dublin, not London. As director of organisation he sought to quell dissent from backbenchers over the party's failure to end partition (its founding pledge). Instead, he wanted to instil a more gradualist approach.[203]

With the IRA recommencing raids on British Army barracks in 1954, he was particularly keen to head off any expressions of solidarity from the party rank and file. He did so by tinkering with a resolution from Fianna Fáil Donegal West calling for unification to be achieved by peaceful means. Lemass altered the resolution by inserting a reference to the central role of the party's National Executive in achieving this goal. A National Executive Standing Committee on Partition Matters was duly created, with Lemass, as he had intended, its chairman.[204]

Lemass was to use this body as a vehicle to move towards a more progressive republican outlook on partition. But in these early tentative days he did not want to damage his republican credentials by sticking his head too far above the parapet. This task instead fell to Lionel Booth, a senior member of Fianna Fáil, who in November 1954 wrote to *The Irish Times* criticising the ambivalent attitude towards the IRA: 'Will there be an extradition agreement between the two governments, or will political offenders who escape across the border – in either direction – be treated simply as rather naughty, but forgivable, impulsive children, even in cases of armed assault?'[205]

Booth's letter provoked a lot of dissent within republican circles. Lemass advised him to send out a further letter playing down the first. He wrote to Booth, instructing him to forward his second letter to six regional newspapers who had not yet published it.[206] But a further controversy involving Booth was to erupt in the Dun Laoghaire branch of Fianna Fáil. Booth annoyed its members by defending the flying of the union flag at a regatta in the harbour. Lemass trod carefully on the issue, which caused sharp division. Ultimately, he advised the cumann to stick by their resolution to make the flying of the British flag an act of disloyalty to Fianna Fáil.[207] While ostensibly treading a middle course, Lemass was actually using Booth to test the waters. They were evidently choppy.

Between 1956 and 1962 the issue of the Republic's attitude to Northern Ireland was brought to the fore by the IRA's Border Campaign.[208] The escalation of the campaign brought out Lemass's real views on modern republican violence. On New Year's Eve 1957 IRA volunteers Seán South and Feargal O'Hanlon were killed during a raid on the RUC barracks in Brookeborough, County Fermanagh. Lemass was inundated with letters of support for the IRA. He was,

Lemass does cabaret, as imagined by C.E.K., *Dublin Opinion*, December 1955.

however, horrified by 'the outbreak of violence around the old emotions'.[209] Responding to a letter from a South Cork TD who looked favourably on the IRA's actions, Lemass condemned the IRA as 'wrong-headed men' wrecking the prospect of reunification.

> We must put the emphasis on the current economic position. This is a far more urgent question than Partition. Nobody would have the neck to urge the Six-Counties to come in until we can lick this economic problem.[210]

The central plank of Lemass's policy towards reunification – the recognition that a united Ireland would be attractive to northerners only if standards of living in the Republic improved – had been articulated by de Valera long before. Nonetheless, Lemass was not only more willing to implement cooperation *practically*, but also benefited from the *perception* that de Valera's stale anti-partitionism would go with him when he inevitably retired as Taoiseach.

That very question – exactly what would change when Lemass succeeded de Valera – was becoming more and more pressing. In the period of opposition between 1954 and 1957 de Valera was already, as Lemass was to describe him to British Prime Minister Harold Macmillan in 1959, 'very blind and only able to distinguish objects quite close to him'.[211] De Valera was also out of his depth on economic issues and had swung back to supporting the economic conservatism of MacEntee against Lemass.

In many ways, the tired old Lemass/MacEntee rivalry was still being played out on the same lines. Lemass, for instance, continued to lament the fact that all the Irish banks were 'constrained to maintain the bulk of their cash and short-term reserves in London'.[212]

'Shong Lee Mah', by C.E.K., *Dublin Opinion*, January 1953.

The two ministers disagreed sharply over budgetary policy in general and methods of taxation and spending in particular.[213]

In other respects, the goalposts had shifted. Lemass knew that he no longer had the same powers to direct economic development centrally, as he explained to a County Louth solicitor who wrote to him to complain about the lack of industrial development there:

> You do not appear to appreciate that the government has no power 'to direct' industries promoted by private persons to any locality, and is opposed, as a matter of policy, to exercising the control over private industry which would be necessary if powers of direction were desired.[214]

This was a far cry from the broad, confident strokes of his early ministerial career and indeed from the tone of his famous Clery's Ballroom speech of October 1955. In this address Lemass proposed a development plan that would create 100,000 jobs in five years. It bore all the hallmarks of the forthright developmentalism favoured by Todd Andrews and Lemass. But it was a blueprint for full employment made from opposition, and in specifying deadlines and targets invited easy criticism.

In the wake of that landmark speech, an article in a Wexford newspaper pointed out that under Lemass's stewardship the numbers in industrial employment in 1951 were lower than they were in 1926. 'During that quarter century emigration went on year by year in an unabated tide. That doesn't give Mr Lemass much "form" for the people to go on.' Lemass wrote a reply in which he admitted that his achievements 'proved not to be enough to end unemployment and emigration'. He explained that Fianna Fáil viewed a lack of investment as the main problem. He now proposed greater state and private investment. Industrial development was key to national recovery and ending emigration: 'If we get even 1,200,000 people in industrial employment in this country our population will have more than doubled by then.'[215]

The Clery's speech was attacked by the government for its conspicuous omission of the agricultural sector.[216] Prior to delivering the speech Lemass wrote to a party worker in west Cork explaining that 'detailed plans for improving the efficiency of production in agriculture are an integral part of the whole idea' but conceding that 'these plans have yet to be publicised'.[217] Clearly, he still wanted wide-ranging structural change in agriculture and had complained about the 'extraordinary inflexibility of agricultural production'.[218] But the illiberal licence which the Emergency afforded was long gone. It was politically prudent to leave agriculture on the back burner instead of tackling it head on.

As demonstrated by a 1955 correspondence, Lemass still held a conviction in the efficacy of 'compulsory acquisition' of land by the state (in other words, the eviction of unproductive farmers from their land). Lemass thought this was the best way to improve farm productivity and speed up afforestation. He had learned, however, that 'compulsory acquisition can result in very considerable difficulties if local feeling is strongly against it'.[219] Lemass had come to realise that the reorganisation of the sector would have to include a nod towards vocational endeavour as well as state direction. He envisaged the creation of farmers' councils, which would have 'the attraction that its members would be his own neighbours elected by himself'; they would also enjoy 'wide powers in the matter of providing credit', resulting in 'more efficient production'.[220]

In the wake of the Clery's speech Fianna Fáil representatives clambered to recover lost ground by emphasising that Lemass did possess at least some plans for agriculture. In a speech printed in *The*

Irish Press in March 1956 Brian Lenihan elaborated on the party's plans for the sector: drainage, land reclamation and afforestation.[221] Lemass thanked him, writing: 'Fine Gael is trying to give the impression that we are interested only in urban employment and that this has to be countered. Your remarks were very much to the point.'[222]

Yet in a 1956 letter to a colleague in County Louth Lemass revealed that his overriding concern remained employment *outside* the agricultural sector.

> The Fianna Fáil Full Employment proposals contemplate placing the main reliance on expansion of agricultural output ... It is recognised, however, that agricultural output could be very greatly expanded without a corresponding expansion of agricultural employment, and that new jobs to end unemployment and emigration must of necessity be found *outside* agriculture.[223]

Addressing the Federation of Irish Manufacturers back in February 1945 Lemass had elaborated on the aim of self-sufficiency. 'We do not use the term in the absurd sense . . . as involving a Robinson Crusoe type of economy . . . self-sufficiency, as we understand it, is synonymous with full employment.'[224] He remained committed to this policy. In a letter to a party member in County Limerick written shortly before the Clery's speech Lemass conceded that too much state investment could increase inflation, but when it came down to the fundamentals he argued: 'I would much rather see the Country faced with problems now arising in Britain from over-full employment and excessive internal consumption than our present problem of continuing emigration.'[225]

He added: 'I believe that if we were to bring about a situation in which private capital would be seeking investment openings in Ireland, it would result in developments in directions which could not now be foreseen.'[226] This was a clear assertion of the 'economic turn' Lemass was to oversee on his final return to power. To Patrick Kavanagh, such eagerness to attract inward investment resembled 'prostitution' to the Yank; but to Lemass, the social pay-off was the prospect of better living standards as a result.

The prospect of the 'economic turn' away from protectionism raised questions about the future role of the state in Irish life. To Liam Skinner – Lemass's first biographer, who was writing at this time – new thinking on economic direction could not gloss over his subject's great sin: the rapid expansion of the state. 'Seán Lemass has not yet surrendered all the powers given to him by emergency legislation,' Skinner wrote. These 'dictatorial powers' marked 'the road leading to abuse of power, corruption, public scandal, and the undermining of democracy'.[227]

To Skinner, Lemass's use of the state could not be divorced from 'an evil and pernicious tendency in our time, when the movement towards a "Welfare State" threatens to steamroll the rights of the family and the individual. The "Welfare State" is the euphemistic title of State control in the absolute.'[228] 'They can't help us without fettering us!' Skinner declared. 'If bureaucrats have their way, our people will become patterned in one common mould. Individuality quickly becomes a crime in the omnicompetent State.'[229] He went on to attack Noël Browne's Mother and Child Scheme and praised a 'vigilant hierarchy' for their success in 'thwarting these staggering designs'. To Skinner, the choice facing Ireland was 'to remain a free people or to become mere serfs of the State'.[230]

Skinner's concerns echoed those of Archbishop of Dublin John Charles McQuaid, who in 1956 expressed his concern that Lemass, de Valera and Aiken were 'socialising' the economy. Skinner and McQuaid need not have been so alarmed. Adjusting to the realities of the post-war world, Lemass recognised sooner than his cabinet colleagues that the creation of the British welfare state increased the pressure on Irish policy-makers to move in a similar direction. And yet he was no welfarist. There is evidence that his 'Victorian' conception of the ills of idle poverty persisted. While Lemass thought that the state should be responsible for putting an end to large-scale unemployment, he still regarded some of the Irish unemployed as 'work shy'.[231] In 1955, a Westmeath county councillor wrote to him proposing a cottage garden cultivation scheme, where tenants of council cottages would receive a small amount of free seeds and fertilisers to encourage them to garden. Lemass replied: 'Few people put any value on what they get for nothing' and concentrated on the punitive side of the scheme, dismissing it because 'penalties on a tenant who failed to use his garden properly would be very difficult to enforce'.[232] There was no 'omnicompetent State' in evidence here. Incidentally, Lemass's erstwhile scheme of 'Military service or a period in a labour corps', precipitated by the removal of dole payments, was to remain the preferred method of dealing with 'the unemployable' for the Knights of Columbanus.[233]

Neither was Lemass as close to Noël Browne as Skinner made out. Browne joined Fianna Fáil in 1953, a move which was met with hostility from the Fianna Fáil rank and file. This was demonstrated by a 1956 letter from Browne's solicitor to a party member who had made a speech at the party's Ard-Fheis suggesting he was a communist. The letter, a copy of which was sent to Lemass, affirmed that Browne was a 'practising Catholic'.[234] Lemass entertained Browne initially but, when asked about his Mother and Child Scheme later in life, was dismissive. 'In a matter of two or three years', Lemass claimed, Fianna Fáil had implemented a similar scheme 'more expertly'.[235]

'More expertly' was a euphemism for 'less comprehensively'.[236] Fianna Fáil's 1953 Health Bill was paltry by comparison to Browne's. It addressed the burden of motherhood by establishing free pre- and post-natal care but retained the old system of having to pay for doctors' visits. In negotiations with the bishops Lemass – who was the acting head of government in de Valera's absence for eye treatment – had played the good Catholic, dutifully listening to McQuaid's claims that socialised medicine was contrary to Church teaching.[237] It was neither the first nor the last time that he would appease McQuaid's outrageous conservatism in the name of political pragmatism.

The Health Bill succeeded, nonetheless, in giving Fianna Fáil the radical tinge which Lemass cherished. He had upset the bishops in discussions over its implementation, describing motherhood as a recurrent 'hazard', a burden which often spanned fifteen years of married life.[238] Although it did not come within his specific brief, Lemass was receptive to health issues and in 1955 replied to a query about facilities for mentally ill children in Ireland by frankly admitting that they were 'entirely inadequate'.[239]

The fact remains that in the critical showdown between the forces of progress and those of conservatism Lemass had remained tight lipped, focused on party political advantage. He viewed the passionate Browne as an 'inept' politician.[240] Lemass laid it down as a maxim to his young protégés that election promises became invalid the day after the count.[241] Browne came from outside the party fold, possessing an 'inept' lack of tutelage in this cynical principle. Lemass's opinion of Browne may have been coloured by the fact that the fastidious Lemass regularly sent him clippings from local newspapers from different counties to provide him with material for speeches he was making around the country. The headstrong Browne never wrote back to Lemass to thank him or discuss these issues.[242]

Lemass's essentially conservative social outlook is demonstrated in an exchange of letters between him and the secretary of a Cork party branch in June 1956. Lemass declared himself in favour of a reorganisation of the income tax code to include a 'marriage dowry' scheme. Under the proposal, after a wage earner turned twenty-one a 'five-year plan' was activated. If the worker married within the five-year period all the income tax accrued by the exchequer would be paid back as a 'marriage dowry'. The scheme would renew itself every five years and end when the individual was forty-five. It would encourage people to wait until they were twenty-six to marry, meaning they would be able to 'help parents for a reasonable time after growing up'.[243] Lemass was thinking in new ways economically, but socially he still conformed to a conservative idiom.

Lemass's social conservatism, often obscured by his populist baiting of the Labour Party, was perhaps the most reassuring facet of his character in the eyes of contemporary observers. His standing as the likely successor to the devout de Valera raised hopes but also concerns. These concerns centred on what exactly Lemass's brand of materialism represented. To commentators like Skinner, Lemass's materialism raised the spectre of the 'omnicompetent State'. To others, the least desirable aspect of Lemass's materialism was the vision of shallow individualism evoked by Kavanagh.

In terms of the latter, the rise of Charles Haughey under Lemass's wing demands consideration. Haughey was a young Commerce graduate of UCD. An accountant by trade, he became involved in Fianna Fáil in 1948. In 1951 he married Maureen, Lemass's eldest daughter. Haughey's early political career was disappointing. He ran unsuccessfully for the Dáil in Dublin North East in 1951 and 1954. He was co-opted onto Dublin Corporation in 1953 but suffered the ignominy of losing his seat at the local elections in 1955.

Lemass's nakedly opportunistic son-in-law was not well liked within the party. Frank Aiken regarded him as a wolf in Fianna Fáil garb. Lemass was better disposed towards Haughey and worked closely with him in the task of reorganisation. Their correspondence from this period shows that Lemass addressed Haughey 'Dear Charlie' when writing to him, but on occasion did not shirk from adopting the same impatient tone, bordering on rudeness, that he often struck with organisers elsewhere in the country.[244]

In early 1955 Lemass received a letter from George Colley, secretary of the party's Dublin North East branch, threatening his resignation. His anger had been aroused by the nomination of a certain unnamed party member as a candidate. Colley and others regarded this man as corrupt. Colley felt so strongly about the issue that he told Lemass that to stay on as secretary 'would be condoning bribery and corruption in public life'.[245] Colley insisted that the candidature of this individual 'implicates the whole organisation unless the action is completely repudiated' and that he should 'not have been ratified by the National Executive'.[246] These robust opinions are likely to have made Lemass feel very uncomfortable: Haughey was a member of the same cumann as Colley. Frustratingly, Lemass's reply to Colley does not survive. Evidently, Lemass smothered the issue privately. It is consequently unclear to whom Colley was referring.

Two years later Colley's father, Harry Colley, was to lose his seat to the ambitious Haughey, the latter's fourth attempt to win a seat in the Dáil.[247] Months later, at the AGM of Fianna Fáil's Dublin North East operation, it was noted with disgust that the party in that area had been subjected to 'infiltration by individuals whose interests were more personal than patriotic'.[248] 'The self-seeker will soon see that Fianna Fáil is an organisation of service and not a ladder for his ambition and he will soon steal away,' the report claimed.[249] Horgan claims that it was Haughey who authored this report.[250] However, the tone of the report suggests that it was Colley who wrote it, with Haughey in his sights. Even if Haughey did author the report, it was clearly intended to quell concerns centring on his character.

Within the party Lemass was obviously aware of the distinction between 'decent men' and 'less desirable types', as he put it himself.[251] He was certainly conscious of the bad rumours that attached themselves to Haughey. Lemass's 'dictatorial' role in vetoing the candidacy of people like the unfortunate Mrs Drennan from Carlow begs an obvious question. Why did he not do more to stunt Charles Haughey's rise within Fianna Fáil?

The familial tie was undoubtedly very important. But, most significantly, Haughey represented the new ethic Lemass was keen to instil in Fianna Fáil: he was young and good at cultivating business contacts. During the 1950s Lemass came to realise the limits of protectionism and state intervention and encouraged the attributes of self-reliance and enterprise instead. As well as injecting a certain dynamism, this general transition would result in the emergence of 'less desirable types' in the party. But it was a gamble Lemass was willing to take in his efforts to shake things up.

Haughey's leading role in the establishment of the new 'special Central Branch' of the party – 'Comh Chomhairle Átha Cliath' – shows that Lemass recognised that Haughey possessed the qualities he was keen to instil. This new branch did not, as Lemass described it, have 'any function in fighting elections'. Instead it would recruit 'a number of fee paying associate members'.[252] Lemass's standards precluded any such flaunting of the party's business contacts. The new branch aimed, in his words, to 'extend the contacts of the organisation amongst influential people in *all classes*'.[253]

In real terms, however, the new body sought to establish links with businessmen whose direct association with the party may have been viewed as a conflict of interest. Lemass confessed that he was 'worried' about finance at this time;[254] a number of cumainn were falling short or failing altogether to raise funds for the party's national collection; to put it simply, a cash cow was needed. In a letter to Haughey, Lemass spoke more frankly about Comh Chomhairle's membership. It would be composed of 'people who are unable, for personal or business reasons, to take a more active part'.[255] Lemass disliked ostentation but at the same time recognised that the suave, personable Haughey was certainly the man for this sort of endeavour.

Lemass evidently set up the new branch as an elite, Dublin-centric vehicle to influence policy direction. The members of the organisation's provisional committee wanted it renamed 'Forum Fáil' in order to indicate its influence on formulating party policy, but this suggestion was quashed.[256] The branch's 'special status' was nonetheless affirmed by its leadership, which was appointed by the National Executive. De Valera was president and Lemass, MacEntee and Oscar Traynor were named as vice-presidents.[257] Its list of guest speakers included de Valera, Lemass (twice) and the president of the National Farmers' Association.[258] Ordinary branches up and down the country had asked Lemass for speakers of such standing, only to receive negative replies. Haughey noted that 'discussions which followed the reading of the papers were not of a very high standard'. This was not a problem because the branch's main function – fund-raising – proved more effective. The subscriptions of the branch's 'associate members' swelled the party's coffers.[259]

Haughey's ambition was nauseating, but he had youthful energy in abundance. This attribute was thrown into relief for Lemass when health problems again consigned him to hospital for a number of months between 1956 and 1957. In February 1957, just before the general election, Lemass wrote to Ned Cotter, a Fianna Fáil deputy for Bantry, County Cork. Cotter's health was ailing and Lemass reminded him that if he was re-elected it would mean 'regular attendance at the Dáil'.[260] In doing so he must have privately hoped that his own health would not again become a reason for lengthy absences from politics.

Ar Ais Arís

By 1957 a slowdown in the building industry, rising unemployment and fuel shortages were aggravating a sense of economic despair. Divisions in the second inter-party government were increasingly apparent and John A. Costello moved for a general election in March of that year. Lemass masterminded Fianna Fáil's election campaign, adopting the typically energetic slogan 'Let's Get Cracking!' The content of Lemass's 1955 Clery's speech was the keynote of his party's election campaign.[261] Before the election he instructed that copies of a similar address of his, entitled 'Proposals for Recovery', be distributed for discussion to every cumann in the country.

Lemass redoubled his energetic efforts as director of organisation during the campaign. According to James Ryan, on one occasion Lemass undertook the then arduous journey from Dublin to Tralee and back in one day, motoring down there to speak and then getting back in his car and returning to Dublin immediately afterwards. He kept tiredness at bay by continuously eating bars of chocolate.[262] He used the 1957 election campaign to distance himself from his record during the Emergency. A decade earlier wartime survival was his main election message. He now insisted that Fianna Fáil did not believe in methods of compulsion, whether compulsory tillage, wage regulation, or undue influence on private business – 'none of these forms any part of our plans'.[263]

The coalition having collapsed in on itself, Fianna Fáil reaped the benefits at the polls and were able to form a majority administration comfortably. Sticking to his conviction that coalition governments were doomed by their very nature, Lemass viewed the government's defeat as 'the consequence of their own actions', blaming the government's policy of import restriction.[264] With Fianna Fáil's victory de Valera again became Taoiseach and Lemass was re-appointed Tánaiste.

Fianna Fáil, back in power. *Dublin Opinion*, April 1957.

Archbishop McQuaid was one of the first people to send Lemass a message of congratulation. Lemass wrote back, expressing his 'deep thanks' to McQuaid, and signing off 'Your Grace's Obedient Servant'.[265]

The old guard may have been back in office, but that did not mean that the knives had been put away. Lemass was now openly in favour of abandoning the economic nationalism a generation had grown used to. His enthusiasm for the coalition government's application to join the rapidly emerging European Free Trade Area (EFTA) bloc – a British alternative to the emerging European Economic Community (EEC) – drew opposition from Gerald Boland, who refused to drop the principle of industrial development based on native resources. Lemass responded by drawing the dagger: he was instrumental in de Valera's decision to drop his long-time colleague Boland from the cabinet in 1957.[266]

For Lemass, of course, there was a more significant scalp than Boland's to be had. With the party back in power de Valera acceded to Lemass's insistence that MacEntee, his oldest rival, vacate the Finance portfolio to make way for the milder James Ryan. After losing ground in the early 1950s, Lemass's ascendancy in this personal battle was now confirmed. All this time, he was busy firming up party adherence to the Central Committee's line; this mostly involved compelling deputies to withdraw motions by 'explaining' the position to them. On one occasion, just before he was made

Taoiseach, his son Noel was obliged to withdraw a motion urging that it be made easier to import vintage cars after receiving a dreaded 'explanation' from his father.[267]

Despite relinquishing his position as director of organisation, Lemass did not idly revel in the party's success. Instead he wrote to each cumann in the country, telling them that 'the overwhelming victory of Fianna Fáil at the general election has created a new spirit of confidence in the minds of the people', before getting to his main point: the need to raise funds through collections after Mass in order to maintain 'a live and effective organisation which will be the eyes and ears of the government throughout the country'.[268]

Back at his desk at Industry and Commerce's impressive Kildare Street HQ, the centre of operations he had fought for and seen realised, he contented himself with a notable increase in national industrial production. In order to sustain this growth, Europe was now the overriding goal. As the British Trade Commissioner noted in a 1957 memorandum, Irish moves to enter the EFTA placed industrial development highest on the agenda. In a nutshell, 'the infinitely wider market which membership of the area would offer to Irish goods would make investment in Irish industry much more attractive to foreign investors'.[269] At the same time, British sources recognised that Lemass did not want to plunge Ireland head first into a free trade zone. He wanted 'special treatment' – the ability to preserve selective protective tariffs 'for so long as might be necessary'.[270] As with the evolution of Lemass's other policies, the 'turn' away from protectionism would be a gradual process.

Domestically as well, Lemass's stance was changing. During the Emergency he had overseen a cessation in private motoring; now he acquiesced in the demise of public transport. Previously, he had indicated that he was opposed to any diminution of the rail network. In July 1948 the 'Dáil Reporter' declared his opposition to the cuts to stations and branch lines that had occurred in Britain, blaming them on transport planning based around the 'concentric zone' urban land use model of the American sociologist Ernest Burgess.[271] In the mid-1950s, too, Lemass supported the campaign of the County Monaghan Fianna Fáil organisation against line closures[272] and tried to secure the reinstatement of sacked railway workers in County Louth.[273] In 1958, however, CIÉ took the devastating step of closing down train lines and stations that were considered un-economic. The long-term impact was the dislocation of communities

Lemass's enthusiasm for air travel features in *Dublin Opinion's* 'Children's Art Competition', February 1958.

and the ascendancy of the motor car over public transport in rural Ireland. The closures were overseen by Lemass's old colleague Todd Andrews, the chairman of CIÉ, and his younger brother Frank, general manager of the company, who had been agitating for such cuts for years.[274]

If Lemass had really wanted to prevent the closure of railway branch lines he could have done, but he did not.[275] In broader ideological terms, this reflected the fact that Lemass's famous impatience was taking on new forms. He was, by this point, more firm in his adherence to post-war American modernisation theory.[276] This theory rested on the assumption of a dichotomous relationship between traditional and modern societies and Lemass was determined to place Ireland in the latter. For Lemass, the totalising brush stroke of 'modernisation' was positive, anything that got in its way was trite, stuffy and negative.

Andrews justified the closure of 700 miles of railway lines and over 300 stations in Lemassian terms. This was an uncomfortable step to take, he said, but modernisation had to take precedence over sentimentalism based around 'folklore', 'landscape', and 'the mind of rural Ireland'.[277] Lemass may have lamented the diminution of the Irish rail network in the early 1950s but, as suggested by the depiction of the sun-god Lugh launching aeroplanes from the walls of his HQ, his real passion was for air travel. In pursuing its growth, some of

The party succession
issue, *Dublin Opinion*,
February 1959.

the Haughey attitude seems to have rubbed off on him. Brendan O'Regan, who managed Shannon Airport, remembers Lemass telling him: 'If I could get the industrial zone going as I had promised I could have the land for a shilling an acre and 35 years tax exemption.'[278] As the chintzy slogans beloved of Lemass and the new commercial Ireland suggested, he felt the country was finally 'going places'; this forward momentum had to be kept up at all costs.

The teleological characterisation of Lemass and the economist T. K. Whitaker as the modernising saviours of Ireland requires some qualification, nonetheless.[279] Not only were Ireland's fortunes linked to international economic developments, but in promoting economic change Lemass was much less strident in challenging the social and cultural norms of old Ireland than has been assumed. In early 1959 Liam Skinner visited Lemass at home and composed a pipe-and-slippers portrait of the future Taoiseach at fifty-nine years of age.

> [The Lemasses] live quietly in the quiet south city suburb of Rathfarnham in a modest bungalow, typically suburban. They entertain but little, and attendance at a dance or other social events is infrequent. Seán Lemass relaxes during the week-end, with his pipe and a book, usually a historical novel, although he has gathered a library of books on political science and economics. He took to the pipe during the Truce, in 1921, but does not drink. Fine weather sometimes tempts him to the golf links at Skerries, where his club handicap was twelve. It is the only outdoor game he has ever played, and he says himself that he is only a 'fair weather' golfer. A Saturday afternoon race meeting more frequently attracts him, with his wife and a few intimate friends . . . He has a strong, well-knit figure, above

medium height, and with powerful shoulders. His weight I
estimate at about twelve stone. His face has filled out in recent
years. It indicates strength and power, both in expression and
outline. The long, pointed nose over the clipped, slight
moustache is in harmony with the determined mouth and jaw.
The raven-black hair, innocent of greyness, is brushed straight
back from the wide sweep of brow. The expressive brown eyes
seem to twinkle at times, to detract a little from the stern aspect
of the clear-cut features. His smile is attractive, perhaps because
of its rarity. He well deserves his reputation as the best-dressed
member of the Government. The vivacious mentality is
reflected in his frequent changes of suits, and his favourite is a
grey-striped dark brown. In recent years he has taken to
wearing the black broad-rimmed hat named after Sir Anthony
Eden. Lemass walks quickly, taking short, snappy steps, but
speaks slowly.

This portrayal is far removed from the image of the dynamic leader
waiting in the wings. But de Valera's increasingly embarrassing
irrelevance to modern Irish life meant the whiff of change was in
the air. In January 1959 the chief announced his intention to retire.
Just six months later he was gone.

The Fianna Fáil parliamentary party and National Executive met
on 22 June 1959 to elect a new leader. Lemass was proposed by
MacEntee and seconded by Aiken. The following day he was
officially elected Taoiseach by the Dáil. No national leader, or Prime
Minister, north or south of the border, before or since, has spent as
long as an elected representative before assuming the highest office.
At last, the succession was complete.

6

Taoiseach

The Early Winds of Change

Seán Lemass was elected Taoiseach by the Dáil on 23 June 1959, shortly before his sixtieth birthday. Tom Garvin holds a rose-tinted view of Lemass's accession to power; a national coming-of-age that happened to coincide with his own coming-of-age: 'I was nearly sixteen in that beautiful summer month and I remember walking down the Rathmines Road in Dublin with a friend, who remarked, "You know, Tom, we might not have to emigrate."'[1]

Economic growth during Lemass's term as Taoiseach coincided with that arbitrary yet influential way of compartmentalising historical time: the turn of a new decade. The bleak 1950s were about to give way to the Swinging Sixties. Ireland was building and the economy was booming. But Garvin goes further, seeing the crucial national change initiated by Lemass in his period as Taoiseach as *cultural*, claiming that Lemass unleashed the social and psychological forces of change as well as the economic.[2] This, it is argued below, is a lopsided appraisal of Lemass's impact as Taoiseach.

Nonetheless, it was evident that things would be different under Lemass.[3] His premiership was influenced by a key document authored by the top civil servant at the Department of Finance, Thomas Kenneth (T. K.) Whitaker. Published in 1958, Whitaker's *Economic Development* advocated a sea change in Irish economic policy: the replacement of protectionism with free trade.[4] The main argument of Whitaker's survey, which James Ryan brought to cabinet, was that the country needed to greatly increase capital investment. In terms of broad national direction, the '1958 turn' provided the final confirmation that the economic status quo of a generation had failed and was now to be abandoned.

Later that year, Lemass's government published its first *Programme for Economic Expansion* based on *Economic Development*. In his first speech as Taoiseach on 24 June 1959 the erstwhile Minister for Industry and Commerce affirmed the centrality of this new economic programme to government policy. Unemployment and emigration were the national priority: as he was the man to tackle both, there would be no quick general election.

Lemass (fourth from right), seated opposite de Valera at the latter's last Cabinet meeting in 1959. Courtesy *The Irish Press*.

For Fianna Fáil, a party that was essentially populist in its reflexes, the attention Lemass gave to *Economic Development* firmly elevated the role of programmatic politics in internal decision making. Moreover, his manner of implementing such decisions represented a pronounced change to de Valera's leadership style. Des O'Malley recalls:

> When I was in my early twenties and living at home the telephone would ring in the evening. About once a month at least. I'd be sent out to answer the phone. It would be Lemass himself, not a secretary. The first time I went back and told my father 'there's some chancer on the phone pretending to be Seán Lemass'. But after a few calls I realised it was genuine. I asked my father, who was a solicitor, 'why is he ringing you?' My father replied that Lemass had several people around the country in different walks of life whom he would use as a sounding board for various ideas. When he wanted to know what the Irish people were thinking he got on the telephone and asked them. Unlike Dev, of course, who only had to consult his heart.[5]

Around the cabinet table Lemass encouraged his ministers to develop policy within their own departments, but gave them little opportunity to debate. Whereas de Valera would allow meetings to

Lemass's first Cabinet meeting, 24 June 1959. Seán McEntee is seated on Lemass's right, with James Ryan, Erskine Childers and Jack Lynch to his left. Courtesy *The Irish Press.*

continue for hours, Lemass was 'brusque and peremptory', as Jack Lynch described his style.[6] He could be stubborn, too. Neil Blaney, a young minister in Lemass's cabinet, recalled that 'once he did not speak to me for six to seven months after I told him in writing what I thought about his refusal to meet a deputation from the flour millers' association'.[7]

This approach extended to his former empire. In swapping the Department of Industry and Commerce for the Department of the Taoiseach Lemass was not prepared to let anyone get their hands on the ministerial powerhouse he had created. As with many imperial withdrawals, he resorted to divide and conquer, quickly announcing the break-up of Industry and Commerce.[8]

At Lemass's instruction public discussion by party members of certain issues, such as expenses, was banned because of the 'unfavourable political reactions' it would cause.[9] At parliamentary party meetings, his role in ensuring discipline shifted from ministerial 'explanation' to 'intimation'. Despite the change in terminology noticeable in the party papers, Lemass's 'intimations' still held decisive sway over these gatherings. But the terminology had changed in another significant way. Whereas de Valera was always recorded as 'the chief' in these minutes, Lemass was referred to as 'An Taoiseach'. Clearly, there could only ever be one chief. Todd Andrews observed that the bond of loyalty that had existed under de Valera disappeared when Lemass became Taoiseach.

> Snide remarks about one another were common enough. Accounts of Cabinet meetings were leaked and often discussed with outsiders. In Dev's time it would have been impossible to

imagine cabals within the Cabinet or the party, but they were certainly organized during Seán Lemass's time . . . there was always personal tension within his Cabinet which finally crystallized in the contest for the succession.[10]

In the popular imagination, the businessman had replaced the dreamer. The most flamboyant cabal in Lemass's cabinet did little to dispel this impression. Charles Haughey, Brian Lenihan and Donogh O'Malley – dubbed the 'three musketeers' or 'the men in the mohair suits' – brazenly canoodled with speculators and builders in Dublin bars and restaurants. These young men's gross flaunting of political influence was punctuated by more endearingly boisterous high jinks (such as stealing a duck from St Stephen's Green and bringing a street busker and his dog into the exclusive Shelbourne hotel for dinner).[11] Their actions are stained by elitism nonetheless. Relative to de Valera's earthiness, Lemass brought a whiff of commercial exclusivity to office. He was accused of nepotism when his ambitious son-in-law was appointed parliamentary secretary to the Minister for Justice, Oscar Traynor, in 1959. According to Haughey, Lemass advised him not to take the post. The fact remains that Traynor was bitterly opposed to Haughey's appointment and Lemass personally rejected three other potential candidates for the job.[12]

According to Des O'Malley, Haughey 'craved the approval of the older generation'. When he attended the funerals of the old guard – such as James Ryan, who predeceased Lemass by a year – he made sure to bring a photographer with him.[13] The sort of naked personal ambition that Haughey symbolised sat uneasily with what many regarded as the Fianna Fáil ethos, encapsulated a few years earlier by Lemass in a letter to a Fianna Fáil supporter in Offaly:

> The qualifications and personalities of candidates are becoming of increasing importance in securing electoral success, but there can be no question that for Fianna Fáil the overriding consideration must always remain their understanding of and loyalty to party policy.[14]

Lemass, it seems, ignored these traits in his son-in-law because he placed a greater value on the necessity for youthful dynamism to shake up a conservative inaction politically and economically.[15] Young men like Haughey represented an alternative to what Lemass described as 'a tendency' in some government departments 'to wait for new ideas to walk through the door'.[16]

Lemass breaks up his old department.
Dublin Opinion, August 1959.

Lemass, as new Taoiseach, goes Christmas shopping.
Dublin Opinion, December 1959.

But for all these early signs of change, the cynical Lemass remained the consummate political operator. By the time he was Taoiseach, he had lost his early fervour for radical Seanad reform;[17] as a political manager, Lemass had come to recognise that the upper house had its uses. In the discussion over his nomination as Taoiseach, Fine Gael's John A. Costello attacked what he saw as Fianna Fáil's effort to use populism to alter the character of Irish democracy. The party had unsuccessfully attempted to replace proportional representation with a first-past-the-post system by coinciding the vote with the presidential referendum, which elevated de Valera to Áras an Uachtaráin.[18] Lemass, one of the most outspoken advocates of the first-past-the-post system, was integral to this manipulation of the national interest for party political reasons, viewing proportional representation (rather than partition) as 'Lloyd George's worst legacy' in Ireland.[19] But with voting reform defeated by popular vote, Lemass as Taoiseach would have to make do with the old system.

As Taoiseach, Lemass felt the distrust surrounding his 'business-man' image keenly. He insisted that the economic 'turn' would not impact cultural integrity. Responding to concerns about the cultural cost of economic change, he mentioned in his first speech as Taoiseach that the revival of the Irish language was integral to progress.[20] He would later oppose Fine Gael's plans to abolish compulsory Irish in schools.[21] If this fidelity to the language jars with the popular image of Lemass-the-moderniser, it is clear that from the earliest stages as Taoiseach he was keen to make up ground he felt he had lost on de Valera. He knew that some prominent public figures, such as the Cork-based writer and cultural protectionist Daniel Corkery, did not trust him, believing no Dubliner should be Taoiseach because they simply did not understand the rest of the country.[22] Admitting that his 'urban mentality' had been criticised, Lemass asserted: 'I had to be born somewhere.'[23] He felt this sense of grievance keenly enough to mention it to Macmillan as well. When the British Prime Minister asked what part of Ireland he was from 'Mr. Lemass said that he and his family all came from Dublin: this had indeed been advanced as an argument against his becoming Prime Minister.'[24]

If this provides a rare example of Lemassian anxiety, he still exhibited the same ruthless willingness to shift position and loyalty when political need took precedence over principle. He was, of course, a long-standing critic of Fianna Fáil's approach to land settlement and agricultural productivity.[25] In 1958 Erskine Childers junior upset the traditionalists in the party by advocating large commercial farms and the cessation of the allotment of land to the landless. Lemass essentially agreed with Childers on this issue, but it was unpopular with the party's rearguard. To quell dissent Lemass relegated Childers to Minister for Transport and Power on becoming Taoiseach.[26]

Lemass's early changes as Taoiseach were not always so decisive. Garvin argues that Lemass was responsible for fostering competition among the young blood of the party such as Haughey, George Colley and Donogh O'Malley, ridding it of the old de Valeran 'gerontocracy'.[27] But as a veteran of 1916, the Independence struggle and the Civil War, Lemass himself embodied the old guard like no other. Rather than a 'breath of fresh air', as de Valera saw him,[28] he was viewed by the opposition – and many sections of Irish society – as offering more of the same. When de Valera retired in 1959 there were still four members of his original 1932 cabinet in office: Lemass, Seán MacEntee, Jim Ryan and Frank Aiken. Lemass frankly admitted to conservativism when it came to ministerial appointments. He was unwilling to execute a rejuvenative cull and these 'boys of the old brigade' remained intact until 1965, a year before his own retirement.

Even his young guns relied on familial ties. Kevin Boland, whom Lemass appointed Minister for Social Welfare in 1959, was the son of Gerald Boland. Neil Blaney, the son of an IRA commandant from Donegal, was kept on as Minister for Local Government by Lemass; he had been given a cabinet position by de Valera in 1957. Brian Lenihan, appointed Minister for Justice in 1964, was the son of Paddy Lenihan, a friend of Lemass's whom he had installed as a textiles manufacturer in Athlone in the 1930s.[29] Son-in-law Haughey, Lemass's only new appointment to the cabinet after the 1961 election, became Minister for Justice. Army officer Jack O'Brien, the husband of Lemass's daughter Peggy, was appointed aide de camp to the new Taoiseach in 1959. Of course, like these young men, Lemass, in his early political career, relied on a prominent relative as his key asset.

Europe and the Coming of Free Trade

If the early stages of Lemass's premiership delivered a mixture of change and continuity, the decision of the Fianna Fáil government to seek membership of the European Economic Community (EEC) signalled the clearest break yet from protectionism towards export-led industrialisation and economic cooperation with Europe. Lemass was moving the country towards free trade, dismantling the protectionist structures he himself had erected. This was, by any standards, a remarkable U-turn. Politically, it threatened the hallowed nationalist principle of Irish ownership of industry. Economically, it presented an unwelcome threat to both the Irish bourgeoisie and workers in protected industries.

On the first score – the charge of a 'sell out' of republican principles – Lemass had secured the political death of his principal opponent and old comrade Gerald Boland in 1957.[30] On the second score, it is evident from his speeches as Taoiseach that Lemass sidestepped a good deal of opposition by dealing with free trade and foreign investment as separate issues. His keenness to separate the two issues demonstrates that Ireland's economic transition was not as seamless as has been suggested.[31] John Leydon, Lemass's erstwhile quiet and faithful sidekick, came out strongly against opening up the economy too rapidly. Industry and Commerce, as usual, engaged in mudslinging with Finance over the wisdom of the policy. There was an inconsistency in Lemass plumping fully for free trade while his old department provided the main opposition to this policy.[32] Finance protested too; but the robust criticism Whitaker faced from within his own department did not stop him teasing Industry and Commerce over its defensive attitude.

In meetings in London in 1958 and 1959 Lemass discussed the British initiative of an Economic Free Trade Area. Cardinal John D'Alton, the head of the Catholic Church in Ireland, had recently unveiled a well-received and eponymous 'plan' which proposed that Ireland rejoin the Commonwealth as an independent republic, like India, for trade reasons, whether or not Britain, Ireland or both gained or were refused entry to the Common Market.[33] The Knights of Columbanus, too, welcomed the EFTA as a 'bulwark against communism'.[34] And de Valera, just prior to his retirement, was secretly sounding out British opinion on a united Ireland joining the Commonwealth.[35]

For Lemass, however, the European Common Market was the more attractive option, though he did not want to sacrifice precious Anglo-Irish trade to European tariffs. In the end Lemass ruled out rejoining the Commonwealth but declared himself open to the EFTA. Membership of a free trade Europe raised the possibility of ending dependence on the British market: a consistent, long-term goal of Lemass's. But Ireland's very application to be part of the club rested on the success of Britain's. Effectively, Ireland could only end dependence on the British market by hanging on to Britain's coat-tails.

A British government memorandum advising what line to take with the Irish in trade talks between the two countries conveyed how close and, to an extent interdependent, the economic relation-ship between Britain and Ireland was:

> We need to be at pains in the trade negotiations that lie ahead to bear in mind the possible political importance, in terms of closer relations with the Republic, of not giving the Irish too raw a deal. They are a very substantial market of ours and their prosperity is, therefore, of some concern to us, they provide a substantial amount of our labour force ... and we are, of course, of the greatest importance to them as we take their cattle etc.[36]

Lemass's own position at this pivotal stage was summarised neatly in the memo. It went on to discuss the costs to Ireland of hastily joining the EEC:

> They [the Irish] appreciate that they would lose the benefit of preferences in the United Kingdom for their industrial exports and that they could not hope to attain compensating benefits in Europe, either through improved industrial or agricultural exports ... a hint was dropped to the Irish that the Irish as a peripheral must not go very fast in giving up protection for their industry.[37]

At this stage the British government was wary of 'the Six', the coun-tries who had established a European common market through the 1957 Treaty of Rome: Belgium, France, Germany, Italy, Luxembourg and the Netherlands. It was keen to maintain existing bilateral trade arrangements with Ireland and did not want to jeopardise them by committing to the fast-track abolition of tariffs. British negotiators noted that their reluctance to embrace European free trade 'was, of course, agreeable to Lemass',[38] who recognised that abolishing tariffs too quickly could be very damaging to the Irish economy.

The British judged that Lemass regarded the EFTA 'on balance in the long run to be beneficial'.[39] Senior British officials thought him

> a practical, down to earth man, I think well-disposed towards us (not for historical, but for practical reasons). As a boy he was in the 1916 Rising. But he is not dominated by the sense of grievance and frustration which characterises so many of the older generation of Irish politicians and I have always had the feeling that we could do quite a lot of business with him.[40]

Macmillan and Lemass in 'Harold Dear' by J.O.D.
(James O'Donnell). *Dublin Opinion*, August 1961.

And yet, to the British imagination, the dichotomy between Lemass and de Valera appeared much greater than it actually was. Lemass may have held a more pragmatic disposition towards Britain, but he was eyeing Common Market Europe as the 'long run' option, not the EFTA.

At a meeting chaired by Lemass and attended by four ministers on 27 April 1961 the decision was taken that if Britain applied to join the EEC, Ireland would too. Protests came in from a number of Irish industrialists and, more cuttingly for Lemass, from Leydon. The opposition of his most faithful work partner pained Lemass. He was, however, resolute in his conviction that the days of protectionism were numbered, whether through bilateral agreement with Britain or within a European framework.[41]

Commenting on their discussions concerning British and Irish entry to the Common Market held in July 1961 the British Conservative Prime Minister Harold Macmillan recalled: 'I found Seán Lemass particularly helpful, and enjoyed my meetings with him.'[42] Speaking in Brussels on 18 January 1962 Lemass presented Ireland's application to join the EEC. He had learned his lesson from the criticism of the Clery's Ballroom speech in 1955: when discussing economic matters he turned first to agriculture.[43]

If Lemass's primary focus remained industrialisation, the *First Programme* had earmarked agriculture as the most dynamic sector for growth.[44] The concerns over this sector that were evident in the 1958 talks between Britain and Ireland persisted. The Department of Agriculture worried that the development of multilateral trading blocs in Europe would harm Irish preferences in the British market. Lemass headed talks in 1959 and 1960 that sought to establish a common agricultural policy between Ireland and Britain, but in the early 1960s Britain imposed further restriction on Irish access to its market.[45] The limitations of the British market for Irish agriculture strengthened Lemass's determination to gain admission to the EEC. At the same time he knew that Britain would also have to become a member if Ireland was to make it in and reap the benefits. If Ireland joined the EEC without Britain, as the National Farmers' Association (NFA) was urging, the 'special relationship' between British and Irish agriculture was likely to collapse. And, as the MP for South Fermanagh Cahir Healy wrote in January 1962: 'Has he [Lemass] any alternative market for his cattle, pork, and eggs?'[46]

These concerns were blown out of the water when French premier Charles de Gaulle vetoed British, and with it Irish, entry to the EEC. Wearily, Lemass returned to bilateral talks with the Tory government and in 1963 he presented Macmillan with proposals for

Lemass, tied to Harold Macmillan, prepares to take the plunge into the Common Market. *Dubin Opinion*, June 1961.

virtual free trade between the two countries.[47] By 1964 Lemass was gravitating towards Harold Wilson's Labour Party. In March he travelled to London to meet Wilson, the leader of the British opposition, for private talks. While they both emitted thick plumes of pipe smoke, Wilson and Lemass discussed areas of future cross-border cooperation, including nuclear energy.[48] The coming to power of Wilson's Labour government later that year was greeted optimistically by Lemass. After an initially rocky patch the Anglo-Irish Free Trade Agreement was signed in 1965. The deal removed virtually all the protection enjoyed by Irish manufacturers against competitive imports of British goods.

Lemass enjoyed the opportunity for travel abroad that came with being Taoiseach, but his redirection of the economy onto a free trade footing would not have been possible without substantial conflict and consensus domestically. As national leader, Lemass paid more attention to the agricultural sector than he had ever done before. And yet his government faced considerable unrest from the farming community. He sought to create markets for the nation's farmers, but Ireland remained effectively frozen out of the European market. One of Lemass's weaknesses in this sphere was the perception that he held a dismissive attitude towards agriculture in general. Like most political caricatures, this was based on more than a scintilla of

"*Kathleen, me daughter, you'll be marrying into a strong family, and many's the fine match was made with a man the girl never seen.*"

truth. Paddy Smith, Lemass's Minister for Agriculture, resigned in 1964 over what he perceived as Lemass's urban bias. The resignation was a landmark, the first that Fianna Fáil had suffered over an openly political division of opinion in the party's history. As Todd Andrews noted, the edifice of unity under de Valera was starting to crumble. Kevin Boland thought Smith had grown tired of being Lemass's fall guy.

> He'd come in every year and fight like hell for the farmers, and then a Cabinet decision would be taken, and he'd have to go out and use the same arguments against the farmers as had been used against him in Cabinet . . . Then the farmers would go behind his back to Jim Ryan and Lemass, and Ryan would end up saying 'we'll have to do something for them'; Smith would get all the blame.[49]

Lemass moved quickly, replacing Smith with his son-in-law, who knew even less about agriculture than Lemass himself. In response to the charge that agriculture had been 'left out in the cold' in a Finance Bill of 1958 Haughey replied – with impressive candour – 'I know very little about agriculture'.[50] His appointment to one of the most important cabinet posts was a clear promotion for Haughey. He never made any secret of his desire to become Taoiseach and in appointing him to Agriculture Lemass was giving him the chance to get rural Ireland, an essential support base for anyone aspiring for the top job, on his side.

By the autumn of Lemass's leadership, agricultural prices had fallen as Ireland started to feel the consequences of being outside the

EEC. Farmers protested against Haughey outside Government Buildings. As the protest continued, the cabinet contemptuously dubbed the NFA the 'Nine Frozen Arses'.[51] By September 1966 Haughey had become embroiled in a dispute with RTÉ over airtime given to the NFA. With his leadership chances appearing dashed his father-in-law came to his aid, dressing up self-interest in the language of self-righteousness. These farmers were of the old, selfish 'rancher' class that Fianna Fáil had initially challenged, Lemass implied. Responding to accusations that the government was censoring the press on the issue, Lemass asserted that RTÉ was not independent and that the government had a right to intervene in the public interest.[52] In October 1966 he launched a crushing rejoinder to the NFA, accusing them of challenging 'the elementary principles of democracy' through their protest.[53] Despite his moves to incorporate different sectors of Irish society in the 1960s, Lemass, it seems, still subscribed to the Fianna Fáil adage that the NFA were just 'Fine Gael on tractors'.[54]

Smith blamed his decision to resign on Lemass's unwillingness to take on the trade unions. If Leydon and certain sections of the civil service clung dear to protectionism, the support of the Irish trade unions for free trade and export-led development was critical in securing Ireland's industrial expansion in the 1960s. In contrast to his lack of dialogue with farmers, Lemass launched industrial productivity councils and development councils, geared towards greater employment and the adoption of free trade. He also oversaw a greater use of the international media, intended to put the new, modernising industrial Ireland on the map.

In securing the unions' support Lemass, Gary Murphy claims, established a 'proto-corporatist social democracy' in Ireland.[55] He expected the unions to achieve wage discipline in return for a consultative role in policy-making and held a genuine belief that class war was futile. Set up under his auspices, the Committee on Industrial Organisation (CIO) was an initiative that united bosses and workers behind the free trade ethos of the EEC. Similarly, the Employer–Labour Conference was formed in 1961 after a major strike by employees of the ESB.

Lemass relied on the support of Ireland's unions to ensure his economic policies were successful. Consequently, the national wage agreements he oversaw as Taoiseach were relatively generous. Famously, the National Pay Deal of 1964 granted wage increases

Lemass greets Joan Kennedy, wife of US Senator Ted
Kennedy, November 1964. In the background are
Lemass's wife, Kathleen, and son-in-law Charles Haughey.
Courtesy *The Irish Press*

amounting to 12 per cent over two years. Whereas in the past Lemass
had shown his willingness to apply the big stick to the unions, he
now recognised that with the upheaval to traditional structures
through the reorganisation of the economy it was vital to keep them
onside.

Politically, Lemass was accused of placing self-interest above
national economic interest.[56] In 1961 he could only secure a minority
government, entering power with independents. Fianna Fáil's vote
dropped from seventy-eight seats to seventy in that year as the party
won the general election by a narrow margin. Several seats 'were
won and lost after very close counts, reaffirming Lemass's disdain for
the PR system.[57] He only remained in power due to the support of
Labour, a party he was fond of disparaging, throwing his intervention
in the 1964 wage agreements into sharp relief. The government's
generous package was certainly delivered to the unions with that
year's forthcoming election in mind.

When it came to state ownership, the same 'evil and pernicious
tendency' detected by Liam Skinner was discussed in the iconic
Time magazine article of 1963, which noted that

> one third of all industrial enterprises in Ireland are bankrolled
> by the Government, which has gone even further towards

nationalization than even Britain's socialists advocate. Lemass says he shares the attitude towards socialism that was expressed in the late Pope John's encyclical *Pacem in Terris*: that no political system is undesirable if it benefits the people.[58]

Significantly though, in the 1960s interest groups such as unions did not become part of the state, as envisaged by the vocationalist or corporatist thinkers of the 1930s and 1940s whom Lemass so vigorously opposed. Rather, under the social partnership arrangements of the CIO, bosses and unions were represented by two separate bodies: the Adaptation Councils and the Trade Union Advisory Boards, respectively. However, these boards rarely met. And while union leadership was keen to gain a stronger hand in national economic management, its membership was more restless. Ireland had the highest strike rate in Europe in the 1960s.[59] Such diverse occupational groups as teachers, power workers and the Gardaí all caused economic disruption by striking. In August 1964 a builders' strike in Dublin culminated in Minister for Industry and Commerce Jack Lynch, Lemass's eventual successor as Taoiseach, intervening to meet their demands for shorter hours, establishing the forty-hour week.

In pursuit of full employment, Lemass encouraged his top civil servants and state company heads to take on extra staff. He viewed their operations as a vehicle to increase employment in Ireland. In 1964 the government published the *Second Programme for Economic Development*. Lemass ignored the concerns of commentators and government colleagues that its targets were too ambitious, comments which must have evoked personal memories of the scorn for his '100,000 jobs' Clery's speech in 1955. Instead he drew up some idiosyncratic alternative titles for the programme: 'Ahead to 1970', 'Operation Speed Up' and 'Target: One Billion Going Up'.[60] All were eventually dropped.

Like de Valera, Lemass regarded class conflict as 'un-Irish'. But by the time of his resignation in 1966, industrial relations were in a state of considerable disarray. These strikes are not important merely as examples of how the social partnership rhetoric Lemass used in the 1960s masked social divisions in the country. They also represented mass involvement in the transformative experience of striking. In major disputes, such as the ESB strike, workers defied the instruction of union leadership not to strike. For Irish labour, this was certainly cultural revolution, but not the sort Garvin identifies.

The strike rate during Lemass's premiership denoted greater rank-and-file confidence in the labour movement, but also dissent linked to the new economic conditions. Like most politicians, Lemass was guilty of brusquely talking up the economy. Foreign direct investment flowed into Ireland during the 1960s, but not at the rate he claimed. Likewise, total employment rose under Lemass, but there was also a haemorrhaging of jobs as the old tariffs were dismantled.[61] Garvin claims that a 'historically unprecedented' growth rate of 8 per cent was recorded in 1961 and net migration was lower between 1961 and 1966 than at any other inter-censal period since independence.[62] Total employment in 1961 was, however, lower than it had been a decade earlier,[63] and emigration continued to blight the nation.[64] The old problems had not gone away.

Stars, Stripes and the Fourth Green Field

The pursuit of EEC membership aside, Lemass played a more active role in the formulation of Irish foreign policy than his biographers have registered.[65] Back in 1931, on the verge of assuming power, Lemass unsuccessfully proposed to the Fianna Fáil party that Ireland cement its isolation from global currents by withdrawing from the League of Nations.[66] Thirty years on, he attached greater importance to Ireland's position as an actor on the world stage and worked to move Ireland towards a more definite pro-western stance.

For most of his career Lemass followed de Valera's statesmanlike handling of foreign affairs, as demonstrated in the controversy over the declaration of the Republic. In 1955, under the second inter-party government, Ireland was admitted to the United Nations. Between 1955 and 1957 Ireland aligned with western, Christian, anti-communist countries in line with the hope of attracting American investment.[67] This changed when Fianna Fáil returned to power in 1957. Resuming his brief at External Affairs, Frank Aiken ruffled feathers and raised the status of the Irish delegation at the UN.[68]

Supported by the Irish mission's most able spokesman, Conor Cruise O'Brien, Aiken faced down Anglo-American pressure and moved Ireland closer to the UN's Afro-Asian block, promoting decolonisation, the rights of small nations, and nuclear non-proliferation.[69] In his initial speeches on foreign affairs, Lemass championed the independent furrow Aiken had ploughed. In a speech to the Cambridge University Liberal Club in January 1960 he described Ireland as an 'independent' country at the General Assembly, like Sweden.[70] Later that year, a visit to newly independent Nigeria with wife Kathleen signalled Ireland's identification with decolonisation in Africa.[71] Lemass, however, was soon to abandon Ireland's autonomous, activist stance at the UN.

In 1960 the United Nations became involved in a peacekeeping exercise in central Africa when the mineral-rich province of Katanga attempted to secede from the Congo. Lemass approved the deployment of Irish troops to the region, kick-starting a tradition of the use of Irish troops as UN peacekeepers. Noël Browne responded by accusing Lemass of 'walking into trouble'. He claimed that the deployment had helped boost Belgian imperialism by bolstering Congolese partition.[72] Lemass knew that he had taken a gamble, but maintained that the mission was 'inspired by the fundamental precepts of our Christian Faith'; Ireland was playing 'the good Samaritan', he claimed.[73] Fifteen Irish troops were killed in the Congo, whom Lemass commemorated by presenting gallantry medals to their next of kin.[74] Luckily for him, their deaths resulted in a surge of pride, rather than anger, at home.

Browne also charged Lemass with washing his hands of Conor Cruise O'Brien, by this time the Special UN Representative in the Congo. O'Brien was convinced that the superpowers had an interest in uniting Katanga with Rhodesia for financial and security gain.[75] Lemass deliberately distanced himself from O'Brien at the time, insisting he was a UN (rather than an *Irish*) representative. He later told British Commonwealth Secretary Duncan Sandys that he had 'great respect' for O'Brien's 'intellectual qualities' but 'doubted whether he was well suited for a practical operation like that undertaken in Katanga'.[76]

Lemass may have looked down on O'Brien as an intellectual rather than a 'man of action', but broader economic objectives were also at play in his attitude. Ultimately, these held sway in his views on international injustices. Notwithstanding the dictates of realpolitik and the imperative to attract foreign investment, this was – at times – a mean attitude.

Following Ireland's censure of apartheid at the UN in 1960 Lemass fretted about the repercussions for Ireland's minimal trade with South Africa and was anxious not to offend trade delegations from that country.[77] Elsewhere, he supported Ireland's condemnation of China's invasion of Tibet in 1959 not as a matter of principle but on the grounds that it would make Ireland appear more anti-communist in the eyes of the Americans.[78] The shift in Ireland's position at the UN from an independent, or Scandinavian-style, delegation to an American satellite was confirmed in late 1960 when Lemass, imagining a potentially devastating war between East and West, asked: 'if they [the western powers] needed to mobilise the total resources of the free world to succeed, and if we were convinced that help from us was vital for their victory, could we in the last resort refuse it to them?' adding: 'Nobody who knows our people, their deep religious convictions and love of freedom could ever think of us as neutral.'[79]

Lemass was content to grant Frank Aiken freedom at External Affairs; when he was away at the UN he was not getting beneath Lemass's feet. At the same time, under the Taoiseach's influence, Irish foreign policy became resolutely pro-western. This shift was particularly noticeable from 1961 onwards.

As early as 1953 Lemass had hinted that a *united* Ireland might subscribe to the North Atlantic Treaty Organisation (NATO).[80] In power as Taoiseach, he quietly dumped this anti-partitionist clause and pushed for the Republic's entry into the military bloc. Typically, he tried to alter Ireland's neutrality policy fundamentally without going to the bother of consulting his cabinet. Irish public opinion, Lemass implied, should fall in line with this new departure. Unwisely, he used Micheál Ó Moráin, his Minister for Lands and something of a buffoon,[81] in one of his famous 'kite-flying' exercises to sound out whether NATO membership could be sold to the public. Lemass scolded the Dáil over the subsequent disquiet about this flirtation with NATO. Such talk would harm Ireland's pursuit of EEC membership, he warned the assembled deputies.[82] His 'Sinn Féin' outlook now firmly consigned to the past, Lemass was looking over his shoulder to 'Big Brother'. However, he faced similar opposition to the idea of joining NATO from his own parliamentary party. Lemass was forced to issue a reassurance that Ireland would not be joining NATO in order to 'clear the air'.[83] On this occasion the kite had foundered.

Ireland's voting at the UN was coloured by Lemass, who stressed that economic considerations came before moral ones. He advised that Irish rhetoric be toned down on Algerian self-determination in order to please French premier Charles de Gaulle.[84] Likewise, in

Lemass meets a fellow card sharp, the then US Vice-
President Richard Nixon (left). Courtesy *The Irish Press*.

1961, he was anxious not to offend the Italians over South Tyrol and,
with an eye firmly on the Yankee dollar, opposed China's membership
of the UN.[85] The following year, during the Cuban Missile Crisis,
Lemass authorised the searching of eastern bloc aircraft at Shannon.
It is evident that his attitude towards colonialism and international
peacekeeping had evolved into a resolutely pro-western stance. He
admitted to finding the atmosphere at the United Nations 'very
unreal'. And, quite amazingly given his anti-colonial protectionist
record, he told the British Commonwealth Secretary that he could
not understand why newly independent Afro-Asian countries at the
UN were so suspicious of receiving capital from 'the more advanced
countries'. Relative to de Valera, contemporary accounts give the
impression that Lemass was a nervous Taoiseach when it came to
foreign affairs, anxious not to offend the western powers.[86]

The Americanisation of Lemass's approach to foreign affairs
crystallised with the visit of John F. Kennedy to Ireland in the
summer of 1963. Lemass is roundly praised for his disdain for the
misty-eyed sentimentality of Irish politics. Yet, ironically, several set-
piece occasions in his premiership are consistently invoked in that
very spirit. Kennedy's visit, the most enduring of these, was coated

in an extra layer of sentimentality after the president's assassination five months later.

Symbolic of the exaggerated deference that greeted Kennedy was the presidential garden party at Áras an Uachtaráin, described by a foreign journalist as 'part rugby scrummage and part adoring struggle for the Presidential handshake'.[87] Kennedy turned in a bravura performance as the returning son of Erin. His security men were less willing to tone down the braggadocio, however. Reportedly, a minister's wife was bustled out of the way in one incident and in another, a fracas in Dublin's Intercontinental Hotel, one of Kennedy's men drew his gun. The CIA's report on Lemass for the purposes of the trip was patronising, describing him as 'an inveterate gambler' and noting 'he has at times been involved in serious financial difficulties'.

Speaking on the trip, Kennedy praised Ireland's intermediary role in foreign affairs between the West and the Third World. According to George Gilmore, Lemass's secretary in his first 'ministerial' post in the ghost cabinet of 1925, Lemass's 'struggle against the Anglo-American pressure to make him abandon his attempts to create an independent Irish economy' was, by this point, unravelling under American pressure. 'President Kennedy was bullying Lemass into the present attitude of subservience.'[88]

Lemass, however, did not need bullying. At this stage he was keen to use Kennedy's trip to bring Ireland more intimately into the western fold. He was openly in favour of compromising Ireland's independent position, moving the country towards an uncritical pro-western, pro-Christian stance. From the 1950s on even Lemass's correspondence showed a conversion to American spelling conventions and turns of phrase. As mentioned, during the Cuban Missile Crisis the previous year Lemass had sanctioned interference with aircraft at Shannon to appease the United States. He also worried that the anti-nuclear demonstrations outside the American embassy at the time would upset the Americans and the protest, led by Noël Browne, was broken up by Gardaí using dogs.

The meeting between president and Taoiseach brought two ruthless political tacticians face to face. Lemass had steered Ireland's foreign policy towards closer alignment with the self-appointed guardians of the free world. Now he hoped that on his Irish trip Kennedy would agree to greater American involvement in Northern Ireland, as a mediator between Britain and Ireland. Kennedy,

Lemass beside West German Chancellor Konrad Adenauer (left), October 1962. Courtesy German Bundesarchiv.

however, ignored his approaches.[89] For all the razzmatazz, JFK was at heart an Anglophile and ruled out any discussion of Irish reunification.

This was a blow to Lemass, who envisaged a role for America over Northern Ireland. He was reluctant to press for UN intervention north of the border because, as he explained to Patrick Hillery, he thought that the inevitable British veto at the UN Security Council that would follow any attempt would secure partition 'for all time'.[90] He repeated this view to northern nationalist MP Cahir Healy in 1962, when the possibility of registering grievances at the UN was again raised.[91]

Lemass had inherited this attitude from de Valera, who thought a partition resolution at the UN was 'foolish' and an 'impossible request'.[92] Unlike Lemass, Frank Aiken was not against the idea of raising the matter at the UN.[93] In late 1960 he had highlighted partition during a debate on colonialism in the UN's General Committee. Yet this speech underlined the futility of the international community's capacity to facilitate a solution to partition. Aiken merely reiterated the habitual Fianna Fáil message of a hope that the 'unity of Ireland would be recovered with reasonable speed and in a peaceful and orderly manner'.[94] By early 1962 Aiken, too, had come to the conclusion that the raising of partition at the UN was a fruitless exercise.[95]

A photograph of Lemass alongside West German Chancellor Konrad Adenauer in 1962 highlights the parallel between partitioned Ireland and partitioned Germany that existed at the time, not least

Lemass arriving in West Germany, October 1962.
Courtesy German Bundesarchiv.

in Lemass's thinking.[96] Lemass proudly received the Grand Cross of the Order of Merit of the Federal Republic of Germany while on his trip there. He had learned some German during his Civil War internment[97] and he and Adenauer stayed up all night discussing the Bay of Pigs invasion and the Vietnam War.[98] According to Lemass's daughter Peggy, when her father met with Adenauer and de Gaulle both had supported Lemass's insistence that Britain withdraw troops from Northern Ireland as a condition of both countries entering the EEC together.[99] But Lemass, as we have seen, was instrumental in shifting the emphasis in Irish government thinking on partition from London to Belfast and this condition was not pursued.

In fact, a British government memorandum of 1958 commended Lemass for what was regarded as his progressive attitude. In contrast to de Valera, the memo argued, 'Already Mr Lemass, though in very general terms, has adjured his people to stop sulking about Partition and concentrate on improving relations with the North and has added (something that would not have been practicable earlier) that he would be very glad to see Lord Brookeborough [Prime Minister of Northern Ireland] in Dublin.'[100]

Lemass was also changing de Valera's preferred policy of non-recognition, becoming more gradualist in his approach over time and seeking to foster cross-border trade links.[101] Lemass never acknowledged the principle of consent – which deemed that Irish unity could not be achieved without the consent of the 'majority' within Northern Ireland – enshrined in the Ireland Act (1949). But, moving with the changed conditions it created, he ended the policy of de facto non-recognition and rejected calls for Ireland to rejoin the Commonwealth as a precursor to unification. A united Ireland would be created from within Ireland, not outside.[102]

His first major policy development on Northern Ireland as Taoiseach was to propose a 32-county free trade area for domestic goods produced in both territories, which he announced in Oxford in 1959.[103] Stormont refused this offer on the grounds that Dublin was doing little to stop IRA activity and did not recognise Northern Ireland's right to exist.[104] Basil Brooke, then Prime Minister of Northern Ireland, complained to British Home Secretary R. A. Butler that Lemass had made much of his 'strict' attitude towards IRA men while playing down the fact that the sentences handed out had been paltry. Brooke was suspicious of 'the United Ireland of which Mr Lemass is dreaming' and did not want to 'rush into any embrace which may end in a bear's hug'.[105]

Brooke's accusation of leniency towards the IRA sheds light on the difficulties posed by militant republicanism. Lemass recognised that the IRA campaign of 1956–62 was carried out by young men who were the product of the trenchant attitudes towards partition in official and unofficial political culture in the Republic. He had, of course, once taken up the gun in the name of the Republic himself. He felt that punishing IRA men by military tribunal, as Fianna Fáil had done during the Emergency, would 'create a spirit of martyrdom which he was trying to avoid'.[106] Frustratingly for Lemass, though, the conciliatory attitude he attempted to foster as Taoiseach was effectively hamstrung until the IRA ceased military activity in February 1962.

With the spirit of militant republicanism alive and well, the insensitive whims of the British royal family presented an unwelcome, if relatively trivial, foreign policy intrusion. As James Ryan recalled:

> The Queen Mother was always fishing for a trip to Dublin, especially for the Horse Show. She once threatened our ambassador in London that she'd arrange for her plane to break down on a visit to Belfast and we'd have to let her. Princess Margaret was just a headache: we could hardly prevent her without a formal thing of some kind.[107]

C.E.K.'s depiction of Lemass in Oxford, where he delivered his famous speech on partition. *Dublin Opinion*, November 1959.

During the frustrating period of IRA activity, Lemass oversaw a shift in terminology. He never officially sanctioned the replacement of the term 'Six Counties' with 'Northern Ireland' in official parlance, but under his leadership the evolution of language more acceptable to the unionist community was marked. Lemass could be ambiguous; in February 1961 he used both 'Northern Ireland' and 'Six Counties' in the same Dáil debate.[108] Yet this very ambiguity was a brave departure from de Valera's attitude, which was to refuse to acknowledge that Northern Ireland existed.[109]

The transition, subtle though it was, was later seized upon in the Dáil by the hawkish left-wing TD Jack McQuillan. He asked Lemass 'whether the Government believed that the abolition of Partition was the responsibility of the British Government; whether this view still holds; and, if not, when the change took place'.[110] The change had taken place gradually. As with Lionel Booth, the TD who had publicly criticised the tendency to view the IRA as 'naughty, but forgivable, impulsive children', Lemass made extensive use of young party men for 'kite-flying exercises' on Northern Ireland. He sent Jack Lynch and Charles Haughey to Belfast in 1962 to explore the possibility of free trade; and also leaned heavily on George Colley to assess the reception to more controversial initiatives.

In April 1963 Lemass used Colley, a Protestant backbencher and future Tánaiste, to announce that independent Ireland had always recognised Northern Ireland de facto (in reality) if not *de jure* (legally). Having sent Colley over the parapet, Lemass waited for

Stormont's response. When it came, it was negative. Next, Lemass decided to go 'over the top' himself. In a July 1963 speech in Tralee he claimed to accept the genuine fear of unionists over the dismantling of partition. Although Lemass referred to Northern Ireland as an 'artificial area', the speech amounted to a reiteration of de facto recognition. This was a significant milestone for a Taoiseach.[111] Delivered in a republican heartland, this address was intended to provoke notice from unionists. Again, the response from Northern Ireland was only muted.[112] Undeterred, in September 1963 Lemass responded to a conciliatory speech by Terence O'Neill – Brooke's replacement as northern Prime Minister – by writing to all government departments asking them to draw up a list of areas where cross-border cooperation could be beneficial.[113]

A month later, however, Lemass undid much of this work by pandering to the Irish-American lobby. In October 1963 he set off on a state visit to the USA. There, conscious of American press attention, the tone of his speeches was more truculent. His address at Boston College concerned the American Civil War. John F. Kennedy had emotively evoked this conflict on his trip to Ireland in July 1963. In a 'stirring speech' met with 'thunderous applause' Kennedy had impressed the assembled deputies by lauding the heroism of the Irish Brigade at the Battle of Fredericksburg.[114] Lemass, invoking Abraham Lincoln's speech when inaugurated as president in 1861, claimed no minority had the right to vote itself out of the nation.[115] In an earlier speech to the National Press Club in Washington Lemass congratulated Britain for accepting the winds of change in granting independence to its African colonies and then asked British political leaders: 'Will you make a clear statement that there is no British interest in maintaining partition when Irishmen want to get rid of it?'[116]

The Tralee speech and the American speeches appear poles apart. Juxtaposition of them ignores the fact that in Lemass's conception of the nature of partition (a viewpoint that appears unbending in the wake of the 1998 Good Friday accords but was normal at the time) there was no inconsistency between the two.[117] Speaking in an Irish town, Irishmen (as he viewed the unionist majority in Northern Ireland) were addressed. Speaking on foreign soil, the colonial occupier (Britain) would be his focus. The following year Lemass further irritated unionists by publicly stating that Britain 'did not want' Northern Ireland.[118]

Lemass's pragmatism is often represented as triumphing over archaic prejudices. But to Seán MacEntee (albeit, by no means an impartial observer), deep down Lemass's nationalism was 'hard and dour, almost . . . implacable'.[119] The tone of his American addresses not only represented a retreat from his earlier attempts to mollify unionists but could easily have undermined the progress made in technical meetings between civil servants from both administrations in the early 1960s. These meetings constituted the unglamorous but crucial groundwork to the summit meetings between Lemass and Northern Ireland Prime Minister Terence O'Neill in 1965.[120]

The Lemass/O'Neill episode was the last time the Prime Ministers of Ireland's two states met officially until the Bertie Ahern–Ian Paisley handshake of 2007. Consequently, the occasion has been relayed with all the breathless excitement of a literary romance. On a cold January morning in 1965 a single black Mercedes carrying Lemass wound its way through the winter snow to Belfast while O'Neill waited on the steps of Stormont on tip-toes.[121] Garvin's account of the meeting strikes a salacious tone – 'Lemass didn't tell Kathleen; O'Neill didn't tell his wife'[122] – and the two premiers marked the occasion with champagne.

The mutual presence of T. K. Whitaker and O'Neill at World Bank and International Monetary Fund (IMF) meetings helped facilitate the get-together. The election of a British Labour government under Harold Wilson in late 1964 – one which looked less favourably on unionism than its Tory predecessor – also proved decisive. Most significant, however, was the context of moves towards European integration. As Lemass stated in an interview with the BBC: 'The political implications of the Border will diminish very considerably when we are all in the European Free Trade Area.'[123]

O'Neill explained how the meeting had come about:

> You may recall that I was asked by Harry Diamond [Nationalist MP for Belfast] if I would meet Mr Lemass when he came to address the Literific [the Queen's University Belfast debating society]. This came very shortly after the playwright John Antrobus had undressed on the stage. I felt I was entitled to dissociate myself from this suggestion! My messenger to Dublin made it plain that I could not meet him in association with a visit to the Literific but that if he would like to come to lunch at Stormont I would be very happy to meet him. To his

credit he immediately accepted my offer and, as you will have noticed, has since declined to come to the Literific. As I have stated in public I think this was an act of great courage on his part. Once he had come through the gates of Stormont he had virtually given de facto recognition to the Government of Northern Ireland, and while there will be many problems in the days that lie ahead and while there will be many setbacks I feel and hope that it is true to say, as he said on his return to Dublin, that nothing will ever be quite the same again. If the Prime Minister of Holland, a predominately Protestant country, can invite the Prime Minister of Belgium to lunch I felt it was time that the Prime Minister of Northern Ireland could do the same.[124]

Lemass himself played down the 'great courage' involved. At the Fianna Fáil Ard-Fheis that year he said he was 'at pains to discourage any exaggeration of the significance of the meeting'.[125] In an effort to appease republican hardliners, he even delivered a tub-thumping address to party members in Sallynoggin the following year, a speech which again alerted unionists to what they saw as Lemass's duplicity.[126]

Nonetheless, the sheer volume of letters both Lemass and O'Neill received illustrated the popularity of the handshake on both sides of the border. O'Neill adjudged this evidence of the 'general public support for the action which I decided to take'.[127] He found the 'many kind notes which have come in from 'representatives of the various Protestant Churches ... particularly encouraging'.[128] Prominent unionist naysayer Ian Paisley was denounced by an anonymous letter signed 'the decent Protestant minority' as an 'antichrist' and a 'bigot'.[129] The minister of a Congregational Church in England wrote that the meeting would 'give the Angels in Glory an excuse to have a drink all round!'[130] O'Neill even received a letter of congratulation from Lemass's old comrades, the Leinster Association of the Old IRA, and replied thanking them, adding: 'I had never expected to receive a letter from the IRA.'[131]

Ultimately, however, the meeting was to provide the symbolism, but not the kiss, of peace. The previous year Lemass had rejected a resolution at the Ard-Fheis that Fianna Fáil participate in politics in Northern Ireland. This had been de Valera's consistent line over three decades. Essentially, Lemass rehashed de Valera's federalist plan for Stormont's Westminster functions to be transferred to Dublin, a proposition that remained unattractive to most within the unionist community. He also left behind no coherent, long-term Northern Ireland policy which his successor Jack Lynch could comfortably call his own. This would be painfully exposed during the turbulent years of 1969 to 1971, when the Irish government imploded over whether or not force should be used to alleviate the suffering of northern Catholics.

Although he regarded partition as 'an absurdity' and was aware of the 'second class status' of northern nationalists,[132] Lemass's desire for greater cross-border cooperation was principally trade-driven. This view displayed a certain disregard for the discrimination suffered by the nationalist community north of the border. After meeting him Eddie McAteer, the leader of the Nationalist Party in Northern Ireland, 'came away with the conviction that as far as Seán Lemass was concerned, the Northern Irish were very much on their own'.[133] With Lemass, as under de Valera, northern nationalists would be frozen out of the formation of Dublin's policy. Lemass's great departure was viewed dimly by the Ulster Unionist Party rearguard as well. William Douglas, of Ulster Unionist headquarters, viewed Lemass's 'vague offers of trade concessions' as unwelcome because 'he has quite openly stated they are promoted to try and bring about eventual reunion in Ireland. We in Northern Ireland will have none of it.'[134]

A Programme for Social Development?

With hindsight, it is clear that Lemass's redirection of Ireland towards the European and international mainstream jolted the state out of its relative insularity. At the same time, as with other transitions in the Lemass premiership, the subject of Church–state relations provides little evidence that he was a 'cultural revolutionary'. It has been noted that Lemass subjected the Church–state relationship to re-evaluation, rather than confrontation.[135] But even this re-evaluation had its distinct boundaries. Garvin claims that Lemass was 'not much of a religious believer'.[136] While this may be true of his convictions in the revolutionary period (1919–23), Lemass proved a pious man in his later years.

As Taoiseach, he presented very little opposition to ecclesiastical power and was viewed favourably by Ireland's bishops. His relation-ship with Archbishop John Charles McQuaid was, as mentioned earlier, closer than has been assumed. From Drumcondra, on Dublin's northside, the authoritarian prelate exercised a control that Lemass was, at best, tentative in challenging. The Second Vatican Council (1962–5) may have raised the prospect of a more compassionate Catholicism and the ending of the authoritarianism of bishops, but McQuaid continued as if nothing had changed. Lemass still corresponded with McQuaid in tones of customary fawning reverence. The Taoiseach and the archbishop regularly exchanged good wishes and saw a lot of each other, at Masses, state functions, and receptions hosted by Lemass and his wife, Kathleen.[137] The volume of Lemass's correspondence with McQuaid is smaller than that of his colleagues Seán T. O'Kelly and Éamon de Valera. Neither was the obsequiousness of Lemass's addresses that unusual. The letters do not, however, suggest that Lemass was significantly less Catholic in his observance and views than the majority of his political contemporaries, as is implied in the Lemassiography.

As Taoiseach, Lemass held meetings with the arch-conservative McQuaid on a monthly basis.[138] In 1960 Lemass submitted a proposal from the director of the National Library for a book-sharing agreement with Trinity College, but he dropped the issue as soon as McQuaid opposed it on his usual sectarian grounds. After the meeting a contented McQuaid wrote to Cardinal John D'Alton, primate of all Ireland: 'I am glad to report that today I saw the Taoiseach and that the proposal to conjoin TCD new library and the National Library will not be heard of again.'[139] In the same year McQuaid wrote to Cardinal D'Alton reporting that he had secured Lemass's agreement that the Charities Bill (1957) be amended so that gifts at Mass were recognised under civil law as valid charitable donations: a 'completely satisfactory' outcome 'thanks to the cooperation of Mr Lemass'.[140] After the reburial of Roger Casement, whose remains were brought back to Ireland in 1965, Lemass gushingly thanked McQuaid for presiding at the requiem Mass.[141] On retirement as Taoiseach in August 1966 he wrote to McQuaid to thank him for 'the unfailing good will and encouragement which you gave me during my term in the Government' and promised to pray for him.[142]

In 1960, again at the urging of McQuaid, Lemass made 'pressing representations' to the Spanish authorities to ensure the Irish hierarchy received compensation for the transfer of Church property, including the College of Irish Nobles in Salamanca, to the Spanish

Lemass and John,
Cardinal D'Alton.
Courtesy *The Irish Press*.

state.[143] He even wrote to General Francisco Franco to secure the money, expressing to him 'my most sincere good wishes for Your Excellency's personal happiness and wellbeing and for the continued success and prosperity of Spain and the noble Spanish people'.[144] Lemass eventually secured the due compensation for the Irish Church. By this point, however, the value of the peseta had fallen so much that the transaction involved a loss to the Irish hierarchy.[145]

The following year Dublin hosted the Catholic Church's Patrician Week. Speaking at the closing ceremony, Lemass said that Ireland was honoured by the visit of so many princes of the Church to her shores.[146] The Great Patrician Week hosting at Croke Park resembled the Eucharistic Congress a generation earlier. Amid a sea of military pomp and twee national costumes the leaders of Church and state lined up stiffly for High Mass and the arrival and departure of the papal legate. An immaculately attired Lemass was repeatedly snapped alongside de Valera and the assembled cardinals.[147] Later that year, in November 1961, Lemass travelled to the Vatican for anniversary celebrations on Pope John XXIII's coronation and eightieth birthday. Speaking on Vatican radio, he referred to the 'intimate connection that always existed between Irish national aspirations and religious beliefs' and to the power of the Church's teaching in solving the world's problems.[148] These were neither the words nor actions of an agnostic.

March 1954: Lemass, switches on the ESB supply to the 100,000th consumer of the rural Electrification Scheme at Ballinamult, County Waterford. Also present were (left) Rev. Fr Peter F. Walsh, PP, Ballinamult, and (right) R. F. Browne, Chairman of the ESB. *Cork Examiner*

Lemass admitted to being so awed when meeting John's predecessor, Pope Pius XII, that it was only when the pontiff retired briefly and Lemass heard the sound of running water that he realised he was human.[149] In 1962 the distinction of the Holy See was bestowed on Lemass and he wrote to McQuaid to express his thanks.[150] In February 1965 Lemass was granted another private audience at the Vatican, this time with Pope Paul VI. At the meeting, the pope made three suggestions to Lemass for the expansion of the church's role in Irish society. The first was that Lemass oversee the establishment of a Catholic radio station in Ireland capable of transmitting programmes to Britain. Secondly, he wanted a college to be set up in Ireland for the education of priests from developing countries. Lastly, the pope requested that periodic international conferences be held in Ireland to 'lessen the risk of newly developing countries coming under Communist influence'.[151] Lemass brought all three of these proposals before cabinet where, after a lengthy discussion, the second initiative was approved.[152]

Lemass is said to have been on good terms with Cardinal William Conway, who replaced D'Alton as archbishop of Armagh and cardinal primate of all Ireland in 1965. Lemass was in the congregation in St Peter's to hear the pope salute the elevation of Cardinal Conway as a sign of the 'unflagging faith and worldwide apostolate of the Irish'.[153] Contemporary newsreel shows Lemass kneeling on the tarmac of Dublin Airport, poised to kiss the episcopal ring as the rotund Conway steps off the plane from Rome.

Evidence from Cardinal Conway's papers, which remain closed to the public, illustrates the closeness between the two men. In the Conway–Lemass correspondence one document in particular stands out. Beneath a pile of exchanges between the two is a long letter Conway wrote to Lemass on his retirement as Taoiseach. This document is particularly telling about the closeness of Lemass to the cardinal and, by extension, the Irish Church to the Irish state. At length, Conway described the personal warmth between them and heaped praise on Lemass for

> the enormous contribution you have made to our national life both as Minister and as Taoiseach . . . [which] constitutes a service to Ireland for which, I am certain, future generations of Irish will be grateful . . . I should like to take this opportunity to thank you also for the understanding and helpfulness which you showed at all times in Church-state relations and for your unfailing kindness to me personally.[154]

Unlike McQuaid, Conway declared himself open to the reforms of Vatican II. But Conway, whose reputation has taken a pummelling since it emerged that in 1972 he colluded with the British government to protect bomber priest James Chesney from prosecution, remained opposed to post-war social liberalisation. A contemporary remembered Conway displaying his true colours at a meeting of the bishops in Booterstown in the early 1960s. 'As Conway lashed into the postprandial brandy he became more and more right wing. Eventually the Bishop of Cloyne had to come to my help.'[155] It is obvious that Conway saw Lemass, who liked to think of himself as the left wing of the Fianna Fáil party, as an ally of the Irish episcopate. Their relationship was one of conservative coalescence in a decade in which rapid social change was outstripping the gradualism of both men.

Shortly before his resignation Lemass spoke of his hope that the future generation would eliminate the 'slave spirit and the inferiority complex' and emphasised Ireland's 'cultural contribution' to the world. He insisted that Ireland's 'august destiny' – as proclaimed in

1916 – 'meant not military power or conquest or economic predominance, but our capacity to attain moral strength ... in demonstrating the applicability of Christian principles'.[156] While Lemass consistently appreciated the role of cultural confidence in national progress, he was unwilling to take on the monolith of the Catholic Church in Ireland in any meaningful way.

At the same time, Lemass played his part in paving the way for a more progressive social outlook in Ireland. In 1965 he made enquiries, through Brian Lenihan, as to the Church's position on a change in the constitutional status of divorce.[157] McQuaid, once again, provided robust resistance and the matter was dropped. Yet after his resignation as Taoiseach, Lemass set up an informal cross-party committee on the Constitution. He supported the committee's far-sighted recommendations, including that civil divorce be made available to Protestants and that the name of religions be deleted from the Constitution.[158]

There were even instances where Lemass got the better of McQuaid. Typically, Lemass made contradictory noises about drinking, in a 1946 Dáil debate describing the consumption of alcohol as an 'ordinary need' but in 1959 describing drunkenness as 'a sin'.[159] But prior to his defeat on the book-sharing proposal, Lemass's liberal side won through when he faced down McQuaid on the latter's attempts to introduce more stringent controls on pub opening hours. Later, in 1966, he allowed Donogh O'Malley (incidentally a great drinker) to implicitly challenge the Church's role in education by announcing free secondary schooling.[160]

John Horgan has argued that it would be ahistorical to regard Lemass's acceptance of McQuaid's opposition to change in divorce legislation as evidence that Lemass accepted ecclesiastical diktats meekly.[161] Nevertheless, for a man considered progressive, Lemass's steps in the social sphere were tentative. As a politician, he appointed reformers at the highest ranks of the legal profession. As a pragmatist, he recognised that social and cultural change had to come with modernisation. But as a social conservative, he was nervous about the pace of change. Unlike the grand plans for economic modernisation, a social development strategy was conspicuous by its absence during Lemass's premiership.

In a broader sense, Lemass was an old man and out of step with the pivotal social events of the decade. The black civil rights movement in America had proved an inspiration for protests by the nationalist community in Northern Ireland. Lemass, however, underestimated the political resolve behind these developments, predicting that it would only take a wet weekend to dampen the enthusiasm of activists in the North for civil rights.[162] He remained Victorian in his attitude to the technological advances which the 1960s heralded. Enthusiastic about air travel, he was nonetheless out of touch with new electronic media. He viewed television with blatant suspicion and insisted on referring to the radio as a 'hurdy gurdy'.[163] There has been much emphasis on the deliberations involving Lemass over whether television in Ireland would be a public or private venture.[164] Lemass favoured commercial broadcasting, but as Taoiseach oversaw the establishment of a television service under a public statutory authority. Senior civil servant Leon Ó Broin described this as 'an extraordinary *volte face*'[165] but in Lemass's eyes there was little contradiction. As either a public or a private venture (or, more aptly, a mixture of both) television – like much else in Ireland – would conform to his designs.

Recognising the influence that this new medium had, Lemass kept close watch to ensure that Telefís Éireann did not develop the liberal independence typical of the BBC. At Telefís Éireann's inauguration the Taoiseach paid lip service to the 'new ideas' and 'new fashions' that television would acquaint Irish people with, before warning of the 'proper regard to the spiritual and national values which should always guide our behaviour'.[166] When RTÉ deviated from these values, most notably in broadcasting programmes revealing the sorry extent of emigration, Lemass was swift to rebuke.[167]

The guarded welcome Lemass gave television resembled that of the Irish bishops, who issued a joint statement in late 1959 welcoming television if it reflected 'the true spirit of the Irish people' but urging against 'the broadcasting of programmes which offend all reasonable standards of morals and decency'.[168] The Executive Committee of the Knights of Columbanus, likewise, urged that broadcasters pay heed to the papal encyclicals.[169] Lemass went as far as passing on a message from McQuaid to the broadcaster Éamonn Andrews requesting that a priest be appointed religious adviser to RTÉ[170] and met with the archbishop in 1962 to go over a list of 'subversive' individuals working in television. He did not, however, agree to McQuaid's plan to have a number of such 'liberals' removed from the broadcasting authority.[171]

Tom Garvin has commented on the 'general syndrome of un-intellectual or even anti-intellectual thinking' in Ireland at the time. This attitude privileged 'can do' and 'common sense' over academic commentary.[172] Garvin claims that by the late 1950s Lemass had turned a corner and accepted that intellectuals needed to be consulted in formulating policy.[173] While this is evident in the mellowing of Lemass's jealous dislike of the IDA, it was less obvious in other areas. Sociology, for instance, was still more of a clerical preserve than a social science in 1960s Ireland. In 1964 the Limerick Rural Survey, a major research project on the Irish agricultural economy, was published. Its sociological observations radically departed from the norm by emphasising class divisions in rural communities and favouring voluntary organisations over the various 'paternalistic' government agencies working in the sector.[174]

This bold social investigation went against conventional civil service wisdom, however, and Lemass launched the study in November 1964 by quoting from the papal encyclical *Mater et Magistra*. He hoped that the survey would be followed by other academic surveys so that 'the Irish social structure, particularly in rural areas, will eventually conform to the ideas so clearly enunciated for our guidance by a great Pope'.[175] This was, at least, a nod to intellectual wisdom. But in citing a papal encyclical – a common trait in Irish political discourse at the time – Lemass's speech reproduced precisely the safe, old, Catholic metanarrative from which the Irish humanities in general and the study in particular were trying to move away.

In terms of broader social policy, Lemass's finely tuned political instinct prevailed over any commitment to social justice. In 1969 he dismissed the Democratic Programme of the First Dáil, the imple-mentation of which had been an original constitutional aim of the Fianna Fáil party, as 'not a very serious document'. This sort of language was reminiscent of Kevin O'Higgins, his political enemy as Minister for Justice in the 1920s, who famously dismissed the document as 'mostly poetry'.[176]

Fundamentally, Lemass was most willing to furnish the social card when the political need arose. Social provision in the Republic was obviously lagging behind that in the United Kingdom and Lemass saw that that political hegemony was shifting leftward in general. In 1963 he claimed that Fianna Fáil were the party of 'social progress' and that economic development was motivated by social

Sean Lemass and
socialist republican
Peadar O'Donnell (left).
Courtesy *The Irish Press*.

goals.[177] He was frustrated when, the next day, his speech was over-shadowed by the news that his wife, Kathleen, had injured herself slipping on ice.[178] It was not until 1964, following the victory of Harold Wilson's Labour Party in Britain, that Lemass seriously pressed for the improvement of social welfare at policy level. Moves in this direction faced decisive resistance from the departments of Social Welfare and Finance.[179] In an attempt to see off the Labour Party challenge during the 1965 election campaign and to counter Fine Gael's 'Just Society' initiative, Lemass made a series of speeches on his party's commitment to social services in Ireland.[180] There were also tentative moves to formulate an embryonic social develop-ment programme. After Fianna Fáil's electoral victory, however, the social welfare theme was largely discarded.

Art and Commemoration

Throughout Lemass's term as Ireland's leader, the fiftieth anniversary celebrations of the Easter Rising loomed large. The occasion was seen by some as a self-referential celebration of violence by the state and helped kick-start much pungent revisionism surrounding the Rising.[181] Wisely, Lemass did not deliver any jingoistic speeches about the legacy of 1916 as the anniversary came around. In his few speeches he used the jubilee celebrations to advance the cause of modern Ireland, describing the 1966 events as 'a time of national stocktaking, as well as for trying to look ahead into the mists of the future and see the right road leading to the high destiny we desire for our nation'.[182] In a speech at the King's Inns in February 1966 he indicated that he had finally come around to the progressive republican view of Irish combatants in the First World War articulated by his rival Michael O'Mullane in 1924. These men were, Lemass stated, 'generous young Irishmen'.[183]

There were limits to Lemass's 'progressive' outlook on 1916, nonetheless. He vetoed Todd Andrews' idea that, as part of the fiftieth anniversary and as a recognition to Irishmen who fought in the British Army, a bridge be built across the Liffey linking the Phoenix Park to the War Memorial Park.[184] He also bowed to pressure from the sectarian McQuaid once again and abandoned plans for an ecumenical service to mark the opening of the Garden of Remembrance.[185] In March 1966 a splinter faction of the IRA blew up Nelson's Pillar on O'Connell Street, ensuring the commemoration of the fiftieth anniversary of the Rising took place without the imperial admiral looking down on events. The explosion left Nelson's doric column as a stump. The recently retired director of the National Gallery, Thomas McGreevy, wrote to Lemass to try and secure the preservation of the remainder of what he described as one of the finest examples of a neoclassical column in Britain or Ireland.[186] The appeal fell on deaf ears. Lemass regarded Nelson's Pillar as a national embarrassment and had himself raised the prospect of Nelson's removal at cabinet level in November 1960. In 1964 James Ryan suggested a statue of Patrick Pearse be erected in time for the anniversary of the Rising. Lemass poured cold water on this idea. His favoured replacement provides evidence of his rarely displayed piety: he wanted Nelson replaced by a statue of Saint Patrick in time for the Patrician Year, 1961.[187]

For all his desire for Irish people to overcome their history complex, Lemass evidently had strong views about national commemoration. The sculptor Edward Delaney remembered the unveiling of his statue to Thomas Davis on Dublin's College Green in the year of the Rising commemoration. Lemass, de Valera and Aiken sat stiffly beside one another, their War of Independence medals pinned proudly to their chests. Delaney, whose modernist rendering of Davis the cabinet had originally deemed unacceptable, recalled his strong feeling that these men were disconnected from

December 1952: Lemass at the unveiling of the monument at Ahiohil, County Cork, commemorating Richard (Dick) Barrett, who was executed during the Irish Civil War on 8 December 1922, on the order of the Minister for Justice, Kevin O'Higgins. *Cork Examiner.*

modern Ireland.[188] However, to Delaney's satisfaction, Lemass instructed that his sculpture of Wolfe Tone, which was unveiled the following year, be placed in its central position on St Stephen's Green rather than in the Phoenix Park.[189]

Speaking about the ideals of the 1916 leaders, Lemass identified more closely with the cultural nationalism of Patrick Pearse than the socialism of James Connolly. He discounted Connolly's views as 'out of date' but cited the ending of partition and language revival as 'unfinished national tasks'.[190] Talking about the Rising in 1969 he affirmed his adherence to an essentially Pearsean view of the rebellion as providing a 'reawakening' for the next generation.[191] He genuinely hoped that the Irish people would, in 'the spirit of 1916', leave their sectional interests aside and pull together in the interest of national economic development. As Mary Daly has commented, the wave of strikes in 1966 suggests that this hope was not fulfilled.[192]

Sticking to old prejudices, Lemass privately fumed at RTÉ's decision to broadcast a dramatisation of Seán O'Casey's *The Plough and the Stars* to mark the anniversary of the Rising. When asked at a press conference two years previously whether the Church's conservatism towards literature would 'drive out another Seán O'Casey' he pointedly refused to answer the question.[193] In 1966 Lemass, a member of the Commemoration Committee, emphatically instructed the broadcaster that he wanted 'No O'Casey'.[194] However, this hope, too, was not fulfilled.

As Taoiseach, Lemass was brought into more regular contact with the literary world in general. In late 1961, for example, he opened an exhibition devoted to the famous Indian author Rabindranath Tagore, praising his contribution to literature and thought.[195] Beyond speeches written for him on occasions like this, Lemass was generally uninterested in arts and culture. He nonetheless held an unbending view on what constituted acceptable national artistic expression. Having himself pursued a brief acting career prior to independence, he disliked the iconoclastic approach to the modern Irish state of newer playwrights.[196] Lemass's biographers perfunctorily note that as a young man he played the part of Sir Lucius O'Trigger in a production of Richard Brinsley Sheridan's comedy *The Rivals* performed at the Abbey Theatre. The character's calculated fortune-hunting was received by audiences in Georgian London as an attack on the Irish. Lemass, however, was happier with this sort of stage-Irishman than the jig-dancing drunkards of Seán O'Casey and Brendan Behan, whom he could not stand.

Behan, the contemporary embodiment of rugged, rebellious Irish masculinity, was at the height of his fame as a playwright during Lemass's premiership. Myles na Gopaleen, in his 'Cruiskeen Lawn' column, could not help comically juxtaposing the two Dublin men.

> What in the world, I said to myself the other morning, is going to happen to us with Seán Lemass being fined five shillings for being drunk in a public place in London, told to pay fifteen shillings to a doctor, and to behave himself. And his black eye? Not caused by the cops at all . . .
>
> I had become confused and mixed up Mr Seán Lemass, the Taoiseach, and Mr Brendan Behan . . .
>
> Here we have a problem of appearance, ability and political intent. The present Taoiseach is a man of a considerable sort of mercantile talent and he is a holy terror in a game of poker. Yet in appearance he looks much like that American creation, the tired businessman. He has never written a play (heavens almighty, I have done that myself!) and so far as I know he can't sing. He drinks not at all – a mortal sin in the eyes of those who appraise the Irish and admire them. True, he plays the ponies, but to a limited extent in recent years. Summarising all this, his ceremonial function is limited . . .
>
> The trend of my dissertation is surely clear enough. Lemass, as Taoiseach, should sack at least half of his present Ministers

. . . He should then have another referendum providing for a Constitutional amendment creating the office of Assistant President. To that office, once created, he should elevate himself. And the next Taoiseach? Brendan Behan, of course. Probably he would appoint myself privy counsellor and general factotum, with uninhibited command of the purse strings.[197]

Lemass was not laughing at Behan's antics, however. Behan's *The Hostage* was enjoying success in Britain at the time. The play was full of bawdy singing and dancing and, among other things, depicted an IRA veteran-turned-brothel keeper. The following year Lemass was invited to address the Muintir na Tíre rural week at Rockwell College in County Tipperary, where he made one of his rare public forays into discussion of art and culture. Lemass used his speech to voice his disdain for Behan's version of the stage-Irishman. He could not understand the popularity of Behan's characters, viewing them as the protagonists in an 'anti-Irish propaganda campaign'. 'We are not a nation of drinkers,' he insisted.[198]

In his debut address as Taoiseach to the Fianna Fáil Ard-Fheis in 1959 Lemass replied to a motion calling for censorship of stage plays as an urgent necessity. Indecent or pornographic material was banned, he said, because it should be treated as 'putrid meat or contaminated milk'. Stage censorship, on the other hand, would amount to 'the censorship of ideas' and was therefore prohibited under the Constitution. Nonetheless, he shared 'the resentment at offensive references in plays and books to the nation or national leaders'. 'The best censorship to apply to plays of this kind is a strong reaction from public opinion. If the public does not go to these plays then these playwrights will soon disappear.'[199]

But the offending playwrights did not disappear. In a letter to the editor of *The Irish Times* in 1961 Behan replied to Lemass's criticism by pointing to the economic and cultural factors underlying emigration. Attacking the 'Irish bourgeoisie . . . the craw-thumpers, orange and green, who run the island', he went on:

Mr Lemass engaged in some theatrical table talk about myself at Rockwell College last August; in view of the census figures, he must now be as expert on emigration as he is in dramatic criticism, so, marrying his dual talents, he may produce an answer to this question – why Irish playwrights leave home.[200]

The spat was insignificant, but along with Na Gopaleen's article it highlights a major disconnection between the dynamic Irish image Lemass wanted to forge and the rough-hewn but more endearing cultural stereotype. His youthful anxiety about cultural threats to 'the principles of Irish nationality' persisted.[201] Lemass ultimately criticised the 'mad period' of the Censorship Board during which works by Behan and other Irish writers were banned.[202] But when confronted with a stage-Irishman that was not in his image he seems to have been reluctant to meet him with an ironic shrug.

Lemass's broader position on the arts as Taoiseach is another area of his career which has escaped attention and is relevant in assessing his status as a 'cultural revolutionary'. It has been summarised negatively by Ciarán McGonigal, son of the artist Maurice McGonigal, who was a contemporary of Lemass. McGonigal argues that Michael Scott, the architect, and Fr Donal O'Sullivan, a Jesuit priest, held disproportionate influence on Lemass.

> Scott of course was good friends with Lemass, who would support Scott whenever there was an opportunity. Lemass was not all that interested in the arts but when he became Taoiseach, Scott and his friends on the Arts Council, including Donal O'Sullivan, were effectively state control of the arts.[203]

Did Lemass facilitate what amounted to 'state control of the arts' in the 1960s? Previously unpublished documents from the Arts Council Archive shed further light on McGonigal's claim. The Arts Council, established in 1951, remained a very small body by the time Lemass became Taoiseach, employing five permanent staff and a part-time board composed of a handful of men headed by the director, Seán Ó Faoláin. The famous writer resigned as director shortly before Lemass was made Taoiseach. In a long memo he explained his decision.

The duty of the council, as Ó Faoláin saw it, was to make a 'frequent impact on the public mind'. It had a strong role to play in preventing emigration, especially in the provinces. To this end, it 'should extend exhibitions to every town where council has contact' and make a greater effort to assist 'active arts groups throughout the country'. However, the council's small size and lack of funds meant it could not carry out this task. Its administrative set-up was laughable. If the government would not increase its size and funding then it should at least appoint a 'full time director'. 'He should be an active, inventive organiser, not more than forty years old, with practical knowledge of at least one of the arts.'[204]

Ó Faoláin's memo spurned artistic elitism for pragmatic social and economic objectives and a call for youthful dynamism. It reads like a vision Lemass would identify with. But Ó Faoláin's resignation as director in 1959 increased the influence of Scott and O'Sullivan – Lemass's 'good friends' on the Arts Council. Writing in 1958 Ó Faoláin had noted the complicity of this pair. He also noted that other board members felt that Scott's presence on the council represented a conflict of interest because the architect was a 'practising professional'.[205] Scott and O'Sullivan were great drinking pals who had first met during the Emergency. Scott had subsequently introduced O'Sullivan to Lemass.

Scott's state-sponsored commissions continued to roll in with Lemass at the country's helm. He designed RTÉ studios at Donnybrook (1960) and the Abbey Theatre (1966). Scott's influence on Lemass's Ireland was affirmed by the famous 1963 *Time* magazine article – 'Lifting the Green Curtain' – in which he was pictured above a caption that read 'Architect Michael Scott, here before his glass-sheathed TV center, plans everything from new Abbey Theater to hospitals'.[206]

This appraisal was not too far wide of the mark. Unsurprisingly, then, Ó Faoláin's recommendations for the Arts Council fell on deaf ears with Lemass as Taoiseach. A week after taking office Lemass appointed Monsignor Pádraig de Brún as director of the Arts Council.[207] De Brún was the brother-in-law of Seán MacEntee, who was Minister for Health at the time. The appointment drew accusations of jobbery. De Brún, aged seventy, was certainly a conservative choice and far removed from the 'active, inventive organiser, not more than forty years old' Ó Faoláin envisioned. When De Brún died, shortly after his appointment, Lemass promoted yet another Catholic priest to the directorship – his pal Donal O'Sullivan.[208] Assuming yet another state board position, his old colleague Todd Andrews took O'Sullivan's place in the Arts Council hierarchy.

The first meeting between the Arts Council and Lemass occurred a year and a half after he was elected Taoiseach. The council deputation was composed entirely of Lemass's acolytes: Scott, O'Sullivan and Todd Andrews. They presented Lemass with a very watered-down version of Ó Faoláin's 1959 recommendations. This met with a corrective from Lemass stressing the priorities of Ireland Inc. Lemass grudgingly consented to a small pay rise for the council secretary but dismissed a query about the aesthetics of advertising hoardings in rural Ireland as a matter for Bord Fáilte. Most significantly, Lemass dismissed Ó Faoláin's vision of bringing the arts to the plain people of Ireland, arguing instead that funds were being 'dispersed too widely among small groups throughout the country'.[209]

At a subsequent Arts Council meeting the Taoiseach's line was toed obediently. The council decided to give more funds to the visual arts and less to 'music, drama, literature, hall building', concluding that 'it is but commonsense to have regard to the general wishes of the existing Government in this regard'.[210] The shift in the Arts Council's priorities from those of Ó Faoláin to those of Lemass was demonstrated the following year in a letter from its exhibition officer, Desmond Fennell, to O'Sullivan.

Fennell advised that 'key groups should be aimed at rather than the broad mass of the people'. Elite exhibitions showing works of 'the very highest calibre' would achieve a 'certain economy' that 'the shifting of a lower quality exhibition around to many small places' could not. Fennell elaborated: 'By "key groups" I mean . . . creative artists, architects, city dwellers, bishops and priests, students, hoteliers, designers, department store buyers and so on.'[211]

Lemass hated the snobbish decadence of opera and ballet[212] and much preferred a backroom card school to a dinner dance.[213] And yet the Arts Council would conform to the pretensions of Ireland Inc.; it would be a small, elite body targeting these bourgeois and intellectual 'key groups'. As demonstrated by O'Sullivan's appointment, Lemass did not regard Catholic priests overseeing the state's arts agency as inappropriate.[214] Predictably enough, under O'Sullivan's control the independence of the Arts Council from the state was compromised. Former director Seán Ó Faoláin strove hard to establish the organisation's independence, but under Lemass its freedom was obviously diminished.

A 1963 memo from Arts Council secretary Mervyn Wall demonstrated the extent to which Ó Faoláin's vision for the Arts Council had been quashed by Lemass. He noted that the Arts Council had the 'right to intervene in any matter involving public taste' but that 'some years ago the council tried to get industrial interests to agree to cease from erecting advertising hoardings in rural areas. The Government [Lemass] expressed the opinion that in acting in this way the Council were exceeding their legal powers.' The annual grant from the Dáil remained 'so small' and the organisation was headed by a priest who occupied a part-time position, got paid £1,000 a year, and was not obliged to attend meetings. The Arts Council could not appoint staff without the Taoiseach's consent and its current staff numbered just four people. The Taoiseach also had right to withhold grant payments if he was 'not satisfied with the way the council are behaving'.[215] Lemass did eventually grant a small annual increase in the Arts Council's budget. However, by the end of his term, the equivalent body in Northern Ireland was receiving grants amounting to £118,000 a year whereas the Arts Council received just £30,000 annually.[216]

In 1960 Lemass transferred the Arts Council's responsibility for industrial design to the Export Advisory Board. His priorities in doing so were scorned with delicious savagery by the leader of Fine Gael, James Dillon:

> I think if we manufacture a sufficient volume of shiny blackthorns, with right-angle pieces at their tops, and china leprechauns with red hats through which a white clay pipe is preferably stuck, they may prove to be extremely popular, excellent sellers in the popular market. But I understood the whole purpose of inviting the Arts Council to concern itself in this business of industrial design was to dissuade the producers of Irish souvenirs from manufacturing shiny blackthorn sticks with right-angle tops, and china leprechauns with white pipes in their hats, with worsted stockings and buckled boots, with perhaps for good luck miniature blackthorns thrust under their oxters.[217]

The implication was clear. Lemass disdained the ever-so-troublesome peasants of rural Ireland, but was reluctant to dispense with the image of old Ireland because, after all, it was good for commercial tourism. Dillon lampooned what he saw as the end result — the dilution of Irish design with a sanitised stage-Irish image. To a certain extent this was an accurate criticism, as demonstrated by correspondence between Lemass and Thomas Bodkin, the former director of the National Gallery, shortly after Lemass became Taoiseach.

In the summer of 1959 Lemass and Bodkin exchanged letters about the return of pictures in the Hugh Lane collection to Ireland from Britain, a matter of 'vicious controversy . . . which has embittered so many people in both Ireland and England'.[218] Lane was a former director of the National Gallery who, before his death in 1915, had bequeathed a number of important paintings to Ireland. Lemass asked Bodkin to act as the government's adviser on whether the estimates of the value of the paintings drawn up by the National Gallery in London were 'fair'.[219] Bodkin obliged, privately providing Lemass with his expert opinion on the provenance, value and authenticity of several paintings after examining them in London.

Lemass's balance-sheet mentality came across strongly in the correspondence that followed. He was preoccupied with how much the government was going to have to pay for the pictures. While this was understandable, he felt obliged to inform Bodkin of the obvious point that 'we would not be disposed to query a valuation on the ground that it is too *low*'.[220] Lemass was evidently worried that Bodkin's academic integrity would ruin a good deal and was anxious to apply some wheeler-dealing.

In August 1959 Bodkin wrote to Lemass informing him that he thought a painting in the collection ascribed to the French painter often referred to as the 'father of impressionism', Jean-Baptiste-Camille Corot, was certainly genuine. Lemass wrote back making clear that for the purposes of valuation the mere ascription of the painting to Corot was fine as this would mean paying the British a lower price.[221] Later, however, when the paintings were secured for display in Ireland, Lemass wrote to Bodkin: 'I need not remind you that you felt that it should be described as *being* by Corot'.[222] 'It should be labelled as being by Corot, and not attributed to him . . . when the picture is eventually hung here'![223]

Lemass professed to have found his chats with Bodkin on art 'so very interesting and informative that I did not note the passage of time'.[224] Bodkin provided Lemass with books on art and art history and wrote to Lemass telling him that 'it was very flattering to me to hear from you that you had been reading my book on Lane and his pictures'.[225] When the paintings were unveiled at Dublin's Municipal Gallery in 1961 (now the Hugh Lane Gallery) Lemass paid tribute to Lane's 'astonishing taste'.[226]

Nonetheless, in his attitude to the arts as Taoiseach Lemass evidently paid less attention to a central argument of Bodkin's, one he had expressed in a 1949 report on the state of the arts in Ireland. 'We have not merely failed to go forward in policies concerning the arts, we have in fact regressed to arrive, many years ago, to a condition of apathy about them'; 'no country of western Europe cared less, or gave less, for the cultivation of the arts,' Bodkin wrote.[227] In their exchange of letters in 1959 Bodkin tried to impress on Lemass 'the great importance of encouraging the production of good design for industry and good pictorial publicity for tourism', claiming that 'no Government in Europe has so dreadfully neglected the cultivation of the visual arts as we have done in the last fifty years'.[228]

In transferring this responsibility from artists to businessmen, it seems Bodkin's appeal was not heeded by Lemass. When it comes to his relationship with the arts as Taoiseach, it is hard to avoid the conclusion that he was influenced by priests, businessmen and friends rather than artists. This did little to mitigate his general ignorance of the importance of organic and independent artistic and cultural initiatives to national progress.

The Drama of Resignation

In 1965 James Ryan departed from the cabinet and, despite his resistance, Lemass succeeded in getting his old rival MacEntee to resign as well. Of de Valera's original warriors only Aiken and Lemass remained. Lemass knew, however, that his health would force his retirement soon enough. He was increasingly weary and had started to suffer blackouts.[229] At a reception in late 1963 his ailing health was displayed in public when he was taken quite seriously ill. The press were told that it was an allergy and Lemass laughed it off by saying he had an 'allergy to work'.[230] But the signs of declining health were there to see. As a man in his mid-sixties who did not drink, his pipe gave him great comfort. The rituals of scraping it, cleaning it and filling it with tobacco were reassuring. If asked an uncomfortable question at a meeting Lemass could always go about lighting his pipe, giving him time to think. Yet the health effects of smoking copious amounts of strong pipe tobacco for over forty years were beginning to show as well.

At a special meeting of the Fianna Fáil party in September 1966 Lemass referred to press speculation about his retirement. These rumours were not 'maliciously inspired', he contended, and he 'would have to retire sooner or later'.[231] Brushing aside the issue, he went on to emphasise the need to strengthen the party organisation at all levels. But in allaying the rumours, he knew he was trying to play a hand with no cards in it. News of Lemass's impending resignation was leaked in *The Irish Press*. Speculation and uncertainty persisted until Lemass confirmed his resignation just a week later.

In one of his earliest political articles, written in 1966, Bruce Arnold, the journalist who later became the scourge of Charles Haughey, wrote of Lemass as '*le Roi*' of the Fianna Fáil party, describing his exercise of power in imperious terms:

> Lemass managed to achieve one of the strangest pieces of political wizardry ever seen in Ireland: he took the two party system – which for all that P.R. could do, or the existence of a third political 'Left-wing' group – was the natural residue of the Civil War, and he used it according to the American system of a separated executive and legislature. One witnessed, often with amazement, usually with great admiration, and always with the knowledge that it could not really fail – this single-handed Government of the country, his own party, and even his occasionally dissident Ministers. Even when his majority in the House was down to one the man himself remained un-worried, unflustered and unhurried in his manipulation of state affairs.
>
> And when he announced his resignation and sat facing his biggest-ever press conference, he remained as inscrutable as he had always been, and – so used had the press got to his ability to outmanoeuvre them – he did not even get asked any 'rubbing' or 'scratching' questions. It was one of the most perfect examples of democratic dictatorship ever known.[232]

The democratic dictator's decision to retire was taken in good grace by most within the parliamentary party. Those in the inner sanctum knew that Lemass had been suffering from growing hoarseness for some time; in fact, it was assumed that the Taoiseach had contracted throat cancer.[233] However, and perhaps predictably, he faced criticism from his old cabinet-room enemy MacEntee, who claimed Lemass's resignation was a poorly timed blow to a party at its lowest ebb. Taking his old rival's claim to health on face value, MacEntee demanded 'a more credible justification' for the decision. Amazingly, the embers of one of the longest-running Irish political rivalries were not quite dead. Lemass was 'washing his hands' of responsibility for the country's affairs, MacEntee asserted. The party and the state were 'tottering towards anarchy': Lemass had not just 'squandered' de Valera's legacy, he was 'deserting in the face of the enemy'.[234]

MacEntee's outburst was cutting if not uncharacteristic. It demonstrated a personal enmity built up over many years. Significantly, MacEntee also voiced dissatisfaction with the ascent of 'personal interest' over loyalty in the party under Lemass's leadership. But for all his bluster, MacEntee also displayed nervousness. Fianna Fáil had never before held a leadership contest. To the party, the whole affair was frighteningly new.

Lemass's resignation represented a tacit acceptance that his influence upon national development and economic recovery had been significant but – amid the winds of social and cultural change that the 1960s generated – was limited. Anxious to avoid accusations of nepotism, Lemass did not express a preference when meeting the three candidates for succession – George Colley, Jack Lynch and Charles Haughey. He maintained an aloof stance in the unfolding drama, which was seen by most people as a clash between the slick, ambitious Haughey and the cleaner Colley.

There are rumours that Lemass secretly shared the general dislike of Haughey. On the other hand, there are rumours that he initially led journalists to believe that he was supporting George Colley because he thought this would help Haughey by discouraging others from entering the race.[235] Whatever his private convictions, Lemass eventually backed Jack Lynch, Cork hurling hero and Finance Minister. Lynch was not just the 'compromise candidate' between Colley and Haughey, but also the alternative to Neil Blaney. Lemass had praised Blaney on his nomination as a candidate in the 1949 Donegal by-election as 'a very fine type of Irishman, combining high educational qualifications and considerable administrative experience with a very intimate knowledge of the area'.[236] But despite these qualities, Blaney gave off the malodour of unreconstructed Donegal republicanism.[237]

Throughout the succession drama Lemass exuded his own, at times studied, air of chauvinistic paternalism. He barracked Lynch and George Colley for consulting their wives before taking major decisions. Lemass, displaying a more Victorian approach to conjugal relations, had not discussed his resignation with Kathleen beforehand. Every morning Kathleen served her husband breakfast in bed while he read the papers; then he would get dressed and depart for work. He was always home by 5 p.m. for dinner; if he was forced to stay on

Lemass receives an honorary Law doctorate from Trinity
College Dublin, July 1965. *Courtesy The Irish Press.*

a minute longer than scheduled in the Taoiseach's office he became
agitated.[238] True to form, he merely came home one day at 5 p.m.
and told Kathleen he had resigned as Taoiseach, before settling down
to dinner.

   When the leadership ballot was held, Lemass remarked that the
battered old shoebox used to collect votes was a 'queer receptacle for
such a momentous decision'.[239] A queer receptacle, perhaps, but the
shoebox was a rare example of a certain innocence to the party, an
innocence that was starting to drain out of Fianna Fáil under Lemass's
leadership. It was Jack Lynch who eventually triumphed. With the
succession complete, Lemass continued as a TD until 1969. He spent
most of his later years on the golf course, at home, or sitting on
company boards. Between 1966 and 1968 he was given no fewer
than eight business directorships – a reflection of the scale of the
patronage he had built up over his years in public office. These
included board membership of big Fianna Fáil donors Unidare,

Electrical Industries of Ireland, Irish Security Services; the chairmanship of a new company set up to manage the Beamish brewery in Cork, and the vice-chairmanship of the tourist company of party colleague Dermot Ryan.[240] On his retirement from politics in 1969, Haughey arranged a special presentation to Lemass by members of the Oireachtas.[241]

Lemass had claimed on resignation in 1966 to be in good health, but it was an open secret that this was not the case. Throat cancer had been suspected then, but in later years he suffered increasingly from lung problems. David Andrews, a young member of Lemass's retirement project, the informal cross-party committee on the Constitution, recalled that at these meetings the former Taoiseach was often obviously struggling to catch his breath.[242]

Towards the end of his life, consigned to hospital, Lemass insisted on maintaining a neat appearance and having his hair oiled. He also refused drugs to deal with the pain because he wanted to 'stay in control'. During his last illness he suffered a collapsed lung; 'I've had enough,' he is rumoured to have said. Efforts to re-inflate the organ failed and he died on 11 May 1971.[243] At his funeral the Dublin brigade of the Old IRA provided a guard of honour as his coffin, flanked by troops of the Irish Army, passed the GPO on its way to the Church of the Good Shepherd, Churchtown, and on to Deansgrange Cemetery.

How should Lemass's legacy as Taoiseach be appraised, then? When his political career ended in 1969 many of Lemass's associates looked upon his record as Taoiseach with some scepticism. This was in part due to his plain, matter-of-fact, stoical way of doing his job and addressing the public. He had little time for flowery rhetoric and derided the polished language of his great adversary MacEntee by referring to him as a 'minor poet'.[244] Relative to de Valera, he was a liberal, reforming Taoiseach. As in a great number of other countries, Ireland experienced social change in the 1960s, most notably in a growing anti-clericalism. And Lemass, an ageing soldier of destiny, proved receptive to these conditions.

He denied that civil servants took decisions, but his thinking was certainly influenced by the civil service machine, one which was increasingly a commentary on world trading opportunities and how Ireland was responding to them.[245] At the same time, the closeness of T. K. Whitaker and Lemass in this head-first modernisation project has been overstated.[246] While both men thought that foreign capital

Lemass's grave, Deansgrange Cemetery.

should be allowed in to Ireland, Lemass's expansionist Keynesianism clashed with Whitaker's bleak deflationary approach, which viewed social spending as an 'unproductive investment'. Lemass's was a gradual and conditional liberalisation of economic thought, never to be full throttle.

While some Irish businesses inevitably lost out with the abandonment of protection, the new state subsidies for foreign firms predominately went to companies who did not threaten to displace native capitalists.[247] Lemass did not wholeheartedly follow Whitaker, who favoured cutbacks in public spending, whereas the Taoiseach favoured expansion through expenditure. Neither did he merely abandon his verve for state control for a deregulatory agenda. Although the 'turn' was signalled most clearly by *Economic Development*, Lemass imposed tariffs up until 1963.[248] Lemass and Whitaker did not single-handedly kick-start Irish economic growth in this period, then; rather, they worked to reposition the country, signalling

Ireland's willingness to take advantage of bigger developments in the international economy.[249] The Irish economy's growth in the next few years did not occur as a direct result of the publication of these documents. The new economic direction had been coming for some time. As we have seen, Lemass was preparing for the transition since at least the early 1950s.

Socially and culturally, the majority of changes in 1960s Ireland happened despite, not because of, Lemass, who was forced to work within the parameters he had played a leading role in establishing. While he was unleashing economic liberalisation, he neglected to engage social and cultural liberalisation with the same enthusiasm. Lemass understood that Ireland's new multinational companies were effectively setting in train trends 'contrary to our way of life', such as the employment of women. Yet the stifling hegemony of the Catholic Church still remained.

Lemass maintained a distance from the obnoxious new set embodied by Taca, an alcohol-soaked boys' club of businessmen, who paid £100 a year for the ears of young ministers at ostentatious dinners. However, the break between the old soul of Fianna Fáil and the ostentatious new attitude towards wealth and power was evident well before Lemass stepped down as leader. Devoid of the mohair suit and Dom Pérignon dynamic of his son-in-law, Lemass was, nonetheless, of the same paternalist political stable. He never identified fully with the laissez-faire ethos, but had come to place a rather dogmatic premium on the values of 'enterprise' and 'risk-taking' in public life. Arguably, he had unleashed the forces of commercial modernisation while addressing the social and cultural backwardness of Ireland from a relatively narrow ideological perspective. When he stepped down as Taoiseach the economic revolution may have been well under way, but the Irish cultural revolution had a long way yet to go.

Conclusion

The Real Measure of the Man

In his satirical play *The Mundy Scheme* Brian Friel provided an allegory of the commercial priorities of Ireland Inc. First performed in 1969, Friel portrayed an Ireland suffering the 'spiritual and economic depression' caused by economic planning dependent on western investment. The stage Taoiseach promises escape from bankruptcy by endorsing a scheme drawn up by an Irish-American millionaire, Homer Mundy, to buy up huge swathes of the west of Ireland to use as an international cemetery. Ireland is effectively sold to the highest bidder.

Friel did not seek to satirise Lemass exclusively, but in parts the lampoon is unmistakeable.[1] Similarly, Gerry Boland, Lemass's long-time colleague, paid him a backhanded compliment when he described him in 1968 as 'different' from his old party colleagues; he was, stated Boland, 'a real businessman'.[2] Symbolic of this was the destruction of much of Georgian Dublin under Lemass's premiership, replaced by glass-faced office blocks and rented back to the government at a tidy profit by the developers and speculators that grew up around Fianna Fáil in the 1960s.[3] Noël Browne recalled going to visit an old hospital on Dublin's northside in the early 1970s which he had campaigned to keep open. 'It had been demolished and converted into a modern office block called Seán Lemass House. Such are our priorities.'[4]

The majority of historical appraisals of Lemass have conformed to a modern Irish version of 'Whig history'. In this approach, a narrative of modernisation-at-all-costs explains away the unsavoury by-products of the 'priorities' Browne identifies. Implicitly, the negative aspects of Lemass's developmentalism are excusable once the well-worn dichotomy between the 'old' and the 'new' Irelands is rolled out. Whatever his faults, at least Lemass delivered one in the eye for twee auld Ireland. As Tom Garvin enthuses: 'When Lemass affected a de Valeran fondness for the green fields he loved so well, it concealed his real love: driving across them.'[5]

This is a far cry from the political ethic some of the literary works Ernie O'Malley recalled Lemass quoting enthusiastically while they were imprisoned in 1923. Peter Kropotkin, whom O'Malley

CONFIDENTIAL

LEMASS, SEAN   died May 1971

Businessman and former Taoiseach.

Born 1899 in Dublin. Educated in Christian Brothers' Schools. Took part in 1916 Rising and taken prisoner at the G.P.O. but released because of his youth; fought again in 1916 Rising and interned until 1921; fought with de Valera on anti-Treaty side in the Civil War (HQ staff; imprisoned twice and escaped once); T.D. (Sinn Fein and, from 1926, Fianna Fail) for Dublin South 1924-48 and for Dublin South Central 1948-69; Fianna Fail Director of Elections 1927-32; Minister for Industry and Commerce 1932-9; Minister for Supplies 1939-45 and Minister for Industry and Commerce, 1941-8 (Tanaiste 1945-8); Managing Director, Irish Press Ltd., 1948-51; Tanaiste and Minister for Industry and Commerce, 1951-4 and 1957-9; Taoiseach 1959-66.

Chairman of Cement Roadstone Holdings Ltd.; Unidare Ltd.; Wavin Pipes Ltd.; Beamish and Crawford Ltd. (a subsidiary of Canadian Brewers). Deputy Chairman of Ryans Tourist Holdings Ltd. Director of Electrical Industries of Ireland, Ltd., Waterford Glass, etc.

Mr. Lemass was, from an early age, Mr. de Valera's right hand man. He is said to have suggested the formation of Fianna Fail in 1926 and was immediately put in charge of the party machine. His concentration on Industry and Commerce once the party came into power reflected the early Fianna Fail conviction that Ireland must be made economically as well as politically independent. Mr. Lemass was the architect of the Irish airlines, the peat industry, mineral exploitation and the sudden extension of the electricity, sugar and shipping industries. His isolationist views soon changed, and he has become a supporter of Irish entry to the E.E.C. and its corollary, the reduction of protection. It was largely through his initiative that negotiations for the Anglo-Irish Free Trade Area Agreement were undertaken and successfully completed in 1966.

It is said that during the 1939-45 War, Mr. Lemass privately supported Ireland's association with the Allied cause.

Mr. Lemass' views on partition are orthodox, but his approach is pragmatic. In the early 1960s he made it clear that he deplored the excessive Irish preoccupation with past grievances and hoped reunification could come about through economic co-operation and mutual tolerance. In 1965, he took the unprecedented step of visiting Stormont for talks with the Northern Prime Minister, an act which started to melt the ice between Dublin and Belfast. In 1970, he gave his support to Mr. Lynch's policy towards the North.

CONFIDENTIAL

Mr. Lemass' main task was to usher out of power the Old Guard, de Valera's comrades, and replace them with the younger men who now govern Ireland. The change was abrupt but successful. The men who now govern Ireland reflect his personality and ideals.

Mr. Lemass retired from politics in 1966 through bad health, but has since led a very active business life. He is an active Chairman of the Irish Council of the European Movement, and invariably chairs meetings where prominent E.E.C. personalities address Irish audiences.

Despite his revolutionary background, Mr. Lemass is not a typical Irishman (his family is said to be of Jewish origin – his father was a Dublin tailor). He is sensible, courageous, cool-headed and at heart a businessman. His outlook has always been wider and more pragmatic than that of his contemporaries in politics. He is pleasant but lacks charm; he commanded the devotion of his officials and now claims the respect of most businessmen.

Married in 1924, Kathleen Hughes, an agreeable lady whose interests are confined to her family and domestic affairs. They have one son, Noel (q.v.), Parliamentary Secretary to the Minister for Finance (in charge of Board of Works), and three daughters, one of whom is married to Mr. Charles Haughey (q.v.) and another to Commandant John O'Brien, A.D.C. to the Taoiseach. The third, Mrs. Sheila O'Connell, is active in Fianna Fail politics in south Dublin.

Confidential British file on Lemass, 1971. NAUK FCO 33,1599.

mentions, was an anarchist Russian writer with a rural, rather than industrial, vision, opposed to centralised state planning and control; Upton Sinclair, another early favourite of Lemass's, was an American socialist who depicted the injustices of capitalism. The other writer whom O'Malley recalls Lemass's admiration for, Thomas Carlyle, wrote of the necessity of 'heroes' taking control of society; only these dynamic individuals could master events. This vision is closer to Lemass's vigorous, highly centralised, headstrong exercise of power. He had all the nerve of a card sharp, wrapped up within an unshakeable, self-righteous conviction that he was the man to build modern Ireland.

The hatter's son was Taoiseach for just seven of his forty-six years as a politician. And yet the vast majority of literature on Lemass concerns his performance in this figurehead role. As Michael Kennedy has observed, the airbrushing of the less liberal, pre-1959 Lemass has much to do with his ownership by T. K. Whitaker, to whom everyone goes to talk about Lemass.[6] This has obscured the influence of John Leydon, Lemass's lieutenant for the best part of three decades before Whitaker. Leydon was described by Todd Andrews as 'the greatest public servant of our time' and 'the crutch on which Lemass leaned'.[7] And Leydon's scrupulous professionalism as a civil servant ensured he attributed all his achievements to Lemass exclusively.

Similarly, the Lemass–de Valera relationship was much closer than conveyed in the Lemassiography. 'The whole of our political and social activity is based on the knowledge that mankind has a spiritual destiny ... more important than factories, power stations and material wealth.'[8] These were the words of Lemass, not de Valera, speaking in 1952 after recovering from illness. Lemass followed his chief's lead, and occasionally his turn of phrase, for most of his political life. Theirs was a relationship based not only on loyalty but also shared aspiration.[9] Garvin places Lemass close to Charles Stewart Parnell. But Lemass, like de Valera, was far removed from the liberal, professional, secularised political leadership of Parnell. Lemass saw Catholicism as offering a desirable social model while ignoring the economic recommendations of social Catholicism such as distributism, voluntarism and vocationalism. Garvin has little time for either the idealism of the old Ireland or the commerce-driven authoritarian bureaucracies of the new Ireland.[10] But in reality, Lemass's footprints are perceptible in both of these camps.

In much the same way that Lemass and de Valera have been almost clinically separated by Lemass's admirers, his role in Charles Haughey's political ascent has been downplayed. Haughey was to amass great personal wealth, but at the expense of an impoverished reputation. Lemass's reputation, by contrast, has undoubtedly been enhanced not only by his own financial probity but also by his son-in-law's financial profligacy. And yet towards the end of his political career Lemass placed a high value on the money-making capacity of vacuous rogues like Haughey. According to a contemporary, Lemass – who did not invest his money wisely – confided that he 'admired Haughey because of his ability to make money, which he hadn't got himself'.[11] From the point of view of historical judgement, Lemass was lucky that Haughey was not seen as his successor. He was also fortunate that his resignation as Taoiseach in 1966 occurred before the resumption of serious unrest in Northern Ireland and its political consequences in the Republic.

Veteran politician and academic Michael D. Higgins briefly joined Fianna Fáil in 1966 aged twenty-five, as Lemass's term as

Taoiseach was coming to an end. Higgins' view of Lemass is resoundingly negative. He sees Lemass as 'Taoiseach of the new money', resembling the leaders of today's Asian 'Tiger' economies, with 'economic progress incubated by a quasi-authoritarian state'. He regards Lemass as 'unlike most of his early republican comrades; he was not a non-inheriting son of the farm, but a "mover and shaker" of the embryonic speculative class, a member of the metropolitan elite'. Higgins sees the popular image of Lemass as facing a decision between the traditionalist route of protectionism, on the one hand, and the modernist route of free trade, on the other, as simplistic, a symptom of what the sociologist Max Weber termed the 'iron cage' – the teleological pursuit of efficiency, rationalisation and bureaucratisation in western capitalist societies. This dichotomy, according to Higgins, ignores the 'missing conception': the broader application of egalitarian, inclusive civic republicanism in Ireland. Lemass had no commitment to this ideal of citizenship, he claims. The flip side of Lemass's celebrated pragmatism, argues Higgins, was a 'philistine impatience' with complex matters.[12]

But if Lemass had faith in the dynamism of enterprise, he was more of a dirigiste and does not belong to the ultra free-market liberalism of the post-Soviet world. In modern Fianna Fáil, Lemass is celebrated as a pragmatist among rustic republican cranks. At policy level, his name lives on in the 'Lemass Forum', a policy group established in March 2010. But Lemass could not be further divorced from the model of 'light-touch regulation' instituted by his admirers in modern Fianna Fáil. Lemass remained sceptical of the financial sector for most of his political career and criticised what he termed 'uncontrolled bank policy'. Commercial banking should 'march in accord with national policy', he insisted.[13] While he came around to the idea of greater foreign capital investment in Ireland, he did not see the role of the Irish state as subservient to it. Neither did he manufacture credit for himself through utilising the political marketing techniques beginning to emerge as he was bowing out of public life.

Throughout his career Lemass established a variety of welfare initiatives and doggedly pursued the goal of full employment. As Taoiseach he wanted the civil service to become 'more commercially oriented in respect of some of their activities', but not to the *detriment* of the state sector.[14] Lemass used the radical juggernaut of state intervention to expand Irish industrial development greatly and, with it, living standards. His legacy, then, comprises more than soulless office blocks or, to quote his long-time collaborator Todd Andrews, the worship of 'the bitch goddess, success – an image that has many aspects, the most common being the acquisition and appreciation of fine food, exquisite wine and the limousine one dreams of'.[15]

At the same time, Lemass and Andrews laid the foundations for the later triumph of this materialistic attitude in Ireland. Lemass was preoccupied with the consolidation and maintenance of power over nation and party. Like his chief, he frequently manipulated Ard-Fheis procedures to get his own way. As Dick Walsh put it: 'No one, as far as we know, ever asked Lemass about Machiavelli's *Prince*, but he played the part at least as often and arguably with more success than Dev.'[16] But unlike de Valera, who had the common touch, Lemass's economically focused Ard-Fheis speeches often went over the heads of the crowd.[17] He was more skilled as a political tactician than a political orator.

As a political operator, Lemass was not a political pluralist. He held the view that it was unpatriotic not to vote for Fianna Fáil. Only *his* party could deliver national progress and it would be on *their* terms. In implementing this view, Lemass was capable of innovation but also sophistry. He was adept at dressing up self-interest in the language of self-righteousness, in disguising tribalism as high-mindedness. Although scrupulous in pursuing his nationalistic conception of the 'common good', a quasi-corporatist cronyism developed under him. When he was in power, the grand narrative of national economic progress allowed little time for free thinkers who challenged state authority.

If the title 'architect of modern Ireland' is to be given to Lemass then he must take the blame for some of the negatives as well as the positives of life in modern Ireland. Lemass's energetic determination to spearhead national regeneration has to be weighed against his negative points, like his weak commitment to pluralism and his authoritarian and populist reflexes. He personally adhered to the classical values of Irish social and political culture such as state bureaucracy, authoritarianism and personalism. To view him as the 'father' of more recent phenomena such as the ending of organised religious control over social spheres, liberalism, pluralism and relativism is glaringly anachronistic.

In summary, it seems many historians have fallen under the spell of the *Time* cover story of 12 July 1963. On that classic magazine cover a leprechaun pulls back a shamrock curtain to reveal Lemass's film noir facial features against the backdrop of a busy factory. While Lemass's energy as Taoiseach imbued 'New Spirit in the Ould Sod', this process was less revolutionary and less personalised than has hitherto been claimed. Neither should Lemass's period as Taoiseach obscure his long and eventful political career up to that point. It is high time we acquainted ourselves with Ireland's Democratic Dictator.

References

Introduction

1 These are Brian Farrell, *Seán Lemass* (Dublin, 1983); Michael O'Sullivan, *Seán Lemass: A Biography* (Dublin, 1994); John Horgan, *Seán Lemass: The Enigmatic Patriot* (Dublin, 1997); Robert Savage, *Seán Lemass* (Dundalk, 1999); Tom Garvin, *Judging Lemass: The Measure of the Man* (Dublin, 2011). See also the collection of chapters in Brian Girvin and Gary Murphy (eds), *The Lemass Era: Politics and Society in the Ireland of Seán Lemass* (Dublin, 2005) and Paul Bew and Henry Patterson's *Seán Lemass and the Making of Modern Ireland, 1945–66* (Dublin, 1982).

2 Martin Mansergh, 'The Political Legacy of Seán Lemass', in Mansergh, *The Legacy of History for Making Peace in Ireland* (Cork, 2003), p. 330.

3 Albert Reynolds, *My Autobiography* (Dublin, 2009), p. 13; Bertie Ahern, *The Autobiography* (Dublin, 2009), p. 19.

4 Brian Cowen, speech at the launch of *Judging Lemass* in the Royal Irish Academy, Dawson Street, Dublin, 29 September 2009.

5 Sir Anthony O'Reilly's comments to the author on Seán Lemass, 17 June 2010.

6 Tom Garvin, *Preventing the Future: Why was Ireland So Poor for So Long?* (Dublin, 2004), p. 63.

7 Tim Pat Coogan, *De Valera: Long Fellow, Long Shadow* (London, 1993), p. 629.

8 J. J. Lee, 'Seán Lemass', in J. J. Lee (ed.), *Ireland 1945–70* (Dublin, 1979), p. 22.

9 See Diarmaid Ferriter's introductions to his *The Transformation of Ireland* (Dublin, 2005) and *Judging Dev: A Reassessment of the Life and Legacy of Éamon de Valera* (Dublin, 2007).

10 'Lifting the Green Curtain' *Time*, 12 July 1963.

11 Liam Skinner, 'Seán Lemass: Nation Builder', unpublished manuscript, University College Dublin Archives, P161/93.

12 Garvin, *Judging Lemass*, p. 256.

13 Tim Pat Coogan, *A Memoir* (London, 2008), p. 282.

14 'Lemass: The Man Who Made Modern Ireland', broadcast RTÉ 1, 16 February 2010.

Chapter 1: The Shadow of a Gunman

1 Census material accessible at www.census.nationalarchives.ie

2 *Thom's Directory* (Dublin, 1909).

3 Skinner, 'Seán Lemass: Nation Builder', p. 169.

4 www.census.nationalarchives.ie

5 School records, courtesy of the Allen Library.

6 Seán Lemass to Michael Mills, *The Irish Press*, 21 January 1969.

7 School records, courtesy of the Allen Library.

8 Biographical details on Bracken are taken from Charles Edward Lysaght, *Brendan Bracken* (London, 1979).

9 Allen Library, O'Connell School register, 1904–1918. Dalton's presence at the school has escaped Lemass's biographers because he was listed in the school register (possibly as a result of the school registrar's identification with the leader of the futile rising of 1803) as 'Robert Emmett Dalton'.

10 Allen Library, O'Connell School register, 1908–1917.

11 Emmet Dalton papers, National Library of Ireland (NLI) Manuscripts Collection (MS) 46, 687 (6). Dalton was also stationed in Belgium, Salonika, Greece, Macedonia and Egypt.

12 Lemass to Mills, *The Irish Press*, 21 January 1969.

13 Quote from Coogan, *Long Fellow, Long Shadow*, p. 69.

14 Michael Laffan, *The Resurrection of Ireland: The Sinn Féin Party, 1916–1923* (Cambridge, 1999), p. 45.

15 Garvin's claim that MacNeill recognised the Lemass lads is unfounded; they would have recognised him. Garvin, *Judging Lemass*, p. 47.

16 Lemass to Mills, *The Irish Press*, 20 January 1969.

17 Seán Haughey in 'Lemass: The Man Who Made Modern Ireland', broadcast RTÉ 1, 16 February 2010.

18 See Skinner, 'Seán Lemass: Nation Builder', p. 172.

19 Tom Garvin in 'Lemass: The Man Who Made Modern Ireland', broadcast RTÉ 1, 16 February 2010.

20 Lemass to Mills, *The Irish Press*, 20 January 1969.

21 See Dan Breen, *My Fight for Irish Freedom* (Tralee, 1973), p. 77.

22 Lemass to Mills, *The Irish Press*, 20 January 1969. The garrison's hunger was exacerbated by the unnecessarily mean rationing system operated by Desmond Fitzgerald in the GPO.

23 Lemass to Mills, *The Irish Press*, 20 January 1969.

24 Lemass, 'Account of Rising', courtesy of Seán Haughey.

25 Bertie Ahern, *The Autobiography*, p. 19.

26 Seán Lemass, 'Account of Rising', courtesy of Seán Haughey. Connolly was, of course, quite a heavy man, which impeded the stretcher bearers' progress.

27 Skinner, 'Seán Lemass: Nation Builder', p. 173.

28 'Lifting the Green Curtain', *Time*, 12 July 1963.

29 Lemass to Mills, *The Irish Press*, 20 January 1969.

30 Lemass to Mills, *The Irish Press*, 21 January 1969.

31 *Ibid.*

32 Garvin claims that by this early stage Lemass was already sceptical about Pearse's militaristic romanticism. See Garvin, *Judging Lemass,* p. 47.

33 Lemass to Mills, *The Irish Press*, 21 January 1969.

34 NLI, Thomas MacDonagh papers, MS 33,567/10.

35 MacDonagh was the sister of Grace Gifford, bride to Joseph Plunkett, another leader of the Rising executed in 1916. See Philip B. Ryan, *Jimmy O'Dea: The Pride of the Coombe* (Dublin, 1990), p. 41.

36 Lemass to Mills, *The Irish Press*, 21 January 1969. For more on Moore see NLI, Colonel Maurice Moore papers, MS 9,712. Moore was the brother of the novelist George Moore.

37 Lemass to Mills, *The Irish Press*, 21 January 1969.

38 Skinner, 'Seán Lemass: Nation Builder', p. 176.

39 *Ibid.*

40 Diary of Lieutenant Emmet Dalton, 6th Leinster Regiment, 3 February 1918. NLI, Dalton papers, MS 46,687 (1).
41 Dalton Diary, 26 February 1918, NLI, MS 46,687 (1).
42 Dalton Diary, 27 February 1918, NLI, MS 46,687 (1).
43 Dalton Diary, 25–27 March 1918, NLI, MS 46,687 (1).
44 Dalton Diary, 25 January 1918, NLI, MS 46,687 (1).
45 Dalton Diary, 28 January 1918, NLI, MS 46,687 (1).
46 Dalton Diary, 3 February 1918, NLI, MS 46,687 (1).
47 Lemass to Mills, *The Irish Press*, 21 January 1969.
48 John Horgan Archive (JHA), notes on Noel Lemass. Noel is cited as drilling in Derry in February 1920.
49 *The Irish Times*, 25 October 1920.
50 *The Irish Times*, 11 November 1920.
51 Military Archives (MA), Civil War prisoner index, no. 8774.
52 Tony Woods, in Uinseann MacEoin, *Survivors* (Dublin, 1987), p. 312.
53 *Ibid.*
54 O'Sullivan, *Seán Lemass*, p. 20.
55 The assassinations prompted the brutal retaliation by Black and Tans at Croke Park later that day. The author's grandfather, a spectator supporting the Tipperary team, managed to escape the slaughter, suffering only the loss of a shoe.
56 *Irish Independent*, 27 October 1997.
57 Breen, *My Fight for Irish Freedom*, p. 128.
58 See MA, Bureau of Military History, WS 413 (Patrick McCrea).
59 Michael Foy, *Michael Collins's Intelligence War: The Struggle Between the British and the IRA, 1919–1921* (Stroud, Gloucestershire, 2006), p. 193.
60 See MA, Bureau of Military History, WS 413 (Patrick McCrea). McCrea returned home after the killing and told his wife he had been out fishing. Later that day his wife, in floods of tears, produced a newspaper detailing the killing. 'Was this the fishing trip you were on?' she asked. 'Yes, and don't you see we had a good catch,' he drily replied.
61 Horgan, *Enigmatic Patriot*, pp. 17–18.
62 See Foy, *Michael Collins's Intelligence War*, p. 193. The testimony of the volunteer, Matty MacDonald, is included in the Ernie O'Malley notebooks, held in UCD Archives at P17b/105 (75–76). His is the only witness statement to mention Lemass.
63 Garvin, *Judging Lemass*, p. 48.
64 See, for instance, William J. Stapleton, 'Michael Collins's Squad', *Capuchin Annual* (1969), pp. 368–77.
65 See the statement of Colonel Joseph Leonard at NLI, MS 33,700. According to Leonard the main members were Paddy O'Daly, himself, Ben Barrett and Seán Doyle. He also mentions four Tipperary men 'attached for a time' – Seán Treacy, Dan Breen, J. J. Hogan and Séamus Robinson. Bringing the 'apostles' up to full number were Mick McDonald, Tom Keogh, Jim Slattery, Vincent Byrne and Martin Savage. Leonard also cites the involvement of Tom Kehoe, Frank Bolster, Eddie Byrne, Ben Byrne, Mick O'Reilly and Mick Kennedy. Patrick McCrea, who was interviewed by the Bureau of Military History as

a 'Squad' member repeats this list, also mentioning himself, Paddy Griffin, Séamus Brennan, Bill Stapleton and Paddy Drury as members who joined later on. See MA, Bureau of Military History, WS 413. None of the many testimonies collected by the Bureau of Military History in the 1940s and 1950s mentions Lemass's involvement.

66 Leonard, NLI, MS 33,700.

67 *Ibid.*

68 JHA, IRA 'A' company 3rd battalion reunion dinner, 2 October 1948.

69 Interview with Ulick O'Connor, 27 July 2010. O'Connor met a range of men involved in the Bloody Sunday killings, including such protagonists as Vincent Byrne and William Stapleton.

70 *The Irish Times*, 15 March 1921.

71 Lemass to Mills, *The Irish Press*, 22 January 1969.

72 Horgan, *Enigmatic Patriot*, p. 21.

73 See National Archives of Ireland (NAI), Industry and Commerce files (IND)/ EMR/1/3.

74 JHA, interview with Charles Haughey, 24 October 1994.

75 Patrick Murray, *Oracles of God: The Roman Catholic Church and Irish Politics, 1922–37* (Dublin, 2000), p. 37.

76 Lemass to Mills, *The Irish Press*, 22 January 1969.

77 *Ibid.*

78 *Ibid.*

79 Description of Lemass at the Four Courts in C. S. Andrews, *Dublin Made Me* (Dublin, 2001), p. 238.

80 Ernie O'Malley, *The Singing Flame* (Dublin, 1978), p. 71.

81 NLI, Thomas O'Reilly papers, MS 40, 224/1.

82 Garvin, *Judging Lemass*, p. 50.

83 C. Desmond Greaves, *Liam Mellows and the Irish Revolution* (London, 1971), p. 268. Gallacher had been introduced to Rory O'Connor, Cathal Brugha and Liam Mellows by Labour Party leader Tom Johnson.

84 See *Dáil Debates*, 19 December 1921–7 January 1922.

85 Garvin, *Judging Lemass*, p. 50.

86 *Ibid.*

87 Horgan, *Enigmatic Patriot*, p. 23.

88 Lemass to Mills, *The Irish Press*, 22 January 1969.

89 *Ibid.*

90 De Valera is reputed to have made this remark to a Labour Party delegation in April 1922. Cited, in this instance, by John Paul McCarthy, *Sunday Independent*, 23 January 2011.

91 Laffan, *The Resurrection of Ireland*, p. 424.

92 O'Malley, *The Singing Flame*, p. 84.

93 *Ibid.*, p. 97.

94 Michael McInerney, *Peadar O'Donnell: Irish Social Rebel* (Dublin, 1974), p. 105.

95 O'Malley, *The Singing Flame*, p. 103.

96 *Ibid.*, p. 78.

97 Lemass to Mills, *The Irish Press*, 20 January 1969.

98 O'Malley, *The Singing Flame*, p. 125.

99 Garvin, *Judging Lemass*, p. 50.

100 Lemass to Murphy, 25 February 1950. Courtesy of Seán Haughey. In his letter Lemass also recalled that 'there was not much bitterness between the contending forces at that time although it developed subsequently'.
101 O'Malley, *The Singing Flame*, p. 126.
102 Lemass to Mills, *The Irish Press*, 22 January 1969.
103 *Ibid.*
104 O'Malley, *The Singing Flame*, p. 136.
105 *Ibid.*, p. 137.
106 Lemass to Mills, *The Irish Press*, 22 January 1969.
107 O'Malley, *The Singing Flame*, p. 142.
108 Murray, *Oracles of God*, p. 76.
109 Seán Dowling, in MacEoin, *Survivors*, p. 409.
110 Andrews, *Dublin Made Me*, p. 278.
111 O'Malley, *The Singing Flame*, p. 236.
112 MA, Civil War prisoner index, no. 8834.
113 MA, Civil War Prisoners Collection, CW/P/09/08.
114 *The Irish Times*, 14 October 1963.
115 *The Irish Times*, 15 October 1923.
116 *The Irish Times*, 16 October 1923.
117 *Ibid.*
118 Uinseann MacEoin, *The IRA in the Twilight Years, 1923–1948* (Dublin, 1997), p. 84.
119 *The Irish Times*, 4 August 1923.
120 *The Irish Times*, 23 October 1923.
121 *Ibid.*
122 Peter Pyne, 'The Third Sinn Féin Party: 1923–1926', *Economic and Social History Review*, 1, 1 (October, 1969), p. 31.
123 O'Malley, *The Singing Flame*, p. 236.
124 Lemass to Mills, *The Irish Press*, 22 January 1969.
125 *The Irish Times*, 30 July 1923.
126 *Dáil Debates*, 27 July 1923, vol. 4, col. 1537.
127 *The Irish Times*, 28 July 1923.
128 *Ibid.*
129 *Ibid.*
130 *The Irish Times*, 26 September 1923.
131 *The Irish Times*, 15 October 1923.
132 *Ibid.*
133 *The Irish Times*, 23 October 1923.
134 *The Irish Times*, 16 October 1923.
135 *Southern Star*, 22 December 1923.
136 *Irish Independent*, 11 June 1925.
137 Attorney General of the Irish Free State v. Murray, NLI, Seán O'Mahony papers, MS 44,071/1.
138 *Ibid.*
139 *Irish Independent*, 11 June 1925.
140 *The Irish Times*, 27 October 1923.
141 *The Irish Times*, 11 October 1923.
142 *The Irish Times*, 23 October 1923.

143 *The Irish Times*, 28 July 1923.

144 *The Irish Times*, 23 October 1923.

145 *The Irish Times*, 15 November 1923. -

146 *The Irish Times*, 27 October 1923.

147 Statements of Maud McKeever, Kathleen McAuliffe and Constance Hope Benson, 10 November 1922. NAI, Department of Justice (JUS)/H169a (1).

148 See NAI, Department of the Taoiseach (DT) S/1411 and DT S/3307.

149 Horgan, *Enigmatic Patriot*, p. 27.

150 *The Irish Times*, 23 February 1927.

151 *Ibid.*

152 *Ibid.*

153 Lemass to Mills, *The Irish Press*, 21 January 1969.

154 Francis Stuart, *Black List, Section H* (London, 1975), p. 89.

155 *The Irish Times*, 12 August 1922.

156 Eoin Neeson, *The Civil War, 1922–1923* (Dublin, 1989), p. 191.

157 MA, Civil War prisoner index, no. 8774.

158 Horgan, *Enigmatic Patriot*, p. 27.

159 Ministers Kevin O'Higgins and Richard Mulcahy are generally regarded as pushing most strongly for the execution policy. Ulick O'Connor, however, was informed by Ernest Blythe that it was Professor Eoin MacNeill, whom Noel and Seán met in the Dublin mountains on Easter Monday 1916, who was most enthusiastic about the policy. Hugo MacNeill, one of his sons and an acquaintance of the Lemass brothers, had gone against the Treaty and had been killed three weeks prior to the Hales killing. Interview with Ulick O'Connor, 27 July 2010.

160 See Ulick O'Connor's account of Donnelly's confession in *Irish Independent*, 17 February 2002.

161 Emmet Dalton to Hazel Lavery, 15 November 1922, cited in Sinéad McCoole, *Hazel: A Life of Lady Lavery, 1880–1935* (Dublin, 1996), p. 105.

162 Hazel Lavery to Emmet Dalton, 22 November 1922, Dalton papers, NLI, MS 46,687 (6).

163 *Ibid.*

164 Tim Pat Coogan, *Michael Collins* (London, 1990), p. 294.

165 In late July 1922 Michael Collins urged the publication of letters that ostensibly demonstrated that Harry Boland was bent on aggression and civil war. These were published in the *Irish Independent* on 1 August 1922, the same day that news of Boland's death was reported. See Brian P. Murphy, 'Nationalism: The Framing of the Constitution of the Irish Free State, 1922 – the Defining Battle for the Irish Republic', in Joost Augusteijn (ed.), *The Irish Revolution, 1913–1923* (Basingstoke, 2002), pp. 135–50.

166 Coogan, *Michael Collins*, p. 454n.

167 JHA, interview with Moll Lemass, 27 February 1995.

168 Tom Barry, *Guerilla Days in Ireland* (Cork, 1962), p. 168.

169 *The Irish Times*, 24 October 1923.

170 Marcus Bourke, 'Shooting the Messenger: Colonel Costello and the Murray case', NLI, Seán O'Mahony papers, MS 44,071/1.

171 Interview with Ulick O'Connor, 27 July 2010. Ennis's involvement in the Bloody Sunday killings is detailed by 'Squad' member Vincent Byrne, who led

the raid on Upper Mount Street with him in which two British intelligence officers were executed. See MA, Bureau of Military History, WS 423 (Vincent Byrne).

172 O'Sullivan, *Seán Lemass*, p. 22.

173 Interview with Seán Haughey, 25 November 2009.

174 Dalton papers, NLI, MS 46,687 (3).

175 Dalton compared his appreciation of Collins to David's lament for Jonathan when 'the beauty of Israel' was felled by Philistine archers; compared him to St Paul; and imagined a young army captain calling Collins his 'darling', 'a term not commonly applied as between men, but I loved him as I never loved a girl in my youth'. See Dalton papers, NLI, MS 46,687 (4).

176 For accounts of Lemass's boyhood and family background displaying this narrative tendency see Horgan, *Enigmatic Patriot*, pp. 1–9; Garvin, *Judging Lemass*, pp. 37–40; O'Sullivan, *Seán Lemass*, pp. 1–5.

177 Patrick O'Shea, *An Phoblacht*, 16 October 1925.

178 Horgan, *Enigmatic Patriot*, pp. 28–9.

179 Lemass to Murphy, 25 February 1950.

Chapter 2: Emerging from the Shadows

1 See Pyne, 'The Third Sinn Féin Party', pp. 29–49.

2 Lemass apparently held Mellows in high regard and in later life occasionally drove his family to see his grave in County Wexford.

3 'Irregular "Re-organisation Committee H.Q". 15 College Green', 28 July 1923, NAI, JUS/8/675.

4 See Richard Dunphy, *The Making of Fianna Fáil Power in Ireland* (Oxford, 1995). See Richard English's 'Paying No Heed to Public Clamour: Irish Republican Solipsism in the 1930s', *Irish Historical Studies*, 28, 112 (1993), pp. 426–39 for a haughtily revisionist take on republican ideology in this period and after.

5 'Irregular "Re-organisation Committee H.Q"', NAI, JUS/8/675.

6 *The Irish Times*, 15 October 1923.

7 Lemass to Mills, *The Irish Press*, 23 January 1969.

8 Lemass to Mills, *The Irish Press*, 21 January 1969.

9 Ernie O'Malley remembered Philip Cosgrave fondly when interned in Mountjoy Prison in 1923, where Cosgrave was governor. He describes Cosgrave as a melancholy, rotund, heavy-drinking character who was deeply disturbed by the Free State's execution of republican prisoners. See O'Malley, *The Singing Flame*, pp. 206–7.

10 Lemass to Mills, *The Irish Press*, 21 January 1969.

11 *Irish Independent*, 3 March 1924.

12 IRA Intelligence Report, 9 August 1924, UCDA, Moss Twomey papers, P69/179.

13 J. H. Whyte, *Church and State in Modern Ireland, 1923–1979* (Dublin, 1980), p. 109.

14 *Irish Independent*, 12 March 1924; 15 April 1924.

15 Diary of Charlotte Despard, 13 March 1924, Public Record Office of Northern Ireland (PRONI), D2479/1/8.

16 Diary of Sighle Humphreys, 14 March 1924, UCDA, P106/909. The independent candidate, O'Neill, was also responsible for denting Cumann na nGaedheal's majority in the area.

17 Diary of Sighle Humphreys, 6 April 1924, UCDA, P106/909.

18 O'Sullivan, *Seán Lemass*, p. 26.

19 Garvin, *Judging Lemass*, p. 80.

20 *The Irish Times*, 10 November 1924.

21 *Freeman's Journal*, 17 November 1924.

22 O'Malley, *The Singing Flame*, p. 148.

23 Garvin, *Judging Lemass*, pp. 37–55.

24 *Irish Independent*, 14 November 1924.

25 *Irish Independent*, 10 March 1924.

26 See Cumann na mBan minutes 1924 and 1925, UCDA, Humphreys papers, P106/1105 and 1106.

27 *The Irish Times*, 16 August 1960.

28 *Freeman's Journal*, 14 November 1924.

29 Diary of Charlotte Despard, 19 November 1924, PRONI, Despard papers, D2479/1/8.

30 De Valera to Frank Aiken, 20 February 1925, UCDA, Moss Twomey papers, P69/181 (132).

31 Agreement between de Valera and Aiken, 20 February 1925, UCDA, P69/181 (130).

32 De Valera to Aiken, 24 February 1925, UCDA, P69/181 (130).

33 See UCDA P69/179.

34 'Irregular "Re-organisation Committee H.Q."', NAI, JUS/8/675. Mayo-born Ernie O'Malley was the director of organisation and acting assistant chief of staff of the IRA at the time.

35 'Irregular Split', 16 July 1923, UCDA, Desmond Fitzgerald papers, P80/847.

36 Lemass to Aiken, 24 February 1925, UCDA, P69/181 (129).

37 Aiken to Lemass, 25 February 1925, UCDA, P69/181 (135).

38 *The People*, 11 February 1925, UCDA, P69/181 (136).

39 Aiken to Lemass, 26 February 1925, UCDA, P69/181 (127).

40 *Irish Independent*, 8 October 1925.

41 Minutes of meeting of Comhairle na dTeachtaí, 22 June 1925, UCDA, Éamon de Valera papers, P150/1946.

42 Lemass to chief of staff, IRA, 14 March 1925, UCDA, P69/181 (103).

43 Chief of staff to Lemass, 24 March 1925, UCDA P69/181 (105).

44 Lemass to chief of staff, IRA, 24 March 1925, UCDA P69/181 (104).

45 Chief of staff to Lemass, 24 March 1925, UCDA P69/181 (105).

46 Minutes of Army Council meeting, 19 March 1925, UCDA P69/181 (108).

47 Agenda for Convention, 1925, UCDA P69/179.

48 Horgan, *Enigmatic Patriot*, p. 41. The defining departure of IRA officers to sole membership of Fianna Fáil took place in May 1927 in the run-up to the general election.

49 IRA Executive election, General Army Convention, 14–15 November 1925, UCDA, P69/179 (190).

50 *Ibid.*

51 Minutes of meeting of Comhairle na dTeachtaí, 15 November 1925, UCDA, P150/1946.

52 *Ibid.*

53 Aiken to Army Council, 18 November 1925, Moss Twomey papers, UCDA, P69/181.

54 Brian Hanley, *The IRA*, 1926–1936 (Dublin, 2002), p. 114.

55 Lemass to Aiken, 2 March 1925, UCDA, Moss Twomey papers, P69/181 (124).

56 Aiken to Lemass, 3 March 1925, UCDA, Moss Twomey papers, P69/181 (120).

57 'Murders and Principal Outrages Committed by Irregulars Since the "Ceasefire" Order, April 1923', in Department of Justice Report on unlawful and dangerous associations, August 1931, NAI, DT S/5864 A.

58 MacEoin, *The IRA in the Twilight Years*, p. 909.

59 'Murders and Principal Outrages Committed by Irregulars Since the "Ceasefire" Order, April 1923'.

60 Andrews, *Dublin Made Me*, p. 210.

61 McInerney, *Peadar O'Donnell*, p. 102.

62 *The Voice of Labour*, 17 January 1925.

63 'Report by No. 70 to Director of Intelligence', 19 January 1925, UCDA, Fitzgerald papers, P80/847.

64 See UCDA, P80/847.

65 See *Irish Independent*, 11 March 1924; 13 November 1924; 15 November 1924; 20 November 1924.

66 Diary of Charlotte Despard, 9 November 1924, PRONI, Despard papers, D2479/1/8.

67 *Irish Independent*, 20 November 1924.

68 *Freeman's Journal*, 10 November 1924. Around the same time Lemass was denouncing the 'poppy day jamboree' as imperialist and after entering office he, and Fianna Fáil, continued to oppose the commemoration.

69 Cited in Brian Hanley, 'Poppy Day in Dublin in the '20s and '30s', *History Ireland* (spring, 1999), pp. 5–6.

70 Cited in Murray, *Oracles*, p. 117.

71 'No. 161 to Director of Intelligence', 21 March 1925, UCDA, P80/847.

72 'Report by No. 70' (undated), UCDA, P80/847.

73 'No. 161 to Director of Intelligence', 21 March 1925; intelligence report dated 29 March 1925, UCDA, P80/847.

74 Advisory Council Agreement for Formation, UCDA, Twomey papers, P69/182 (1).

75 See *An Phoblacht*, 18 September 1925; 9 and 23 October 1925; 22 and 29 January 1926; 5 February 1926.

76 *Nenagh Guardian*, 28 November 1925.

77 Patrick O'Shea, *An Phoblacht*, 16 October 1925.

78 *Meath Chronicle*, 4 October 1924.

79 Intelligence Reports, October–February 1926, UCDA, P80/847.

80 See UCDA, de Valera papers, P150/1948.

81 Sinn Féin Policy, index of reports, 11 February 1926, UCDA, P80/847.

82 Cited in Murray, *Oracles*, p. 303.

83 Cited in Horgan, *Enigmatic Patriot*, p. 34.

84 Southern Command intelligence report, 1 April 1926, UCDA, P80/847.

85 Micheal McInerney, *Éamon de Valera* (Dublin, 1976), p. 55.

86 De Valera's celebrity status is conveyed in an intelligence report of a Sinn Féin meeting at Rathmines Town Hall in January 1926. Lemass and Seán MacEntee provided the 'warm-up' speeches for de Valera, who received an 'enthusiastic reception' from the 1,500-strong crowd, among which 'there was not a dissenting voice', intelligence report, 7 January 1926, UCDA, Fitzgerald papers, P80/847.

87 Minutes of meeting of Comhairle na dTeachtaí, 15 November 1925, UCDA, P150/1946.

88 *Ibid.*

89 Farrell, *Seán Lemass*, p. 18.

90 Eastern Command monthly summary, March 1926, UCDA, P80/847.

91 Dunphy, *The Making of Fianna Fáil Power in Ireland*, p. 74. Garvin endorses this view in *Judging Lemass*, pp. 91–3.

92 Ferriter, *The Transformation of Ireland*, p. 310.

93 Boland cited in Horgan, *Enigmatic Patriot*, p. 37; C. S. Andrews, *Man of No Property* (Dublin, 2001), p. 56. Both Boland and Andrews were political colleagues of Lemass and sat on the party's National Executive in the 1930s.

94 Kevin Boland, *The Rise and Decline of Fianna Fáil* (Cork, 1982), pp. 18–19.

95 See 'Petty Cash, 1929–38', UCDA, P176/740.

96 Kevin Boland, cited in Horgan, *Enigmatic Patriot*, p. 45; Boland, *The Rise and Decline of Fianna Fáil*, p. 18. Boland often found that wherever he went himself, his brother Harry had been before on work for either the IRB, the IRA, Sinn Féin, the GAA, or all four. Harry Boland was a senior figure in the Irish revolutionary period and a close friend of Michael Collins. Boland opposed the Treaty and was killed during the Civil War.

97 Lemass and Boland to National Executive, 21 March 1927, UCDA, P176/351.

98 Lemass and Boland to each cumann, 25 July 1927, UCDA, P176/351.

99 Lemass and Boland to each candidate, 13 May 1927, UCDA, P176/351.

100 John A. Murphy, 'Fifty Years of Fianna Fáil: The Historical Perspective and the Early Years', *The Irish Times*, 19 May 1976.

101 Founding documents and constitution of the Fianna Fáil party, Seán MacEntee papers, UCDA, P67/90/1.

102 De Valera, speech to initial Fianna Fáil Ard-Fheis, cited in Kieran Allen, *Fianna Fáil and Irish Labour: 1926 to the Present* (London, 1997), p. 16.

103 Hanley, *The IRA*, p. 113.

104 *Ibid.*, p. 119.

105 Seán MacBride, *That Day's Struggle: A Memoir, 1904–1951* (Dublin, 2005), p. 96.

106 *Irish Independent*, 22 June 1926.

107 *Irish Independent*, 24 June 1927.

108 *The Irish Times*, 12 July 1927.

109 McInerney, *Peadar O'Donnell*, p. 94.

110 *The Irish Times*, 12 August 1927.

111 Coogan, *Long Fellow, Long Shadow*, p. 405.

112 *The Irish Times*, 17 September 1927.

113 Cited in Bill Kissane, *The Politics of the Irish Civil War* (Oxford, 2005), p. 188.

114 See records of the Fianna Fáil parliamentary party, UCDA, P176/452 and 453.

115 Mary Daly, *Industrial Development and Irish National Identity, 1922–1939* (Dublin, 1992), pp. 4–5.
116 *Irish Independent*, 10 February 1928.
117 Daly, *Industrial Development*, p. 41.
118 *The Irish Times*, 9 November 1927.
119 Cited in Dunphy, *The Making of Fianna Fáil Power in Ireland*, p. 106.
120 *Dáil Debates*, 14 February 1930, vol. 33, col. 389.
121 *The Irish Times*, 1 March 1927.
122 Frank Gallagher papers, NLI, MS 18,339, p. 19.
123 See *Dáil Debates*, 12 February 1930, vol. 33, col. 164.
124 See *The Irish Times* report of a Lemass speech in County Roscommon, 21 October 1929.
125 Dunphy, *The Making of Fianna Fáil Power in Ireland*, p. 78.
126 Lemass, 'Notes for a Specimen Speech', circa 1929, UCDA, P176/351.
127 *Ibid.*
128 Patrick Hogan to Michael Fogarty, 5 January 1928, cited in Murray, *Oracles*, p. 112.
129 *The Irish Times*, 1 March 1927.
130 *The Irish Times*, 20 April 1927.
131 Lemass, 'Notes for a Specimen Speech', circa 1929, UCDA, P176 / 351.
132 Frank Gallagher papers, NLI, MS 18,339, p. 1.
133 See Garvin, *Judging Lemass*, pp. 124–8.
134 Horgan, *Enigmatic Patriot*, pp. 51–3. Horgan also queries Lemass's assumptions of stability in international economics and his remarks on agricultural productivity
135 Frank Gallagher papers, NLI, MS 18,339, pp. 8–9.
136 Frank Gallagher papers, NLI, MS 18,339, pp. 13–15.
137 Frank Gallagher papers, NLI, MS 18,339, p. 27.
138 Frank Gallagher papers, NLI, MS 18,339, pp. 1–5.
139 Frank Gallagher papers, NLI, MS 18,339, p. 14.
140 Frank Gallagher papers, NLI, MS 18,339, p. 31.
141 Daly, *Industrial Development*, p. 13.
142 *The Irish Times*, 22 January 1930.
143 Other material in the same collection of papers in the National Library ostensibly suggests a desire for trade liberalisation also; in 1943, for instance, he wrote of his desire to one day 'burst everything wide open'. However, this, like the 1929 memorandum, demands proper contextualisation. It was written apologetically in the context of the heavily regulated market overseen by Lemass to Stephen O'Mara, businessman and brother of the 'bacon man' James, whose request for a licence to expand his business he had just turned down. Lemass to Stephen O'Mara, 29 May 1943, NLI, MS 18,349 (9).
144 *Irish Independent*, 28 March 1928.
145 *Anglo-Celt*, 19 November 1927.
146 Lemass to each TD, 6 November 1928, UCDA, P176/352.
147 See *Irish Independent*, 14 June 1928; 17 November 1928.
148 *Irish Independent*, 27 February 1928.
149 *The Irish Times*, 2 September 1927.
150 *The Irish Times*, 17 May 1929.

151 *Irish Independent*, 6 July 1928.

152 *Dáil Debates*, 14 March 1929, vol. 28, col. 1370.

153 *The Irish Times*, 17 May 1919.

154 *The Irish Times*, 7 September 1927.

155 *The Irish Times*, 12 September 1927.

156 *Dáil Debates*, 22 February 1928, vol. 22, col. 140.

157 Richard English, *Ernie O'Malley: IRA Intellectual* (Oxford, 1999), p. 74.

158 *Dáil Debates*, 2 April 1930, vol. 34, col. 318.

159 Hanley, *The IRA*, p. 123.

160 Ireland was obliged to raise land annuity payments to cover the loans raised in England that had been used to buy out Anglo-Irish landlords under the Land Acts around the turn of the century. Refusing payment was a policy which Peadar O'Donnell and Colonel Maurice Moore advocated in 1925 when they advised farmers in Donegal to withhold payment.

161 Dunphy, *The Making of Fianna Fáil Power in Ireland*, p. 97.

162 Gilmore, in MacEoin, *Survivors*, p. 564. Gilmore, who went on to negotiate with the Soviet Union on behalf of the IRA, held a high opinion of Lemass until the 1950s, when he thought Lemass had buckled under foreign policy pressure from Washington. Interestingly, Arthur Griffith had taken the same approach as Lemass in relation to Larkin when imprisoned in England during the War of Independence. See Robert Brennan, *Allegiance* (Dublin, 1950), p. 222.

163 *Irish Independent*, 21 August 1925.

164 Minutes of meeting of Army Council, 11 April 1927, UCDA, P69/48 (107).

165 Meeting of representative individuals of republican bodies to consider Army Council proposals for co-ordination for general election, 26 April 1927, UCDA, P69/48 (107).

166 Dunphy, *The Making of Fianna Fáil Power in Ireland*, pp. 78–80.

167 Horgan, *Enigmatic Patriot*, p. 20.

168 Garvin, *Judging Lemass*, p. 45.

169 Columban na Banban, 'Ghosts – Other Ghosts or The Priests and the Republic' (1922), Ó Fiaich Memorial Library and Archive (OFMLA), Patrick O'Donnell papers, box 5.

170 *The Derry Journal*, 25 February 1925.

171 *The Irish News and Belfast Morning News*, 26 February 1925.

172 *Irish Independent*, 3 March 1925.

173 *Irish Independent*, 11 March 1925.

174 *Irish Independent*, 14 March 1925.

175 'No. 70 to Director of Intelligence', 19 March 1925, UCDA, P80/847.

176 'No. 114 to Director of Intelligence', 24 February 1926, UCDA, P80/847.

177 Murray, *Oracles*, p. 303.

178 Dermot Keogh, *The Vatican, the Bishops and Irish Politics 1919–39* (Cambridge, 2004), p. 248.

179 Lemass to Byrne, 8 July 1927, cited in Savage, *Seán Lemass*, p. 63.

180 Cahir Healy to Joe Devlin, 8 February 1928, Cahir Healy papers, PRONI, D2991/A/1/75.

181 Peter Livingstone, *The Fermanagh Story* (Enniskillen, 1969), p. 394.

182 Frank Gallagher papers, NLI, MS 18,339, pp. 29, 33.

183 *Ibid.*

184 Horgan, *Enigmatic Patriot*, p. 53.

185 Sandra L. McAvoy, 'The Regulation of Sexuality in the Irish Free State', in Greta Jones and Elizabeth Malcolm (eds), *Medicine, Disease and the State in Ireland, 1650–1940* (Cork, 1999), pp. 253–66. The sale of contraceptives was prohibited by Fianna Fáil in 1935.

186 *Dáil Debates*, 18 October 1928, vol. 26, col. 637.

187 *Dáil Debates*, 18 October 1928, vol. 26, col. 638.

188 *Dáil Debates*, 18 October 1928, vol. 26, col. 639.

189 The most prominent of these dubious decisions was probably the ban on Eric Cross's *The Tailor and Ansty* in 1942. In his 1929 speech on censorship Lemass stressed that 'evil' in newspapers was much more prevalent than in books. However, it is reasonable to assume that he would have disliked Cross's book for its depiction of a rural mindset he found tiresome.

190 *Dáil Debates*, 8 March 1929, vol. 28, col. 1188.

191 Marcus O'Sullivan, *Dáil Debates*, 8 March 1929, vol. 28, col. 1169.

192 Mary MacSwiney, *An Phoblacht*, 8 March 1930.

193 See de Valera papers, UCDA, P150/1946–8, where Mannix's name recurs; also Keogh, *The Vatican*.

194 Lemass to Mills, *The Irish Press*, 23 January 1969.

195 Farrell, *Seán Lemass*, pp. 22–3.

196 Allen, *Fianna Fáil and Irish Labour*, p. 22.

197 Anne Dolan, *Commemorating the Irish Civil War: History and Memory, 1923–2000* (Cambridge, 2006), p. 185.

198 *Dáil Debates*, 21 March 1928, vol. 22, col. 1615.

199 John McCann, RTÉ radio interview, 11 May 1996. Cited in Horgan, *Enigmatic Patriot*, p. 46.

200 Andrews, *Man of No Property*, p. 82.

201 *The Irish Times*, 21 May 1927.

202 Record of honorary secretaries' report, 3rd Fianna Fáil Ard-Fheis, October 1928, UCDA, P176/742.

203 Record of honorary secretaries' report, 4th Fianna Fáil Ard-Fheis, October 1929, UCDA, P176/743.

204 Record of honorary secretaries' report, 3rd Fianna Fáil Ard-Fheis, October 1928, UCDA, P176/742. It appears that de Valera quashed these initiatives, as Lemass did with similar ideas when he became Taoiseach. Ultimately, the extension of the party to Northern Ireland came second to the consolidation of power in the twenty-six counties.

205 O'Sullivan, *Seán Lemass*, p. 64.

206 Charles Lysaght, 'Seán Lemass: Ireland's Saviour had a Ruthless Streak', *Sunday Independent*, 22 November 2009.

207 *Dáil Debates*, 27 February 1929, vol. 32, col. 1615.

208 *Dáil Debates*, 14 March 1929, vol. 28, col. 1380.

209 *Dáil Debates*, 14 March 1929, vol. 28, col. 1399.

210 Pyne, 'The Third Sinn Féin Party', p. 35.

211 Lemass to Mills, *The Irish Press*, 28 January 1969.

212 Cited in Farrell, *Seán Lemass*, p. 30.
213 Garvin, *Judging Lemass*, p. 83.
214 *Ibid.*, p. 80.
215 *The Irish Times*, 28 December 1991.

Chapter 3: Free State Minister

1 Skinner, 'Seán Lemass: Nation Builder', p. 119.
2 Record of honorary secretaries' report, 7th Fianna Fáil Ard-Fheis, November 1932, UCDA, P176/746.
3 Breen, *My Fight for Irish Freedom*, p. 100.
4 De Valera, cited in George Gilmore, *The Irish Republican Congress* (Cork, 1978), p. 11.
5 Lemass to Mills, *The Irish Press*, 24 January 1969.
6 See NAI, Office of Public Works (OPW) files, Department of Industry and Commerce files at B15.
7 Horgan, *Enigmatic Patriot*, p. 66.
8 Conor Cruise O'Brien, *Memoir: My Life And Times* (Dublin, 1999), p. 189.
9 Andrews, *Man of No Property*, p. 74.
10 See NAI, DT/S2470 A.
11 Lemass to Mills, *The Irish Press*, 24 January 1969.
12 Leydon to Department of Finance, 23 November 1932, NAI, OPW A 15/1/20/37.
13 Dunphy, *The Making of Fianna Fáil Power in Ireland*, p. 157.
14 *Dáil Debates*, 15 July 1932, vol. 43, col. 1188.
15 Lemass to de Valera, 15 July 1932, UCDA P150/2226. Accessible at www.difp. ie.
16 See Ronan Fanning, *The Irish Department of Finance, 1922–58* (Dublin, 1978), pp. 218–20.
17 Horgan, *Enigmatic Patriot*, p. 70.
18 Cited in Farrell, *Seán Lemass*, p. 38.
19 Mary Daly, *The First Department: A History of the Department of Agriculture* (Dublin, 2002), p. 165.
20 Farrell, *Seán Lemass*, pp. 38–9.
21 Tom Feeney makes this point throughout his *Seán MacEntee: A Political Life* (Dublin, 2009).
22 Lemass to Mills, *The Irish Press*, 24 January 1969.
23 Hanley, *The IRA*, p. 124.
24 According to Seán MacBride the IRA was in very close contact with Lemass at this point and the campaign in Dublin was 'run practically entirely by IRA officers'. See MacBride, *That Day's Struggle*, p. 121.
25 Conor Foley, *Legion of the Rearguard: The IRA and the Modern Irish State* (London, 1992), p. 102.
26 Lemass to Mills, *The Irish Press*, 24 January 1969.
27 *The Irish Press*, 12 January 1933.
28 *The Irish Press*, 9 January 1933.
29 JHA, interview with James Ryan, 25 July 1967.

30 James Henry Thomas, 'Irish Free State: Political Situation', February 1932, National Archives of the United Kingdom (NAUK), Cabinet files (CAB)/24/228.

31 James Henry Thomas,'Position in the Irish Free State', 23 March 1932, NAUK CAB/24/229.

32 James Henry Thomas, 'Irish Situation Committee', 21 June 1932, NAUK CAB/24/231.

33 Thomas, 'Position in the Irish Free State'.

34 James McNeill to de Valera, 7 July 1932, NAUK CAB/24/231.

35 National Executive minute book, 22 May 1934, UCDA, P176/444.

36 Maurice Manning, *James Dillon: A Biography* (Dublin, 2000), p. 84.

37 *Dáil Debates*, 18 April 1934, vol. 51, col. 1862.

38 O'Duffy, in *United Ireland*, 6 January 1934, cited in Fearghal McGarry, *Eoin O'Duffy: A Self-Made Hero* (Oxford, 2005), p. 236. Although Lemass liked to criticise the formal attire of his political rivals, the wit James Montgomery had levelled the same accusation at the Irish delegation to Ottawa, contrasting Lemass and company's donning of morning suits for the occasion with their plainer appearance at the Eucharistic Congress: 'Cloth caps for Christ the King and toppers for King George,' he quipped. Cited in Tony Farmar, *Privileged Lives: A Social History of Middle-Class Ireland, 1882 to 1989* (Dublin, 2010), p. 154.

39 Andrews, *Man of No Property*, p. 74.

40 *Ibid.*

41 Boland, *The Rise and Decline of Fianna Fáil*, p. 62.

42 Horgan, *Enigmatic Patriot*, pp. 27–9.

43 Daly, *Industrial Development*, p. 179.

44 JHA, interview with Eugene McCague, 28 February 1995.

45 Conference between OPW and Leydon, 8 March 1933, NAI, OPW A15:1.

46 Summary of progress, new government offices: Kildare Street, NAI, OPW A 15/1/20/37.

47 *Ibid.*

48 W. J. Veale to Leydon, 22 October 1940, NAI, OPW A 15/1/20/37.

49 Fearghal McGarry, *Irish Politics and the Spanish Civil War* (Cork, 1999), p. 128.

50 Daly, *Industrial Development*, p. 104.

51 Cabinet minutes, 6 April 1934, NAI, DT S/2470 A.

52 Angela Rolfe, *The Department of Industry and Commerce, Kildare St, Dublin* (Dublin, 1992), p. 18.

53 *Ibid.*, p. 21.

54 Leydon to OPW, 10 March 1937; 2 April 1937, NAI, OPW A 15/1/20/37.

55 Lemass to Flinn, 13 July 1937, NAI, OPW A 15/1/20/37.

56 Flinn to Lemass, 28 April 1937, NAI, OPW A 15/1/20/37.

57 J. W. Nolan to Leydon, 27 September 1940, NAI, OPW A 15/1/20/37.

58 Leydon to secretary, OPW, 27 February 1937, NAI, OPW A 15/1/20/37.

59 Leydon to J. W. Nolan, 3 March 1939, NAI, OPW A 15/1/20/37.

60 *The Irish Press*, 4 January 1939.

61 *Dáil Debates*, 23 March 1938, vol. 70, col. 774.

62 Daly, *Industrial Development*, p. 178.

63 Garvin, *Judging Lemass*, p. 135.

64 *Ibid.*, p. 130.

65 Minutes of Finance Committee, 22 October 1934, UCDA, P176/358.

66 Mick Price, cited in Foley, *Legion of the Rearguard*, p. 140.

67 America was the major centre of distress and as Fianna Fáil won power in 1932 banks were collapsing across the United States. The Soviet Union, which had insulated itself from the global economy, was little affected but was undergoing a bloody internal clash between the regime and the peasantry.

68 British Board of Trade, 'Effects of Possible Retaliatory Action on United Kingdom Export Trade', 24 June 1932, NAUK CAB/24/231.

69 Lemass to Mills, *The Irish Press*, 24 January 1969.

70 Boland, *The Rise and Decline of Fianna Fáil*, p. 63.

71 Thomas, 'The Irish Free State Situation', November 1934, NAUK CAB/24/251.

72 *Ibid.*, my emphasis.

73 *Ibid.*

74 See NAI, IND, TID/1207/322.

75 See, for example, E. M. Forde to Irish Free State high commissioner, 19 July 1935, NAI, IND/258/84.

76 JHA, interview with Kevin Boland, 24 November 1994.

77 Daly, *Industrial Development*, p. 109.

78 See NAI, IND/TID/1207/1178.

79 Lemass to Mills, *The Irish Press*, 24 January 1969.

80 See Leydon to Munster Simms, 31 October 1933, NAI, IND/TID/1207/347.

81 See correspondence in NAI, IND/TID/1207/347.

82 Interview with Harold Simms, 15 October 2009.

83 *The Irish Times*, 11 May 1937.

84 Garvin, *Judging Lemass*, p. 131.

85 Thomas, 'The Irish Free State Situation'.

86 Diary of London conferences, January–April 1938, UCDA, P150/2513.

87 Lemass to Mills, *The Irish Press*, 24 January 1969.

88 David Johnson, *The Interwar Economy in Ireland* (Dublin, 1989), p. 41.

89 Lemass to Mills, *The Irish Press*, 24 January 1969.

90 Aodh de Blacam, *From a Gaelic Outpost* (Dublin, 1932), p. 40.

91 Department of Education, memorandum for circulation to members of Gaeltacht sub-committee of the cabinet, 17 November 1937, NAI, S 744/A.

92 Department of Industry and Commerce, memorandum on the Gaeltacht, 10 April 1935, NAI, S 744/A.

93 *Ibid.*

94 Andrews, *Man of No Property*, p. 246.

95 The ILO was established after the First World War at the Paris Peace Conference to discuss labour issues and to dampen enthusiasm for radical social change.

96 Daly, *Industrial Development*, p. 127.

97 Ferriter, *Judging Dev*, p. 238.

98 Daly, *Industrial Development*, p. 123.

99 Horgan, *Enigmatic Patriot*, pp. 84–6.

100 Rosemary Cullen Owens, *A Social History of Women in Ireland, 1870–1970* (Dublin, 2005), p. 206.

101 Daly, *Industrial Development*, p. 132.
102 Farrell, *Seán Lemass*, p. 89.
103 Garvin, *Judging Lemass*, p. 133.
104 Conference between representatives of United Kingdom and Éire, 4 March 1938, cited in David S. Johnson, 'Northern Ireland as a Problem in the Economic War, 1932–1938', *Irish Historical Studies*, 22, 86 (1980), p. 153. The emphasis is my own.
105 Brian Girvin, 'Church, State and the Moral Community', in Girvin and Murphy (eds), *The Lemass Era*, p. 126.
106 Cited in Farrell, *Seán Lemass*, p. 45.
107 Pius XI, *Quadragesimo Anno* (Rome, 1931), point 80. Text consulted http://www.vatican.va/holy_father/pius_xi/encyclicals/documents/hf_p–xi_enc_19310515_quadragesimo–anno_sp.html on 11 January 2010.
108 *Quadragesimo Anno*, point 49.
109 Cited in Horgan, *Enigmatic Patriot*, p. 92.
110 See NAI, DT S/9715.
111 Horgan makes this point in *Enigmatic Patriot*, p. 90.
112 See Lemass to de Valera (undated), NAI, DT S/10160.
113 Dermot Keogh, *Ireland and the Vatican: The Politics and Diplomacy of Church–State Relations, 1922–1960* (Cork, 1995), p. 93.
114 Keogh, *Ireland and the Vatican*, p. 94.
115 Evelyn Bolster, *The Knights of St Columbanus* (Dublin, 1979), p. 34.
116 Directives reminding knights to use secret 'signs and passwords' when meeting each other are detailed in OFMLA, D'Alton papers, box 24.
117 Bolster, *The Knights of St Columbanus*, p. 34.
118 *The Irish Times*, 6 September 1927.
119 *The Irish Press*, 12 April 1934.
120 Bolster, *The Knights of St Columbanus*, p. 71.
121 Fianna Fáil parliamentary party minutes, 20 July 1933. UCDA, P176/439.
122 Cited in Bolster, *The Knights of St Columbanus*, p. 71.
123 Report of the CTSI, 1927, cited in Maurice Curtis, *A Challenge to Democracy: Militant Catholicism in Modern Ireland* (Dublin, 2010), p. 54.
124 In research for this book the order was contacted in an attempt to ascertain whether records of Lemass's membership exist. The order said that no records referring to Lemass exist and that older members could not recall Lemass ever being a member.
125 *The Irish Times*, 30 March 1935.
126 *Meath Chronicle*, 30 March 1935.
127 *Irish Independent*, 18 March 1935.
128 *The Economist*, 2 January 1937, cited in Daly, *Industrial Development*, p. 122.
129 Cited in Mary E. Daly, 'The Modernization of Rural Ireland', in David Dickson and Cormac Ó Gráda, *Refiguring Ireland: Essays in Honour of L.M. Cullen* (Dublin, 2003), p. 359.
130 See Farrell, *Seán Lemass*, p. 41; Garvin, *Judging Lemass*, p. 131; Allen, *Fianna Fáil and Irish Labour*, p. 40.
131 See NAI, IND/TID/1207/187.
132 *The Irish Times*, 25 January 1932.

133 Lemass, undated letter, NAI, DT S/9715A.
134 Claude Warner's memoir of Bord na Móna (1937–45) in Todd Andrews papers, UCDA P91/45.
135 JHA, interview with Peggy and Jack O'Brien, 13 February 1995.
136 Daly, *Industrial Development*, p. 87.
137 See NAI, IND,TID/1207/361.
138 Skinner, 'Seán Lemass: Nation Builder', p. 97.
139 Dunphy, *The Making of Fianna Fáil Power in Ireland*, p. 147.
140 Conference on Legislative Proposals in Relation to the Home-Grown Tobacco Industry, 24 January 1934, NAI, IND/TID/11/23.
141 Memo from P. J. Carroll Ltd. to Industry and Commerce, 22 May 1934, NAI, IND/TID/11/23.
142 Lemass to James Ryan, March 1934, NAI, IND/TID/11/23.
143 *The Irish Press*, 16 April 1934.
144 Lemass also established a control board for the tobacco trade, but with membership determined by him.
145 See, for instance, *Sunday Tribune*, 11 July 2010.
146 The policy to develop Shannon as integral to the North Atlantic route was inaugurated under Cosgrave's administration, and Lemass's predecessor Patrick McGilligan also deserves more recognition for his role in this crucial area. In July 1930 it was he who told the Dáil that Shannon would be first port of call for all east-bound transatlantic flights.
147 'Transatlantic Air Services: Instructions to Saorstát Representatives in Discussions in Ottawa and Washington', 7 November 1935, NAI DT/S8238.
148 Skinner, 'Seán Lemass: Nation Builder', pp. 23–35.
149 A large number of Aiken's inventions survive in his papers, deposited in UCD Archives at P104.
150 Andrews, *Man of No Property*, p. 118.
151 Alex Findlater, *Findlaters: The Story of a Dublin Merchant Family* (Dublin, 2001), p. 299.
152 In the late 1930s Lemass also signalled his support for an Irish film industry. See Roddy Flynn, 'A Semi-State in all but Name? Seán Lemass's Film Policy', in Girvin and Murphy (eds), *The Lemass Era*, pp. 166–90.
153 Brian P. Kennedy, *Dreams and Responsibilities: The State and the Arts in Independent Ireland* (Dublin, 1990), p. 33. The *Capuchin Annual* displayed a clear allegiance to Fianna Fáil's version of Irish nationalism. It was simultaneously heavily Catholic in subject and tone, describing the June 1932 Eucharistic Congress, which was held in Dublin, as 'the greatest day in Ireland's history' and carrying articles with titles such as 'The Communistic Antichrist' and 'Christ or Communism?'. See Alice Curtayn, 'The Story of the Eucharistic Congress', *Capuchin Annual* (1933), pp. 74–88; Fr Cuthbert, 'The Communistic Antichrist', *Capuchin Annual* (1934), pp. 84–89; Fr James, 'Christ or Communism?', *Capuchin Annual* (1934), pp. 166–78.
154 JHA, interview with Ben Kiely, 2 May 1995.
155 Like Lemass, Scott had started out as an actor. He had played Clitheroe, the bricklayer and Citizen Army commandant in Seán O'Casey's *The Plough and the Stars*, but as a child had in fact seen his father fight against the rebels during the Easter Rising. As an architect, Scott designed a number of cinemas, houses

and hospitals in the 1930s. In 1935 he entered the competition to design the new Department of Industry and Commerce building but was unsuccessful. See Dorothy Walker, *Michael Scott, Architect, in (Casual) Conversation with Dorothy Walker* (Kinsale, 1995), p. 22.

156 Clair Wills, *That Neutral Island: A Cultural History of Ireland during the Second World War* (London, 2007), p. 18.

157 See NAI, IND, TID/2/95; NAI, IND, TID/2/124.

158 Andrews, *Man of No Property*, p. 177.

159 Donal Clarke, *Brown Gold: A History of Bord na Móna and the Irish Peat Industry* (Dublin, 2010), pp. 30–2.

160 Lemass to de Valera, 17 November 1938, NAI, DT, S10927.

161 *Ibid.* The emphasis on 'voluntary' is my own. Unemployment assistance was withheld from unemployed men who refused to work on employment schemes but always after refusal and not as an incentive, as Lemass envisaged.

162 156 (23 March 1940) Dublin Garda Index to Special Files, 1929–45, private collection.

163 De Valera to Irish Trade Unions Congress representatives, 14 May 1941, NAI, Irish Trade Union Congress collection, 6100.

164 Wages for turf cutters were kept at artificially low levels because, in the words of turf controller Hugo Flinn: 'If the turf wage is set at a higher level than the agricultural wage, then there is going to be competition between the two, to the detriment of agriculture.' *Dáil Debates*, 16 April 1942, vol. 86, col. 634. From 1943 onwards, wages improved.

165 Aiken memo., 22 October 1935, NAI, DT/S8203.

166 Department of Defence memo., 31 January 1939, NAI, DT/S8203.

167 Memorandum on interdepartmental committees on essential materials, NAI, Department of the Taoiseach (DT), S 8203.

168 Memorandum from H. French, head of British Food Department, November 1937, MA, Secret Files (S)/49.

169 'Record of Activities', NAI, IND/EHR/3/15, p. 2.

170 Department of Industry and Commerce, 'Department of Supplies. Historical Survey of Work Dealing with Rationing, Miscellaneous Supplies and Control of Exports, 1938–1945', NAI, IND/EHR/3/C1. Part I, pp. 1–3.

171 Memo. on interdepartmental committees on essential materials, NAI, DT, S/8203. See also cabinet minutes, 7 February 1939, NAI, DT/S8203.

172 Gerald Boland and William Quirke, honorary secretaries' report, 14th Fianna Fáil Ard-Fheis, December 1939, UCDA, P150/2060.

173 Daly, *Industrial Development*, p. 61.

174 Diary of Éamon de Valera, UCDA P150/304 and 305. Most notably, the 'chief' was gone from March to May 1936 for eye treatment in Zurich; from September to October 1938 as president of the assembly of the League of Nations; and for the duration of March 1939 for a number of European visits.

175 J. Peter Neary and Cormac Ó Gráda, 'Protection, Economic War and Structural Change: The 1930s in Ireland', *Irish Historical Studies*, 27, 107 (1991), pp. 252–5.

176 *Statistical Abstract*, 1940.

177 *Ibid.*

178 *Statistical Abstracts*, 1932–9.

179 Cormac Ó Gráda, *A Rocky Road: The Irish Economy Since the 1920s* (Manchester, 1997), pp. 1–8.
180 Horgan, *Enigmatic Patriot*, p. 95.
181 Garvin, *Judging Lemass*, p. 130.

Chapter 4: The Great Dictator

1 *Dáil Debates*, 2 September 1939, vol. 77, col. 7.
2 Department of Supplies, 'Record of Activities', NAI, IND, EHR/3/15, Appendix I.
3 Ronan Fanning, *Independent Ireland* (Dublin, 1983), p. 148.
4 Skinner, 'Seán Lemass: Nation Builder', p. 48.
5 Horgan, *Enigmatic Patriot*, p. 110.
6 'Record of Activities', NAI, IND/EHR/3/15, p. 11. The legal term 'corporation sole' refers to the fact that the department was a body legally authorised to act as a single individual, having authority to preserve certain rights and powers in perpetual succession. A corporation may be either aggregate, comprising many individuals, or sole, consisting of only one person and his or her successors, like a monarch.
7 Farrell, *Seán Lemass*, p. 64.
8 Ryan to de Valera, 13 January 1941, NAI, DT S/11402B.
9 See UCDA P176/445.
10 See NAI, OPW A15/1/54/41.
11 Horgan, *Enigmatic Patriot*, p. 107.
12 'Record of Activities', NAI, IND/EHR/3/15, p. 48.
13 The installation of the department's state-of-the-art telephone communication system is detailed in NAI, FIN S53/12/39 and NAI, FIN S53/13/39.
14 'Record of Activities', NAI, IND/EHR/3/15, pp. 48–50.
15 *Ibid.*, p. 50.
16 *Ibid.*, p. 31. Mary Daly records that the turf quota which the department set for each county tended to be 'unrealistically high'. See Daly, *The Buffer State: The Historical Roots of the Department of the Environment* (Dublin, 1997), p. 265.
17 After the Nazi invasion of France in 1940 the government drew up plans for decentralised administration. Lemass authorised the transfer of central powers to the local officials of the department 'in the event of hostile military operations', allowing them to disregard the usual checks and residency requirements when giving out dole payments. He also issued a 22-page *Guide to the Social Services* to each regional commissioner. Department of Industry and Commerce, memo on unemployment insurance and unemployment assistance, 23 July 1940, NAI, INDC/EMR/4/5.
18 'Record of Activities', NAI, IND/EHR/3/15, Appendix II.
19 *Ibid.*, p. 56.
20 Skinner, 'Seán Lemass: Nation Builder', p. 9.
21 Department of Supplies, 'History and Organisation of the Inspection Branch', NAI, IND/EHR/3/4, p. 1.
22 'Inspection Branch', NAI, IND/EHR/3/4, p. 1.
23 *Ibid.*, p. 3.

24 *Ibid.*, p. 4.
25 Leydon to J.W. Nolan, 9 September 1941, NAI, OPW A 15/1/20/37.
26 Notes of conference, 7 October 1941, NAI, OPW A 15/1/20/37.
27 Lemass memo., 15 December 1941, NAI, OPW A15:1. See also Angela Rolfe's pamphlet *The Department of Industry and Commerce*, accessible in the Irish Architectural Archive, R.P.D.189.2.
28 NAI, OPW A15/1/17/36.
29 NAI, OPW A15/1/66/42.
30 *The Irish Times*, 31 October 1942.
31 NAI, OPW A15/1/17/36.
32 'Historical Survey'. NAI, IND/EHR/3/C4, part XI, p. 475.
33 *Ibid.*, p. 475.
34 *Ibid.*, p. 476.
35 *Ibid.*, p. 477.
36 *Ibid.*, p. 496.
37 *Ibid.*, p. 498
38 *Ibid.*, p. 479.
39 *Ibid.*, p. 490.
40 Censor's report for April 1941, UCDA, Frank Aiken papers, P104/3480.
41 Report of meeting at the Dominions Office, 30 April 1940, UCDA, de Valera papers, P150/2571.
42 Memorandum from H. French, head of British Food Department, November 1937, MA, Secret Files (S)/49.
43 Report of meeting at the Dominions Office, 30 April 1940, UCDA, de Valera papers, P150/2571.
44 *Ibid.*
45 Lemass to Mills, *The Irish Press*, 25 January 1969.
46 Geoffrey Roberts, 'The British Offer to End Partition, June 1940', *History Ireland* (spring 2001), pp. 5–6.
47 See biography material on de Valera, UCDA LA10/D/201.
48 Roberts, 'The British Offer', p. 6.
49 John Williams to de Valera, 23 August 1940, NAI, Department of Foreign Affairs (FA)/P25.
50 Interdepartmental memorandum on proposed trade agreement with Great Britain, 19 September 1940, NAI, FA/P25.
51 Untitled memorandum, 19 September 1940, NAI, FA/P25.
52 'Record of Activities', NAI, IND/EHR/3/15, pp. 22–3.
53 *Ibid.*, p. 81.
54 Maffey to Machtig, 4 March 1941, NAUK, DO 130/21.
55 Farrell, *Seán Lemass*, p. 61.
56 For a history of the Irish mercantile marine during the Emergency see Frank Forde's *The Long Watch* (Dublin, 2000).
57 Lemass to Mills, *The Irish Press*, 25 January 1969.
58 Skinner, 'Seán Lemass: Nation Builder', p. 56.
59 'Record of Activities', NAI, IND/EHR/3/15, p. 101.
60 *Ibid.*, p. 31.
61 Daly, *Social and Economic History of Ireland Since 1800* (Dublin, 1981), p. 158.
62 Joseph Carroll, *Ireland in the War Years* (New York, 1975), p. 83.

63 *The Irish Press*, 17 January 1941.

64 *Ibid.*

65 'Record of Activities', NAI, IND/EHR/3/15, p. 27.

66 'Historical Survey', NAI, IND/EHR/3/C1, part III, pp. 103–4.

67 'Tea – Maintenance of Supplies', NAI, IND/EHR 3/13, p. 19.

68 'Historical Survey', NAI, IND/EHR/3/C4, part XI, p. 501.

69 *Ibid.*, p. 605.

70 *Ibid.*

71 *Ibid.*, p. 606.

72 Leydon memo., 10 March 1942, NAI, FA/P58.

73 Leydon memo., 12 March 1942, NAI, FA/P58.

74 Leydon memo., 1 April 1942, NAI, FA/P58.

75 Leydon memo., 6 May 1942, NAI, FA/P58. Leydon's reports on his trips to London between 1942 and 1945 are accessible at NAI, INDC/EMR/19/4.

76 Leydon, report on discussions in London, 17–19 November 1942, NAI, FA/P58.

77 Leydon memo., 28 November 1942. Leydon's response probably reflected his anger at Britain's reneging on the 1938 deal. The ostensibly principled British stance against barter arrangements was also bunk. See, for just one example, NAI, FA/P23 (i) for British attempts to secure Irish labour on a briquetting plant in Wales considered too 'dirty' for British workers. In exchange Ireland would receive extra briquette exports.

78 Report of meeting at Department of Supplies, 11 March 1943, NAI, FA/P58.

79 See, for instance, Minister for Agriculture James Ryan's plea for a softer approach in order to secure more fertilisers and agricultural machinery in his memorandum to Leydon, 22 June 1943, NAI, FA/P58.

80 Department of Supplies memorandum to cabinet, 22 September 1943, NAI, FA/P58.

81 Supplies memo. to cabinet, 22 September 1943, NAI, FA/P58.

82 Department of Industry and Commerce, 'Observations Regarding Price Control', report of the Committee of Inquiry into Taxation on Industry (Dublin, 1955), p. 115.

83 *Ibid.*

84 *Ibid.*, pp. 10–11.

85 'Record of Activities', NAI, IND/EHR/3/15, p. 33.

86 Dunphy, *The Making of Fianna Fáil Power in Ireland*, p. 218.

87 'Historical Survey', NAI, IND/EHR/3/C2, part VIII, p. 340.

88 JHA, interview with Kevin Boland, 24 November 1994.

89 Lemass to C. K. Mill, 6 November 1943, NAI, FA/P58.

90 Supplies, memo. on Control of Profits and Prices, p. 2. NAI, DT, S/13545.

91 *Ibid.*, pp. 3–4.

92 Eric Lyde Hargreaves and Margaret Gowing, *History of the Second World War: Civil Industry and Trade* (London, 1952), p. 578.

93 Horgan, *Enigmatic Patriot*, p. 101.

94 Supplies, memo. on Control of Profits and Prices, p. 5. NAI, DT, S/13545.

95 Seán MacEntee, memo. on proposed establishment of Industrial Efficiency Bureau, 4 March 1946, NAI, DT, S/13545

96 *Dáil Debates*, 22 October 1947, vol. 108, col. 732.

97 The Control of Manufactures Act (1932) was designed to build up Ireland's industries and capital behind tariff walls. Later in that decade Lemass identified key sectors of the economy and established a number of 'semi-state' or 'state-sponsored' companies with a monopoly on the Irish market in those areas. These included Comhlucht Siúicre Éireann (1933), Aer Lingus (1936) and the Irish Tourist Board (1939).

98 'Record of Activities', NAI, IND/EHR/3/15, p. 132.

99 *Ibid.*, p. 13.

100 Skinner, 'Seán Lemass: Nation Builder', p. 65.

101 *Irish Independent*, 20 February 1946.

102 *Ibid.*

103 *Dáil Debates*, 16 January 1941, vol. 81, col. 1312.

104 'Historical Survey', NAI, IND/EHR/3/C4, part XI, p. 556.

105 *Dáil Debates*, 1 July 1941, vol. 84, col. 551.

106 *Irish Independent*, 19 October 1939.

107 'Historical Survey', NAI, IND/EHR/3/C4, part XI, p. 562.

108 *Ibid.*, p. 563.

109 Notes of conversation between Shanagher, Williams and O'Shea (Supplies) and Malone and Gallacher (Censorship) regarding adverts for certain goods, 22 October 1941, MA, Office of the Controller of Censorship/2/57.

110 Robert Fisk, *In Time of War: Ireland, Ulster and the Price of Neutrality, 1939–45* (London, 1983), p. 384.

111 These timber joint purchase companies were Timber Exports (Dublin) and Timber Exporters Ireland (south and west).

112 'Historical Survey', NAI, IND/EHR/3/C2, part V, p. 220.

113 *Ibid.*, p. 221.

114 Wills, *That Neutral Island*, p. 241.

115 'Historical Survey', NAI, IND/EHR/3/C2, part V, p. 222.

116 *Ibid.*, p. 223.

117 *Dáil Debates*, 12 May 1943, vol. 90, col. 2.

118 'Salvage – Vessels', MA, Central Registry Files (CRF), 2/62922.

119 Séamus Ó Murphy, Department of Industry and Commerce memorandum, 20 June 1940, MA, CRF, 2/62922.

120 Ó Murphy, 20 June 1940, MA, CRF, 2/62922.

121 Lieutenant Owen Quinn (retd), 'Salvaged Rubber', 29 October 1991, MA, CRF, 2/62922.

122 *Ibid.*

123 Lemass stood apart from his party colleagues in his modernising outlook. At the time, this was seen by some as indicating a preference for the base materialism of the sort associated with the planned economies of the Soviet Union. See Garvin, *Preventing the Future*, p. 145.

124 Seán Lemass to the National Convention of Retail, Grocery, Dairy and Allied Trades' Associations, 29 November, 1944, NAI, Hilda Tweedy papers, 98/17/5/5/43.

125 'Historical Survey', NAI, IND/EHR/3/C1, part I, p. 5.

126 *Ibid.*, p. 24.

127 Jonathan Swift, *A Critical Essay upon the Faculties of the Mind* (London, 1709), cited by Nick Cohen, 'Comment', The Observer, 13 November 2008.

128 *Statistical Abstracts*, 1938–46.

129 *The Irish Press*, 6 August 1939.

130 Department of Supplies, 'Tea – Maintenance of Supplies and Equitable Distribution during the Emergency', NAI, IND/EHR 3/13, p. 11.

131 Bernard Share, *The Emergency: Neutral Ireland* (Dublin, 1978), p. 11.

132 *The Irish Press*, 20 September 1939.

133 See *The Irish Press*, September–December 1939.

134 *Irish Independent*, 28 September 1939.

135 *Meath Chronicle*, 13 July 1940.

136 *Irish Independent*, 28 September 1939.

137 *Munster Express*, 15 November 1940.

138 *Irish Independent*, 12 October 1940.

139 James Dillon, cited in *Irish Independent*, 9 November 1939.

140 Editorial, *Southern Star*, 18 November 1939.

141 *The Irish Press*, 20 September 1939.

142 *The Irish Press*, 21 September 1939.

143 See J. McCarthy, 'Is the Legal Price a Purely Penal Regulation?' *Irish Ecclesiastical Record*, vol. 62 (July–December 1943), pp. 269–70.

144 E. J. Hegarty, 'The Black Market', *Irish Ecclesiastical Record*, vol. 64 (July–December 1944), p. 42.

145 *Ibid.*

146 *Irish Independent*, 8 May 1942.

147 Emmet O'Connor, *A Labour History of Ireland, 1824–1960* (Dublin, 1992), p. 137.

148 Daly, *Social and Economic History of Ireland Since 1800*, p. 157. Liam Kennedy's estimate exceeds O'Connor but falls short of Daly's by putting these figures at 27 per cent and 70 per cent respectively. See Kennedy, *The Modern Industrialisation of Ireland 1940–1988* (Dublin, 1989), p. 6.

149 *The Irish Press*, 17 January 1941.

150 'Record of Activities', NAI, IND/EHR/3/15, p. 26.

151 'Historical Survey', NAI, IND/EHR/3/C1, part II, p. 27.

152 Farrell, *Seán Lemass*, p. 60.

153 *The Irish Press*, 2 January 1941.

154 *The Irish Press*, 3 January 1941.

155 *The Irish Press*, 6 January 1941.

156 *The Irish Press*, 10 January 1941.

157 *The Irish Times*, 22 February 1942.

158 *Irish Independent*, 10 July 1942.

159 'Record of Activities', NAI, IND/EHR/3/15, Appendix VIII.

160 Wills, *That Neutral Island*, p. 241.

161 'Tea – Maintenance of Supplies', NAI, IND/EHR 3/13, p. 27.

162 *Anglo-Celt*, 2 December 1939.

163 Barney Heron, 'Winning the Turf', *The Bell*, 2, 6 (September 1941), p. 35.

164 *Dáil Debates*, 8 April 1943, vol. 89, col. 1834.

165 *Statistical Abstract*, 1945, p. 162.

166 *The Irish Times*, 6 February 1943.

167 *Dáil Debates*, 9 July 1943, vol. 91, col. 574.

168 'Record of Activities', NAI, IND/EHR/3/15, p. 46.

169 *Irish Independent*, 19 December 1942.

170 'Inspection Branch', NAI, IND/EHR/3/4, p. 11.

171 *Irish Independent*, 16 January 1943.

172 'Inspection Branch', NAI, IND/EHR/3/4, p. 11.

173 *Ibid.*

174 *Ibid.*

175 *Irish Independent*, 19 November 1942.

176 See, for instance, *Munster Express*, 11 September 1942.

177 *The Irish Times*, 13 December 1941.

178 *Munster Express*, 25 September 1942.

179 *Irish Independent*, 16 October 1942.

180 *Irish Independent*, 4 February 1944.

181 *The Irish Press*, 26 June 1942.

182 *Munster Express*, 14 July 1944. If Nora Barnes had been living in Nazi Germany at this time she might have faced the hangman's noose for engaging in the black market, a fact which – in line with the government's pursuance of moral economy – censorship officials allowed to creep in to newspaper reports.

183 Cornelius Meaney, 'Cereal Prices', *Dáil Debates*, 23 July 1941, vol. 84, col. 2360.

184 Ina Zweiniger-Bargielowska, *Austerity in Britain: Rationing, Controls, and Consumption* (Oxford, 2000), p. 176.

185 Wills, *Neutral Island*, p. 247.

186 John W. Blake, *Northern Ireland in the Second World War* (Belfast, 1956), p. 101.

187 *The Irish Times*, 13 May 1942.

188 Lemass, cited in *Irish Independent*, 27 June 1946.

189 Alan S. Milward, *War, Economy and Society, 1939–45* (London, 1977), p. 282.

190 'Record of Activities', NAI, IND/EHR/3/15, p. 52.

191 Lemass, cited in the *Cork Examiner*, 20 February 1940.

192 Fianna Fáil's emphasis on tillage had its roots in Sinn Féin's socio-economic hostility to large-scale grazing, itself a product of nineteenth-century nationalism. During the economic war, trade restrictions also meant stock was not earning what it once did. Consequently, for both ideological and material reasons it had been government policy vigorously to encourage wheat-growing in the years preceding the Emergency.

193 *Dáil Debates*, 8 November 1939, vol. 77, col. 921.

194 James Ryan, 'Emergency Powers (No. 234) Order, 1942 – Motion to Annul', *Dáil Debates*, vol. 89, col. 1013, 4 March 1943.

195 *Dáil Debates*, 22 January 1947, vol. 104, col. 64.

196 *Ibid.*

197 Minutes of Fianna Fáil parliamentary party meeting, 23 February 1944, UCDA P176/445.

198 *The Irish Times*, 2 July 1942.

199 James Dillon to editor, *The Irish Times*, 1 April 1940.

200 'Historical Survey', NAI, IND/EHR/3/C4, part XI, p. 607.

201 Clement Attlee to Irish high commissioner, 8 March 1942, NAI, FA/P58.

202 Blake, *Northern Ireland and the Second World War*, p. 410.

203 Lemass, 'Memorandum on Full Employment', UCDA, MacEntee papers, P67/264 (4).

204 *Ibid.*
205 *Ibid.*
206 *Ibid.*
207 De Valera to Lemass, 9 July 1942, NAI, DT/S12882A.
208 Lemass memo., June 1942, NAI, DT/S12882A.
209 Lemass, 'Memorandum on Full Employment', UCDA, P67/264 (4).
210 *Ibid.*
211 Lemass, 'Memorandum on Full Employment Policy', 17 January 1945, NAI, DT, S 13101 A.
212 James Larkin, *Dáil Debates*, 28 March 1944, vol. 93, col. 396.
213 Fianna Fáil parliamentary party papers, May 1940–May 1942, UCDA, P176/440, cited in Daly, *The First Department*, p. 229.
214 James Ryan, 'Observations of the Minister of Agriculture on the Memorandum by the Minister for Industry and Commerce', UCDA, P67/264 (5).
215 *Ibid.*
216 James Ryan, 'Memorandum on Full Employment', 14 March 1945, NAI, DT, S 13101 A.
217 Ryan, 'Observations of the Minister of Agriculture on the Memorandum by the Minister for Industry and Commerce', UCDA, P67/264 (5).
218 Lemass, 'Observations on Memorandum Circulated to Cabinet Committee by the Department of Finance on the British White Paper on Employment Policy', 21 November 1944, NAI, DT, S 13101 A.
219 Ryan, 'Observations of the Minister of Agriculture on the Memorandum by the Minister for Industry and Commerce', UCDA, P67/264 (5).
220 Ryan, 'Memorandum on Full Employment', 14 March 1945. NAI, DT, S 13101 A.
221 Garvin, *Judging Lemass*, p. 51.
222 Horgan, *Enigmatic Patriot*, p. 115.
223 *Statistical Abstract*, 1945.
224 Garvin, *Judging Lemass*, p. 51.
225 Industry and Commerce memo on Emergency Powers, October 1945, NAI, IND/EMR/8/39.
226 Tom Feeney, in *Seán MacEntee* (pp. 105–6), describes de Valera's enthusiasm for the Construction Corps. However it was Lemass, not his 'Chief', who pursued the scheme most vigorously.
227 See Bryce Evans, 'The Construction Corps, 1940–48', *Saothar*, vol. 32 (2007), pp. 19–31.
228 *Irish Independent*, 4 March 1943.
229 Andrews, *Man of No Property*, p. 180.
230 Dublin Garda Index to Special Files, 1929–45.
231 *Ibid.*
232 Mary Daly, *The Slow Failure: Population Decline and Independent Ireland, 1920–1973* (London, 2006), p. 146.
233 Seán MacEntee, untitled memo., 30 September 1942, NAI, DT, S 13029 A.
234 Lemass, untitled memo., 13 May 1942, NAI, DT, S 13029 A.
235 Lemass, memorandum for the government, October 1942, NAI, DT, S 13029 A.
236 Lemass, memo., October 1942, NAI, DT, S 13029 A.
237 *Ibid.*

238 E. J. MacLaughlin to Hugo Flinn, 8 May 1942, NAI, DT, S 13029 A.

239 Emergency Powers (no. 243) Order 1942, NAI, DT, S 13029 A.

240 Seán MacEntee, 'Observations of the Department of Finance on British White Paper on Employment Policy', 31 October 1944, NAI, DT, S 13101 A.

241 *Irish Independent*, 28 March 1945.

242 McQuaid to De Valera, 24 January, 1946, DDA, AB/B/XVIII/4/6/291.

243 Dick Walsh, *The Party: Inside Fianna Fáil* (Dublin, 1986), p. 51.

244 Lemass to William O'Keeffe, 30 September 1956, UCDA, P176/282.

245 *Report of the Commission on Vocational Organisation* (Dublin, 1944), p. 45.

246 *The Standard*, 9 March 1945.

247 See John Cooney, *John Charles McQuaid: Ruler of Catholic Ireland* (Dublin, 1999), pp. 169–70.

248 McQuaid to Leydon, 30 September, 1943, Dublin Diocesan Archives (DDA), McQuaid papers, AB8/B, Supplies.

249 McQuaid to Leydon, 1 December 1943, DDA, AB8/B, Supplies.

250 Lemass to McQuaid, 28 July 1942, DDA, AB8/B, Industry and Commerce.

251 NAI, INDC/EMR/15/1.

252 Lemass to McQuaid, 14 September 1942, DDA, AB8/B, Supplies.

253 O'Doherty to McQuaid, 14 July 1944, DDA, AB8/B, Supplies.

254 McQuaid to Lemass, 15 July 1944, DDA, AB8/B, Supplies.

255 Leydon to McQuaid, 13 November 1941, DDA, AB8/B, Supplies.

256 McQuaid to Leydon, 15 November 1941 (not sent), DDA, AB8/B, Supplies.

257 Details of the relief contained in NAI, INDC/EMR/18/4.

258 Betjeman to W. C. Hankinson, 21 March 1943, NAUK, DO 130/33.

259 *Irish Independent*, 27 October 1945.

260 *Ibid.*

261 Farrell, *Seán Lemass*, p. 78.

262 See NAI, DT/S11 750B.

263 Dunphy, *The Making of Fianna Fáil Power in Ireland*, p. 302.

264 Bew and Patterson, *Seán Lemass and the Making of Modern Ireland*, p. 12.

265 Minutes of Fianna Fáil parliamentary party meeting, 23 January 1947, UCDA P176/445.

266 *Dáil Debates*, 19 September 1944, vol. 94, col. 1547.

267 *Irish Independent*, 16 March 1944.

268 *Irish Independent*, 3 May 1944.

269 *Irish Independent*, 14 March 1944.

270 *Irish Independent*, 19 May 1944.

271 *Irish Independent*, 20 June 1944.

272 Farrell, *Seán Lemass*, p. 136.

273 *Ibid.*, p. 70.

274 Industry and Commerce memo on various state-controlled companies, 1947, NAI, IND/EMR/8/81.

275 It was also where the Irish vernacular for the Second World War – the 'Emergency' – originated.

276 The international crisis also prompted Fianna Fáil to introduce internment without trial. During the Emergency six IRA men were hanged and four left to die on hunger strike.

277 'Historical Survey', NAI, IND/EHR/3/C1, part I, p. 24

278 Farrell, *Seán Lemass*, pp. 51–63.

279 O'Leary, *Vocationalism*, p. 130.

280 Diarmaid Ferriter, 'A Peculiar People in Their Own Land: Catholic Social Theory and the Plight of Rural Ireland 1930–55' (unpublished PhD thesis, UCD, 1996), p. 88.

Chapter 5: Mischief-Maker

1 Minutes of Fianna Fáil parliamentary party meeting, 14 November 1947, UCDA, P176/445.

2 For the 'rise and fall' of the Labour party during the Emergency see Niamh Puirséil, *The Irish Labour Party 1922–73* (Dublin, 2007), pp. 71–109.

3 Allen, *Fianna Fáil and Irish Labour*, p. 94.

4 Lemass to Mills, *The Irish Press*, 27 January 1969.

5 Minutes of Fianna Fáil parliamentary party meeting, 19 February 1948, UCDA P176/445.

6 Record of meeting of the Fianna Fáil parliamentary party, 26 February 1948, UCDA, P150/2944.

7 Minutes of Fianna Fáil parliamentary party meeting, 26 February 1948, UCDA, P176/446.

8 Party Central Committee minutes, 27 February 1948, UCDA, P176/451.

9 See NAI, OPW A15/1/53/41.

10 Interview with Niall Tierney, 15 September 2010.

11 JHA, interview with Douglas Gageby, 21 February 1995.

12 JHA, interview with Jack McQuillan, 18 November 1994.

13 JHA, interview with Eoin Ryan, 18 January 1995.

14 JHA, interview with Sheila and John O'Connor, 30 November 1994.

15 *The Irish Press*, 26 February 1948.

16 Horgan, *Enigmatic Patriot*, p. 137.

17 See Farrell, *Seán Lemass*, pp. 80–4; O'Sullivan, *Seán Lemass*, pp. 115–22; Horgan, *Enigmatic Patriot*, pp. 135–48; Garvin does not treat the 1948–51 period separately but is critical of Lemass's condemnation of the IDA (*Judging Lemass*, pp. 180–2). See also Mark O'Brien, *De Valera, Fianna Fáil and the Irish Press* (Dublin, 2001), pp. 82–4.

18 See, for instance, *The Irish Press*, 23 February 1949.

19 *The Irish Press*, 29 September 1948.

20 *The Irish Press*, 7 April 1948.

21 *The Irish Press*, 9 June 1948.

22 *The Irish Press*, 28 April 1948.

23 *The Irish Press*, 19 May 1948.

24 *The Irish Press*, 12 January 1949.

25 *The Irish Press*, 7 April 1948.

26 *The Irish Press*, 21 July 1948.

27 *The Irish Press*, 25 August 1948.

28 Cited in Bill Kissane, 'Majority Rule and the Stabilisation of Democracy in the Irish Free State', *Irish Political Studies*, vol. 13 (1998), pp. 1–24.

29 Fanning, *The Irish Department of Finance*, p. 389.

30 *The Irish Press*, 21 April 1948.
31 Minutes of Fianna Fáil parliamentary party meeting, 30 June 1948, UCDA, P176/446.
32 *The Irish Press*, 2 June 1948.
33 *The Irish Press*, 26 May 1948.
34 *The Irish Press*, 5 May 1948; 30 June 1948.
35 *The Irish Press*, 11 August 1948.
36 *The Irish Press*, 18 August 1948.
37 J. J. Lee, *Ireland 1912–1985: Politics and Society* (Cambidge, 1989), p. 301.
38 *The Irish Press*, 8 September 1948.
39 *The Irish Press*, 15 September 1948.
40 *The Irish Press*, 8 September 1948.
41 *The Irish Press*, 27 April 1949.
42 *The Irish Press*, 1 June 1949.
43 See, for instance, *The Irish Press*, 5 January 1948.
44 *The Irish Press*, 14 July 1949.
45 *The Irish Press*, 25 May 1949.
46 *The Irish Press*, 23 June 1948.
47 *The Irish Press*, 25 March 1948.
48 *The Irish Press*, 22 June 1949.
49 *The Irish Press*, 24 November 1948.
50 *The Irish Press*, 16 March 1949.
51 *The Irish Press*, 9 February 1949.
52 *Ibid.*
53 Fanning, *The Irish Department of Finance*, p. 465.
54 *The Irish Press*, 29 June 1949.
55 *The Irish Press*, 10 November 1948.
56 *The Irish Press*, 9 March 1949.
57 *The Irish Press*, 2 February 1949.
58 *The Irish Press*, 1 July 1949.
59 Noël Browne, in his *Against the Tide* (Dublin, 1986) confirms Lemass's appraisal of Norton.
60 *The Irish Press*, 26 January 1949.
61 *The Irish Press*, 16 February 1949.
62 *Ibid.*
63 *The Irish Press*, 16 February 1949.
64 Lemass's trip was reported in *The Irish Times*, 10 April 1948.
65 *Dáil Debates*, 23 November 1950, vol. 123, col. 1212.
66 Minutes of Fianna Fáil parliamentary party meeting, 21 June 1950, UCDA P176/446.
67 Interview with Ulick O'Connor, 27 July 2010.
68 *Ibid.*
69 Garvin, *Judging Lemass*, p. 181.
70 *Dáil Debates*, 16 November 1950, vol. 123, col. 926.
71 *Dáil Debates*, 16 November 1950, vol. 123, col. 932.
72 Eugene McCague, *My Dear Mr McCourt* (Dublin, 2009), p. 49.
73 Cited *Ibid.*, p. 37.
74 Bew and Patterson, *Seán Lemass and the Making of Modern Ireland*, p. 57.

75 Horgan, *Enigmatic Patriot*, p. 149.
76 *The Irish Press*, 23 March 1949.
77 *The Irish Press*, 6 April 1949.
78 *Dáil Debates*, 4 May 1950, vol. 120, col. 1785.
79 Horgan, *Enigmatic Patriot*, p. 148.
80 *The Irish Press*, 30 March 1949.
81 *The Irish Press*, 20 April 1949.
82 National Executive minute book, 4 May 1951, UCDA, P176/347.
83 *The Irish Press*, 17 May 1951.
84 See *The Irish Press* throughout May 1951.
85 *The Irish Press*, 8 May 1951.
86 See Lemass's speeches as covered in *The Irish Press*, 15 May 1951; 18 May 1951; 19 May 1951.
87 *The Irish Press*, 7 May 1951.
88 *The Irish Press*, 24 May 1951.
89 *The Irish Press*, 23 May 1951.
90 *The Irish Press*, 24 May 1951.
91 *The Irish Press*, 26 May 1951.
92 *The Irish Press*, 29 May 1951.
93 *The Irish Press*, 21 May 1951; 22 May 1951;
94 *The Irish Press*, 14 May 1951.
95 *The Irish Press*, 25 May 1951.
96 *Fianna Fáil, 1926–1951: The Story of Twenty-Five Years of National Endeavour and Historic Achievement* (Dublin, 1951).
97 See NAI, OPW, A15/1/95/51.
98 Andrews, *Man of No Property*, p. 207.
99 National Executive minute book, 22 October 1951–9 June 1952, UCDA, P176/347.
100 Minutes of Fianna Fáil parliamentary party meeting, 28 February 1952, UCDA P176/446.
101 See UCDA, P176/446.
102 De Valera to Lemass (dictated), 9 October 1952, courtesy of Seán Haughey.
103 Bew and Patterson, *Seán Lemass and the Making of Modern Ireland*, p. 66.
104 *Dáil Debates*, 31 October 1952, vol. 134, col. 855.
105 Michael Kennedy, Division and Consensus: *The Politics of Cross-Border Relations in Ireland, 1925–1969* (Dublin, 2000), p. 132.
106 *Ibid.*, p. 151.
107 Lemass speech, Ottawa, Canada, 25 September 1953. See NAI, DFA 305/14/192A.
108 *Kavanagh's Weekly*, 1, 1 (12 April 1952).
109 *Kavanagh's Weekly*, 1, 10 (14 June 1952).
110 *Kavanagh's Weekly*, 1, 1 (12 April 1952).
111 *Dáil Debates*, 26 March 1952, vol. 130, col. 601.
112 *Dáil Debates*, 26 March 1952, vol. 130, col. 605. For a fairer appraisal of Lemass's input into the Irish tourism industry in the 1950s see Irene Furlong, 'Tourism and the Irish State in the 1950s', in Dermot Keogh, Finbarr O'Shea and Carmel Quinlan (eds), *The Lost Decade: Ireland in the 1950s* (Cork, 2004), pp. 164–86.

113 *Kavanagh's Weekly*, 1, 1 (12 April 1952).

114 *Kavanagh's Weekly*, 1, 12 (28 June 1952).

115 OFMLA, D'Alton papers, box 24. Supreme secretary of the Knights of Columbanus, 'Evaluation of Comics', 1954. The evaluation was drawn up by the Waterford provincial grand knight and circulated around the country. It recommended just 17 comics and listed 123 as 'not recommended'.

116 Superman was replaced with Irish cartoons such as the awful 'Monster of Shandon Hill', in which a man and his two nephews strive to avoid dinosaurs marauding inexplicably across the Irish countryside, and 'Éire Ar Aghaidh', a cartoon strip telling the story of Irish independence through the eyes of a Fianna Éireann recruit.

117 See *Kavanagh's Weekly*, 1, 2 (19 April 1952).

118 *Kavanagh's Weekly*, 1, 11 (21 June 1952).

119 *The Irish Times*, 24 January 1953.

120 British ambassador's report on Ireland, 5 May 1953, NAUK, DO35/7906.

121 JHA, interview with Tim O'Driscoll, 22 February 1995.

122 Minutes of Fianna Fáil parliamentary party meeting, 24 June 1954, UCDA, P176/446.

123 *The Irish Press*, 8 September 1948.

124 *The Irish Press*, 15 June 1969.

125 Lemass to Jack Lynch, 24 September 1954, UCDA P176/290. Martin Harvey carried out much of the organisation work alongside Lynch.

126 Lemass to Dave Shanahan, 9 March 1956, UCDA, P176/271.

127 Lemass to Kieran Kenny, 9 March 1956, UCDA, P176/271.

128 Lemass to Noel Griffin, 2 March 1957, UCDA, P176/291.

129 Lemass to Phil Glavin, 18 December 1954, UCDA, P176/288.

130 Lemass to Oliver Greene, 26 November 1954, UCDA, P176/269.

131 Lemass to Michael Dore, 4 July, 1955, UCDA, P176/296.

132 Farrell, *Seán Lemass*, p. 89.

133 Minutes of Fianna Fáil Central Committee, 17 August 1954, UCDA P176/451.

134 Lemass to Bernard Cunniffe, 30 August 1954, UCDA, P176/299.

135 Secretary of the National Executive to John C. Leahy, Walkinstown cumann, 28 September 1954, UCDA, P176/281.

136 Lemass to James Coyne, 1 May 1955, UCDA, P176/300.

137 See, for instance, 'Report of Special Meeting of Clondalkin Comhairle Ceanntair', 24 November 1954, UCDA, P176/281.

138 Lemass to Seamus Murcadha, 23 October 1956, UCDA, P176/273.

139 Seamus Murcadha to Lemass, 19 October 1956, UCDA, P176/273.

140 Michael Moran to Lemass, 23 July 1954, UCDA, P176/304.

141 Lemass to William McMahon, 15 December 1954, UCDA, P176/285.

142 Kevin Boland, 'Report of Annual General Meeting of Dublin South East CC', 28 February 1956, UCDA, P176/284.

143 Frank Grady to Tommy Mullins, 15 September 1957, UCDA, P176/81.

144 Lemass to Joe Kennedy, 30 October 1954, UCDA, P176/269.

145 Lemass to Denis Curran, 4 April 1955, UCDA, P176/294.

146 Lemass to P. Gaffney, 25 March 1955, UCDA, P176/266.

147 Lemass to Erskine Childers, 5 January 1955, UCDA, P176/270.

148 Lemass to Industry and Commerce, 2 January 1956, UCDA, P176/266.

149 Lemass to Patrick Kennefick, 14 May 1956, UCDA, P176/288.

150 Lemass to Thomas O'Riordan, 20 January 1955, UCDA, P176/288.

151 John Moher to Lemass, 10 March 1956, UCDA, P176/288.

152 Lemass to Dave Shanahan, 23 March 1956, UCDA, P176/271.

153 Lemass to Patrick Teehan and Martin Medlar, 20 December 1956, UCDA P176/274.

154 Lemass to Florence Begley, 4 September 1954, UCDA, P176/286.

155 *The Irish Press*, 13 October 1948.

156 Lemass to Vincent Conroy, 7 July 1955, UCDA, P176/268.

157 Minutes of Fianna Fáil parliamentary party meeting, 7 October 1958, UCDA P176/447.

158 Lemass to Kieran Kenny, 8 October 1954, UCDA, P176/271.

159 Fianna Fáil election funds, 1953–9, UCDA, P176/888.

160 Seán Ó Muireadhaigh to Lemass, 20 January 1955, UCDA, P176/266.

161 Lemass to Vivion de Valera, 26 January 1955, UCDA, P176/266.

162 Lemass to Daniel Kenny, 1 November 1954, UCDA P176/285; Lemass to Leo McAlinden, 5 March 1956, UCDA, P176/306.

163 Lemass to Vivion de Valera, 5 September 1954, UCDA, P176/308.

164 Lemass to Christy Cowen, 12 December 1955, UCDA, P176/271.

165 Christy Cowen to Lemass, 29 May 1956, UCDA, P176/271.

166 He wrote to one practitioner of 'an béal bocht' (the poor mouth) to inform him that 'I have never succeeded in representations to CIÉ on behalf of workers who were dismissed'. Lemass to J. J. Carroll, 22 August 1956, UCDA, P176/278. To another, a Cork man who wrote to Lemass lamenting that 'all I have in this wourld is the dole, the land and house that I am in is belong to my brother, I will have to get out from him very soon, I have no money and I am 53 years old', Lemass's reply was characteristically curt. Lemass to Patrick Mahony, 17 February 1955, UCDA, P176/289.

167 Walker, *Michael Scott*, p. 132.

168 Lemass to Cormac Breslin, 15 September 1954, UCDA, P176/308; Lemass to Joe Brennan, 24 October 1954, UCDA, P176/308.

169 Seán Ó Ceallaigh to Lemass, 10 March 1957, UCDA, P176/298.

170 For examples of Lemass's ambiguous public pronouncements on the issue of foreign capital see Bew and Patterson, *Seán Lemass and the Making of Modern Ireland*, pp. 87–93.

171 Lemass to Éamon Hoy, 1 November 1954, UCDA, P176/266.

172 Patrick Hillery to Lemass, 23 September 1954, UCDA, P176/298.

173 Lemass to Hillery, 25 September 1954, UCDA, P176/298.

174 See, for instance, Kieran Kenny to Lemass, 16 December 1955, UCDA, P176/271. In this letter Kenny urged Lemass to investigate the transfer of a County Offaly Bord na Móna employee whom he felt had been the victim of a Fine Gael 'whispering campaign'.

175 Lemass to Mark Killilea, 21 January 1955, UCDA, P176/300.

176 Lemass to Frank Loughman, 24 February 1956, UCDA, P176/293.

177 Hon. secretary to Fr T. Hill, 16 May 1956, UCDA P176/289; Lemass to Seamus Ó Maoldomhnaigh, 30 January 1956, UCDA, P176/291. In 1957 this hard-headed attitude was to come up against the redoubtable opposition

of Cardinal Joseph D'Alton, archbishop of Armagh and primate of all Ireland, who refused Fianna Fáil permission to fund-raise in his archdiocese, citing the 'many complaints from both priests and people about the embarrassment that is caused'. See OFMLA, D'Alton papers, box 33, D'Alton to Joseph Farrell, 5 February 1957.

178 Maureen Haughey, cited in *Sunday Independent*, 6 January 1980.

179 Fianna Fáil Dublin North West Ladies' Committee minutes, 15 June 1955; 25 November 1955; 14, 20, 28 December 1955; 20 January 1956; 10 February 1956; 23 March 1956; 15 May 1956, UCDA, P176/282.

180 Lemass to William Lenihan, 26 March 1955, UCDA, P176/291.

181 *Irish Independent*, 29 January 1966. Incidentally, Lady Gregory had herself heaped praise on O'Casey's representation of 1916 for its 'overpowering quality', saying: 'I felt at the end as if I should never care to look at another; all others would seem so shadowy to the mind after this.' Cited in Charles Townshend, *Easter 1916: The Irish Rebellion* (London, 2005), p. 348. It is likely that Lemass went along with Ernest Blythe's opposition to the play.

182 Lemass to Michael Hilliard, 28 July 1954, UCDA, P176/272.

183 Lemass to Vivion de Valera, 17 August 1954, UCDA, P176/267.

184 Lemass to Pa McGrath, 22 September 1954, UCDA P176/290.

185 Fan McCracken to Lemass, 14 March 1955, UCDA, P176/290.

186 See R. M. Douglas, *Architects of the Resurrection: Ailtirí na hAiséirghe and the Fascist 'New Order' in Ireland* (Manchester, 2009).

187 Lemass to McCracken, 18 March 1955, UCDA, P176/290.

188 McCracken to Lemass, 21 March 1955, UCDA, P176/290.

189 The diligent Mrs McCracken later wrote to Lemass informing him that a friend of hers had once witnessed Fianna Fáil TD Pa McGrath's rival as Lord Mayor for Cork, Labour's Seán Casey, singing 'The Red Flag' on a bus trip to Killarney.

190 Lemass to McCracken, 25 March 1955, UCDA, P176/290.

191 Lemass to P. McGetrick, 29 August 1956, UCDA, P176/268.

192 This sweeping conviction is undoubtedly based on Maureen Haughey's recollection that Lemass occasionally read 'pulp fiction' such as the 'Roy Rogers' books. JHA, interview with Moll Lemass, 27 February 1995.

193 JHA, List of Lemass books at Hillside Drive, Rathfarnham.

194 See UCDA, P176/266.

195 Lemass to Brian Lenihan, 7 September 1954, UCDA, P176/299.

196 Lemass to each cumann in Laois/Offaly, 23 March 1956, UCDA, P176/268.

197 See, for instance, Lemass to Aiken, 28 September 1954 and 7 October 1954, UCDA, P176/266; Lemass to James Phelan, 26 October 1954, UCDA, P176/268.

198 Lemass to Gerald Boland, 14 January 1957, UCDA, P176/299.

199 Minutes of Fianna Fáil Central Committee, 10 April 1956, UCDA P176/451.

200 Pádraig Ó Cadhla to Tommy Mullins, 7 October 1956, UCDA, P176/73.

201 Lemass to William Kenneally, 12 October 1954, UCDA, P176/291.

202 Lemass to Ted O'Sullivan, 1 September 1954, UCDA, P176/289.

203 This section owes much to Stephen Kelly's excellent dissertation on 'Fianna Fáil, Partition and Northern Ireland, 1938 to 1966' (UCD, unpublished PhD thesis, 2010).

204 See *Ibid*; Record of meetings of Fianna Fáil National Executive, 1951–4, UCDA, P176/347; Meeting of the parliamentary party, 27 October 1954, UCDA P176/446.
205 For further information on Booth on Northern Ireland see Kelly, 'Fianna Fáil, Partition and Northern Ireland', pp. 150–1; *The Irish Times*, 2 November 1954.
206 Lemass to Booth, 15 and 22 November, 1954, UCDA, P176/277.
207 Lemass to Diarmuid Ó hAlmhain, 6 October 1955, UCDA, P176/277.
208 For more on Fianna Fáil grass-roots reaction to the Border Campaign see Stephen Kelly, 'Conditioned Constitutionalists: The Reaction of Fianna Fáil Grass-roots to the IRA Border Campaign, 1956–1962', in William Sheehan and Maura Cronin (eds), *Riotous Assemblies: A History of Riots and Public Disorder in Ireland* (Cork, 2011), pp. 210–26.
209 Lemass to Michael O'Connor, 15 January 1955, UCDA, P176/287.
210 Lemass to Seán McCarthy, 25 January 1957, UCDA, P176/286.
211 Minutes of meeting between Lemass and Harold Macmillan, 13 July 1959: 'Visit to England of Mr Lemass, the Irish Prime Minister', NAUK/CON 20/9/28.
212 Lemass to Michael Dore, 30 November 1955, UCDA, P176/2966.
213 Lemass, memorandum on fiscal policy, 1955, UCDA, MacEntee papers, P67/468.
214 Lemass to Donal O'Hagan, 9 February 1954, UCDA, Frank Aiken papers, P104/2133 (45).
215 Lemass to Eoghan Uas Mac Cuirtin, 20 October 1955, UCDA P176/276.
216 *Irish Independent*, 24 October 1955.
217 Lemass to Proinnsías Uas Ó Lionáin, 26 September 1955, UCDA P176/289.
218 *The Irish Press*, 18 January 1952.
219 Lemass to Séamus Dolan, 7 September 1955, UCDA, P176/309.
220 Lemass to Erskine Childers, 10 January 1956, UCDA, P176/270.
221 Brian Lenihan, 'Full Employment', speech delivered to Fintan Lalor cumann, Rathmines, Dublin, 6 March 1956, UCDA, P176/269.
222 Lemass to Brian Lenihan, 9 March 1956, UCDA, P176/269.
223 Lemass to Pádraig Faulkner, 12 April 1956, UCDA, P176/266.
224 *Irish Independent*, 8 February 1945.
225 Lemass to Michael Dore, 21 September 1955, UCDA, P176/296.
226 *Ibid*.
227 Skinner, 'Seán Lemass: Nation Builder', p. 91.
228 *Ibid.*, p. 89.
229 *Ibid.*, p. 100.
230 *Ibid.*, p. 101.
231 Lemass to Michael Dore, 21 September 1955, UCDA, P176/296.
232 Lemass to Carley, 22 July 1955, UCDA, P176/269. By contrast, earlier in the year Lemass had backed a similar scheme initiated by a cumann in Schull, County Cork, encouraging private landowners to grow trees. Lemass to Thomas Derrig, 19 January 1955, UCDA P176/274.
233 OFMLA, D'Alton papers, box 24, Knights of St Columbanus supreme secretary's annual report, 1953.
234 McCann, White and Fitzgerald to Francis Clarke, 30 November 1956, UCDA P176/284.

235 Lemass to Mills, *The Irish Press*, 27 January 1969.

236 Lemass to Pádraig Faulkner, 24 October 1956, UCDA, P176/266.

237 See Savage, *Seán Lemass*, pp. 66–75.

238 Diarmaid Ferriter, *Occasions of Sin: Sex and Society in Modern Ireland* (Dublin, 2009), p. 295.

239 Lemass to Proinnsías Uas Ó Lionáin, 22 June 1955, UCDA, P176/289.

240 Lemass to Mills, *The Irish Press*, 27 January 1969.

241 James Downey, *Lenihan: His Life and Loyalties* (Dublin, 1998), p. 105.

242 Lemass to Noël Browne, 14 September 1954; 5 and 9 November 1954, UCDA, P176/284.

243 Patrick Cronin to Lemass, 16 June 1956, UCDA, P176/286.

244 Lemass to Haughey, 3 March 1955, UCDA, P176/280.

245 George Colley to Lemass, 20 May 1955, UCDA, P176/280.

246 *Ibid.*

247 Bruce Arnold, *Haughey: His Life and Unlucky Deeds* (London, 1993), p. 33.

248 Report of annual general meeting of Dublin North East Comhairle Cheanntair, 13 January 1956, UCDA, P176/280.

249 *Ibid.*

250 Horgan, *Enigmatic Patriot*, p. 161.

251 Lemass to John Moher, 10 January 1957, UCDA, P176/288.

252 Lemass to Andreas O'Keeffe, SC, 20 September 1954, UCDA, P176/283.

253 Lemass to O'Keeffe, 20 September 1954, UCDA, FF P176/283. My italics.

254 Lemass to William McMahon, 15 April 1955, UCDA, P176/285.

255 Lemass to Haughey, 1 December 1954, UCDA, P176/283.

256 O'Keeffe to Lemass, 17 November 1954, UCDA, P176/283.

257 Lemass to Haughey, 16 December 1954, UCDA, P176/283.

258 General Michael Costello, who had been involved in the Murray case surrounding Noel Lemass's death, also addressed the group.

259 Charles Haughey, 'An Chomh Chomhairle Atha Cliath Report to the Director of Organisation', 3 March 1956, UCDA, P176/283.

260 Lemass to Ned Cotter, 6 February 1957, UCDA P176/289.

261 Niamh Puirséil, 'Political and Party Competition in Post-War Ireland', in Girvin and Murphy (eds), *The Lemass Era*, p. 17.

262 JHA, interview with James Ryan, 19 February 1968.

263 *The Irish Times*, 1 March 1957.

264 Lemass to John Kennedy, 18 September 1956, UCDA, P176/293.

265 Lemass to McQuaid, 26 June 1957, DAA, AB/B/XVIII/9/2/66.

266 Walsh, *The Party: Inside Fianna Fáil*, p. 78.

267 Minutes of Fianna Fáil parliamentary party meeting, 10 June 1959, UCDA P176/447.

268 Lemass to every registered cumann, 26 May 1957, UCDA, P176/81.

269 'Summary by the British Trade Commissioner of a Statement Made by Mr Lamass [sic]', 22 May 1957, NAUK, Mutual Aid Department, 611/604.

270 *Ibid.*

271 *The Irish Press*, 7 July 1948. In 1949 Lemass remarked that 'the railway problem began with the development of the motor car'. *Dáil Debates*, 26 October 1949, vol. 118, col. 71.

272 Lemass to Frank Maguire, 21 November 1955, UCDA, P176/310.

273 Lemass to J. F. McCormack, 3 June 1955, UCDA, P176/266.

274 See NAI, DT S8090.

275 Under the Railways Act (1933) any permanent closure first required the permission of the Minister for Industry and Commerce; see NAI, DT S8090. Moreover, as Taoiseach Lemass allowed Minister of Industry and Commerce Jack Lynch to override CIÉ despite checks against this being in place.

276 Conor McCarthy, *Modernisation, Crisis and Culture in Ireland, 1969–1992* (Dublin, 2000), pp. 14–15.

277 Address by Todd Andrews to Publicity Club of Ireland, Dublin, 13 October 1965, UCDA, Todd Andrews papers, P91/49.

278 JHA, interview with Brendan O'Regan, 3 May 1995. For the similarly generous terms Lemass granted to American investors keen to exploit Ireland's gas and oil reserves see Conor McCabe, 'Sale of the Century: the £500 Deal for Ireland's Gas and Oil', *History Ireland*, 19 (4) July/August 2011, 42–44.

279 Enda Delaney, 'The Vanishing Irish? The Exodus from Ireland in the 1950s', in Keogh, O'Shea and Quinlan (eds) *The Lost Decade*, pp. 80–6.

Chapter 6: Taoiseach

1 Garvin, *Judging Lemass*, p. 205.

2 Garvin, *Preventing the Future*, p. 6.

3 John Horgan's lengthy appraisal of Lemass's term as Taoiseach (*Enigmatic Patriot*, pp. 189–347) remains the most in-depth monograph on his premiership. This chapter discusses (the few) areas that Horgan does not mention in detail, specifically Lemass's impact on foreign policy, the arts and culture, and aspects of his broader social outlook and Northern Ireland policy. I am also indebted to Clara Cullen and her work in compiling an index file containing details of speeches by Seán Lemass during his period as Taoiseach from 1959 to 1966 for the 'Speeches of Seán Lemass as Taoiseach Research Project' as part of the UCD Irish Virtual Research Library & Archive: http://hdl.handle.net/10151/OB_9100021_RP, accessed 26 May 2010.

4 T. K. Whitaker, *Economic Development* (Dublin, 1958), pp. 1–5.

5 Interview with Des O'Malley, 11 November 2009.

6 Jack Lynch, 'My Life and Times', *Magill*, November 1979, p. 40.

7 JHA, interview with Neil Blaney, October 1993.

8 *The Irish Times*, 24 June 1959.

9 Minutes of Fianna Fáil parliamentary party meeting, 16 March 1960, UCDA, P176/447.

10 Andrews, *Man of No Property*, p. 256.

11 Downey, *Lenihan*, p. 44.

12 T. Ryle Dwyer, *Short Fellow: A Biography of Charles J. Haughey* (Dublin, 1995), p. 31.

13 Interview with Des O'Malley, 11 November 2009.

14 Lemass to David O'Shanahan, 11 July 1955, UCDA, P176/271.

15 Lee, *Ireland, 1912–1985*. Lee also notes the appointment of Brian Walsh to the Supreme Court in 1962 as evidence of Lemass's intention to shake up the judicial system. Walsh, as well as being a close personal friend of Lemass's, was a noted reformer.

16 Lemass speech in Killarney, April 1961. Cited in Fanning, *The Irish Department of Finance*, p. 596.

17 Garret Fitzgerald, *All In A Life* (Dublin, 1991), p. 60.

18 *Dáil Debates*, 23 June, 1959, vol. 176, col. 6.

19 Minutes of Lemass/Macmillan meeting, 13 July 1959, NAUK/CON 20/9/28.

20 *Irish Independent*, 24 June 1959.

21 *Irish Independent*, 21 September 1961.

22 Patrick Maume, '*Life That Is Exile': Daniel Corkery And the Search for Irish-Ireland* (Belfast, 1993), p. 138.

23 *Irish Independent*, 24 June 1959.

24 Minutes of Lemass/Macmillan meeting, 13 July 1959, NAUK/CON 20/9/28.

25 See Lemass, 'Memorandum on Full Employment', UCDA, MacEntee papers, P67/264 (4).

26 See Terence Dooley, *The Land for the People: The Land Question in Independent Ireland* (Dublin, 2003), pp. 172–6.

27 Garvin, *Judging Lemass*, p. 214.

28 Patrick Hillery, cited in Garvin, *Judging Lemass*, p. 211.

29 Downey, *Lenihan*, p. 8.

30 Walsh, *The Party: Inside Fianna Fáil*, p. 78.

31 See Bew and Patterson, *Seán Lemass and the Making of Modern Ireland*, pp. 118–44.

32 Gary Murphy, 'From Economic Nationalism to European Union', in Girvin and Murphy (eds), *The Lemass Era*, p. 33.

33 OFMLA, D'Alton papers, box 7, correspondence with Taoiseach, memorandum on 'Commonwealth to Common Market Campaign', 1 March 1962. D'Alton was also open to a united Ireland joining NATO, offered a federal solution to partition, and spoke out against gerrymandering and discrimination in Northern Ireland.

34 Bolster, *The Knights of St Columbanus*, p. 127.

35 See NAUK/Dominions Office (DO) 35/7891 on de Valera and Aiken's 'brief visit to London' in 1958.

36 Memo. prepared for Macmillan on 'Visit to England of Mr Lemass, the Irish Prime Minister', NAUK/CON 20/9/28.

37 *Ibid.*

38 *Ibid.*

39 Minutes of 'Visit to London by Mr. Lemass – Irish Republican Minister for Industry and Commerce – European Free Trade Area Negotiations', April 1958, NAUK, DO 35/8352.

40 Minutes of same, NAUK, DO 35/8352.

41 Henry Patterson, *Ireland Since 1939* (Oxford, 2002), p. 149.

42 Harold Macmillan, *At the End of the Day, 1961–1963* (London, 1973), p. 11.

43 *The Irish Times*, 19 January 1962.

44 Daly, *The First Department*, p. 343.

45 *Ibid.*, p. 360.

46 Cahir Healy to Canon Tom Maguire, 8 January 1962, PRONI, D2991/B/144/138.

47 Lemass to Macmillan, 27 March 1963, NAUK, Prime Minister's Office (PREM) 11/5151.

48 JHA, notes on Lemass/Wilson meeting, 16 March 1964.
49 JHA, interview with Kevin Boland, 24 November 1994.
50 *Dáil Debates*, 28 May 1958, vol. 168, col. 785.
51 JHA, interview with Kevin Boland, 24 November 1994.
52 *Irish Independent*, 13 October 1966.
53 Ryle-Dwyer, *Short Fellow*, p. 76.
54 Gary Murphy, 'Towards a Corporate State? Seán Lemass and the Realignment of Interest Groups in the Policy Process, 1948–1964' (Working paper, Dublin, 1997), p. 8. Murphy argues that by the 1960s this sobriquet was redundant and the NFA had come to be seen as an apolitical group. It is evident, however, that tribalistic sentiments persisted.
55 Murphy, 'Towards a Corporate State?', p. 11.
56 Farrell, *Seán Lemass*, p. 121.
57 JHA, interview with James Ryan, 29 November 1968.
58 *Time*, 12 July 1963.
59 Mary Daly, 'Lemass and Economic Planning', 'The Legacy of Lemass' conference, Humanities Institute of Ireland, 6 November 2009.
60 See Ó Gráda, *A Rocky Road*, p. 78.
61 Daly, 'Lemass and Economic Planning'.
62 Garvin, *Judging Lemass*, p. 218.
63 Daly, 'Lemass and Economic Planning'.
64 Enda Delaney, 'Emigration, Political Cultures, and Post-War Irish Society', in Girvin and Murphy (eds), *The Lemass Era*, pp. 49–65.
65 Maurice Fitzgerald provides a short summary of 'The "mainstreaming" of Irish foreign policy' under Lemass in Girvin and Murphy (eds), *The Lemass Era*, pp. 82–98.
66 Minutes of Fianna Fáil parliamentary party meeting, 5 June 1931, UCDA, P176/443.
67 Joseph Morrison Skelly, *Irish Diplomacy at the United Nations, 1945–1965: National Interests and the International Order* (Dublin, 1997), p. 84.
68 The volume of outraged letters from Irish-American Catholics to Cardinal D'Alton between 1957 and 1959 on occasions when Ireland voted against the USA testifies to the steadfastness of the line that Aiken, with the support of de Valera, pursued. See OFMLA, D'Alton papers, box 7.
69 See Skelly, *Irish Diplomacy*, pp. 86–165.
70 *Irish Independent*, 1 February 1960.
71 *The Irish Times*, 3 October 1960.
72 *Dáil Debates*, 23 November 1960, vol. 185, col. 21 and vol. 185, col. 169.
73 *Dáil Debates*, 23 November 1960, vol. 185, col. 175.
74 *Irish Independent*, 9 November 1961.
75 *The Irish Times*, 7 December 1961.
76 'Visit of Mr Lemass to the UK, March 1964', NAUK, DO 9/180/1.
77 See NAI, DT, S 14851B/61.
78 Skelly, *Irish Diplomacy*, p. 181.
79 *Irish Independent*, 2 December 1960.
80 Farrell, *Seán Lemass*, p. 114.
81 Downey, *Lenihan*, p. 48.
82 *Dáil Debates*, 14 February 1962, vol. 193, col. 7.

83 Minutes of Fianna Fáil parliamentary party meeting, 14 February 1962, UCDA, P176/447.

84 See NAI, DT, S 16057.

85 Skelly, *Irish Diplomacy*, pp. 222–35.

86 These remarks appear in British records of the 'Visit of Mr Lemass to the UK, March 1964', NAUK, DO 9/180/1. Lemass's anxiety on geopolitical issues is captured in Noel Dorr's *Ireland at the United Nations: Memories of the Early Years* (Dublin, 2010).

87 Cited in Ian McCabe, 'JFK in Ireland', *History Ireland*, vol. 2 (Winter, 1993), p. 42.

88 Gilmore to Sighle Humphreys, 28 March 1984, UCDA, Sighle Humphreys papers, P106/698.

89 Cited in McCabe, 'JFK in Ireland', pp. 38–42.

90 Lemass, cited in Anthony J. Jordan, *To Laugh or to Weep: A Biography of Conor Cruise O'Brien* (Dublin, 1994), p. 31.

91 See 1962 correspondence between Cahir Healy and Lemass, PRONI, D2991/B/57.

92 Copy of speech delivered by de Valera at the 1957 Fianna Fáil Ard-Fheis, 19 November 1957, UCDA, P150/2075.

93 This was Conor Cruise O'Brien's understanding of Aiken's views on the subject; see UCDA P104/6116.

94 *Irish Echo*, 17 December 1960.

95 Kennedy, *Division and Consensus*, p. 160.

96 Lemass to Mills, *The Irish Press*, 29 January 1969. Lemass told Mills that he thought that Adenauer, like Charles de Gaulle had held on to power for too long.

97 JHA, *Sunday Review*, 21 October 1962.

98 JHA, interview with Peggy and Jack O'Brien, 13 February 1995.

99 *The Irish Press*, 5 January 1978.

100 'Visit to London by S. F. Lemass, Irish Republican Minister for Industry and Commerce – to discuss the European Free Trade Area Negoatiations', NAUK, DO35/8392.

101 His chief cabinet rival, Seán MacEntee, held an even more realistic attitude towards Northern Ireland than Lemass, recognising as early as 1938 that the territorial claim of Articles 2 and 3 of the Constitution would harm the chances of reunification.

102 For further information on Lemass and the issue of recognition of Northern Ireland see Stephen Kelly, 'The Politics of Terminology: Seán Lemass and Northern Ireland, 1959–1966', in Caoimhe Nic Dháibhéid and Colin Reid (eds), *From Parnell to Paisley: Constitutional and Revolutionary Politics in Modern Ireland* (Dublin, 2010), pp. 139–58.

103 *The Irish Times*, 16 October 1959.

104 *The Irish Times*, 15 January 1960.

105 Basil Brooke to R. A. Butler, 19 February 1960, NAUK, Home Office (HO) 284/42.

106 Record of meeting between Lemass and Butler, 1 February 1960, NAUK, HO 284/42.

107 JHA, interview with James Ryan, 29 November 1968.

108 *Dáil Debates*, 8 February 1961, vol. 186, col. 10. For other examples see Stephen Kelly, 'The Politics of Terminology: Seán Lemass and Northern Ireland, 1955–1966', in Nic Dháibhéid and Reid, *From Parnell to Paisley*, p. 145.

109 Stephen Kelly pursues this argument in more detail in his 'Fianna Fáil, Partition and Northern Ireland, 1938–1966'.

110 *Dáil Debates*, 10 February 1965, vol. 214, col. 5.

111 See Kelly, 'The Politics of Terminology', pp. 147–54.

112 Horgan, *Enigmatic Patriot*, p. 271.

113 Kennedy, *Division and Consensus*, pp. 202–10.

114 *Munster Express*, 5 July 1963.

115 Speech at Boston College, 20 October 1963, cited in Horgan, *Enigmatic Patriot*, p. 273.

116 *Sunday Independent*, 20 October 1963.

117 Arnold draws too much of a distinction between the change in tone of the Tralee speech and the American speeches; see Arnold, *Haughey*, p. 48.

118 *Wicklow People*, 18 April 1964.

119 MacEntee, cited in Farrell, *Seán Lemass*, p. 113.

120 Michael Kennedy, '"A Roadblock Has Been Removed":The Lemass/O'Neill Meetings in the Context of the Development of Cross-Border Relations in Ireland', 'The Legacy of Lemass' conference, Humanities Institute of Ireland, 6 November 2009.

121 This tongue-in-cheek account of the meeting was relayed by Michael Kennedy in his account of 'The Lemass/O'Neill Meetings', 'The Legacy of Lemass' conference, Humanities Institute of Ireland, 6 November 2009.

122 Garvin, in 'Lemass – The Man Who Made Modern Ireland', broadcast RTÉ 1, 16 February 2010.

123 Cited in Farrell, *Seán Lemass*, p. 116.

124 O'Neill to Rev. H. R. Allen, 21 January 1965. Correspondence from the Public in Favour of the Visit of Mr Seán Lemass on 14 January 1965, PRONI, Prime Minister's papers (PM) 5/7/6. Lemass had in fact turned down the 'Literific' before: the first time because of the outrage after the IRA shot an RUC officer in 1961 and the second time, in 1962, because the proposed date coincided with the Fianna Fáil Ard-Fheis.

125 See UCDA P176/722, record of Fianna Fáil Ard-Fheis, 16–17 October 1965.

126 Kelly, 'Fianna Fáil, Partition and Northern Ireland', pp. 276–7.

127 O'Neill to Maureen Best, 21 January 1965, PRONI, PM5/7/6.

128 O'Neill to Rev. D. P. Connery, 21 January 1965, PRONI, PM5/7/6.

129 Letter to O'Neill, 18 January 1965, PRONI, PM5/7/6.

130 Noel Calvin to O'Neill, 16 January 1965, PRONI, PM5/7/6.

131 O'Neill to Leinster Association IRA, 22 February 1965, PRONI, PM5/7/6.

132 The 'absurdity' quote was recorded in *The Irish Press*, 4 April 1960. Lemass referred to nationalists' 'second-class status' in a letter to Ernest Blythe, dated 7 December 1962; see UCDA, Ernest Blythe papers, P24/1421.

133 Cited in Horgan, *Enigmatic Patriot*, p. 288.

134 William Douglas to Daniel McCoy, 8 June 1961, PRONI, Ulster Unionist Council papers, D1327/18/424.

135 Brian Girvin and Gary Murphy, 'Whose Ireland? The Lemass Era', in Girvin and Murphy (eds), *The Lemass Era*, pp. 1–11.

136 Garvin, *Preventing the Future*, p. 33.

137 Lemass letters to McQuaid, 1965 and 1966, DDA, AB/B/XVIII/3/6/460–90.

138 JHA, interview with Peggy and Jack O'Brien, 13 February 1995.

139 McQuaid to D'Alton, 4 May 1960, OFMLA, D'Alton papers, box 14.2.
140 McQuaid to D'Alton, 7 November 1960, OFMLA, D'Alton papers, box 5.2.
141 Lemass to McQuaid, 9 March 1965, DDA, AB/B/XVIII/7/9/449.
142 Lemass to McQuaid, 15 November 1966, DDA, AB/B/XVIII/7/9/454.
143 Lemass to McQuaid, 15 July 1960, DDA, AB/B/XVIII/7/9/424 (a).
144 Lemass to Franco, 15 August 1960, DDA, AB/B/XVIII/7/9/427.
145 Lemass to McQuaid, 12 May 1961, DDA, AB/B/XVIII/7/9/431; Lemass to McQuaid, 21 March 1962, OFMLA, D'Alton papers, box 13.1, Irish College Salamanca.
146 *The Irish Times*, 26 June 1961.
147 *The Standard*, 30 June 1961.
148 *The Irish Press*, 6 November 1961.
149 JHA, interview with Sheila and John O'Connor, 30 November 1994.
150 Lemass to McQuaid, 29 January 1962, DDA, AB/B/XVIII/7/9/349.
151 Lemass to William Conway, 19 May 1965, OFMLA, Cardinal Conway files, 25/2. Collection currently closed to public.
152 'Memorandum regarding suggestions made by Pope Paul VI in the course of the audience which the Taoiseach had with His Holiness on the 27th February, 1965', OFMLA, Cardinal Conway files, 25/2. Collection currently closed to public.
153 *The Times*, 26 February 1965.
154 Conway to Lemass, 8 November 1966, OFMLA, Cardinal Conway files, 25/2. Collection currently closed to public.
155 JHA, interview with Donall Ó Moráin, 30 November 1994.
156 *The Irish Times*, 17 August 1966.
157 Cooney, *John Charles McQuaid*, p. 418.
158 For more on Lemass and the Constitutional Committee see Kevin Boland, *The Rise and Decline of Fianna Fáil*, pp. 145–50.
159 Diarmaid Ferriter, *A Nation of Extremes: The Pioneers in Twentieth-Century Ireland* (Dublin, 1999), pp. 145, 190.
160 For a full discussion of Lemass's record on education as Taoiseach see John Walsh, 'The Politics of Educational Expansion', in Girvin and Murphy (eds), *The Lemass Era*, pp. 146–65.
161 Horgan, *Enigmatic Patriot*, p. 324.
162 *Ibid.*, p. 342.
163 John Horgan, 'Writing Lemass: Roundtable Discussion', 'The Legacy of Lemass' conference, Humanities Institute of Ireland, 6 November 2009.
164 See Horgan, *Enigmatic Patriot*, pp. 310–13; Robert Savage, 'Seán Lemass and the Advent of Irish Television', in his *The Age of Seán Lemass: Ireland 1945–1973* (Dublin, 2005).
165 Leon Ó Broin, *Just Like Yesterday: An Autobiography* (Dublin, 1985), p. 209.
166 *Irish Independent*, 1 January 1962.
167 Horgan, *Enigmatic Patriot*, pp. 314–22
168 OFMLA, D'Alton papers, box 5.2, statement of the hierarchy on the inauguration of the Irish television service, October 1959.
169 Bolster, *The Knights of St Columbanus*, p. 129.
170 Cooney, *John Charles McQuaid*, p. 347.
171 Horgan, *Enigmatic Patriot*, p. 317; Cooney, John Charles McQuaid, p. 347.

172 Garvin, *Preventing the Future*, pp. 220–1.

173 Garvin, speaking at 'Public Intellectuals in Times of Crisis: What Do They Have to Offer?', Royal Irish Academy, 28 November 2009.

174 Peter Murray and Maria Feeney, 'The Market for Sociological Ideas in Early 1960s Ireland: Civil Service Departments and the Limerick Rural Survey, 1961–64', National Institute for Regional and Spatial Analysis Working Paper Series, 53, December 2009.

175 *The Irish Times*, 27 November 1964.

176 Lemass made this remark to Mills in their conversations, later published in *The Irish Press*, 21 January 1969. For O'Higgins reference see R. F. Foster, *Modern Ireland* (1988), p. 521.

177 *The Irish Times*, 9 January 1963.

178 *Irish Independent*, 9 January 1963.

179 Horgan, *Enigmatic Patriot*, p. 292.

180 See *The Irish Times*, 25 and 27 March and 3 April.

181 The state's military commemoration of 1966 contrasted sharply with the more sober celebration of the seventy-fifth anniversary held in 1991. Charles Haughey attended the latter as Taoiseach and oversaw an understated military ceremony. Then, the state feared legitimising the violence of the Provisional IRA, a problem those planning the 1966 commemoration did not have to contend with.

182 *The Irish Press*, 12 February 1966.

183 *Irish Independent*, 19 February 1966.

184 Andrews, *Dublin Made Me*, p. 80.

185 Cooney, *John Charles McQuaid*, p. 378.

186 Micheál Ó Riain, 'Nelson's Pillar: A Controversy that Ran and Ran', *History Ireland* (Winter, 1998), p. 21.

187 *Ibid.*, p. 25.

188 For the cabinet's opinion on Delaney's modernism see NAI, DT, SI 3610D/62.

189 Edward Delaney, *Breaking the Mould: A Story of Art and Ireland* (Dublin, 2010), pp. 160, 189.

190 *Irish Independent*, 19 February 1966.

191 Lemass to Mills, *The Irish Press*, 20 January 1969.

192 Mary Daly, 'Less a Commemoration of the Actual Achievements and More a Commemoration of the Hopes of the Men of 1916', in Mary Daly and Margaret O'Callaghan (eds), *1916 in 1966: Commemorating the Easter Rising* (Dublin, 2007), p. 71.

193 See NAI, DT S 16699 F/95.

194 See Roisín Higgins, '"I am the Narrator Over and Above ... The Caller-Up of the Dead": Pageant and Drama in 1916', in Daly and O'Callaghan (eds), *1916 in 1966*, p. 158.

195 *The Irish Times*, 7 December 1961.

196 Lemass played the part of Father Mangan in T. C. Murray's *Maurice Harte* (1912), a tragedy about the social and economic pressures of Irish peasant life. Lemass's character is 'a bright, genial-tempered warm-complexioned little man of about sixty-five'. Father Mangan is the consistent bearer of bad news in the play and, in his insistence that the reluctant Maurice be ordained as a priest, he bears some of the responsibility for the latter's eventual nervous breakdown.

Lemass and O'Dea's Kilronan Players also produced William Boyle's comedy *The Mineral Workers* (1906). Unlike the rustic *Maurice Harte*, the play is about a mining venture. Industrial relations and issues of foreign-versus-native and public-versus-private ownership therefore make an appearance. Lemass also helped adapt for the stage James Murphy's novel *The Forge of Clohogue* (written in 1885), a ripping yarn set during the 1798 rebellion.

197 Myles na Gopaleen, 'B.B. or S.L.?', *The Irish Times*, 18 July 1959.
198 *Irish Independent*, 20 August 1960. Behan had had a column in *The Irish Press* between 1954 and 1956. On the above evidence it is likely that Lemass disliked it for its depiction of ordinary, non-enterprising Dublin people who enjoyed drink too much.
199 *Irish Independent*, 12 November 1959.
200 Behan to editor, *The Irish Times*, 27 August 1961.
201 *Irish Independent*, 19 November 1925. Lemass instructed delegates at the Sinn Féin Ard-Fheis to 'take action' against 'British propaganda' in cinemas.
202 *The Irish Times*, 28 April 1967.
203 Ciarán McGonigal, interviewed 26 March, 1996; www.archiseek.com
204 Seán Ó Faoláin, Special Report (Director), 26 January 1959, Arts Council Archive (ACA), 15316/1958/1.
205 Ó Faoláin to the Earl of Rosse, 18 December 1958, ACA, 15316/1958/1.
206 *Time*, 12 July 1963. Parenthetically, the chief planning officer on Dublin Corporation at this time was a zealous Knight of Columbanus, Michael O'Brien; see Cooney, *John Charles McQuaid*, p. 339.
207 Kennedy, *Dreams and Responsibilities*, p. 128.
208 Lemass charged O'Sullivan with improving the visual arts. Years later Michael Scott remarked: 'It is quite interesting that Seán Lemass should take this interest in the visual arts ... because he didn't seem to be a fellow who took much interest in any of the arts'; Walker, *Michael Scott*, p. 178. Given his developmentalist disregard for the Irish landscape, there was a certain irony in Lemass's lip service to the visual arts.
209 Meeting between Arts Council and the Taoiseach, 31 October 1960, ACA, 15316/1958/1.
210 Council meeting, 15 November 1960, ACA, 2681/1957/1.
211 Desmond Fennell to Donal O'Sullivan , 17 May 1961, ACA, 2681/1957/1.
212 JHA, interview with Sheila and John O'Connor, 13 February 1995.
213 *Sunday Press*, 6 November 1966.
214 Lemass, *Dáil Debates*, 19 July 1960, vol. 183, col. 1817.
215 Memo by Mervyn Wall, 9 September 1963, ACA, 2681/1957/1.
216 Summary of commitments for financial year, 28 January 1964, PRONI, Arts Council of Northern Ireland records, AC1/1/2. See also Joseph O'Malley to editor, *The Irish Press*, 28 October 1966.
217 *Dáil Debates*, 19 July 1960, vol. 183, col. 1820.
218 Thomas Bodkin to Lemass, 2 September 1959, Trinity College Manuscripts Collection (TCMC), 7003/362c–88a. After years of correspondence between Dublin and London, agreement was reached in 1959 for half of the Lane Bequest to be lent and shown in Dublin every five years.
219 Lemass to Thomas Bodkin, 10 August 1959, TCMC, 7003/362c–88a.

220 Lemass to Bodkin, 14 August 1959, TCMC, 7003/362c–88a. Author's italics.
221 Lemass to Bodkin, 14 August 1959, TCMC, 7003/362c–88a.
222 Lemass to Bodkin, 9 October 1959, TCMC, 7003/362c–88a.
223 Lemass to Bodkin, 13 October 1959, TCMC, 7003/362c–88a.
224 Lemass to Bodkin, 4 September 1959, TCMC, 7003/362c–88a.
225 Bodkin to Lemass, 2 September 1959, TCMC, 7003/362c–88a.
226 *Irish Independent*, 17 February 1961.
227 Cited by Joseph O'Malley, letter to editor, *The Irish Press*, 14 November 1966.
228 Bodkin to Lemass, 2 September 1959, TCMC, 7003/362c–88a.
229 Farrell, *Seán Lemass*, p. 122.
230 JHA, notes relating to a reception on 17 October 1963.
231 Minutes of Fianna Fáil parliamentary party meeting, 21 September 1966, UCDA, P176/448.
232 NLI, Bruce Arnold papers, MS 41,395.
233 JHA, interview with Michael Mills, 22 January 1995.
234 MacEntee, handwritten statement on Lemass's resignation, UCDA, FF P176/734.
235 See T. Ryle Dwyer, *Nice Fellow: A Biography of Jack Lynch* (Cork, 2001), p. 123.
236 *The Irish Press*, 17 November 1948.
237 De Valera, it seems, also preferred Lynch and certainly backed his stance during the arms crisis of 1970.
238 Interview with Seán Haughey, 25 November 2010.
239 Ryle Dwyer, *Nice Fellow*, p. 132.
240 JHA, note on Lemass directorships.
241 Minutes of Fianna Fáil parliamentary party meeting, 15 February 1969, UCDA, P176/448.
242 David Andrews, *Kingstown Republican* (Dublin, 2007), p. 39.
243 JHA, interview with Sheila and John O'Connor, 30 November 1994.
244 Feeney, *Seán MacEntee*, p. 234.
245 Arnold, *Haughey*, p. 51.
246 Garvin, *Judging Lemass*, pp. 187–94
247 Allen, *Fianna Fáil and Irish Labour*, p. 108.
248 Mary Daly, 'Lemass and Economic Planning', 'The Legacy of Lemass' conference, Humanities Institute of Ireland, 6 November 2009.
249 Kennedy, *The Modern Industrialisation of Ireland*, p. 15.

Conclusion

1 Friel's references to the 'Fourth Programme for Economic Expansion' and the scheme's incentives – capital investment, a drop in emigration, full employment, 'new airstrips capable of carrying the biggest jets, a 300% leap in tourism' – are unmistakably Lemassian. Brian Friel, *The Mundy Scheme* (London, 1970).
2 *The Irish Press*, 19 October 1968.
3 Arnold, *Haughey*, p. 53.
4 Browne, *Against the Tide*, p. 145.
5 Garvin, 'Writing Lemass: Roundtable Discussion', 'The Legacy of Lemass' conference, Humanities Institute of Ireland, 6 November 2009.

6 Michael Kennedy, 'The Lemass/O'Neill Meetings', 'The Legacy of Lemass' conference, Humanities Institute of Ireland, 6 November 2009.

7 Andrews, *Man of No Property*, p. 122.

8 *The Irish Press*, 18 March 1952.

9 Bew and Patterson were the first to make this point, in their *Seán Lemass and the Making of Modern Ireland*.

10 Tom Garvin, 'Grey Philistines Taking Over Our Universities', *The Irish Times*, 1 May 2010.

11 JHA, interview with Howard Robinson, 10 September 1994.

12 Interview with Michael D. Higgins, 19 May 2010.

13 *The Irish Press*, 2 November 1956.

14 JHA, interview with Brendan O'Regan, 21 December 1994.

15 Address by Todd Andrews to Publicity Club of Ireland, Dublin, 13 October 1965, UCDA, Todd Andrews papers, P91/49.

16 Walsh, *The Party: Inside Fianna Fáil*, p. 69.

17 David Thornley, *The Irish Times*, 1 April 1965.

Select Bibliography

Primary Sources

Allen Library
O'Connell School records

Arts Council Archive
Files and correspondence relating to the early years of the council

Dublin Diocesan Archives
John Charles McQuaid papers

Irish Architectural Archive
Material on Department of Industry and Commerce building, Kildare Street

Irish Virtual Research Library and Archive
'Speeches of Seán Lemass as Taoiseach Research Project': index file containing details of speeches by Lemass during his period as Taoiseach from 1959 to 1966

John Horgan Archive
Transcripts of interviews carried out for *Enigmatic Patriot*

National Archives of Ireland
Cabinet minutes
Department of Finance files
Department of Foreign Affairs files
Department of Industry and Commerce files
Department of Justice files
Department of Local Government and Public Health files
Department of the Taoiseach files
District Court records
Hilda Tweedy papers
Office of Public Works files
Trade Union collection

National Library of Ireland
Emmet Dalton papers
Frank Gallagher papers
Joseph Leonard papers

Maurice Moore papers
Thomas MacDonagh papers
Seán O'Mahony papers
Thomas O'Reilly papers

Military Archives
Bureau of Military History collection
Central Registry files
Civil War prisoner indexes
Office of the Controller of Censorship files
Secret files

National Archives of the United Kingdom
Board of Trade files
Cabinet files
Colonial Office files
Dominions Office files
Foreign and Commonwealth Office files
Home Office files
Prime Minister's Office files

Cardinal Tomás Ó Fiaich Memorial Library and Archive
William Conway papers
John D'Alton papers
Joseph MacRory papers
Patrick O'Donnell papers

Public Record Office of Northern Ireland
Arts Council of Northern Ireland records
Cabinet papers
Charlotte Despard papers
Cahir Healy papers
Prime Minister's Office papers
Ulster Unionist Council papers

Trinity College Early Printed Books Department
Dublin Opinion, 1932–68

Trinity College Manuscripts Collection
Bodkin–Lemass correspondence

University College Dublin Archives
Frank Aiken papers

C. S. Andrews papers
Ernest Blythe papers
Éamon de Valera papers
Fianna Fáil party papers
Desmond Fitzgerald papers
Sighle Humphreys papers
Seán Lemass papers
Seán MacEntee papers
Moss Twomey papers

Courtesy of Seán Haughey
Seán Lemass miscellaneous papers

Newspapers and Periodicals
An Phoblacht
Anglo-Celt
The Bell
Capuchin Annual
Christus Rex
Cork Examiner
The Derry Journal
Dublin Opinion
Evening Herald
Freeman's Journal
Irish Ecclesiastical Record
Irish Echo
Irish Independent
Irish Monthly
The Irish News and Belfast Morning News
The Irish Press
The Irish Times
Kavanagh's Weekly
Leitrim Observer
Magill
Meath Chronicle
Munster Express
Nenagh Guardian
The Observer
Southern Star
Studies
Sunday Independent
Sunday Tribune
The Sunday Press

Time
The Times
Thom's Directory
Waterford News
Wicklow People

Official Publications
Census of Ireland (1901, 1911)
Dáil Debates
Economic Development (1958)
First Programme for Economic Expansion (1958)
Report of the Commission of Inquiry into Banking, Currency and Credit (1938)
Report of the Committee of Inquiry into Taxation on Industry (1955)
Report of the Commission on Vocational Organisation (1944)
Seanad Debates
Statistical Abstracts

Interviewees
Ulick O'Connor
Seán Haughey
Michael D. Higgins
Des O'Malley
Tony O'Reilly
Harold Simms

Secondary Sources
Ahern, Bertie, *The Autobiography* (Dublin, 2009)
Allen, Kieran, *Fianna Fáil and Irish Labour: 1926 to the Present* (London, 1997)
Andrews, C. S., *Dublin Made Me* (Dublin, 2001)
Andrews, C. S., *Man of No Property* (Dublin, 2001)
Andrews, David, *Kingstown Republican* (Dublin, 2007)
Arnold, Bruce, *Haughey: His Life and Unlucky Deeds* (London, 1993)
Augusteijn, Joost (ed.), *The Irish Revolution, 1913–1923* (Basingstoke, 2002)
Barry, Tom, *Guerilla Days in Ireland* (Cork, 1962)
Bew, Paul and Patterson, Henry, *Seán Lemass and the Making of Modern Ireland, 1945–66* (Dublin, 1982)
Blake, John W., *Northern Ireland in the Second World War* (Belfast, 1956)
Boland, Kevin, *The Rise and Decline of Fianna Fáil* (Cork, 1982)
Bolster, Evelyn, *The Knights of St Columbanus* (Dublin, 1979)
Breen, Dan, *My Fight for Irish Freedom* (Tralee, 1973)
Brennan, Robert, *Allegiance* (Dublin, 1950)
Browne, Noël, *Against the Tide* (Dublin, 1986)
Carroll, Joseph, *Ireland in the War Years* (New York, 1975)

Clarke, Donal, *Brown Gold: A History of Bord na Móna and the Irish Peat Industry* (Dublin, 2010)

Coogan, Tim Pat, *Michael Collins* (London, 1990)

Coogan, Tim Pat, *De Valera: Long Fellow, Long Shadow* (London, 1993)

Coogan, Tim Pat, *A Memoir* (London, 2008)

Cooney, John, *John Charles McQuaid: Ruler of Catholic Ireland* (Dublin, 1999)

Cousins, Mel, *The Birth of Social Welfare in Ireland* (Dublin, 2003)

Cullen Owens, Rosemary, *A Social History of Women in Ireland, 1870–1970* (Dublin, 2005)

Curtis, Maurice, *A Challenge to Democracy: Militant Catholicism in Modern Ireland* (Dublin, 2010)

Daly, Mary, *Social and Economic History of Ireland Since 1800* (Dublin, 1981)

Daly, Mary, *Industrial Development and Irish National Identity, 1922–1939* (Dublin, 1992)

Daly, Mary, *The Buffer State: The Historical Roots of the Department of the Environment* (Dublin, 1997)

Daly, Mary, *The First Department: A History of the Department of Agriculture* (Dublin, 2002)

Daly, Mary, *The Slow Failure: Population Decline and Independent Ireland, 1920–1973* (London, 2006)

Daly, Mary and O'Callaghan, Margaret (ed.), *1916 in 1966: Commemorating the Easter Rising* (Dublin, 2007)

Daly, Mary, 'Lemass and Economic Planning', 'The Legacy of Lemass' conference, Humanities Institute of Ireland, 6 November 2009

de Blacam, Aodh, *From a Gaelic Outpost* (Dublin, 1932)

Delaney, Edward, *Breaking the Mould: A Story of Art and Ireland* (Dublin, 2010)

Dickson, David and Ó Gráda, Cormac, *Refiguring Ireland: Essays in Honour of L.M. Cullen* (Dublin, 2003)

Dolan, Anne, *Commemorating the Irish Civil War: History and Memory, 1923–2000* (Cambridge, 2006)

Dooley, Terence, *The Land for the People: The Land Question in Independent Ireland* (Dublin, 2003)

Dorr, Noel, *Ireland at the United Nations: Memories of the Early Years* (Dublin, 2010)

Douglas, R. M., *Architects of the Resurrection: Ailtirí na hAiséirghe and the Fascist 'New Order' in Ireland* (Manchester, 2009)

Downey, James, *Lenihan: His Life and Loyalties* (Dublin, 1998)

Dunphy, Richard, *The Making of Fianna Fáil Power in Ireland* (Oxford, 1995)

English, Richard, 'Paying No Heed to Public Clamour: Irish Republican Solipsism in the 1930s', *Irish Historical Studies*, 28, 112 (1993)

English, Richard, *Ernie O'Malley: IRA Intellectual* (Oxford, 1999)

Evans, Bryce, 'The Construction Corps, 1940–48', *Saothar*, vol. 32 (2007)

Evans, Bryce, 'Farewell to Plato's Cave: "Moral Economy" in Emergency Ireland, 1939–1945' (unpublished PhD thesis, UCD, 2010)

Fanning, Ronan, *The Irish Department of Finance, 1922–58* (Dublin, 1978)

Fanning, Ronan, *Independent Ireland* (Dublin, 1983)

Farmar, Tony, *Privileged Lives: A Social History of Middle-Class Ireland, 1882 to 1989* (Dublin, 2010)

Farrell, Brian, *Seán Lemass* (Dublin, 1983)

Feeney, Tom, *Seán MacEntee: A Political Life* (Dublin, 2009)

Ferriter, Diarmaid, 'A Peculiar People in Their Own Land: Catholic Social Theory and the Plight of Rural Ireland 1930–55' (unpublished PhD thesis, UCD, 1996)

Ferriter, Diarmaid, *A Nation of Extremes: The Pioneers in Twentieth-Century Ireland* (Dublin, 1999)

Ferriter, Diarmaid, *The Transformation of Ireland* (Dublin, 2005)

Ferriter, Diarmaid, *Judging Dev: A Reassessment of the Life and Legacy of Éamon de Valera* (Dublin, 2007)

Ferriter, Diarmaid, *Occasions of Sin: Sex and Society in Modern Ireland* (Dublin, 2009)

Findlater, Alex, *Findlaters: The Story of a Dublin Merchant Family* (Dublin, 2001)

Fisk, Robert, *In Time of War: Ireland, Ulster and the Price of Neutrality, 1939–45* (London, 1983)

Fitzgerald, Garret, *All In A Life* (Dublin, 1991)

Foley, Conor, *Legion of the Rearguard: The IRA and the Modern Irish State* (London, 1992)

Forde, Frank, *The Long Watch* (Dublin, 2000)

Foster, R. F., *Modern Ireland* (1988)

Foy, Michael, *Michael Collins's Intelligence War: The Struggle Between the British and the IRA, 1919–1921* (Stroud, Gloucestershire, 2006)

Garvin, Tom, *Judging Lemass: The Measure of the Man* (Dublin, 2009)

Garvin, Tom, *Preventing the Future: Why was Ireland So Poor for So Long?* (Dublin, 2004)

Gilmore, George, *The Irish Republican Congress* (Cork, 1978)

Girvin, Brian, *Between Two Worlds: Politics and Economy in Independent Ireland* (Dublin, 1989)

Girvin, Brian and Murphy, Gary (eds), *The Lemass Era: Politics and Society in the Ireland of Seán Lemass* (Dublin, 2005)

Greaves, C. Desmond, *Liam Mellows and the Irish Revolution* (London, 1971)

Hanley, Brian, 'Poppy Day in Dublin in the '20s and '30s', *History Ireland* (spring, 1999)

Hanley, Brian, *The IRA, 1926–1936* (Dublin, 2002)

Hargreaves, Eric Lyde and Gowing, Margaret, *History of the Second World War: Civil Industry and Trade* (London, 1952)

Horgan, John, *Seán Lemass: The Enigmatic Patriot* (Dublin, 1997)

Johnson, David, 'Northern Ireland as a Problem in the Economic War, 1932–1938', *Irish Historical Studies*, 22, 86 (1980)

Johnson, David, *The Interwar Economy in Ireland* (Dublin, 1989)

Jones, Greta and Malcolm, Elizabeth (eds), *Medicine, Disease and the State in Ireland, 1650–1940* (Cork, 1999)

Jordan, Anthony J., *To Laugh or to Weep: A Biography of Conor Cruise O'Brien* (Dublin, 1994)

Kelly, Stephen, 'Fianna Fáil, Partition and Northern Ireland, 1938 to 1966' (unpublished PhD thesis, UCD, 2010)

Kennedy, Brian P., *Dreams and Responsibilities: The State and the Arts in Independent Ireland* (Dublin, 1990)

Kennedy, Liam, *The Modern Industrialisation of Ireland 1940–1988* (Dublin, 1989)

Kennedy, Michael, *Division and Consensus: The Politics of Cross-Border Relations in Ireland, 1925–1969* (Dublin, 2000)

Kennedy, Michael, '"A Roadblock Has Been Removed": The Lemass/ O'Neill Meetings in the Context of the Development of Cross-Border Relations in Ireland', 'The Legacy of Lemass' conference, Humanities Institute of Ireland, 6 November 2009)

Keogh, Dermot, *Ireland and the Vatican: The Politics and Diplomacy of Church–State Relations, 1922–1960* (Cork, 1995)

Keogh, Dermot, *The Vatican, the Bishops and Irish Politics 1919–39* (Cambridge, 2004)

Keogh, Dermot, O'Shea, Finbarr and Quinlan, Carmel (eds), *The Lost Decade: Ireland in the 1950s* (Cork, 2004)

Kissane, Bill, 'Majority Rule and the Stabilisation of Democracy in the Irish Free State', *Irish Political Studies*, vol. 13 (1998)

Kissane, Bill, *The Politics of the Irish Civil War* (Oxford, 2005)

Laffan, Michael, *The Resurrection of Ireland: The Sinn Féin Party, 1916–1923* (Cambridge, 1999)

Lee, J. J. (ed.), *Ireland 1945–70* (Dublin, 1979)

Lee, J. J., *Ireland 1912–1985: Politics and Society* (Cambridge, 1989)

Livingstone, Peter, *The Fermanagh Story* (Enniskillen, 1969)

Lysaght, Charles Edward, *Brendan Bracken* (London, 1979)

MacBride, Seán, *That Day's Struggle: A Memoir, 1904–1951* (Dublin, 2005)

MacEoin, Uinseann, *Survivors* (Dublin, 1987)

MacEoin, Uinseann, *The IRA in the Twilight Years, 1923–1948* (Dublin, 1997)

Macmillan, Harold, *At the End of the Day, 1961–1963* (London, 1973)

Manning, Maurice, *James Dillon: A Biography* (Dublin, 2000)

Mansergh, Martin, *The Legacy of History for Making Peace in Ireland* (Cork, 2003)

Maume, Patrick, *'Life That Is Exile': Daniel Corkery And the Search for Irish-Ireland* (Belfast, 1993)

McCabe, Ian, 'JFK in Ireland', *History Ireland*, vol. 2 (winter, 1993)

McCarthy, Conor, *Modernisation, Crisis and Culture in Ireland, 1969–1992* (Dublin, 2000)

McCague, Eugene, *My Dear Mr McCourt* (Dublin, 2009)

McCoole, Sinéad, Hazel: *A Life of Lady Lavery, 1880–1935* (Dublin, 1996)

McGarry, Fearghal, *Irish Politics and the Spanish Civil War* (Cork, 1999)

McGarry, Fearghal, *Eoin O'Duffy: A Self-Made Hero* (Oxford, 2005)

McInerney, Michael, *Peadar O'Donnell: Irish Social Rebel* (Dublin, 1974)

McInerney, Micheal, *Éamon de Valera* (Dublin, 1976)

Milward, Alan S., *War, Economy and Society, 1939–45* (London, 1977)

Murphy, Gary, 'Towards a Corporate State? Seán Lemass and the Realignment of Interest Groups in the Policy Process, 1948–1964' (Working paper, Dublin, 1997)

Murray, Patrick, *Oracles of God: The Roman Catholic Church and Irish Politics, 1922–37* (Dublin, 2000)

Murray, Peter and Feeney, Maria, 'The Market for Sociological Ideas in Early 1960s Ireland: Civil Service Departments and the Limerick Rural Survey, 1961–64' (Working Paper, 2009)

Neary, J. Peter and Ó Gráda, Cormac, 'Protection, Economic War and Structural Change: The 1930s in Ireland', *Irish Historical Studies*, 27, 107 (1991)

Neeson, Eoin, *The Civil War, 1922–1923* (Dublin, 1989)

Nic Dháibhéid, Caoimhe and Reid, Colin (eds), *From Parnell to Paisley: Constitutional and Revolutionary Politics in Modern Ireland* (Dublin, 2010)

O'Brien, Conor Cruise, *Memoir: My Life And Times* (Dublin, 1999)

O'Brien, Mark, *De Valera, Fianna Fáil and The Irish Press* (Dublin, 2001)

Ó Broin, Leon, *Just Like Yesterday: An Autobiography* (Dublin, 1985)

O'Connor, Emmet, *A Labour History of Ireland, 1824–1960* (Dublin, 1992)

Ó Gráda, Cormac, *A Rocky Road: The Irish Economy Since the 1920s* (Manchester, 1997)

O'Malley, Ernie, *The Singing Flame* (Dublin, 1978)

Ó Riain, Micheál, 'Nelson's Pillar: A Controversy that Ran and Ran', *History Ireland* (winter, 1998)

O'Sullivan, Michael, *Seán Lemass: A Biography* (Dublin, 1994)

Patterson, Henry, *Ireland Since 1939* (Oxford, 2002)

Pius XI, *Quadragesimo Anno* (Rome, 1931)

Puirséil, Niamh, *The Irish Labour Party 1922–73* (Dublin, 2007)

Pyne, Peter, 'The Third Sinn Féin Party: 1923–1926', *Economic and Social History Review*, 1,1 (October, 1969)

Reynolds, Albert, *My Autobiography* (Dublin, 2009)

Roberts, Geoffrey, 'The British Offer to End Partition, June 1940', *History Ireland* (spring 2001)

Rolfe, Angela, *The Department of Industry and Commerce, Kildare St., Dublin* (Dublin, 1992)

Ryan, Philip B., *Jimmy O'Dea: The Pride of the Coombe* (Dublin, 1990)

Ryle Dwyer, T., *Short Fellow: A Biography of Charles J. Haughey* (Dublin, 1995)

Ryle Dwyer, T., *Nice Fellow: A Biography of Jack Lynch* (Cork, 2001)

Savage, Robert, *Seán Lemass* (Dundalk, 1999)

Share, Bernard, *The Emergency: Neutral Ireland* (Dublin, 1978)

Sheehan, William and Cronin, Maura (eds), *Riotous Assemblies: A History of Riots and Public Disorder in Ireland* (Cork, 2011)

Skelly, Joseph Morrison, *Irish Diplomacy at the United Nations, 1945–1965: National Interests and the International Order* (Dublin, 1997)

Skinner, Liam, *Politicians by Accident* (Dublin, 1946)

Skinner, Liam, 'Seán Lemass: Nation Builder', unpublished manuscript (1959)

Stuart, Francis, *Black List, Section H* (London, 1975)

Townshend, Charles, *Easter 1916: The Irish Rebellion* (London, 2005)

Walker, Dorothy, *Michael Scott, Architect, in (Casual) Conversation with Dorothy Walker* (Kinsale, 1995)

Walsh, Dick, *The Party: Inside Fianna Fáil* (Dublin, 1986)

Whelan, Bernadette, *Ireland and the Marshall Plan, 1947–57* (Dublin, 2000)

Whyte, J. H., *Church and State in Modern Ireland, 1923–1979* (Dublin, 1980)

Wills, Clair, *That Neutral Island: A Cultural History of Ireland during the Second World War* (London, 2007)

Zweiniger-Bargielowska, Ina, *Austerity in Britain: Rationing, Controls, and Consumption* (Oxford, 2000)

Index